Six Degrees of Corruption
The Fleecing of a City

L.P. Smith

Six Degrees of Corruption
The Fleecing of a City

"We hang petty thieves and appoint the great ones to public office"
Aesop

The information in this book is presented for historical, journalistic, and educational purposes only. This book is based entirely on documented public records, sworn testimony, and government files. Nothing is included without a source.

Every effort has been made to verify facts through court records, government documents, media reports, and other credible sources.

Nothing in this work is intended to constitute a statement of fact about the private character of any individual. Any descriptions of conduct or events are based on documented sources and are not presented as personal opinion or conjecture.

The author and publisher disclaim any liability for damages resulting from use or interpretation of the material contained herein.

Readers are encouraged to consult the source materials cited in the notes and bibliography for independent verification.

Copyright ©2025 LP. Smith

All rights reserved. No part of this book may be reproduced or transmitted in any form or by any means, electronic or mechanical, including photocopying, recording, or by any information storage and retrieval system, without written permission from the author.

ISBN: 9-798993-347523

www.LPSmithAuthor.com

Printed in the United States of America

Preface

> *"The truth is that all men having power
> ought to be mistrusted."*
> James Madison

They said I was chasing windmills. Like Cervantes' Don Quixote, I was mocked as a fool, tilting at giants that weren't there. That label wasn't just ridicule — it was strategy. If they could make me the story, they could bury the facts. If they could laugh me off, they wouldn't have to answer for what was really happening.

I didn't begin this journey looking to write a book. I began as an investigator following a forged police certification. But the deeper I pulled, the more I uncovered — not just misconduct, but a collapse in governance itself. My work led me through court filings, personnel hearings, FOIA requests, and late-night interviews with those too afraid to speak publicly. Each document, each testimony, each whispered account added another layer to a picture that no one in power wanted drawn.

That's when the attacks came. Instead of confronting the corruption, officials tried to discredit the one pointing to it. I was accused of exaggerating, dismissed as obsessive, portrayed as chasing shadows. But behind the curtain, many of those same officials quietly leaned on my findings to shape their own investigations. They wanted the results without the accountability.

This book is the product of years of that work — of pulling records, connecting threads, and refusing to look away when others chose silence. It is not speculation. It is evidence. And it is not just Methuen's story. What happened here reveals how fragile oversight becomes when politics and fear override responsibility.

If the metaphor of Don Quixote was meant to diminish me, I wear it differently now. Because unlike Cervantes' knight, I wasn't imagining giants. I was documenting them. And though they tried to make me disappear, the record remains.

This is that record.

Before you judge this record, you deserve to know how it was built.

Author's Note

"Because power corrupts, society's demands for moral authority and character increase as the importance of the position increases." John Adams

This book is outrageous, it's eye-opening, and feels like peeling back the wallpaper on a house to find rot in every wall. It's shocking that this happened in a small city — and terrifying because it could happen anywhere.

I did not begin this journey as an author. I began by investigating the trail of a single forged police training record. But once that thread was pulled, it revealed something much larger — a city caught in a cycle of poor leadership, misplaced loyalties, and systemic neglect.

As a combat veteran, retired State Police Sergeant, and certified fraud examiner, I have dedicated my life to serving truth and accountability. What I uncovered in Methuen, Massachusetts, was not just one man's misconduct — it was a case study in what happens when leaders prioritize self-interest over responsibility, and when oversight is compromised by politics, fear, or complacency.

I wrote this book because silence is a form of complicity. Communities cannot defend themselves against corruption if they are denied the facts. What happened in Methuen is not unique — it is a symptom of a larger problem creeping into municipal governments across the country. Incompetent leadership, quid pro quo arrangements, and hesitation to confront hard decisions are not confined to one city. These failures are spreading into town halls, council chambers, and police departments nationwide.

This book is not speculation. It is evidence. Every claim is supported by public records, sworn testimony, and financial documents. Embedded throughout are QR codes that link directly to those sources, allowing you to examine the proof for yourself.

I wrote this because the story demanded to be told. Because Methuen's experience is not just its own — it is a warning for every community that believes it cannot happen there.

L.P. Smith

Prologue

*"Nearly all men can stand adversity,
but if you want to test a man's character,
give him power."* Abraham Lincoln

This is not just the story of Methuen. It is the story of what happens when oversight erodes, when political expediency supplants accountability, and when those in power discover that intimidation and loyalty can be more useful than integrity.

Methuen, a city of 53,000, became a stage for these failures. Leadership decisions elevated loyalty over competence. Difficult choices were delayed until the damage could no longer be ignored. Into this void, one man expanded his influence far beyond what should have been possible. He ruled not by respect, but by fear, humiliation, and the quiet certainty that speaking out carried consequences.

The city's political leadership reinforced this imbalance. Oversight bodies became reluctant to challenge authority. Council chambers echoed with approvals rather than scrutiny. What should have been checks on power became rubber stamps. Each compromise, each silent vote, each unanswered warning chipped away at the safeguards designed to protect a community from abuse.

The police department reflected the culture of the city around it. Promotions rewarded allegiance. Dissent was punished. Evidence management faltered. Resources meant to serve the public became bargaining chips in an environment where personal gain outweighed professional duty.

The cost to Methuen was enormous: millions in wasted taxpayer dollars, civil rights undermined, and public trust destroyed. Yet the deeper tragedy is not what happened here — it is that what happened here can happen anywhere.

This book is not about a single scandal in a single city. It is about the conditions that allow corruption to flourish, and the danger of ignoring those conditions until they become ingrained in culture. Methuen is not an outlier; it is a forewarning.

If this city could be led down such a path, any city can. The only question is whether others will see the warning signs and act — or look the other way, until the damage is beyond repair.

Introduction

*"Power does not corrupt people.
People corrupt power."* William Gaddis

Throughout the long and often sordid history of law enforcement scandals, few had been as staggering-or as brazen — as what unfolded in the quiet city of Methuen, Massachusetts. When the first whispers of corruption began circulating beyond city limits, the reaction was immediate and universal: "That can't be real," and "There's no way that happened." Yet, every word is accurate. At the heart of it all stood a corrupt police chief and a compromised city council chairman, collectively facing 23 counts of fraud, with a criminal trial looming in 2026.

But to the citizens of Methuen, it had been just another day in their city.

Corruption doesn't storm your gates — it walks in smiling, embraced like an old friend returning home. Each morning, it dresses meticulously, buttoning its shirt cuffs, adjusting its tie, and blending seamlessly into Methuen's daily rhythm. Throughout the day, corruption wears the polished face of trust and authority, quietly infiltrating every layer of city government — so finely woven that it becomes indistinguishable from the fabric itself. And when darkness falls, it rests peacefully, its sleep unbroken by guilt, its conscience clear because it has none.

Methuen was never shaken awake by a sudden act of violence; its pockets weren't emptied at gunpoint. Instead, the city was quietly picked clean, piece by piece, through years of calculated deception. The theft was disguised as service, masked as leadership, draining public trust under the careful illusion of integrity and devotion.

That's the insidious brilliance of institutional corruption — it never needs to break laws, because it holds the power to rewrite them.

The Methuen Police Department did not function as a standard law enforcement agency for 18 years. In place of a standard institutional flow chart was a power structure built on the three Fs: fear, favors, and fraud. At the top sat Chief Joseph Solomon, a narcissistic, egotistical, and quick-tempered leader prone to

Introduction

tantrums. He didn't just run the department; he ruled it like the don of an organized crime family, using his badge not to uphold the law but rather, bending it to his will. He hadn't merely been in charge — he had been untouchable. Solomon's leadership was rarely about law and order — it was all about power and control. His outbursts were legendary, his anger unpredictable, and his need for dominance absolute. He demanded loyalty above all else, and when challenged, he retaliated with calculated precision. The message had been clear: fall in line or face the consequences — a mantra repeated to me in virtually every interview.

Those who obeyed the chief without question were rewarded with promotions, inflated salaries, and job security that most officers could only dream of. Those who questioned him faced humiliation, threats, or were forced out. As for those who defied him, Solomon did his best to ensure that their careers, reputations, and personal lives were destroyed.

For nearly two decades, this corruption thrived. Everyone knew it existed. Many fought to dismantle it. Yet, every attempt failed. Early in Solomon's career, the walls had begun closing in on him when a key figure in an investigation abruptly took his own life, effectively shutting down a federal probe — likely sparing Solomon from a federal indictment.

Solomon was fired once by the city for mismanaging federal police grants, yet he somehow managed to claw his way back into power, returning bolder and more brazen than before. Cloaked in a false sense of invincibility, he earned the nickname "Teflon Joe."

After the Civil Service Commission ordered the city to reinstate Solomon as chief, he embarked on what appeared to be a calculated plan to extract every possible dollar from the city's coffers. His methods followed a pattern of boardroom-level genius, including lawsuits, contract negotiations, conferences, side businesses, double-dipping, strategic promotions, and hires. To his credit, investigators have been unable to find any concrete evidence of shakedowns and kickbacks.

It took years and millions of taxpayer dollars to settle Solomon's multiple lawsuits and appeals with the city, all of which ended in his favor, leaving him completely unfettered. After seeing what it cost the city to go after him before, to no avail, no one dared to challenge him now.

Solomon's control extended into the city council, contracts, union negotiations, and even the state's training system. If those avenues didn't work, he found ways around them, using backdoor connections to get what he wanted while circumventing those who could cause him problems.

Over the years, he inserted his family members and those of his loyal followers into nearly every department in Methuen's government. He cultivated favors from politicians and state officials, strategically lending his officers to stints at the DEA, FBI, and other agencies — ostensibly not for their career development, but to keep his foot in the door and an ear open for his unprincipled purposes.

Media was Solomon's playground, and he was the resident bully. Police department blogs, social media, and press releases — the MPD did not publish any form of publicity without his explicit approval. It almost always included his name somewhere in the first sentence. Local newspapers and their reporters would either write favorable stories or face static from his lawyer or henchmen.

Stroking the ego of the mayor at the time — an awkward, socially introverted figure — Solomon nominated him for a national anti-bullying award, brought him into weekly poker nights, and included him in multiple out-of-state police conferences. The reward for the mayor's loyalty was substantial: a salary package that only a handful of police chiefs in the nation could surpass.

Solomon also inserted himself into both sides of the police union contract negotiations — a glaring conflict of interest. In doing so, he helped orchestrate one of the most outrageous municipal union contracts ever signed. The result was staggering. Superior Officers saw their salaries skyrocket, with captains earning nearly half a million dollars annually. Coincidentally, family members of roughly half the city councilors received promotions within the department, while two other councilors quietly secured job offers on the force.

One of those councilors, Sean Fountain, would eventually become Solomon's Achilles' heel. In one of the most brazen public actions of his career, Solomon pinned a badge on an untrained, unqualified cop wannabe, handed him a gun, and unleashed him on the streets of Methuen. It was moronic, reckless,

Introduction

arrogant, and entirely out in the open. And though it would take five more years, that decision marked the beginning of the end. After years of sliding by untouched, the first cracks finally showed in Teflon Joe's armor.

Table of Contents

Preface i
Author's Note iii
Prologue v
Introduction
    Inside a Small-City Power Machine vii

The Rise of Power (2002–2007)
The Year of the Rat
    A Chief Ascends 1
Controlling the Narrative
    Silencing the Local Press 3
Police Work
    Ambition and Loyalty 13
2002–2004
    Appointment, Early Missteps & A Tragic Loss 17
2005   Internal Turmoil and Political Pressure 27
2006   Manzi's Administration and the Cronin Lawsuit 41
2007   Federal Probe, Aiello Arrest, and Suspension 53
    Racism Allegations & the No-Confidence Vote 57
    Fulya Metin's Lawsuit and the Turning Point 68

The Fall and the Fight (2008–2013)
2008   Civil Service Hearings Begin 79
    Manzi's Second Inauguration & Internal Fallout 81
2009   Arbitration Battles and Mounting Legal Fees 107
2010   Stein's Decision and Solomon's Return 125
    The 125-Page Outlier 149
    Solomon Returns, Aiello Trial 154
2011–2012
    Phillips Lawsuit and Solomon Files Suit................... 159
    New Mayor, Old Problems 159
    Settlements, Contracts, and Campaign Cash 186
2013–2014
    McQuillan out, search out for new solicitor................. 179

Introduction

The Reckoning (2015–2020)

2015–2016
    Police Academy and EIS 206
    Promotions and Intermittent Officer Fountain 223

2017–2018
    Chief and Union Contracts 235
    Conventions, Presentations and Awards 249
    Changing of the Guard 267

2019–2020
    Pink Slips, Grand Juries, & Inspector General 294
    "Chuckle" Controversy and Fallout 296
    State Oversight and Public Outcry 344

The Aftermath (2021–2023)

2021–2022
    Retirement and Arbitration Fallout 351

2023
    Civil Service and Ethics Investigations 367
    Formal Charges Filed 382

Epilogue & Appendices

Epilogue – What If… 387
The Fleecing Was Just the Beginning 389
Acknowledgements 393
Author's Call 395
Glossary & Acronyms 397
Character Index 403
Investigator's Dossier (Bibliography) 417

The Cast of Characters, Glossary, and Bibliography are included in the book. Use the QR codes below to access an online version for easy reference on your phone while reading

Cast of Characters

Investigator's Dossier
(Bibliography)

Glossary

The Year of the Rat

"Experience has shown that even under the best forms of government those entrusted with power have, in time, and by slow operations, perverted it into tyranny."
Thomas Jefferson

In the fall of 2020, the winds around the Methuen Police Department were shifting, and Chief Joseph Solomon knew they would soon blow his way. What he failed to anticipate was how quickly a breeze would turn into a hurricane.

Solomon had a checkered past and an air of bravado that suggested he believed the rules did not apply to him. Born in 1961, he fell under the Chinese zodiac sign of the Rat. Fittingly, his final year as police chief was 2020 — also the Year of the Rat.

After reading this book, ask yourself: Was it fate or coincidence that Solomon was born and ended his law enforcement career in the Year of the Rat? My decades as an investigator have shown me that there are no coincidences when it comes to investigations.

The Rat in the zodiac calendar is a symbol of being smart, talented and innovative, with a strong sense of self-awareness. People born under this sign are known to be loyal and optimistic, always striving for success despite any challenges that come their way.

Those born in the Year of the Rat are often said to enjoy good fortune in their careers, with the drive and ambition to rise into positions of power — whether in politics, the military, or business. Their quick thinking and adaptability lend themselves to success in competitive ventures and high-stakes environments. In many ways, Solomon embodied each of these traits.

Rats are known for their resilience and ability to overcome obstacles. Solomon's story is a testament to the determination and drive that rats possess, as he navigates his way through life's challenges to achieve success in his career and financial endeavors.

The Year of the Rat

However, it's important to acknowledge the less favorable traits associated with Rats, all of which Solomon seemed to possess. They can be self-centered, impatient, suspicious, hot-tempered, jealous and somewhat vain.

Allow me to shed some light on Mr. Solomon's character — a man possessing the strategic mind of a brilliant chess player, driven by what seemed like an insatiable desire to exploit the City of Methuen for maximum financial gain, employing any means necessary to achieve his ends.

The story you are about to hear is true.
The names have not been changed,
for they are not the innocent.

Controlling the Narrative

"In the First Amendment, the Founding Fathers gave the free press the protection it must have ... The press was to serve the governed, not the governors. The Government's power to censor the press was abolished so that the press would remain forever free to censure the government."
U.S. Supreme Court Justice Hugo Black -1971

Pulling out all the stops:
The shutting down of Ellen Bahan

It all began with a microwave tower — its looming shadow and potential long-term effects threatening her children's well-being. Successfully challenging the tower's installation opened Ellen Bahan's eyes to the inner workings of Methuen's government and the power players behind the scenes. What she uncovered was deeply unsettling. She realized that nothing was as it seemed; everything was in constant flux, manipulated by a select few who fancied themselves royalty in a one-horse town drowning in corruption.

Rumbo, a fledgling free weekly newspaper, offered her a column and a form of catharsis, a pro bono labor of love. Her headline read *"It's All About Rights!"* and her trademark snarky tone irritated the powerful while endearing her to the everyday citizens.

For eight years, she wrote to create a safer, cleaner community for her family and to warn her neighbors about the corruption their elected and appointed officials were perpetrating — officials who did not have the public's best interests at heart. Sadly, even 25 years later, many of the same characters remained, spinning their schemes in the same murky cesspool.

When Bahan began requesting public records that city officials would rather keep buried, the retaliation was swift. She was met with astronomical fees — price tags so high even Bill Gates would've balked — and delays so long they could be measured by calendar pages flying off the wall.

Her crusade came at a steep personal cost. Challenging Methuen's political elite unleashed their full wrath. Bahan and her

Controlling the Narrative

husband were both interior decorators by trade, and their children lived in a pink Victorian on the main road, in the heart of the historic district. To this home, the city's full force descended: police, fire department, building inspector, city engineer, city solicitor, board of health, and the assessor — all arriving with threats and intimidation.

They were slapped with extensive lists of code violations, dragged into court, hit with a 44 percent tax increase, and routinely followed by police cruisers every time their children left the driveway. This municipal barrage continued for years. Her kids would complain, and Ellen would respond with a wry smile, "How lucky to always have a police escort wherever you go!"

It wasn't any single story that drew the administration's ire — the steady drumbeat of articles, exposés, and accusations of wrongdoing ultimately made her a target. No department or employee was off-limits to Bahan's pen. Whether she was covering the school business administrator's misuse of a city credit card for personal purchases or raising red flags about the construction of an assisted living facility downtown, Bahan reported with equal scrutiny and tenacity.

The city solicitor once dismissed her as a woman full of "random, unconnected thoughts." In true fashion, she turned that slight into something of her own, launching a sporadic, editorial-style column titled "Random Unconnected Thoughts". In that space, she commented on the rumors swirling through the city, speculated on behind-the-scenes maneuverings, and offered commentary — sometimes biting, sometimes bemused — on the goings-on within and beyond city hall walls.

In a final act of defiance, Bahan even ran for Mayor — if only to ensure the incumbent wouldn't go unchallenged. She lost the election but not the fight. She kept writing. Bundles of *Rumbo* would mysteriously disappear on delivery day. Many city officials made attempts to silence her — confronting the newspaper's owner and pressuring advertisers. Some caved. Others stood firm.

Eventually, the pressure took its toll. As she saw her business suffer, Bahan came to a hard truth: You can't save people who don't want to be saved. She and her family finally escaped Methuen — and never looked back. She disappeared so wholly that it took me a year to find her.

Controlling the Narrative

The Campaign of Fear and Intimidation: The Case of Tim Wood

Tim Wood, a local reporter and owner of Methuen newspaper *Loop Weekly*, is a chilling example of the lengths to which corrupt officials will go to silence those who get too close to the truth. Wood's inquiries into Officer Sean Fountain's forged training records put him in the crosshairs of those who wanted the truths hidden.

Wood initially made a public records request on February 6, 2019 for Chief Solomon to confirm when Fountain became a full-time employee and whether Fountain had completed full-time officer training at a police academy.

Solomon initially replied that he couldn't comment on personnel matters and directed Wood to the City Human Resources Director Anne Randazzo. Wood replied that he was simply looking for confirmation of dates of Fountain's full-time employment and his academy training.

In that email, Wood said, "I have made the same information request regarding the training to the MPTC." It's that one line that set in motion a campaign to intimidate and marginalize Wood.

Wood later emailed Randazzo that the MPTC had replied saying they had no record of Fountain completing the required training. After a series of internal communications, Randazzo replied on February 14, 2019 that the "City has no documentation regarding attendance at a police academy. She attached a spreadsheet outlining MPD seniority listing Fountain as a full-time officer with department seniority of 14th out of 67 officers and a civil service date of August 29, 1999.

Initially, the effort to neutralize Wood was subtle yet insidious.

He said he endured six different traffic stops by Methuen police officers over the next three weeks. Through his ownership of *Loop Weekly*, he knew many of the officers who stopped him and said they all told him the same thing.

"Sorry, Tim. Chief's orders."

Each time, he was detained for about 30 minutes without any official warning or documentation of the stop, and none of the stops were recorded by the Department.

Soon after, a doctored social media post was published on a local Facebook rumors page known to be run by one of Solomon's friends, a calculated and carefully orchestrated attempt to ruin his

Controlling the Narrative

reputation. This was no ordinary smear campaign; it was character assassination at its most strategic, designed to discredit him both professionally and personally. The aim was clear: to ruin his credibility as a journalist and isolate him from his peers, sources and advertisers.

However, when this failed to achieve its desired effect, the campaign against Wood escalated to a new level of threat and intimidation.

At first, Wood noticed unmarked cars surveilling his house at all hours. He later confirmed with Methuen police officers that this was ordered off-the-books by "superiors".

The most brazen intimidation occurred as Wood was filling up his car at a local gas station on January 2, 2020. The card reader did not work so Wood went inside to pay cash. When he returned, he noticed the driver's side rear door ajar. When he opened it, there was a strong smell of gasoline coming from the seat where he typically had his toddler son's car seat. As he cleaned up the gasoline, a stranger approached and, before he could react, the man stuck something pointed in his back that Wood said felt like a gun barrel. The man said to not turn around until he left and stated, "This is a warning. Leave the Methuen Police alone or the next time, the gas will be lit."

Wood was unable to get a plate on the car and was denied access to the video surveillance footage from the gas station. Attempts to seek assistance from the Massachusetts State Police (MSP) and the local FBI office were unsuccessful. An unnamed FBI agent responded to Wood saying, "Be careful. He has friends at every level."

This brazen act of intimidation was more than just a threat; it was a terrifying reminder of the physical danger that comes with pursuing the truth in a world of bad guys. Wood was forced into an impossible situation — continue his work and risk the safety of his loved ones, or walk away from his home, business and career, leaving the truth buried in darkness. Faced with such a harrowing choice, Wood ultimately chose to protect his family. He shuttered his newspaper and relocated down south, far from the reach of those who sought to silence him.

Tim Wood's story is a powerful one, a reminder of the dangers faced by journalists who dare to expose corruption. The campaign against Wood was not just an attack on one man; it was an attack on free press and an informed public. In this world of "Hide & Seek," publishing the truth can come at a great personal cost, but it is a pursuit that must continue if justice is ever to prevail.

The Unpublished Exposé: Keith Eddings and the Lawrence Eagle-Tribune

In the profession of investigative journalism, few stories are as explosive or as consequential as the one Keith Eddings was ready to publish in 2018. As a seasoned reporter for the *Lawrence Eagle-Tribune*, Eddings had meticulously pieced together a hard-hitting exposé that would have shed light on the questionable activities of Solomon and his privately owned business enterprise, Eagle Investigation Services (EIS). The report was set to be released as a three-part series, a detailed analysis of the conflicts of interest and possible illegal activities in which Solomon and EIS were allegedly involved.

Eddings' investigation delved far into the tangled web of relationships and transactions that raised serious ethical concerns. At the heart of the story were several troubling business dealings involving intermittent and full-time Methuen police officers who were also employed by EIS. These officers, while representing the City of Methuen at various trade shows, were found to be working the EIS vendor booth instead of fulfilling their civic responsibilities. The city had paid for their attendance, not to promote a private enterprise, but to represent the public interest. This blatant conflict of interest was a key focus of Eddings' investigation.

The exposé also highlighted the establishment of the Northern Essex Community College (NECC) Methuen Police Academy, a venture that should have been a straightforward public service. At the same time Solomon was negotiating with NECC for the academy, he was negotiating for a multi-million-dollar security contract with the college, casting a long shadow over the academy and Solomon's professionalism. The entire arrangement, as Eddings' report would have revealed, reeked of cronyism and corruption. Solomon's decisions, at best, reflected a severe conflict of interest and, at worst, pointed to outright corruption.

Despite the explosive nature of his findings, Eddings' story never made it to print. When he was informed that his investigative series had been killed, reportedly due to political

Controlling the Narrative

pressure to protect Solomon and those aligned with him, Eddings made a principled stand. Disgusted by what he saw as a blatant cover-up, he grabbed his keys, picked up his phone, and walked out of the *Lawrence Eagle-Tribune*, resigning on the spot. Eddings' departure was more than just the loss of a dedicated journalist — it was a symbol of the ongoing struggle between truth and power, and the lengths to which the corrupt will go to protect their interests.

This chapter, and indeed this entire book, aims to shine a light on the dark corners where such corruption thrives. The suppression of Eddings' story is a reminder of the challenges faced by those who seek to hold the powerful accountable. Yet, it is also a testament to the courage of those who refuse to be silenced, who continue to fight for the truth, no matter the personal cost.

The Silencing of Andrea Estes:
When Journalism Collides with Corruption.

Andrea was not just any journalist. She was an award-winning investigative reporter, widely known for her tenacity and commitment to uncovering the truth. Her meticulous work at *The Boston Globe* earned her accolades and respect, earning her a reputation as a fearless journalist who pursued stories with integrity. But when you go up against public corruption, even the most seasoned reporters can become targets when their work threatens the powerful.

On April 6, 2023, Estes and the *Globe* published a riveting article that exposed the forged academy records of police officer Sean Fountain. Less than three weeks later, Estes was abruptly fired from *The Boston Globe* — a move that sent shockwaves through the journalistic community and raised serious questions about the forces at play behind the scenes.

The story Estes broke was a significant one. It detailed how Fountain, a former Methuen police officer, had obtained a legitimate academy certificate from the Methuen Police Department records and used it to forge his own non-existent police academy graduation record. The implications of this forgery were far-reaching, for Fountain did not act alone. Deep-seated corruption within and outside the police department were

Controlling the Narrative

being exposed, raising alarms about the integrity of law enforcement in the region.

The fallout from Estes' article was swift and severe. Just as her story began to gain traction, highlighting the forged records and the corruption surrounding them, she found herself unemployed. According to sources, the reasons given for her termination were flimsy at best — a minor infraction in the newspaper world that under normal circumstances would have warranted nothing more than a small retraction buried deep within the newspaper. Yet, Estes was summarily dismissed, an action that many within the journalism community saw as an apparent attempt to silence her, warn other journalists and stifle further investigation. Mission accomplished.

The Report That Never Saw the Light of Day

To fully grasp the significance of Estes' dismissal, it's crucial to understand the chain of events that immediately preceded it. Shortly before Estes published her explosive article, my company, STIRM Group, finalized a comprehensive 203-page investigative report detailing serious misconduct involving Fountain, the subject central to Estes' reporting.

After submitting this report to Methuen Police Chief Scott McNamara, he quickly recognized the precarious position he faced. Prosecutors, notably from Essex County District Attorney Jonathan Blodgett's office, had repeatedly declined to take meaningful action. Out of sheer necessity — and to circumvent further stonewalling by authorities — McNamara instructed me to discreetly send a copy of the report to Estes via one of my company's anonymous email accounts. This unusual step was intended to ensure the report reached the public eye despite the mounting efforts to suppress it.

The day Estes' article went public, McNamara called Fountain's attorney, instructing Fountain to surrender himself because the story was breaking. Once Fountain was arraigned, DA Paul Tucker's office swiftly acted to impound our investigative report and the related warrant application submitted by Captain Eric Ferreira to the Court. To this day, both the investigative report and warrant remain sealed, locked away from public scrutiny.

During a subsequent conversation, McNamara and I spoke on the phone as things were progressing fast. McNamara told me that

Controlling the Narrative

Tucker was determined to keep the report quiet. The urgency behind Tucker's decision was clear: the report was intentionally and uncompromisingly drafted to expose the unwillingness of elected officials to fulfill their duties. If made public, it would demand accountability for why earlier investigations and charges had been systematically ignored.

The firing of Andrea Estes sent a chilling message to journalists and whistleblowers everywhere. That when it comes to public corruption, even the truth can be silenced if it threatens the wrong people. Estes' story, which had the potential to unravel a network of corruption, was buried along with her career at the *Globe*. The investigative report, which could have served as a critical piece of evidence in prosecuting others involved, was hidden away, its findings locked up under the guise of legal necessity.

A few months later, former MPD Police Chief Solomon was indicted alongside police officer Fountain in the forgery scandal, both facing a combined 22 state charges. No further indictments have been made and those who should have been held accountable continue to operate with impunity. The silencing of Estes and the suppression of the investigative report are not just isolated incidents; they are part of a broader pattern of protecting the powerful at the expense of justice and transparency.

The question remains: if the truth is buried, and those who uncover it are punished, how can the public ever trust the institutions meant to serve them? Andrea Estes' story is a stark reminder that the fight for truth is often met with fierce resistance, but it is a fight that must continue if justice is ever to be served.

Reflection: The Cost of a Silenced Press

In Methuen, silencing the press wasn't an accident — it was a strategy. From the early battles with Ellen Bahan to the intimidation of Tim Wood, from the buried investigation of Keith Eddings to the firing of Andrea Estes, the pattern was unmistakable. When reporters got too close, retaliation followed.

The tactics varied. For Bahan, it was city inspectors swarming her home, police cruisers tailing her children, and tax hikes designed to break her spirit. For Wood, it escalated to traffic stops on the chief's orders and a chilling encounter at a gas station, where a stranger left gasoline on the seat where his toddler usually sat. For Eddings, it was a quiet suffocation — years of reporting killed at the editor's desk. And for Estes, it was a career suddenly ended after she published what officials most wanted hidden: proof of forged academy records.

Each case might look different in the details, but together they form a single truth: corruption thrives when the press is neutralized. Whether through harassment, smear campaigns, or the blunt force of a pink slip, the result is the same — journalists are removed from the field, and the public is left in the dark.

And this is bigger than Methuen. Across America, shrinking newsrooms and political pressure have left local reporters exposed. Newspapers close, reporters are laid off, and those who remain are stretched too thin to fight back when power bears down. The corrupt know this. They don't need to bribe every journalist; they just need to make an example of one. Others will get the message.

A silenced press isn't just a Methuen problem — it's a democratic crisis. The watchdog is muzzled, and the thieves are left to ransack the house in peace. The lesson is stark: if the public does not protect those who tell uncomfortable truths, no one will be left to warn them when corruption comes to their own town.

Police Work

"To protect and serve"
Thomas Houser

Joseph Solomon grew up in the mill city of Lawrence, Massachusetts, the only son among five siblings in a close-knit Lebanese family. They lived in a triple-decker in the Arlington District, a neighborhood straddling the Lawrence-Methuen border, along with their grandparents.

The family attended the nearby Maronite Catholic Church, a cornerstone of their faith and cultural identity. Solomon's father, Eddie, started as a butcher and eventually opened his own market and deli in Lawrence. As the business grew, the family moved to nearby Methuen for a quieter life.

Though they left the Arlington District, Solomon's connection to the area remained strong — his future career would eventually bring him right back to where he started.

He later enrolled at the University of Massachusetts Lowell, earning a bachelor's degree in business management and accounting in 1983. What he didn't yet realize was that the skills he picked up there would eventually become tools — not for building, but for manipulating — laying the groundwork for a career ultimately marred by fraud and self-interest.

Despite his parents' demanding work schedules, particularly his father's long hours at the family business, the Solomon family prioritized unity and togetherness. They made it a ritual to gather for dinner each evening and spend quality time together on weekends, forging strong bonds amidst the hustle and bustle of everyday life. Each of the children, Joe included, eagerly contributed their efforts at the market, actively participating in the family's shared success.

In addition to instilling a strong work ethic, Solomon's parents imparted invaluable lessons about the importance of community engagement and giving back. Whether it was lending a helping hand at church events or taking pride in maintaining the cleanliness of the street outside their market, the Solomons embodied a spirit of civic duty and altruism.

Police Work

These early experiences of communal responsibility and service likely influenced Solomon's career path after college. Drawn to the noble profession of law enforcement, he sought to continue the legacy of giving back to his community instilled by his upbringing, embodying the principles of integrity, justice and service that were woven into the fabric of his family's values.

In 1986, Solomon began his tenure with the Methuen Police Department as a reserve officer, while balancing the responsibilities of a husband and as a father to two daughters and a son. His professional journey took a significant turn when he was partnered with Joseph Alaimo. Over the years, what started as a professional connection blossomed into a deep friendship, entwining their lives both personally and professionally. This bond became a basis of their shared experiences within the law enforcement community, shaping their paths in profound ways.

Within a year, Solomon had distinguished himself at the police academy, graduating at the top of his class, which paved the way for his transition to a full-time officer role within the department. Solomon's ascent through the ranks was marked by both ease and speed. By the turn of the millennium, he had climbed to the positions of Sergeant, then Lieutenant, and ultimately Captain.

Twice during his rise through the ranks, Solomon received notable recognition for his exceptional police work. In 1989, he was honored with the department's Officer of the Year award, and in 1997, he achieved further acclaim as one of only two law enforcement officers in the United States to be recognized by the International Association of Chiefs of Police with the National Shared Vision Award. This prestigious accolade was bestowed upon him for successfully directing a community policing initiative in Methuen's crime-plagued Arlington District — a personal crusade to restore safety in his childhood neighborhood.

In 1995, Solomon became commander of the Community Policing Division, which centered on the Arlington District. In 1998, just a year after his national accolades for cleaning up Arlington, a management study conducted for the City yielded a report critical of his division, describing it as an elite group that earned perks such as take-home vehicles and extra overtime. Chief Bruce MacDougall took this information to the City Council to propose a reorganization of the police department, primarily to disband the Community Policing Division. At this public meeting,

Police Work

Solomon clashed with MacDougall, but to no avail — the division was ultimately dissolved.

However, Solomon's ambitions did not stop at being a Captain. The position of Chief beckoned, and when Solomon sets his mind to a goal, nothing will stand in his way.

2002 – 2004

2002

July 2	Thomas Lussier is fined by the Massachusetts State Ethics Commission
July 24	Police Chief Bruce MacDougall signs a new employment contract with Mayor Sharon Pollard.
Fall	Mayor Pollard appoints Captain Joseph Solomon to the Community Television Advisory Commission.
September 4	Captain Solomon is appointed Acting Police Chief.
November	The City Council approves the creation of a Deputy Chief position. Pollard and Solomon nominate Lieutenant Joseph Alaimo to the role.
December 8-11	Officers Greg Gallant, Michael Pappalardo, and Frank Korn, as well as Sergeants Kris McCarthy and Kathy Lavigne, are promoted.
December 31	The Festival of Trees is established by Mayor Pollard and three collaborators.

2003

January 2	James Jajuga is replaced as Secretary of Public Safety for the Commonwealth of Massachusetts.
May 10	Acting Chief Solomon takes the Civil Service exam for Police Chief.
June	City Council votes to expand the number of intermittent officers.
	Pollard signs a consulting agreement with Crest Associates.
June 11	Pollard and Solomon co-sign a Community Oriented Policing Services (COPS) grant application.
August 4	Solomon is formally appointed permanent Police Chief.
September 7	Officer dies by suicide; the Patrolmen's Union hosts its annual party.
December	The Federal Bureau of Investigation (FBI) launches a probe into Executive Office of Public Safety grants.

2004

January 9	Methuen police install a surveillance camera at the home of Chief Solomon's sister.
February 17	Richard St. Louis of Crest Associates dies by suicide.

2002 – 2004

April 21	Promotions announced for Sergeant Kevin Mahoney, Lieutenant Kathy Lavigne, and Officer Donald Lavigne.
May 12	Timothy Getchell is hired as a Methuen police officer.
June 24	Officer Joseph Aiello is arrested in New Hampshire for forgery.
July	Mayor Pollard instructs Brooks Pharmacy to issue two checks (for the City and Festival of Trees).
July 7	An amendment to the Acts of 1945 is enacted by the Massachusetts State Legislature.
July 20	At a Festival of Trees board meeting, Mayor Pollard announces a $200,000 donation from Brooks Pharmacy for "wall restoration."
August 25	The secretary to the City Solicitor retires.
August 27	Brooks Pharmacy delivers two checks to Mayor Pollard.
September	Fulya Metin relocates from New York to her mother's residence in Massachusetts.
September 20	City Council accepts a $450,000 donation from Brooks Pharmacy.
October 4	Metin begins work as temporary secretary in the City Solicitor's Office.
December 27	Metin is hired permanently.

Passing of the Baton

Methuen has a rich history of political dynamics. In 1917, the town made a significant decision to transition into a city and adopt a mayoral form of government. Just three years later, it was revealed that the process had not been conducted properly, as only supporters of the city/mayor form were notified for the town meeting vote. Therefore, in 1921, another vote was held, resulting in a resounding choice for a town meeting/selectmen system.

This governance structure persisted until 1992 when Michael McLaughlin's[1] controversial tenure as town manager came to an end. His two years in office were fraught with turmoil, marked by accusations of tyrannical leadership. Matters escalated to such a

---

[1] In 2014, Michael McLaughlin was sentenced to federal prison for conspiring to defraud the United States in connection with his role at the Chelsea Housing Authority.

2002 – 2004

degree that the electorate opted to amend the charter once more, changing to the city council/mayoral system their forefathers envisioned 75 years earlier.

Sharon Pollard, a proud Methuen native, was elected mayor in 2000 — the second to serve under the city's new charter. A longtime force in Massachusetts politics, her influence was significant then and remains so today. She served as the representative for the Third Essex District in the Massachusetts Senate from 1977 to 1983 before assuming the role of Massachusetts Secretary of Energy from 1983 to 1989. Even today, Pollard's political clout remains as potent as it was 50 years ago. Aspiring politicians in Methuen are advised to meet with Pollard and "kiss the ring" if they want to gain any traction in local politics.

One of the first acts that Mayor Pollard implemented was to reinstate the Community Policing Division, rebranding it as the Neighborhood Services Division and appointing Solomon as its head.

In August of 2002, Chief MacDougall, a dedicated 27-year veteran of the department and chief for the past seven years, chose to take advantage of an early retirement incentive program provided by the Commonwealth. While publicly stating that the state retirement incentive was his reason for retiring, there's a widespread belief among insiders that the Chief's relationship with the new Mayor was not a harmonious one. Speculations suggest that MacDougall either eagerly embraced the early retirement opportunity or was nudged toward it. One fact that supports the latter theory: MacDougall signed a new contract with Mayor Pollard on July 24, 2002 and then announced his retirement a little over a week later.

Chief MacDougall's Contract

Before MacDougall could pack his bags, the mayor made an unexpected announcement, appointing Solomon as the new Acting Chief. According to witnesses, Solomon was quick to redecorate, entering MacDougall's office and personally packing up the former chief's belongings.

Typically, the appointment of an acting department head is a straightforward affair — a quick swearing-in by the city clerk at

2002 – 2004

Invitation to Swearing-in Ceremony

town hall or the police station, sometimes during a City Council meeting. But Solomon's appointment was anything but typical. A special swearing-in ceremony was organized by Pollard at the local grammar school on September 4th. Invitations, as sought-after as those for a wedding, were extended to all of Pollard's closest allies.

The ceremony culminated with Solomon kissing Pollard on the cheek before raising his right hand and solemnly pledging to uphold the law.

The festivities continued with a celebratory gathering at Pollard's home where a delightful buffet awaited everyone. The evening was capped off with Solomon's buddy, Detective Ron Valliere, popping the question to his fiancée and receiving a yes. Solomon would be tapped for Best Man at their future wedding.

Solomon swiftly implemented changes within the department. By year's end, he had revamped the police force, creating the position of Deputy Chief and elevating his old partner, Lieutenant Joseph Alaimo, to serve as his right-hand man. Furthermore, Solomon introduced a Homeland Security component to the city's drug and gang unit, paving the way for the department to seek more federal grants. By mid-December, he had also promoted six individuals: Officers Greg Gallant, Michael Pappalardo and Michael Havey, Sr. to Sergeant, and Sergeants Kristopher McCarthy, Katherine Lavigne and Frank Korn to Lieutenant.

Pictures of the Swearing in Ceremony

Intermittent Police Force

The Massachusetts State Legislature granted Methuen the ability to have a permanent intermittent police force in 1945 to address the shortage of available police officers during World War II. This allowed the selectmen or the police chief to appoint up to 12 male Methuen citizens as police officers to fill the ranks of the

2002 – 2004

police department as needed. When called into service, these officers shall have all the powers, duties and rights of a regular police officer in Methuen.

The Acts of 1945

Several conditions accompanied this decree. These included situations where no members of the regular or reserve police force were available, and when a requisition had been made to the State's Director of Civil Service, who then certify that no candidates were available from the civil service list. Removal of a person from the list of intermittent officers could be made by the Selectmen [now City Councilors] at any time and for any reason satisfactory to them. Importantly, individuals appointed as intermittent officers were not eligible for retirement benefits.

Chief MacDougall sought an opinion from the State Ethics Commission in March 1997 regarding an issue with an intermittent officer. The resulting Commission written opinion stated that, according to Massachusetts General Laws, reserve and intermittent officers must complete the same training course before exercising police powers.

During his discussions with the Commission, MacDougall explained that intermittent officers are typically called in for road detail work, which is assigned daily. He also mentioned that due to the part-time nature of their police work for the city, intermittent officers need other employment. Unlike full-time regular officers, intermittent officers are not considered "on-duty" at all times, nor are they required or authorized to take reasonable action to preserve the peace or protect life and property when off duty.

However, officers must pass the Civil Service exam and go through the standard hiring process like any other full-time candidate to transition from intermittent to full-time status.

In 2004, Methuen successfully petitioned for an amendment to increase the number of intermittent police officers from 12 to 20. This adjustment occurred during Solomon's second year as Chief of Police and Sharon Pollard's tenure as mayor. According to a statement

The Amendment

2002 – 2004

made to *The Boston Globe* by then-City Council Chair William Manzi III, the MPD was seeking to increase the number due to a need for more officers at road construction sites. It was also thought that a larger police reserve force could play an important role in local homeland security.

The selection of candidates at the local level often allowed for the appointment of intermittent officers as a means to gain favor with friends, family and politicians. Over the decades, Solomon elevated this practice to a quid pro quo art form, ultimately leading to his downfall.

Throughout his tenure as Chief, Solomon would garner a reputation for rewarding unwavering loyalty while swiftly retaliating against the slightest disloyalty.

Over the next couple of years, when retirements in the upper ranks occurred, they often came with 'encouragement' and those who stepped into these vacancies were typically individuals loyal to the Chief. These appointees became known, albeit quietly, as 'Solomon's Posse.'

In the spring of 2004, one notable hire was Timothy Getchell. His recruitment required a "home rule petition," which involves the city petitioning the state legislature and governor for a change or exemption in the city's charter. In this case, it was an exemption, as both he and another candidate exceeded the city's maximum hiring age of 32 for sworn police officers. Coincidentally, Officer Getchell is the husband of Solomon's younger sister, Emily. Another interesting hire was Mark Aiello, the brother of Joe Aiello. These appointments marked the beginning of a pattern of filling the ranks with relatives.

Getchell's Home Rule Petition

At the same time that family ties were beginning to influence hiring decisions, Solomon was preparing to secure his own position at the top. To make his promotion to Chief permanent, he needed to take the civil service police chief exam, held every spring. In order to hold the exam, a minimum of four Captains must sign up to take the test. Given Methuen's limited number of Captains — only three — and the possibility that two of them may not take the exam, it became necessary to extend the eligibility to the

2002 – 2004

lieutenant rank. Scheduled annually in the spring, the exam identifies the candidate with the highest score for the position.

As it turned out, Solomon was the only candidate to sit for the test — and how that came to be remains open to speculation. The prevailing explanation is simple: the others just didn't show up on exam day. Regardless of the reason, Solomon achieved his goal and secured the position of permanent Chief.

In August 2003, the Methuen City Council confirmed the appointment of 43-year-old Solomon as Police Chief with a 5-2 vote. The two councilors who opposed the appointment were Kenneth Henrick and Todd Woekel, the latter a mayoral candidate. Solomon's position became protected by civil service, ensuring he would hold the job for life or until he retired. This protection proved to be a shield throughout his tenure, repeatedly tested over the next twenty-plus years, earning him the moniker "Teflon Joe."

Solomon's 2nd Swearing in Ceremony Photo

A Life Cut Short

Tragedy struck the police station just a month after Solomon's permanent appointment. On September 7, 2003, the patrolmen's union members held a private party, with Solomon, Alaimo and Pollard making appearances at some point. While some rumors described the event as rowdy – with MPD motorcycles doing wheelies in the street – others claimed it was more of a family affair, complete with a moonwalk, a clown painting children's faces, and llama rides. According to one source, the party was held at Officer Scott Lever's home to save the union some money.

Three shots rang out in Lawrence that evening, on the top floor of a triple-decker. Two Methuen patrolmen lived at that residence, each on a separate floor. Both had been at the party earlier that day. Some said the two were seeing each other and had a fight at the party — fueled by too much alcohol.

Those officers decided to spend the remainder of the night in their respective apartments. That's when the young patrolwoman allegedly picked up her gun, fired two shots into the window, and then turned the weapon on herself, delivering the fatal shot. To

2002 – 2004

this day, details remain unclear around the suicide. Although officially ruled a suicide, questions lingered. Investigators documented three shots fired — based on bullet holes and shell casings — even though only one was fatal. One caller reported hearing just a single gunshot, adding to the uncertainty. While no evidence ever implicated the other officer, his presence in the building underscored the unanswered questions surrounding that night. It should be noted that he was never considered a suspect, and no evidence has ever tied him to the death.

When her mother picked up the death certificate, she was startled to see the cause of death listed as pending investigation. But what investigation? In an interview with *Rumbo*, a local newspaper, the mother described the difficulties she encountered in her search for answers. Trying to separate gossip from fact, she went to the MPD for clarification. The Chief was unavailable at the time of her arrival at the station. Undeterred, she visited the records department to obtain a copy of the police report, only to learn that the records were classified and kept in the Chief's office. So, she went back to Solomon's secretary and scheduled an appointment for the following day.

When you're going through severe grief, your mind isn't at its best. Understanding this, she brought a friend to ensure she asked all the necessary questions and could remember the answers she received. However, upon arrival, Solomon informed the friend that she could not attend the meeting, citing his own policy. He told the grieving mother she could return with a lawyer or someone he approved of.

Note: In all my years in law enforcement, I can't imagine telling the grieving mother of one of my employees that — by my own rule — she's not allowed to bring a friend for comfort unless I personally approve of them.

The *Rumbo* columnist, seeking answers, called Essex County District Attorney Blodgett's office to inquire about the investigation and the availability of the investigative and autopsy reports. The DA's office spokesman stated that those reports could only be released to the family but confirmed that no foul play had been discovered.

The following day, the reporter attempted to verify the information, calling again to speak to a higher-up in the office but ended up speaking with the same person. The spokesman

2002 – 2004

reiterated his previous statement but added that the investigation was still ongoing, and they were awaiting toxicology results. Later newspaper reports cite alcohol as a possible factor in this sad story.

Regardless of the cause, a young life was cut short that evening, one of MPD's own. Solomon compounded that grief by treating the mother of his fallen officer poorly and with more emphasis on policy than empathy, which speaks volumes about his character.

2005

January	City Solicitor Maurice Lariviere is reappointed to a two-year term by the City Council.
February 10	Officer Joseph Aiello pleads guilty to tampering with a public document.
February 15	City Hall employee Fulya Metin reports allegations of sexual harassment by Solicitor Lariviere to police.
February 16	Captain Randy Haggar installs a surveillance device in the Solicitor's Office; Lariviere resigns the same day.
February 23	Metin's final day working at City Hall.
March 8	Metin begins an 11-week unpaid leave and files a complaint with the Massachusetts Commission Against Discrimination (MCAD), citing emotional disability.
April 1	*The Eagle-Tribune* files suit against the City for the release of the surveillance recording (Lariviere tape).
April 28	Chief Solomon appears as a guest on *Jimmy Kimmel Live*.
May	The City terminates Metin's employment.
May 2	Mayor Sharon Pollard is publicly criticized by the City Council over the $200,000 check from Brooks Pharmacy.
May 3	Officers Randy Haggar, Michael Pappalardo, and James Jajuga Jr. are promoted.
June	Peter McQuillan is appointed as the permanent City Solicitor.
	Metin begins receiving workers' compensation and later settles for a lump sum of $33,900.
June 4	Last day the City issues payroll payments to Metin.
June 24	The Festival of Trees returns the $200,000 donation to the City.
July 1	Former Solicitor Lariviere files a civil lawsuit against the City of Methuen, Chief Solomon, and Deputy Chief Alaimo.
July 7	Metin files a formal claim for workers' compensation.
July 20	A workers' compensation hearing is held in Metin's case.
September 2	Lariviere's lawsuit is transferred to the U.S. District Court.
October 20	Melanson Heath submits the first of a two-part audit report regarding municipal grant programs.
October 21	Lariviere files an amended complaint with the court.

2005

February

Maurice Lariviere, a Methuen native and the son of a retired Methuen police officer, served as the Methuen City Solicitor for 20-plus years. He was widely regarded by his colleagues as a municipal law savant. Lariviere's steadfast commitment to upholding the rule of law forged positive relationships with many, although it also earned him adversaries. The significance of the Solicitor in ensuring compliance with the law and preserving the city's integrity was so valued that the position, along with that of the City Auditor, were made employees of the City Council rather than under the mayor's purview – underscoring the importance of their roles in maintaining the city's legal and ethical standards without political interference.

On February 15, 2005, the newly hired secretary in the solicitor's office filed a complaint of sexual harassment within her workplace to the MPD. Solomon contacted Mayor Pollard that evening, seeking her authorization to conduct an investigation within City Hall.

"At that point, I was not given any details nor did I ask for them," stated Pollard in an interview with a *Boston Globe* reporter. "I permitted the police to take whatever actions they deemed necessary upon receiving an allegation of physical and sexual assault."

Pollard's quote raises questions, as she referenced sexual assault, while the complaint was filed as sexual harassment. These are very different issues in the eyes of the law. Did Pollard misspeak, or was she fanning the flames for the masses?

The following day, Solomon and Deputy Chief Alaimo had a hidden camera installed in Lariviere's outer office.

Later that morning, the camera captured Lariviere attempting to kiss and fondle the secretary while two officers waited in the nearby restroom watching the video feed. Solomon and Alaimo waited in the mayor's office and later confronted Lariviere with the video evidence. They asserted that he offered to resign and subsequently signed a one-sentence resignation paper. Pollard informed reporters the next day that she arranged a check for his unused sick and vacation time, as there was no opportunity to place him on administrative leave.

2005

"When confronted with the allegation, he resigned because he knew what he was doing was wrong," stated Pollard.

She added that she was not involved in the decision to install the surveillance camera.

"I know that the police checked with the district attorney's office prior to proceeding, but this is exactly the type of decision you want the police and not the politicians to make."

Indeed, the motive behind that unsolicited statement remains open to speculation.

Lariviere swiftly departed City Hall and sought legal representation. By July, he informed the City Council of his intention to contest his resignation in court, alleging that it was coerced. Additionally, he planned to file lawsuits against the officials involved in pressuring him to resign, citing violations of his civil rights. Ultimately, Lariviere faced no criminal charges, and the Essex County District Attorney's office opted not to pursue prosecution, largely because the woman involved declined to press criminal charges.

Was the solicitor a womanizer or set up by the administration? There are strong opinions on each side. Some believe the story as it played out and argue that Lariviere's resignation was justified. Others believe that the book-smart, street-naive solicitor was truthful when he said the relationship was consensual and that Solomon and Alaimo took turns yelling at him for two hours, threatening to drag him out of City Hall in handcuffs if he did not resign on the spot.

Lariviere's Resignation

Some further claim the plot was orchestrated by Mayor Pollard to get Lariviere out of the solicitor's office and that Pollard took advantage of the fact that Lariviere's longtime secretary had retired and instead of replacing her with the internal candidate that had certification as a paralegal, Pollard chose to hire an attractive woman from a temp agency. That temp was a single mother who had just moved to the area, had a fiancé in jail and, most importantly, was in financial need.

At the time, a brewing controversy involving Pollard was beginning to unfold — one that would have required the city solicitor to defend her.

2005

Questions arose concerning mitigation funds provided to the city by the Brooks Pharmacy chain during this period. The story dates back to the spring of 1999, before Pollard assumed the mayoral office. Osco Drug presented a proposal to construct a store on Howe Street. As part of the application process, Osco offered the city $650,000 to address any traffic concerns arising from the store's operation. However, the project was rejected at that time. Fast forward to 2004, when the new owners of Osco, Brooks Pharmacy, revived the proposal. Once again, the $650,000 traffic mitigation fund was offered. This time, the Community Development Board approved the project, along with the full mitigation fee, in June 2004.

A few weeks later, Mayor Pollard, through her staff, instructed Brooks Pharmacy to issue two separate checks: one for $450,000 payable to the City of Methuen and another for $200,000 payable to the Methuen Festival of Trees — a nonprofit organization that Pollard herself had founded in 2002.

The $200,000 payment was publicly presented the following month at a Festival board meeting, where Pollard personally announced the contribution. The organization's charitable purpose was to "raise awareness and funds to benefit historic preservation in the City of Methuen." The problem is clear: as mayor, Pollard directed mitigation funds — money that legally belongs under the city's control — to her own nonprofit venture. Under Massachusetts General Laws Chapter 44 (Municipal Finance Law), all mitigation funds must be deposited with the city treasurer and appropriated for municipal use. Having a private nonprofit, even one dedicated to a civic cause, intercept those funds at the mayor's direction was improper and unlawful.

In short, instead of the city controlling and accounting for the funds as required by law, Pollard diverted nearly half a million dollars in mitigation money — $200,000 of which went directly to an organization she created and controlled.

The Methuen City Council officially accepted their $450,000 check from Brooks during the September 20, 2004 meeting. Mayor Pollard, during that meeting, referred to it as a "gift to the city." When a councilor sought clarification about the nature of the "gift," the mayor incorrectly stated that the money could be "expended for any purpose at the city's discretion." She then

2005

proposed various ideas for how the money could be spent, including park improvements and playing fields.

At no point during the meeting did the mayor mention the second check given to the Festival of Trees. However, rumors quickly began circulating about the large donation received by the Festival from Brooks Pharmacy. This issue was brought up at the May 2, 2005 City Council meeting, where Pollard was called to account for diverting city funds to her private non-profit organization.

The Matter of Sharon Pollard

On June 24, 2005, nine months after receiving the check, the Festival of Trees returned the $200,000 to Brooks Pharmacy, which then issued a replacement check, this time payable to the City of Methuen.

Pollard justified her original decision by stating that she believed the city had already addressed traffic issues in the area and that the funds should be allocated to various civic projects, including wall restoration.

Although Essex County District Attorney Jonathan Blodgett initiated an investigation into the gift, he did not press charges against Pollard. However, the State Ethics Commission did fine her $4,000 for conflict-of-interest violations in 2007 in the matter.

If this were you or me, let's be honest — there wouldn't have been a token $4,000 fine. There'd be a 6 a.m. knock at the door from my former colleagues, armed with a search warrant for my financial records and every electronic device I own. And more likely than not, they'd be carrying an arrest warrant and a shiny pair of bracelets to haul me off to court for arraignment. Rules for thee and rules for the politically connected.

Conflict of interest investigations were not something new to Pollard's household. In July of 2002, her husband, Thomas Lussier, former executive director of the Massachusetts Retirement Teacher's Board (MTRB) also faced consequences from the State Ethics Commission. He was fined $5,000 and required to pay $3,500 in restitution due to his misuse of the MTRB's credit card for personal expenses.

The Matter of Thomas Lussier

2005

Replacing Lariviere would have served Pollard's agenda, and the timing of the secretary's hiring was either remarkably coincidental — or conveniently strategic.

Solicitor Fights Back

Lariviere, wanting to clear his name and get his job back, filed a civil rights lawsuit on July 1, 2005 in Lawrence Superior Court against Solomon, Alaimo and the City. A few months later, the case was moved to the U.S. District Court of Massachusetts. His amended complaint and demand for a jury trial were filed in October 2005. In the complaint, Lariviere provided his side of the story, outlining the contentious relationship he had with Mayor Pollard. As an appointed employee under the purview of the City Council, he was not beholden to or under the control of the mayor.

Lariviere provided examples of the acrimonious relationship, stating the mayor repeatedly became angry when he refused to disclose confidential communications with city councilors. He maintained that documents such as ordinances or resolutions prepared for either a councilor or the mayor were kept confidential until the 'client' went public with them.

In one instance, a dispute arose among the City Council regarding raises for department heads. A councilor had Lariviere draft a salary increase ordinance only for the heads of the Department of Elder Affairs and Department of Veteran's Service, excluding other department heads. Consistent with his previous practice, Lariviere did not discuss this draft ordinance with anyone, including the mayor. After learning of the ordinance, Pollard allegedly screamed at Lariviere for not disclosing it to her. He responded that it had always been his policy not to breach attorney-client confidentiality, even refraining from telling councilors when he did work for her. Pollard screamed over the phone, "You scare me!" and hung up, according to Lariviere.

Lariviere's Court Complaint

Pollard's resentment toward the solicitor began in 2004 when a political opponent and critic of Pollard was involved in an accident while exiting her driveway and received a citation related to the incident. This woman also wrote a column in a local newspaper that was highly critical of Pollard and her staff. After the columnist filed a complaint with the police, claiming the citation was politically motivated, Pollard directed Lariviere to conduct a thorough inquiry. Lariviere did so and concluded in his report that the woman had been improperly ticketed and that the accident was actually the fault of the other driver.

Shortly thereafter, while Lariviere was on vacation, he received a call from a city councilor informing him that the mayor wanted him to discard the report and rewrite it, deleting all references to her opponent not being at fault. When Lariviere did not comply, Pollard ordered him and the councilor to a meeting where she attempted to force Lariviere to change the report. He refused, and Pollard reportedly left the meeting angry and disgusted.

In yet another instance, Solomon ordered a police officer to City Hall during a council meeting to issue tickets to persons parking in areas with time-limited parking signage. Two tickets were issued: One to a political opponent and another to a city councilor on the mayor's bad side. The following day, upon learning about the tickets, Lariviere went to the police station and advised Solomon that the ticketing was illegal. Solomon informed Pollard of Lariviere's interference, which reportedly outraged her. The tickets were subsequently withdrawn.

These examples illustrated that, despite Lariviere being hired by and reporting directly to the City Council, Pollard repeatedly came into conflict with him. The evidence suggests that Pollard wanted to remove him and replace him with someone loyal to her, a tactic she had already executed with most of the city department heads. It was common knowledge that she had enough votes on the council to get her preferred candidate hired.

Then there's the hiring of the secretary. When his long-time assistant retired, Lariviere, according to his court complaint, wanted to change the position from a secretarial position to a litigation paralegal role. Through the interview process with the human resource director, a highly qualified internal candidate was chosen. In his court complaint, Lariviere stated that the mayor, without explanation, refused to hire the selected candidate and delayed the process. After six weeks with the position unfilled, the human resource director informed him that he could hire a temporary employee until a second round of interviews could take

2005

place. This is how the temp secretary in question, Fulya Metin, started with the city.

After a few days of working in the office, Lariviere returned from lunch and was informed that the new secretary did not know anyone in the area and had gone to Burger King to eat alone in her car. The next day, Lariviere invited Metin to lunch. The conversation was pleasant, and she talked openly about her previous failed marriage, life problems and intimate details of her life. She divulged that she had money problems and had to move to her mother's home in Haverhill.

Emails between Metin and Lariviere

They began a routine of going to lunch Monday through Thursday, unless Lariviere had a court appearance. At Metin's insistence, they joined a gym and would either work out or go to lunch. Sometimes, they would go on shopping trips when she needed things for herself. This continued from October 2004 to February 2005.

Shortly after Metin started, Lariviere put a hold on the interview process to see if she would be a good fit, as she had indicated her interest in the position. He mentioned that she began to call him "Archangel" because he had helped her with many problems. In November 2004, after she agreed to obtain a paralegal certificate, Lariviere recommended her for the job to the human resource director, who agreed. The recommendation then went to the mayor, who also approved the hire.

He stated that Metin was so happy that she jumped into his arms with such force that she almost knocked him over, repeatedly hugging and kissing him while thanking him for the position. From then on, she would often thank Lariviere for the job, repeatedly saying he was the best boss she ever had and that he was training her well. She even mentioned that she did not want to leave the job and that when her fiancé Anthony, a Seabee serving in Iraq, returned home, she would convince him to move to Massachusetts. In reality, Anthony was in jail in New York for conspiracy to commit armed robbery.

She would spend at least an hour per day in the City Council office next door, making photocopies, taking breaks or having coffee with the staff there. Metin shared with them the same

2005

stories she told Lariviere about her personal, financial and other intimate troubles. At no point did she mention to the City Council staff that Lariviere was approaching her in an unwanted or sexual manner or that he made her uncomfortable.

The office on the other side of the solicitor's office was the Human Resource Department. She also became friends with an employee there, and they would often talk about life in general. Their friendship grew to the point where they discussed attending dating service parties or going out for the evening. At no time did she confide in that friend about any inappropriate conduct happening in her workplace.

According to his complaint, as time went on, Metin became bolder. After getting a tattoo, she offered to show it to Lariviere and proceeded to pull the sides of her top down, exposing her breast and bra and new tatoo. She also asked him for help managing her financial problems, prompting Lariviere to call his credit union to help her get a consolidated loan. When she needed money to buy a prescription, he lent her the money, which she paid back a week later.

On the day of his resignation, February 16, 2005, Lariviere described the events according to his recollections. Upon learning that he had won a large federal court case on behalf of the city — the largest and most important of his career — he called the secretary at home to share the good news, as well as calling Solomon and Pollard.

The next morning when Metin came to work, she appeared sad, which he assumed was due to her ulcers causing her pain. He asked her to make copies and prepare envelopes for the councilors to inform them of the successful case outcome. As he was returning to his office, Metin said, "You are a good attorney."

He came back, and they talked about the case some more. As she had done to him before, he leaned over and kissed her on the cheek, followed by a peck on her lips. She looked slightly downwards.

"Are you okay?" he asked.

She answered, "Yes, I am just tired."

Leaning over, he placed his right arm on her left shoulder as a sign of support, stating what he often told her.

"I am here for you to help you, my friend."

2005

They talked a bit more before she stood up. They briefly kissed again. As she began to leave, he stood up and again asked if she was okay. Metin replied yes and started to walk past him. He inquired about her stomach, pointing to and then touching the right front area, asking, "Is it [her ulcer] okay?" She again replied yes. After a few moments, she left and went outside. He said that she never gave any indication that the contact was unwanted or inappropriate.

Next thing he knows Solomon and Alaimo arrived in his office. Lariviere assumed they had come to talk about his court victory, but he couldn't have been more wrong. The two men had stern looks on their faces and asked him to go to the second-floor conference room. Lariviere initially thought they might have planned a surprise party for his victory in court.

The conference room was empty besides Solomon and Alaimo, but Lariviere assumed people would join them shortly. However, Alaimo began reading him his Miranda rights, and only then did Lariviere realize his fantastic day had turned upside down. The duo informed him that Metin had filed a complaint of sexual assault, alleging that he had fondled her breasts.

Solomon then placed two tape recorders on the table and started recording. Feeling exposed, Lariviere wanted to explain his side of the story to the two men he had worked with closely for years. He admitted he had blurred the line between boss and employee in his friendship with Fulya but insisted it was nothing close to what they were alleging. Hoping to handle things privately, he asked them to turn off the recorders, thinking he could appeal to them personally before the situation spiraled further out of control.

According to Lariviere, Solomon and Alaimo then began berating him, saying, "[The secretary] wants you out of here; you cannot work here anymore, you are finished." Solomon then expressed how much it hurt him to have to do this and how he couldn't sleep the night before.

Both Lariviere and the officers knew that Methuen had a sexual harassment policy in place, which included a complete review process. Nevertheless, they demanded he resign and waive his right to a hearing to avoid criminal prosecution. Solomon added,

> "If you resign, I know [the secretary] will not press charges based on my talking to her just a little while ago. However, the Mayor wants you fired and prosecuted. I

> *can talk to her; as you know, we have let people have [paid administrative] leave and then they just go away. I will talk to her [the mayor] about this."*

Confused and devastated, Lariviere thought he was attending a victory party but found himself facing criminal accusations. All he wanted to do was go home, talk to his wife, and decide what to do.

"You will not leave. Resign or I will arrest you right now," said Solomon before leaving the room to consult with the mayor.

Being the two top law enforcement officials in the city and the mayor's strongest supporters, Solomon and Alaimo had no interest in hearing Lariviere's side of the story. They knew the solicitor had due process rights concerning his job, but that did not matter to them. It was either waive his rights and resign or be arrested.

Solomon and Alaimo repeated Metin's allegations that Lariviere had molested the secretary, fondled her breasts, and stalked her. When pressed about the stalking accusation, they referenced the call he had made to her the night before. Lariviere explained that the call was about the court case. Solomon admitted, "I was there for the second call and heard it." Lariviere responded, "Joe, if you did, then you know all I talked about was the court case and then hung up."

As Alaimo stood over the seated solicitor, Solomon repeatedly stated, "Sign the resignation or I will arrest you, handcuff you and drag you out of this building in front of people you know."

He continued the intimidation.

> *"When we arrest you it will be all over the papers. We will then ask council to terminate you. If you quit now it will be kept quiet and no one will know. I will instruct my people not to talk about this. Your choice. Make it now."*

After just under two hours of being attacked by Solomon and Alaimo, Lariviere snapped. All he could think about was his family and the potential harm that could come to them and him. He realized the threats, intimidation and coercion were designed to force him to waive his rights, and he felt that presenting his side of the story would be fruitless. Beaten down and wanting to avoid the notoriety that would harm his family and tarnish his name, he told them, "OK, what choice do I have?"

Solomon left the room to get the human resource director, another strong Pollard supporter, who arrived with a short resignation letter, a hearing waiver and a pen.

After Lariviere left the City of Methuen, Peter McQuillan, Esq., who had previously held the position, was again appointed to the City Solicitor.

April

In April Methuen gained national media attention when four men stumbled upon a trove of antique bills while excavating a tree in their Methuen backyard. Their discovery, estimated to be worth approximately $120,000, sparked a week-long flurry of television interviews featuring the men discussing their find. However, these interviews, coupled with an anonymous tip to the MPD, prompted detectives to delve deeper into the men's conflicting statements. Upon questioning, one of the roofers confessed to finding the bills concealed in rusted cans within the beams of an old barn they had been renovating in Newbury, Massachusetts.

Two of the men were to appear on "Jimmy Kimmel Live!" but instead found themselves booked at the Methuen police station on charges of larceny, receiving stolen property, conspiracy, and accessory after the fact.

Taking one for the team, Solomon filled in for them during the interview with Kimmel. When not bantering with actress Fran Dresher, he quipped that they'd be splitting the money and not in trouble with the law if they kept the discovery to themselves.

In another interview on "Good Morning America," Solomon speculated that the men likely stumbled upon the money and concocted a scheme to make their find appear legitimate so they could keep the proceeds. His observation proved astute — by making their story so public, they effectively raised a glaring red flag. After all, how often do people who stumble upon a fortune broadcast it unless they're trying to justify possessing it?

This brief taste of fame seemed to ignite Solomon's narcissistic tendencies, leading to a pattern of seeking media attention whenever possible. Years later, during the Lawrence natural gas disaster, Solomon, not the Lawrence Police Chief, took center stage in early media interviews.

The Chief even directed the department to purchase equipment, including lights and backdrops resembling those used by news reporters, to enhance the appearance of his press conferences and present himself and his team in a more favorable light on camera.

Essex County District Attorney Jonathan Blodgett pursued prosecution against all four treasure hunters not once but twice, attempting to bring the case to two different courts. Both efforts ended in dismissal due to insufficient evidence. The failings of the prosecution prompt a compelling question: why did Blodgett dedicate such persistent effort to this case out of the many under his jurisdiction? At the same time, the property owner initiated a lawsuit against the men, seeking the return of the disputed property. The two sides eventually resolved through an out-of-court settlement.

As a side note, while researching and writing this book, I would naturally share aspects of my findings with my wife. Several months into the project, the story of the treasure trove surfaced in one of our conversations. To my surprise, she got a peculiar look on her face. The family whose barn the money was discovered in was her own family!

Reflections: Weaponizing Scandal

The contrast in how these scandals were handled is striking. We know that Mayor Pollard directed mitigation money illegally, diverting funds from Brooks Pharmacy to her own nonprofit, and for that she received nothing more than a $4,000 ethics fine. Most public officials who used their office that way would have been facing years in prison, not a slap on the wrist.

Maurice Lariviere, by contrast, was treated very differently. The city went to extraordinary lengths — planting hidden cameras and fast-tracking an investigation on the thinnest of claims. His real "crime," it seems, was that he was a threat to Sharon Pollard. As City Solicitor, he took seriously the lawyer's code of ethics — particularly the duty of confidentiality and attorney–client privilege. He would not bend those rules, nor would he betray client confidences to serve a political agenda.

That refusal to "share" information made him dangerous in a political environment where loyalty was often valued above law or ethics. So while Pollard's own misconduct was minimized, Lariviere was subjected to a covert sting operation and pushed out of office.

This is the textbook definition of selective enforcement — where power, politics, and personal alliances dictate consequences rather than the law itself. In Methuen, scandal wasn't simply about uncovering wrongdoing; it was about deciding whose wrongdoing would be punished and whose would be quietly excused.

2006

	Officer Joseph Aiello returns to active duty with the Methuen Police Department after a leave of absence.
January 2	William Manzi is sworn in as Mayor of Methuen.
March	A purchase order for a police patrol boat appears on Mayor Manzi's desk for approval.
March 30	Shaun Cronin files a civil lawsuit against the City of Methuen, Police Chief Joseph Solomon, and Deputy Chief Joseph Alaimo.
April 6	Sergeant Larry Phillips is assigned to investigate a stolen tractor case.
May	Melanson Heath submits the second and final portion of its audit of municipal grant programs.
May 2	Chief Solomon donates $500 to Jon Blodgett's campaign for Essex County District Attorney.
May 11	The Massachusetts State Ethics Commission initiates an investigation into whether former Mayor Sharon Pollard violated conflict-of-interest laws.
May 22	The United States Department of Justice (DOJ) reduces the City's repayment obligation on the Community Oriented Policing Services (COPS) grant to $23,096.
June	The Methuen Police Department purchases a patrol boat from Merrimac Marine.
June 29	An exit conference is held with Melanson Heath to discuss the findings of the grant audit.
June 30	A decision is issued in the case of *Eagle-Tribune v. Methuen*.
July 26	Sergeant Phillips reports that he was instructed not to pursue criminal charges against a relative of Chief Solomon in the stolen tractor case.
August	Federal agents subpoena the City for all grant-related records dating back to 2001.
September	A federal grand jury subpoenas the City Auditor to testify and provide all requested grant documentation.
September 5	Fulya Metin marries Anthony Capanelli.
October 1	Metin reaches a settlement with the City in her workers' compensation claim.

2006

October 3	A heated three-way phone call takes place between Chief Solomon, his attorney Thomas Kiley, and the City Solicitor.
October 8	Chief Solomon's daughter is involved in a hit-and-run accident.
Mid-October	Chief Solomon's scheduled appearance before the federal grand jury is abruptly canceled.
October 29	Solomon receives a formal subpoena from the Department of Justice.
November 7	A show cause hearing is held for Solomon's daughter in connection with the October hit-and-run incident.
November 10	The City hires APD Management to conduct an independent investigation into allegations of abuse of power by Chief Solomon.
December	Chief Solomon launches an internal inquiry to identify Methuen Police Department personnel allegedly cooperating with the Federal Bureau of Investigation (FBI).
December 4	Approximately 250 supporters attend a City Council meeting in public support of Chief Solomon.

January

In 2006, Sharon Pollard's tenure as Mayor of Methuen ended. Term limits required her to step down, and William Manzi III, a former city councilor and the general election winner, took over the corner office at City Hall. Manzi was a man of commanding stature, with nuanced, loquacious, and colorful speaking skills paired with a mildly brusque demeanor.

Manzi's Inaugural Program

March

Shaun and Kimberly Cronin filed a tortious action against the City of Methuen, MPD, Solomon, and Joseph Alaimo in Essex County Superior Court on March 30th.

Shaun Cronin was a Methuen police officer for 17 years and the son of long-time politico and sitting Methuen City Councilor John Cronin. The lawsuit, initiated in 2006, alleged various claims stemming from Cronin's resignation from the department and his purportedly unsuccessful attempts to secure employment

2006

elsewhere. Eventually, the city was removed from the lawsuit, leaving Solomon and Alaimo as the remaining defendants.

The lawsuit's backstory centers on Cronin's disciplinary record during his tenure at the MPD. Throughout his employment, Cronin faced three disciplinary actions: abuse of sick time, an incident involving a family member, and filing a false report. Between the second and third incidents, in 2003, Cronin underwent his annual review by his supervisor, Sergeant Kevin Martin, receiving "above average" ratings in nine out of 14 categories and "good" ratings in the remaining ones. He did not receive any "needs improvement" ratings. Lieutenant Thomas Fram agreed with and signed off on the assessment along with Martin. Solomon, Deputy Chief Alaimo, and Captain Joseph Harb signed the evaluation as required, though they noted their disagreement with the findings.

Cronin's Court Papers

The following month, a disciplinary hearing was scheduled regarding the third incident, filing a false report. However, a hearing was averted when Cronin and the city settled. Cronin would be terminated on January 3rd of the following year after a paid leave of absence and using up all his MPD sick time. In return, Cronin agreed not to sue the city to reclaim his job or seek additional benefits.

When January arrived, Cronin, still aspiring to be a full-time police officer, began applying to local municipalities and other similar employment. In the meantime, needing a paycheck to support his family, he took on various jobs, working as a mall cop, an armored car driver, a transportation security screener and a college security officer. By May 2006, he had settled into a more stable role as a postal carrier.

The lawsuit arose from Cronin's belief that the MPD gave him poor references when potential employers reached out, and these companies subsequently decided not to hire him.

Solomon testified that two potential employers had contacted him about Cronin. The first was a school's police chief, but Solomon could not recall the name or the school. They played phone tag and never managed to speak directly. Solomon said he had talked to Captain Michael Molchan from the Lawrence Police

Department (LPD), who requested all background information on Cronin. Solomon declined to provide any commentary or documentation without a signed release form.

Contradicting Solomon's testimony was an internal LPD memorandum Molchan wrote at the time. It stated that Solomon "would not recommend Shaun Cronin for the position of patrolman in Lawrence" for several reasons. Solomon expressed concerns that Cronin had too many issues and might abuse his authority as a police officer by pulling over Methuen officers and issuing tickets. However, Solomon indicated that Cronin was not corrupt or dirty but was motivated by a desire for medals and recognition.

Cronin further alleged that he encountered a friend, a former Lawrence police officer, who told him that during his application to the LPD, she informed Chief John Romero that she believed Cronin was a good person. Romero reportedly stated to her that it didn't matter. After all, Solomon and Alaimo had "killed" Cronin's chances and the LPD couldn't hire him because nobody had anything positive to say about him. In an affidavit to the court, Romero stated that he did speak with Solomon, who said that beyond providing what was authorized by Cronin to release, he could not comment further on his application for employment. Romero elaborated that at no time did Solomon badmouth or disparage Cronin or comment negatively on his application.

In the deposition of Cronin, Solomon's attorney, Andrew Gambaccini, asked him if he had any "personal information as to whether Solomon had any contact with anyone associated with the Lawrence Police Department."

> "Oh, please. He did. You know it. I know it. Everyone on the planet knows it. You know how it's done," Cronin replied. "Come on. You know exactly what he did. You know exactly how he did it. You're doing your job in defending him, but you know how he did it. It's all back doors. It is all whispers. You know exactly what he did."

October

The saga surrounding former Solicitor Lariviere did not end with his resignation — it continued to escalate. Fulya, his former secretary, informed city officials that she could no longer work in the solicitor's office. She cited the circumstances surrounding his departure, the ensuing media coverage and concerns about the interim solicitor's ties to Lariviere. She declined when city officials offered her alternative positions in another city building. In response, Mayor Pollard placed Fulya on paid administrative leave and arranged for her to see a psychiatrist.

After three months of paying Fulya to stay home, the City Council pressed Pollard about the mounting costs. The inquiry came when Pollard was already under Council scrutiny for accepting the two checks from Brooks Pharmacy. Ultimately, Pollard terminated Fulya's employment. Fulya responded by filing a workers' compensation claim for emotional and physical disability.

At a hearing on July 20, 2005, Fulya testified that on her fourth day working in the office, Lariviere had "grabbed and kissed" her without consent. Despite her immediate objections and disclosing her history of being sexually abused as a child, he reportedly continued these unwanted advances. As part of her case, Fulya provided medical records that documented her experience of "emotional distress and significant stomach issues" resulting from the sexual harassment and what she described as a hostile work environment.

The hearing officer ruled in her favor, awarding her 60 percent of her salary in compensation, effective immediately and retroactive to her termination date in June. However, the city swiftly filed an appeal, prolonging the legal dispute.

Meanwhile, just a week before Fulya filed her workers' comp claim Lariviere fulfilled his promise to file a lawsuit against Solomon, Alaimo, and the City of Methuen in Essex County Superior Court. His suit alleged coercion, civil rights violations, emotional distress, and conspiracy. In response, the defendants filed a "Notice of Removal" to transfer the case to federal court — a move potentially advantageous to the defense due to the possibility of local biases, conflicts with the judge or jury, and the perceived simplicity of federal court procedures. The court granted the motion was granted, shifting the legal battle to a new arena.

Complicating matters further, the *Eagle-Tribune* requested the City release the police videotape involving the former solicitor and his secretary, citing the public's right to access such records. The city, however, declined the request. In response, the newspaper appealed in local court, arguing that the tape qualified as a public record. The judge ultimately ruled in favor of the city, finding that releasing the tape would infringe on the secretary's privacy and could deter future victims of sexual assault from coming forward. The Boston-based lawyer representing the city emphasized to reporters that access to the tape had been "narrowly constrained," with only a few individuals having viewed it — specifically, Fulya, Lariviere, a city official, and the legal representatives for all three parties.

Eagle Tribune v. Solomon Court Papers

By October 2006, the City and Fulya reached a negotiated settlement to avoid a civil trial over the appeal of Fulya's workers' compensation claim. As part of the agreement, Fulya withdrew her claim. However, the specifics of what she received in return remain unknown.

October 8th

On the night of October 8, 2006, Solomon found himself in a situation where media attention was the last thing he desired. At nearly 7 p.m., his seventeen-year-old daughter was driving home from her aunt's house with her sister and a friend. According to Ms. Solomon's account, while driving her 1995 Toyota Camry down Pleasant Street in Methuen, she noticed a man jogging on the side of the road. As she approached him, she applied her brakes to avoid him. However, her car skidded and when it came to a halt, the man ran into the front of her car. She told authorities that despite the shock of the incident, she decided to drive away to seek help, not because her father was the police chief, but because she knew he possessed the necessary training to assist the injured man.

Meanwhile, patrol Officer Lawrence May was parked down the street when he heard what sounded like a crash. Responding quickly, he drove to the accident scene, where he found the 53-

year-old man lying in the road. Officer May promptly called for an ambulance and began assisting the injured individual. Witnesses at the scene informed May that car's driver had stopped briefly before driving off toward the center of town.

Back at the Solomon household, located about a tenth of a mile down the road, Solomon heard a commotion in his kitchen. Upon investigation, he found his daughters and their friend in a state of distress, informing him that there had been an accident and expressing concern that the man involved might be injured.

Reacting swiftly, Solomon and his daughter rushed to the accident site in his police car with the blue lights flashing, taking only about 15 seconds to arrive. Upon reaching the scene, Solomon instructed his daughter to remain in the car while he assessed the situation.

After informing Officer May that his daughter was the driver involved in the accident and that she parked her car in his driveway, May completed his duties at the scene and then proceeded to the Solomon residence. There, he cited the daughter for leaving the scene of an accident that resulted in personal injury.

A just-cause hearing was requested, prompting Solomon to ask Essex County District Attorney Jonathan Blodgett's office to oversee the case. Initially scheduled to be heard in Lawrence District Court, a change of venue was recommended due to Solomon's relationship with the court, a standard measure taken to prevent conflicts of interest.

The hearing was scheduled for November 7, 2007 in Newburyport District Court, with Clerk Magistrate Kathryn Early presiding. Miss Solomon presented her account of the events while the lawyer representing the injured man offered his perspective. Contrary to Miss Solomon's assertion that the man "ran into her car," the lawyer argued that the man was crossing the street after using the ATM when struck by her car. As a result, he sustained injuries to his ankle, head, and face, requiring overnight hospitalization. His injuries were severe enough to necessitate a CAT scan, and he now relies on a cane for walking.

After considering all the testimony, the Clerk Magistrate determined there was no probable cause to charge Miss Solomon for the accident criminally.

Following the hearing, the man's lawyer expressed his client's desire for Solomon's insurance company to cover his medical expenses, which had already exceeded $3,000.

The man's son, who sat through the hearing, told *The Boston Globe* that the case reeked with hypocrisy. "If I was driving and I hit the police chief's daughter, it wouldn't turn out like this," he stated.

Three years after the accident, the injured man filed a lawsuit in Lawrence Superior Court against Miss Solomon for the cost of his medical care resulting from the car accident. The case was settled out of court in 2011 for $30,000.

Court Settlement Papers

November

In August, federal agents arrived at Methuen City Hall with grand jury subpoenas, demanding records of all federal grants awarded to the Methuen Police Department since 2001. During this period, federal authorities actively investigated grant-related misconduct on the state level.

The visit immediately fueled speculation that the feds would summon certain police officers to testify before a grand jury. The scuttlebutt led Solomon to initiate an inquiry to identify any department employees sharing information with the FBI — especially if the discussions involved him personally.

As part of this investigation, six officers — including one subpoenaed to testify before the grand jury, along with Kevin Dzioba, the patrolmen's union president, and Eric Deleon, the union's vice president — were subjected to intense questioning by an MPD lieutenant. During these interrogations, the officers were pressed for information about possible indictments. They asked if they had been approached by law enforcement, including the FBI, regarding potential charges against Solomon or his command staff.

In speaking with *The Boston Globe*, the union's attorney said some of these interrogations extended past midnight, with two officers called in off-duty and compensated with overtime pay. Following these sessions, the patrolmen's union attorney accused

2006

Solomon of abusing power and violating free speech rights, expressing concerns that his actions might interfere with the ongoing federal investigation.

"You can't compel an officer to testify about lawful off-duty conduct, especially if it involves cooperation with a law enforcement investigation, as it could jeopardize the probe," the attorney stated.

The federal statute 18 U.S.C. § 1503 governs what can and cannot be disclosed regarding grand jury proceedings. Simply put, the law prohibits the disclosure of any information related to the grand jury, its investigation, or an individual's involvement in it. Violating this statute by sharing such information can result in felony charges against the person responsible for the disclosure. Solomon's behavior seemed designed to intimidate and interfere with the integrity of the court process. Despite the clear illegality, the U.S. Attorney's office inexplicably overlooked these actions and brought no repercussions against Solomon.

Solomon's supporters argued that he had the right to question the officers, citing regulations against dishonesty. However, City Solicitor Peter McQuillan advised Solomon to cease the internal inquiry, framing it as a "labor relations issue." The chief then ceased his inquisition into what was disclosed by whom before the Grand Jury.

By November, the Methuen City Council, particularly Councilor John Cronin, grew increasingly apprehensive about the grant investigation. Concerns over the allegations of Solomon interrogating his rank-and-file members to gather firsthand knowledge of ongoing federal investigations, questioning the validity of such actions. "With everything going on, [Solomon] might not be effective as a chief anymore," Cronin told *The Boston Globe*. Expressing concern about the questioning of officers related to the grand jury, Cronin said, "It is very, very wrong, and probably illegal."

While Cronin was getting frustrated with Solomon, some councilors were questioning Cronin's actions, which were appearing like a personal vendetta. Cronin's son Shaun, a former MPD officer, was suing the MPD, alleging that Solomon and others were working behind the scenes to prevent him from getting employment in law enforcement. Councilor Cronin expectantly denied that accusation.

2006

Frustrated with the lack of information, Councilor Cronin called a special council meeting to determine whether Solomon should still lead the department. However, the city solicitor swiftly intervened, halting the special meeting within a few days again citing Solomon's interrogations as a labor dispute.

The subsequent council meeting on December 4th drew a full house. The chamber overflowed with 250 supporters of Solomon, adorned with two Lebanese flags. A contingent of captains and lieutenants from the MPD stood shoulder to shoulder, visibly demonstrating solidarity. While some attended of their own volition, others responded to a strong suggestion that they be present. Notably, one officer who made the difficult choice to prioritize their sick child over attending the meeting faced swift and severe retaliation. The consequences were not only painful but also profoundly career-altering.

The crowd eagerly awaited the public participation segment for their chance to voice either support for the chief or concerns about the situation. Later reports suggested that someone in the crowd offered a prayer, wishing eternal life upon those defending Solomon. Stephen Zanni, the council chairman, requested the audience to refrain from clapping after each speaker, instead saving applause for the end of all speeches. However, his request seemed futile as cheers erupted from the crowd during and after each of the twenty supportive speeches. When a lone individual spoke of alleged abuses by the chief to intimidate people, their words garnered a round of boos. Amidst the charged atmosphere, a voice from the crowd accused Cronin and the *Eagle-Tribune* of racial profiling.

After the meeting, City Councilor Deborah Quinn defended Solomon to reporters. "This guy has been crucified," she said. "It's time to show some of the support he has and the good things he has done."

As *Rumbo* newspaper columnist Ellen Bahan left the meeting, she expressed disgust at the evening's display of force. "It had a mob mentality to it ... I have never been more ashamed of being a resident of Methuen," she remarked.

Quinn took exception to Bahan's comment, countering that the gathering was "a step to healing for the Police Department."

Just a month earlier, the department had investigated Solomon for abuse of power after a complaint from a civilian — who,

2006

notably, was the only person at the meeting to speak out against the chief.

Methuen hired Tewksbury Police Chief Al Donovan to conduct the inquest. Donovan owned APD Management, Inc., a law enforcement consulting firm. Eight months later, in August of 2007, Donovan found the claims against Solomon unfounded.

As a consultant, Donovan will spend the next 14 years professionally entwined with Solomon and the MPD.

2007

January	Officer Joseph Aiello replaces Officer Kevin Dzioba as President of the Patrolmen's Union and is promoted to the Detective Unit.
	Lieutenant Wnek is reassigned from Criminal Investigations to Platoon Commander.
January 24	The Massachusetts State Ethics Commission concludes its investigation into former Mayor Sharon Pollard.
February	*The Valley Patriot* publishes an interview with Police Chief Joseph Solomon about discrimination allegations.
February 5	The United States Department of Justice (DOJ) demands the City repay $40,000 related to the Community Oriented Policing Services (COPS) grant.
March	Solomon and Mayor William Manzi meet to discuss disciplinary issues.
March 13	DOJ reduces the COPS repayment demand to $29,976.
March 15	Mayor Manzi issues a formal Notice of Hearing to Chief Solomon.
March 19	Solomon is summoned to the City Council to address the DOJ grant investigation.
March 23	Solomon contacts DOJ Agent Glendinning to inquire about the ongoing investigation.
March 27	The City of Methuen files an appeal contesting the DOJ's non-compliance findings.
April 2	A disciplinary hearing is held for Solomon regarding mismanagement of grant funds.
April 4	Agent Glendinning releases a DOJ report identifying $170,000 in mismanaged Weed and Seed (W&S) grant funds.
April 9	Hearing Officer Michael Marks issues his findings.
April 11	Mayor Manzi notifies Solomon of a three-day suspension.
April 16	Solomon begins his suspension.
April 26	The Massachusetts State Ethics Commission fines former Mayor Pollard $4,000 for a conflict-of-interest violation.
May 18	DOJ sends a letter identifying $170,000 in questionable grant spending.
May 21	The City Council votes 5–3 in favor of a no-confidence resolution against Solomon.

2007

May 23	DOJ accepts the City's appeal and reduces the repayment amount to $23,000.
May 31	The Superior Officers' Union submits a letter to the City Council supporting Solomon.
June	At a City Council meeting, Solomon publicly demands an end to personal attacks.
June 30	Employment contracts for Solomon and Deputy Chief Joseph Alaimo expire.
July	Fulya Metin's fiancé, Anthony Capanelli, is released from jail.
July 20	Fulya Metin (Capanelli) files a discrimination complaint with the Massachusetts Commission Against Discrimination (MCAD).
July 26	DOJ sends a renewed demand letter seeking repayment of $170,000.
August 8	APD Management, the independent consulting firm, finds Solomon did not commit abuse of power.
August 15	City Council instructs the City Solicitor to review the expired contracts of Solomon and Alaimo.
August 24	Solomon finds on-duty officers watching football at the station.
	Solomon's former brother-in-law is subpoenaed to appear before a federal grand jury.
August 25	Sergeant Larry Phillips is placed on administrative leave pending investigation.
August 27	Fulya Metin (Capanelli) files a civil lawsuit against the City of Methuen, Solomon, Alaimo, and former Solicitor Maurice Lariviere.
August 28	Sergeant Phillips testifies before the grand jury.
September 2	The Essex County District Attorney issues a Brady disclosure letter concerning Aiello's credibility.
September 4	City Council votes to cut the pay of Solomon and Alaimo.
September 13	Solomon and Mayor Manzi meet to discuss discipline of four officers.
September 16	Manzi orders Methuen Square to be reopened during a film shoot.
	Solomon meets with Michael Neve regarding bribery allegations against Manzi.
September 19	Solomon and Alaimo file an emergency injunction and lawsuit to challenge their pay cuts.
September 22	Solomon orders Phillips back to full duty with counseling.
September 24	Solomon, Captain Kathy Lavigne, and Officer Michael Pappalardo meet with the District Attorney to discuss the Manzi bribery allegations.

2007

	Solomon sends a letter to Manzi regarding officer discipline.
	Councilor Deborah Quinn warns Solomon that Manzi may be preparing to terminate him.
September 25	Solomon meets with the Federal Bureau of Investigation (FBI) about allegations against Manzi.
September 26	Alaimo contacts Manzi about the revocation of Solomon's city-issued vehicle.
September 27	Michael Neve is subpoenaed to testify before the grand jury.
September 28	Solomon is placed on paid administrative leave over the grant controversy.
	Captain Kathy Lavigne is named Acting Police Chief.
October 1	FBI wires Aiello for a phone call with Manzi.
	City Council passes a Home Rule Petition removing the Police Chief position from Massachusetts Civil Service.
	The Patrolmen's Union votes unanimously not to endorse any mayoral candidate.
October 3	FBI wires Aiello again for a follow-up call with Manzi.
October 7	City Solicitor Peter McQuillan is directed by the Council to review Solomon and Alaimo's contracts.
October 9	Neve provides a written statement to the grand jury.
October 17	Captain Randy Haggar submits a report on the reopening of Methuen Square during the movie shoot.
November 2	Michael Alaimo meets with Manzi to discuss options ("Speech A or Speech B").
	A "Pro-Joe" rally is held at a local function hall in support of Solomon.
November 6	Mayor William Manzi wins re-election.

January

In the first month of the year, the patrolmen's union held elections, resulting in the narrow defeat of President Dzioba. His replacement, Officer Joseph Aiello — a close friend and ally of Solomon — quickly withdrew the union's complaint against the chief, a move many saw as more than coincidental.

Surprisingly, Aiello remained a police officer in good standing, particularly given his legal troubles two years earlier. In a New Hampshire court, he had pleaded guilty to tampering with a

2007

government document, a reduced charge from the original forgery allegation. The case stemmed from issues related to a motorcycle shop he co-owned and opened in 2002.

Aiello's Arrest Records

The incident occurred when a customer, a New York state trooper, asked Aiello to sell his 2002 Harley Davidson motorcycle for $21,500, with Aiello receiving a $500 commission upon sale. Months later, Aiello informed the client that he had found a buyer but at a lower price and advised him that, under New Hampshire law, signing over the title was unnecessary. Suspicions arose when the client received the title from the New Hampshire Registry of Motor Vehicles and discovered someone had forged his signature.

On June 25, 2004, the New Hampshire Highway Patrol and Enforcement Bureau arrested Aiello and charged him with forging his client's name – a felony. In February of the following year, he pleaded guilty to a misdemeanor charge of tampering with a public record and paid a $1,200 fine.

Surprisingly, despite these legal troubles, Methuen took no action against Aiello – likely because he was on leave from the department from 2002 to 2006. However, a Brady letter was issued by the first assistant at the Essex County District Attorney's office, barring Aiello from testifying in court due to his criminal record potentially undermining his credibility.

Aiello's Brady Letter

Regarding Aiello's Brady letter, his disciplinary records were listed in the Massachusetts Peace Officer Standards and Training (POST) database as they should have been. Still, they disappeared from that list at the beginning of 2023. When contacted several years later, the man whose signature Aiello had forged expressed surprise that Aiello was still an active police officer. New Hampshire investigators had informed him that Aiello would no longer work in law enforcement. The opposite happened. Aiello returned full-time to the MPD in 2006 and was elected union president in January 2007. Soon after, he was

2007

promoted to the elite drug unit, where detectives work in plain clothes and receive unmarked cars.

February

Speculation intensified throughout the winter of 2006-2007 regarding the grand jury and Solomon's potential involvement. The *Eagle-Tribune* published numerous stories scrutinizing and evaluating the MPD's grant funding and Solomon's alleged role in it.

In February, tired of the negative press surrounding the grant situation, Solomon sought the assistance of his friend Tom Duggan, a self-publisher of a local commentary publication known for its unique take on local politics, the *Valley Patriot*. Together, they aimed to reclaim the narrative with a headline titled "Methuen's Police Chief Joe Solomon Speaks Out." The article defended the use of grant funds by the MPD and highlighted the positive impact on the Arlington District. Solomon addressed the *Eagle-Tribune*'s focus on the "mere" $27,000 in his travel expenses, attributing the scrutiny to what he believed was a politically motivated agenda influenced by his ethnic background.

"I personally feel this is a racial attack being launched against me by the *Eagle-Tribune*. Every time they run a picture of me, they use an old picture with a mustache and goatee because I am an Arab American," Solomon said. "I have received so much pressure on this goatee thing I finally shaved it off. They have been after me since 9-11 personally because I am an Arab American police chief, and I'm not going to be silent on this any longer."

The most surprising aspect of this situation is that the only person raising claims of racism is Solomon himself. After thorough research, we found no one else has pointed to his ancestry as a factor — only Solomon. His appearance might easily be associated with ethnicities such as Italian, Greek and Puerto Rican, but "Arab" is not the first identity that comes to mind when looking at Solomon.

2007

March

In March of 2007, the Justice Department sent a letter to City Hall, mandating officials to return some of the Homeland Security COPS grant funds allocated to the police department. The letter highlighted that MPD misused $30,000 of a patrolmen-specific $50,000 grant via erroneous overtime pay to superior officers. The city promptly filed an appeal challenging the Justice Department's non-compliance finding.

On March 19th, Solomon was summoned to the city council meeting to address concerns surrounding the Department of Justice's request to repay grant funds.

In preparation, Solomon reached out to Jack Collins, general counsel for the Massachusetts Chiefs of Police Association, seeking advice via email. In that correspondence, Collins suggested that Solomon consider "taking one for the team," but only on the condition that the three-day suspension proposed by Mayor Manzi would be the sole disciplinary action imposed. He reassured Solomon that he believed Manzi would not push for termination, as public opinion would likely oppose such a move.

Collins also proposed a public relations strategy to navigate the situation. He advised that Solomon's attorney work with the city solicitor to secure an agreement guaranteeing no additional disciplinary actions if federal investigators uncovered further accounting discrepancies. The proposed approach would present Mayor Manzi as a strong, proactive leader for suspending the chief, while Solomon could publicly frame the issue as unintentional mistakes made in good faith. By doing so, both parties could signal a commitment to moving past the controversy for the city's sake.

Additionally, Collins assured Solomon that the Association stood ready to mobilize support if needed.

As the grant administration ultimately fell under Solomon's responsibility, Mayor William Manzi convened a full public hearing for Solomon on April 9th. The hearing was presided over by Michael Marks, Esq., acting as the hearing officer.

Andrew Gambaccini, Esq., represented Solomon, while Peter McQuillan, Esq., represented the city. The suspension case marked the inception of a legal relationship spanning decades between Gambaccini and Solomon. The crux of the defense rested on Solomon seeking clarification from the now deceased Richard St. Louis of Crest Associates, the grant administrator, who assured him that supervisory personnel were eligible for overtime. The defense argued that the responsibility for compliance with the grant lay with Crest Associates, not the Chief.

In 2003, Mayor Pollard had hired Crest Associates, a private law enforcement consulting firm, to oversee the Weed & Seed (W&S) grant program. The exact amount paid to Crest is unknown, as the City no longer retains the relevant records. However, it is known that Crest typically received a 20 percent commission for securing grant funding. In addition to this commission, they were paid further fees for administering the grant. In some cases, they received multiple payments by also developing grant-funded programs, acquiring equipment, and providing other services. For instance, in one case where a police department was awarded a $100,000 grant, Crest billed approximately $50,000 — half the grant total — for services that included the finder's fee, administrative costs, and the development of a web portal.

Founded in 1998 by Methuen native Richard St. Louis, Crest Associates quickly established itself as a leading law enforcement consulting and grant management firm. St. Louis, a former Chief of Staff at the Massachusetts Executive Office for Public Safety (EOPS), began his career there as a grant administrator. His tenure with EOPS, where he managed public safety grants, prepared him for future private consultant roles, including his work in Methuen.

One of Crest's earliest clients was North Andover Police Chief Richard Stanley. Over time, the firm expanded its client base to include the Office of the Chief Medical Examiner, the Greater Boston Police Council, the Essex County Sheriff's Association, the North Eastern Massachusetts Law Enforcement Council (NEMLEC), and police departments in Andover, Arlington, Burlington, Concord, Melrose, Oak Bluffs, Peabody, and Wakefield.

In 2002, Crest Associates secured grants through EOPS Secretary James Jajuga, a Methuen resident and longtime associate of St. Louis and Pollard's close friend and political ally. However, when Edward Flynn took over as EOPS Secretary in 2003, significant irregularities in the grant-awarding process were uncovered. Flynn found that Jajuga had used discretionary powers rather than the standard competitive application process to allocate grants to select communities, particularly those managed by St. Louis. This discovery triggered state and federal investigations into Crest Associates for possible misuse of Justice Department grant funds.

As the investigation unfolded, media reports highlighted a network of former EOPS employees connected to Jajuga who had either joined Crest or taken high-paying roles at agencies benefiting from Jajuga's discretionary grants, such as the University of Massachusetts. This apparent patronage system involved newly created, well-compensated positions funded by the awarded grants. Further scrutiny revealed what one source described as "inflated and fabricated" invoices submitted by Crest Associates.

By February 2004, four months into the FBI's investigation into possible grant mismanagement under Jajuga, St. Louis found himself under intense public and media scrutiny. Struggling under the weight of the investigation, he accepted an invitation to visit his brother's home in the South, where, tragically, he took his own life.

Shortly after St. Louis's passing, Crest Associates employees met with government agency clients, including the Methuen Police Department, to return control of the grants to them.

April

A week after Solomon's disciplinary hearing, on April 9th Hearing Officer Marks released his findings. In the determination letter, Marks emphasized that condition No. 2 of the grant explicitly stated, "The funding under this project is for the payment of the overtime hourly rate and fringe benefits expended for **non-supervisory sworn personnel**."

"As noted in the grant application, the additional hours funded under HSOP are intended to reimburse non-supervisory sworn officer ranks," Marks wrote. "Therefore, grantees should not reimburse for overtime expenses for personnel that hold a rank of supervisory nature even if the person is not currently supervising a staff."

To express his exasperation with the flagrant flaunting of the rules, Marks wrote in the findings:

2007

> *"One must torture logic and the English language to arrive at a conclusion that the grant allows payment for supervisory sworn personnel."*

During the hearing, Marks asked Solomon about the number of ranking positions within his department. Solomon responded that in 2003, the department consisted of approximately 50 patrol officers and 25 superior officers. Marks responded with a surprised "Wow."

Hearing Officer Mark's Determination

Marks also pointed out that Solomon had a federal grant specialist contact to address grant-related queries, which the chief stated he did not utilize.

In his opinion, Marks concluded that the city had provided sufficient cause for its assertion of misapplication of funds, warranting a three-day suspension without pay for the Chief.

Manzi's Letter to Solomon

The situation took on an added layer of intrigue. It elicited frustration from some quarters when Deputy Chief Alaimo and the next senior ranking captain, Edward Guy, were not selected as "Acting Chief" during Solomon's suspension period. Instead, Captain Katherine Lavigne, a longtime supporter of Solomon, was chosen for the role. Alaimo's absence was easily explained as a vacation, but the Capt. Guy omission prompted questions. In response, Mayor Manzi's office clarified that Lavigne was the best fit to fill in for the chief.

Throughout his suspension, Solomon maintained that Crest, rather than himself, should bear responsibility for the misapplication of funds. Availing himself of his right to appeal the decision. As the saying goes – dead men tell no tales.

May

The United States Department of Justice initiated the Weed and Seed Grant program (W&S) to empower police departments to

2007

"weed out" crime and to "seed" community revitalization. This grant would be a 5-year program with a total $1 million grant payout. Methuen joined the program in 2001. The city partnered with its neighbor – the City of Lawrence, which also received an identical grant – to assist the Arlington District, which spans the Lawrence-Methuen line. The neighborhood had long struggled with issues such as gang activity, drug trafficking, prostitution, and graffiti.

The task force named then Captain Solomon to helm the Methuen initiative and designated the "Weed and Seed Coordinator," Lt. Joseph Alaimo, the 'Weed Coordinator,' and the Chief's civilian executive assistant, Patricia Giarusso, was appointed as the "Program Assistant." When Solomon and Alaimo earned a promotion in the department, Captain Kristopher McCarthy replaced Solomon, and Sergeant Michael Havey, Sr., became Weed Coordinator.

In May 2007, just one month after Solomon's disciplinary hearing concerning the COPS grant, the U.S. Department of Justice's assistant deputy comptroller issued another letter to City Hall, this time citing a report issued by the Federal Office of Inspector General's Special Agent David Glendinning commonly referred to as the "Glendinning Report," outlining discrepancies in the W&S grant review. MPD failed to substantiate how five superior officers and one civilian employee had completed additional work hours for which they received grant-funded stipends and overtime. As a result, the Justice Department demanded the city repay $170,472. The breakdown of unsubstantiated overtime payments by employee is as follows:

Glendinning Report

- Joe Solomon (before he was named chief): $10,403
- Joseph Alaimo: $12,604
- Captain Kristopher McCarthy: $44,254
- Lieutenant Kevin Mahoney: $25,480
- Sergeant Michael Havey: $32,021
- Patricia Giarusso (Solomon's Secretary): $45,934

According to payroll records, while a broad pool of officers received portions of the W&S grant-funded overtime, a

2007

substantial share went to a select group. Between 2002 and 2006, three officers — Captain Kristopher McCarthy, Lieutenant Kevin Mahoney, and Sergeant Michael Havey Sr. — received 40 percent of the grant's overtime pay, with the remaining 60 percent spread across 40 other officers.

To put this in perspective, MPD payroll records, reviewed by *The Boston Globe* in 2007, showed $70,384 allocated for community policing overtime in 2005. Of this, McCarthy and Mahoney received 60 percent combined, totaling $42,230. In 2006, their collective share increased to 70 percent, amounting to $59,235, with much of this funding sourced from state grants.

Following Justice Department notices, Mayor Manzi and Solomon sought further clarification before deciding whether to repay or appeal the $170,472 reimbursement demand. Despite providing additional documentation as requested, the Justice Department upheld its stance that the city was obligated to repay the funds.

In response, by engaging an external auditing firm, Methuen officials sought an independent assessment of the W&S grant accounts. They hired Melanson Heath & Co. (Melanson), a certified public accounting firm based in Nashua, New Hampshire, which already managed Methuen's annual citywide audits. The hope was that an independent review might uncover evidence to protect Methuen taxpayers from bearing the burden of substantial repayment.

Melanson's auditors had been assigned to review only one grant year — specifically, fiscal year 2005. Their investigation included interviews with Solomon and a thorough review of the W&S grant records, such as payroll files and warrant logs from the MPD. In their final report, Melanson compared the documentation against federal audit standards and ultimately issued a favorable conclusion.

They reported, "No compliance issues with the MPD or the Weed & Seed grant," and stated, "Our tests disclosed no instances of noncompliance or other matters that are required to be reported under Government Auditing Standards."

Although Melanson Heath did not identify any "compliance issues or fraud," a separate audit by the federal Office of the Inspector General similarly found no evidence of fraud but concluded that Methuen had failed to submit "adequate

2007

documentation" for approximately $170,000 in overtime payments.

Methuen eventually lost all appeals to the federal government and had to pay back both mismanaged grant funds, totaling $192,000 in taxpayer funds.

Because of the malfeasance in the MPD under Solomon, the city council was gearing up for a vote of "no-confidence" in him, seen by many as a symbolic gesture. However, if the council voted in favor of the motion, it could erode support for Solomon. Since he and his deputy's contracts were up for renewal in the summer, securing the council's support appeared increasingly uncertain.

The no-confidence vote appeared on the council's agenda in early May, sparking heated debate among members. Supporters argued that a "yes" vote would send a clear message to residents — who ultimately bear the financial burden of the misappropriation — that the council was willing to hold the chief accountable and formally register its disapproval.

"People are fed up. There is a significant issue in the police department, and it must be addressed," one councilor remarked.

Opponents of the vote criticized the council, contending that the chief had already faced discipline and that it was not their place to intervene at this stage, labeling the vote as "a distraction to the city."

Councilor Phil Lahey expressed his frustration, stating that he was incensed by Solomon's decision to appeal his suspension. As printed by *The Boston Globe*, Lahey remarked, "He won't just suck it up and take the punishment."

The vote ultimately passed with a 5-2-1 split. Supporting the measure were Robert Andrew, John Cronin Jr., Larry Giordano, Philip Lahey Jr., and Kenneth Willette Jr. Opposing the vote were Kathleen Corey Rahme and Deborah Quinn, while Joseph Leone III abstained. Council President Stephen Zanni voted "present" rather than abstain or cast a deciding vote.

Despite the outcome, Solomon made it clear he had no intention of resigning, stating that the decision would not alter how he performs his duties.

Both Solomon and Alaimo's employment contracts expired on June 30, 2007. However, due to the ongoing turmoil within the city stemming from issues within the police department, negotiations for new contracts were not initiated. City Hall insiders expected Mayor Manzi would delay negotiations until the feds resolved the investigation into federal grant monies. According to Solomon, Manzi assured him he would continue receiving the contracted salary if Solomon agreed to postpone contract discussions until after the November elections.

From my personal experience, I've learned that searching for truth is rarely a solitary endeavor. It involves navigating multiple perspectives — my side, your side, and the often-conflicting narratives that lie between. Within this intricate intersection, the truth waits to be discovered, shaped by the willingness to explore beyond individual viewpoints.

The City Council decided to take matters into their own hands. At an August meeting, they directed the city solicitor to investigate the contracts to determine whether the city was legally obligated to honor them.

August

The following week, on the evening of Friday, August 24th, a football game was playing on the television in the MPD squad room. Later, Solomon would testify under oath that Friday nights that month had consistently been busy shifts for the department. He would also recall that the patrol officers' union president, Joseph Aiello, had urged him to assign additional officers to patrol duty earlier that week, citing a notable increase in reported criminal activity.

Returning that evening after two consecutive days of training in nearby Andover, Massachusetts, Solomon was unaware that Sergeant Larry Phillips was filling in for Sergeant Tod Himmer on the shift. Around 8:45 p.m., while on his way home from a personal errand, Solomon noticed multiple police cruisers parked outside the station — a spot generally reserved for officers arriving with prisoners or handling major incidents, with typical parking designated behind the building. Without any reports of a significant incident, he decided to stop in and investigate.

Upon entering the station, Solomon observed Sergeant Phillips and Lieutenant Michael Wnek in the Officer in Charge (OIC) room. The booking area seemed routine and undisturbed, besides the sound of a nearby football game in the background. He proceeded to the "roll call" room, where officers generally gathered, and found five patrol officers: Matthew Bistany, Eric DeLeon, Kevin Dzioba, Joseph Rynne and Jamie Moore. The room's television broadcasted the New England Patriots game.

Here is where the accounts of Solomon and other witnesses diverge regarding what happened over the next five minutes.

While Solomon acknowledges that he lost his composure, admitting to swearing out of frustration and anger, Sergeant Phillips presented a different perspective in his testimony. According to Phillips, Solomon entered the station. He headed directly to the squad room, where five officers were absorbed in watching the preseason Patriots game on TV rather than actively patrolling.

Phillips later court testimony described Solomon's reaction as a "tirade" filled with expletives. "He was totally out of control; we actually saw spit coming from his mouth," Phillips testified. Solomon allegedly expressed frustration, attributing a recent spike in criminal activity to the officers' lack of patrol presence. However, Phillips and other officers contended that they were either on authorized dinner breaks or occupied with writing reports at the time.

Following the incident, the officers drafted formal reports recounting the events. Additionally, three officers created "unofficial" memos that they did not include in the formal documentation but instead forwarded directly to the city solicitor.

Later that evening, Officer Aiello — who had been at the station with Officer Thomas McMenamon to discuss union matters — spoke with Solomon to review the events that had transpired. In his testimony, Aiello, the union president, said he was embarrassed his colleagues were caught watching the game in the station, especially after he had recently appealed to the Chief for increased patrol staffing. Aiello suggested to Solomon that disciplinary action should focus on the supervising sergeants if the officers had received permission to be off duty.

During this conversation, Aiello also informed Solomon of certain behaviors exhibited by Sergeant Phillips earlier that evening. Dispatcher Kara Lapides had reported that Phillips commented to her, implying she was "among the privileged" for receiving overtime. Later, following the incident with the television, Phillips allegedly made crude remarks to Detective Keith Frost and Officer McMenamon, telling Frost to "go f' yourself" and following up with a similar comment directed at McMenamon, who replied in a humorous tone, "Thank you, Sarge, I was feeling left out." Phillips later testified that his comments were intended as jokes and that McMenamon's response indicated he took them as such.

The day after the incident, Solomon directed Captain Haggar to remove all televisions from the roll call room and the OIC room. Additionally, he placed Sergeant Phillips on administrative leave, pending a "fitness for duty" evaluation. Solomon sent officers to Phillips' residence to collect his badge and firearm and assigned Captain Lavigne to conduct a high-priority internal affairs investigation into Phillips' conduct.

There was a clear divide in the MPD between members of the "inner circle" and those on the outside. Officers Aiello, Frost, McMenamon, and Lapides (who would later marry McMenamon and join the department as an officer) were part of this close-knit group, while Phillips clearly was not. Sources told us Aiello allegedly tipped off Solomon about the officers watching the football game to assist Solomon in targeting Phillips.

Lieutenant Michael Wnek, who had once been part of the department's inner circle, was the Officer in Charge on the night of the incident and later received a one-day suspension and to work three days without pay for his role in the events.

There is another dimension to this story: just hours before arriving at the station that evening, Solomon learned his former brother-in-law, James Caron, had been subpoenaed to testify before a federal grand jury in a case that Phillips had investigated and was irate and wanted to get back at Phillips for it.

The backstory as to why Phillips was in Solomon's crosshairs started back the previous year in April. Captain McCarthy had assigned Phillips to investigate a report of a stolen tractor. According to Phillips, McCarthy instructed him to avoid involving one of the suspects, James Caron, because Caron was related to Solomon's ex-wife. By July, Phillips had gathered sufficient evidence to charge Caron but claimed that Lieutenant Wnek directed him not to proceed with those charges. Suspecting interference in his investigation, Phillips contacted the FBI and subsequently agreed to serve as a witness in an ongoing federal criminal investigation involving Solomon and other Methuen city employees.

2007

In August 2007, shortly before the incident with the officers watching football, Sergeant Phillips had received a subpoena to testify before a federal grand jury. He immediately notified his superiors about this development. Whether the disciplinary actions taken against Phillips, including his placement on administrative leave and a fitness-for-duty examination, were justified responses or veiled retaliation remains a point of contention. Some argue that Phillips' behavior warranted these measures. In contrast, others interpret them as a message from those in power who are uncomfortable with Phillips' cooperation with federal investigators.

Fulya

Three days after the football game, on August 27th, Fulya, the former solicitor's secretary — now married to her long-time boyfriend, Anthony "Little Anthony" Capanelli — filed a lawsuit in Lawrence Superior Court against the City, Lariviere, Solomon, and Alaimo, alleging that city officials were negligent in dealing with her claims of sexual harassment.

Metin's Court Docket

Let's take a moment to get some background on Mr. Capanelli. Fulya had reportedly told her city coworkers that her fiancé had been deployed to Iraq. In truth, he was serving a federal prison sentence for conspiring to rob the Times Employee Federal Credit Union. This charge stemmed from a 2001 undercover investigation targeting the Genovese crime family. Capanelli, a married father of four and a pressman at the

Anthony Capanelli's Court Papers

New York Times printing plant in Queens, allegedly acted as the "inside man" for mobsters Carmine "Baby Carmine" Russo and Elio "Chinatown" Albanese, whose expertise was in orchestrating robberies. Capanelli created a hand-drawn plant map showing the location of payroll funds. He also provided plant uniforms and parking passes to assist in the planned heist. Though the robbery never took place, Capanelli was sentenced to 51 months in 2003, reportedly breaking down in tears at the sentencing. He was released just one month before he and Fulya filed their joint lawsuit against the city, Lariviere, Solomon, and Alaimo. As with most civil lawsuits, the wheels of justice turn slowly — and much will unfold in Methuen, and for Solomon, long before Fulya's case even reaches opening statements.

September

During the September 4th city council meeting, the council – under the advice of the city solicitor – reduced Solomon and Alaimo's annual pay by thousands of dollars and moved retroactively to July 1st.

Rumors of these pay slashes had been circulating for months, prompting Solomon's lawyer, Andrew Gambaccini, to write a letter to Methuen Solicitor McQuillan. He stated that the pay reduction violated civil service laws and was brought before council by an official with a personal vendetta – namely, City Councilor John Cronin, whose son, Shaun was suing Solomon and Alaimo. However, Cronin Sr. denied any personal feud.

The City Council's frustration with Solomon had been ongoing; earlier in the year, they had already expressed a vote of no confidence in him. Matters escalated when Mayor Manzi suspended Solomon for three days, prompting Solomon to announce his intention to appeal to recoup his lost salary. This decision became a tipping point for several councilors.

Then in August, several councilors sought guidance from the solicitor regarding the expired contracts. On August 15th, McQuillan sent a letter to the full council, stating that the contracts "no longer have any legal force or effect" because each man's contract did not contain an "evergreen clause" that allows the current contract to stand until a new contract can be negotiated. He further explained Massachusetts state law, which dictates that police chiefs earn at least twice the pay of the highest-paid patrolman. According to this law, Solomon's fiscal year pay would be recalculated to $132,685, down from $158,295. Similarly, Alaimo's salary would be eight percent higher than a police captain's salary, amounting to $122,000 from $136,000.

Furthermore, the duo would forfeit many of the perks outlined in their contracts, including longevity pay, vacation pay, and

2007

career incentives, as the city was no longer obligated to provide them.

Filming in the Square

Los Angeles-based director Daryl Silva, originally from Methuen, chose his hometown as the backdrop for his latest film, a mob-themed drama titled "Boys." Silva brought on MPD Captain Randy Hagger as the film's executive producer, and Hagger also co-stars as the mobster Jimmy Gigante.

Before filming began, Silva had met with Mayor Manzi to discuss the project. Captain Hagger then arranged a meeting with Solomon to establish guidelines for the shoot. They worked together to select filming times that would minimize disruption to local businesses in the square and coordinated using police officers and a cruiser for the movie.

On the late morning of Sunday, September 16, 2007, MPD closed the streets leading to the square as the film crew transformed Methuen's small downtown into a Hollywood set. Several officers were present on set, including Officers Ron Valliere and Kevin Abraham, who, though off duty, donned their uniforms and appeared in the film while stationed in city cruisers. Officer Timothy Getchell, Solomon's brother-in-law, was on duty and working the scene, while Sergeant James Gunter served as the safety officer due to a mock shooting planned for the day. All the officers involved were part of Solomon's close-knit inner circle.

Manzi was driving through downtown when he noticed the square was closed. Concerned about an emergency, he pulled over to investigate – only to discover a movie scene being filmed without a city permit.

"There was also a very angry business owner who hadn't been notified, as city ordinance required," Manzi later testified in a later civil hearing.

Allowing the film crew a little time to wrap up, Manzi went to get a coffee and called Solomon, asking him to meet in the square. When Solomon arrived, Manzi ordered him to reopen the street, which Solomon did — at least initially. After Manzi left, Solomon re-closed the street.

In a later memo drafted by Haggar, he reported that after reviewing the day's footage, Silva asked for "one final shot" after

2007

Solomon had departed. Haggar complied, and filming finally wrapped a little after four in the afternoon.

The order Manzi gave to Solomon would be the final words exchanged face-to-face between the two men.

That afternoon a Methuen resident approached Solomon, alleging knowledge of corruption linked to Mayor Manzi. Court documents later identified the resident as Michael Neve, whom Solomon had encountered earlier that day during the film shoot in the town square. Notably, the film featured Neve and his family's restaurant.

In hearing and court testimony Solomon later testified that Neve had asked to meet privately with Solomon, and the two agreed to meet at Solomon's home. The men sat in Neve's car for two hours. Neve nervously explained to Solomon that he had an upcoming variance hearing before the zoning board of appeals (ZBA) and Mayor Manzi had said "he needed to pay him $15,000 for a favorable vote." He asked Solomon if that was legal and if he should pay him the money. Solomon claimed he was flabbergasted.

The following Saturday, Solomon reported this information to Jonathan Blodgett's Essex County District Attorney's office, following up on Monday with a meeting at the district attorney's office and submitting a written report to them. According to an article by Tom Duggan's, the county district attorney referred the case to the U.S. Attorney's Office.

Lavigne's Memo to Solomon

Twenty-four hours later, Solomon met with two FBI agents at a local restaurant to provide a detailed account of the events relayed to him by the resident. Captain Kathy Lavigne, the MPD's Criminal Investigations Bureau commander at the time, accompanied Solomon to both meetings. That same day, Solomon and Alaimo requested the Lawrence District Court to put a preliminary injunction against the city to stop the pay decreases.

That evening, Mayor Manzi publicly spoke out against Solomon. Three days later, on September 28, the mayor placed the chief on administrative leave. Solomon concluded that this was Manzi's retaliatory act, leading him to invoke his protections under the Whistleblower Act. He referenced a statement

2007

previously made by Manzi back on July 30th regarding the Weed & Seed grant, in which Manzi declared he would fight the federal order to repay the money and "would not seek disciplinary action against the Chief."

According to the *Valley Patriot*, Manzi said, "It's my responsibility as mayor not to give the money back or spend money without fully, vigorously using all administrative remedies, the taxpayers ought not to be penalized for alleged administrative deficiencies." Solomon states Manzi was getting back at him for going to the FBI.

Solomon and Alaimo's Court Papers

A hearing was scheduled at the Essex County Superior Court in Lawrence for Tuesday, September 25th, to rule on a preliminary injunction to halt the Solomon and Alaimo pay cuts. The court ordered Methuen's Solicitor McQuillan, Auditor Thomas Kelly, and City Council Chair Stephen Zanni to attend the hearing.

Two hours before the hearing, Mayor Manzi took Solomon's city-owned SUV away from him in a petty move. The mayor claimed that it wasn't a punishment but rather an administrative move due to other departments having a use for it. Manzi further compounded the issue by stating the city never intended the SUV to be the chief's vehicle.

During the hearing before Judge Thomas Murtagh, lawyers Robert Minasian and Andrew Gambaccini, representing Solomon, argued that when the Chief signed his contract in 2004 with Mayor Pollard, the mayor told him that all the terms and conditions of the agreement would persist until a new contract was negotiated and signed. The lawyers also contended that the council ratified the pay reduction without allowing Solomon to defend himself. They asserted that this action was an unjustifiable form of punishment that would tarnish Solomon's community reputation and cause personal financial strain that could render him unable to pay his home mortgage.

Solomon's lawyers submitted a letter from Pollard on behalf of Solomon, wherein she stated that during negotiations in 2004, it was her understanding that his pay would remain in effect even if the contract expired. However, the judge declined to consider the letter, ruling that the pact contained no such language. He emphasized that he could only evaluate the words used in the contract and not Pollard's intentions.

"It certainly doesn't meet evidentiary criteria at this point, someone's beliefs are not something I can consider," Judge Murtagh said during the hearing.

The judge also declined to consider Solomon's finances.

"The fact is, I'm not sure I've heard anything that tells me [the pay cut] is irreparable," Murtagh remarked.

McQuillan, representing the city's defense, pleaded that the matter was a straightforward contract issue.

"This is a simple matter of contract; the contract had simply expired," he argued. "There's no punishment here. There's no retribution. He still holds the position."

Discussion on civil service laws was a significant aspect of the 45-minute hearing. Minasian argued that the pay cut violated civil service laws, which meant there must first be a Civil Service Commission hearing. The lawyer reiterated that the action was retaliatory.

"Lowering a man's salary is a form of discipline," he said.

In response, McQuillan countered that Solomon's contract signing implied his consent to the specified salary. "That contract itself ... is his written consent to receiving those benefits for that period of time," he argued.

In the audience were councilors Joseph Leone, Robert Andrew, and Kathleen Corey Rahme, along with former town manager Robert LeBlanc and the lawyer for former Solicitor Maurice Lariviere.

Within days of the preliminary injunction hearing, Judge Murtagh issued a ruling denying the request to halt the pay reduction for Solomon immediately. While the preliminary injunction failed, the broader lawsuit continued. Ultimately, the parties settled the case out of court about a month later, and the resolution details remain unknown.

On September 28th, a little over a month after the football game incident and three days after the injunction hearing, Manzi, in an interview with the *Eagle-Tribune*, characterized the MPD as an "untenable and dysfunctional" environment, citing the negative publicity surrounding the department. He expressed his concerns that the controversy was consuming the positive developments elsewhere in the city. He placed Solomon on indefinite paid administrative leave to address the ongoing turmoil. Although Mayor Manzi clarified that this action was "not disciplinary," it was necessary to facilitate a proper investigation into Solomon's conduct.

Manzi's letter to Solomon

Solomon was required to surrender his badge, firearms, department vehicles, and keys to the station. Captain Lavigne was once again elevated over her superiors and appointed as the acting chief during Solomon's absence.

By the end of that day, the police department's website was put "under construction," and Solomon's personal website, www.chiefsolomon.com, went offline.

October

In response to the pay injunction hearing, at the October 1st city council meeting, a very frustrated city council voted to approve a home rule petition to exempt the police chief's position from civil service requirements. The vote passed 7-2, with Councilor Rahme opposing it out of concern that civil service protections guard against improper "political influence." Councilor Andrew similarly criticized the decision, calling it a "knee-jerk" reaction.

The Massachusetts legislature enacted the home rule petition on June 20, 2008.

November

The only fact Mayor Manzi and retired Lieutenant Michael Alaimo — father of Deputy Chief Joseph Alaimo — agreed on was that they spoke by phone on November 2, 2007. In a later civil service hearing Alaimo recalled the convesation. There were two calls that day, during the first, Manzi expressed concern about a pro-Solomon rally scheduled for later that evening. He urged Alaimo not to attend, allegedly stating, "I've drawn a line in the sand — whoever goes is his friend, not mine."

2007

Alaimo, a friend of both men, found it difficult to take sides. "Why can't you two get together and make a deal?" he implored.

"What kind of a deal?" Manzi responded, prompting a discussion about what a potential agreement might entail. Manzi responded by floating a possible $50,000 buyout of Solomon's contract. Alaimo agreed to bring the offer to Solomon, who was unaware that Alaimo was making this proposal on his behalf.

During his call with Manzi, Alaimo proposed a plan where Solomon would give one of two speeches at the rally: "Speech A" if no deal was reached, and "Speech B" if both sides came to terms.

After hearing Manzi's offer, Solomon said he needed to consult his attorney before deciding. When he later spoke to Alaimo, Solomon clarified that the proposed $50,000 was unacceptable and "insultingly low."

"I'm 46 years old, and the mayor expects me to settle for $50,000 and the vague promise of a job somewhere down the road?" Alaimo recalled

Solomon estimated that a more appropriate buyout would be closer to half a million dollars, along with concrete support in securing another job.

After speaking with Solomon, Alaimo called Manzi back, Manzi responded with a profanity-laced outburst. According to Alaimo, Manzi said, "Solomon can give his f---ing Speech B or Speech A. What the hell is Speech A supposed to be? What is this bull...t? What does he think, he's going to talk about my sexual exploits? If he wants to use my sexual exploits, he can use them because my wife doesn't give a shit, and I don't give a shit. I'm just human. I'm just a normal man."

Manzi then told Alaimo to deliver a message to Solomon: "F--- you." Alaimo noted that this was the first time he had heard any mention of sexual misconduct in connection with the situation.

Manzi's account of the conversation sharply contrasted with Alaimo's version. His account of that day was also testified to at the later civil service hearing.

While he agreed that the call occurred before the rally, he claimed Solomon had proposed, with Alaimo as the intermediary. He later said in an *Eagle-Tribune* interview that they discussed dollar figures but he "never made a hard offer."

2007

"We discussed a range of figures that were in no way in any proximity to each other, so I would cauterize the talks as not serious."

According to Manzi, Solomon's last offer was that he should reinstate Solomon within one hour of the call; if he failed to do so, Solomon would deliver "Speech B" at the rally that night instead of "Speech A."

When Manzi asked Alaimo what "Speech B" might contain and why it should concern him, Alaimo replied that there was nothing specific but hinted at allegations of sexual improprieties that Solomon could expose if Manzi refused to reinstate him.

Alaimo offered Manzi half an hour to consider the proposal, but Manzi declined, stating he didn't need any time. Instead, he asked if Alaimo would deliver his response directly to Solomon. The response was reportedly so laced with profanity that no exact record of Manzi's words exists.

Manzi later dismissed the sexual allegations as baseless, describing them as an "attempt to bully me, blackmail me, and intimidate me."

Separately that day, City Councilor Deborah Quinn reported being approached by two men at different locations, each making cryptic references to allegations against the mayor — one regarding an affair, the other implying financial misconduct. Neither individual identified themselves, nor there's any evidence tying them directly to Solomon or his supporters. Still, the incidents added tension to an already volatile situation.

That night, over 250 attendees filled a local hall for the rally. Supporters wore "I'm Pro-Joe" buttons, and Solomon family members sported matching shirts. Solomon, in his first public remarks since his departure from the department, addressed the crowd. He criticized city leadership, denied wrongdoing, and pushed back against ongoing lawsuits and federal grant investigations. He defended himself and Deputy Alaimo, particularly against accusations they had forced out the former city solicitor and another officer.

Solomon also reiterated his belief that errors with the COPS and Weed & Seed grants were due to bad data from Crest Associates, despite federal authorities having already rejected those explanations. He thanked former Mayor Sharon Pollard, who

2007

publicly defended him at the event, saying, "There is nothing to indicate he did anything wrong."

Ultimately, Solomon delivered "Speech A." The rally was organized by two Methuen residents with help from Solomon's extended family and featured live music, food, and a bar. Solomon spent time personally thanking attendees.

Weeks later, Alaimo and Manzi met for lunch. When the buyout was mentioned again, Manzi reportedly stated, "I simply don't have that kind of money. The city just can't afford it."

2008

January 6	William "Bill" Manzi begins his second term as Mayor of Methuen.
January 15	First day of civil trial *Lariviere v. Solomon, Alaimo & City of Methuen*.
January 16	Second day of civil trial *Lariviere v. Solomon, Alaimo & City of Methuen*.
January 17	Third day of civil trial *Lariviere v. Solomon, Alaimo & City of Methuen*.
January 18	Fourth day of civil trial *Lariviere v. Solomon, Alaimo & City of Methuen*.
January 22	Fifth day of civil trial *Lariviere v. Solomon, Alaimo & City of Methuen*.
January 23	Officer Joseph Aiello is removed from the Methuen Police Department (MPD) Detective Unit.
January 24	Sixth and last day of civil trial *Lariviere v. Solomon, Alaimo & City of Methuen*.
February	A FOX News reporter informs Mayor Manzi of an ongoing Federal Bureau of Investigation (FBI) probe.
February 19	First day of Solomon's disciplinary hearing.
	Melanson Heath submits a report on MPD grant auditing.
February 20	Second day of Solomon's disciplinary hearing.
March	Mayor Manzi hosts his annual St. Patrick's Day fundraiser.
March 19	Acting Chief Kathy Lavigne calls Joseph Aiello at home; he is later hospitalized.
March 25	Third day of Solomon's disciplinary hearing.
March 31	Deputy Chief Joseph Alaimo retires from the Methuen Police Department.
April 14	Final day of Solomon's disciplinary hearing.
April 16	Aiello files a federal civil lawsuit against Mayor Manzi, Chief Lavigne, and Captain Thomas Fram.
May 5	Hearing Officer Michael Marks issues a final report on Solomon to Mayor Manzi.
May 7	Mayor Manzi terminates Solomon's employment.

2008

May 8	Solomon's MPD locker is forcibly opened and found to contain firearms, evidence, and other materials.
May	Solomon appeals his termination to the Massachusetts Civil Service Commission.
June 4	Attorney Paul M. Stein is appointed as Civil Service Commissioner by Governor Deval Patrick.
June 20	A Home Rule Petition is signed, officially removing the Methuen Police Chief position from Massachusetts Civil Service.
June 25	A hearing is held on a motion for summary judgment in *Cronin v. Solomon & Alaimo*.
July	MPD initiates the Civil Service hiring process to recruit ten permanent reserve officers.
August 19	Officer Ron Valliere accuses Sergeant Larry Phillips of assault during a training session.
September 10	Solomon's former brother-in-law is arrested.
September 12	Solomon has an unemployment benefits hearing with the Massachusetts Department of Workforce Development.
September 15	The City Council votes to rehire Shaun Cronin to the MPD using reserve funds.
September 23	An investigative report on the Valliere–Phillips training altercation is submitted to Acting Chief Lavigne.
October	The Department of Workforce Development issues its ruling on Solomon's benefits case.
October 6	Summary judgment is issued in *Cronin v. Solomon & Alaimo*.
October 7	Day 1 of *Solomon v. Methuen* before Civil Service Commission.
October 10	Day 2 of *Solomon v. Methuen* before Civil Service Commission.
October 13	Day 3 of *Solomon v. Methuen* before Civil Service Commission.
October 14	Day 4 of *Solomon v. Methuen* before Civil Service Commission.
October 16	Day 5 of *Solomon v. Methuen* before Civil Service Commission.
October 21	Day 6 of *Solomon v. Methuen* before Civil Service Commission.
October 28	Day 7 of *Solomon v. Methuen* before Civil Service Commission.

2008

October 30	Day 8 of *Solomon v. Methuen* before Civil Service Commission.
November 6	Day 9 of *Solomon v. Methuen* before Civil Service Commission.
November 13	Day 10 of *Solomon v. Methuen* before Civil Service Commission.
November 25	Day 11 of *Solomon v. Methuen* before Civil Service Commission.
December 4	Day 12 of *Solomon v. Methuen* before Civil Service Commission.

January

The new year marked the start of Mayor Manzi's second term, with his inauguration on January 6th. In his speech, Manzi focused on upcoming projects, including high school renovation and initiatives to make City Hall and the city website more accessible and user-friendly. While he addressed several pressing city issues, he conspicuously avoided any mention of Solomon or the Methuen Police Department.

Breaking tradition, Manzi opted for the fire department's honor guard to participate in the day's events instead of the usual police department honor guard. This decision suggested an effort to shift attention away from the controversy surrounding the police department and keep the spotlight on himself and other city officials, leaving behind the tumultuous events of the previous year.

Nine days later, on January 15th, former City Solicitor Lariviere's lawsuit against Solomon, Deputy Chief Alaimo, and the City of Methuen went to trial in U.S. District Court in Boston. The proceedings centered on a classic "he said, they said" conflict, with both sides firmly sticking to their narratives. Lariviere alleged that Alaimo and Solomon, acting as enforcers for Pollard, were determined to remove him by any means necessary. In contrast, Solomon and Alaimo argued that their actions were entirely by the book.

Pre-trial, Lariviere gave a very emotional excerpt when asked why he didn't ask for a lawyer or why he didn't do other things:

2008

> "Because, by that point in time, they had been on me for an hour and a half, coercing and intimidating me. I'm dealing with two known punks with a history of violence, that I knew that these sons of bitches had, in fact, beaten up people, and I thought that I was their next candidate, especially after what they had been doing to me."

Elaborating further:

> "We were not sitting in a room where there is peace. I'm sitting in the room with a guy that had been charged on numerous occasions with beating the shit out of people, and he is two inches away from my face, about to cream into me, and I am going to sit there and think through the thought process?"

In opening statements, Lariviere's lawyer, Carmen DiAdamo, told the jurors, "They [Solomon and Alaimo] walked over a good guy and walked hard. The mayor wanted to get rid of him. His life was ended for what, a political favor?"

When it was the defense's turn, Gareth Notis, Solomon and Alaimo's attorney, told the jury that Lariviere was well aware of his actions when he signed the resignation paper – he was resigning to protect himself and his pension.

Solomon and Alaimo testified that Lariviere asked the two officers if he could voluntarily resign and signed the resignation letter. In contrast, Lariviere testified that the duo threatened to arrest him if he did not sign the paper. Given that Lariviere was a municipal lawyer and would have seen many resignation letters cross his desk over the years, it is a fair assumption that he would want to draft his resignation letter, not a short one that Solomon typed up in the adjoining office.

While both sides agreed that the 2-hour videotape, which DiAdamo described as rated PG-13, should be played for the jury, the defense wanted to close the courtroom to the public for the showing – citing privacy. Judge Edward Harrington ruled lawyers should show the tape in public session.

After seven days of testimony and evidence, including police surveillance footage, a federal jury concluded that the officers had not coerced Lariviere into resigning. This verdict effectively

2008

ended Lariviere's bid to reclaim his $96,000-per-year position, marking a definitive close to his legal challenge.

During the trial, Lariviere expressed deep frustration with the events.

"That was the biggest mistake I ever made in my entire life," he said. "The minute I had [them] turn it [tape recorder] off, the politics started, the threats began, and the pressure to resign escalated."

He also reflected on the emotional toll the situation had taken.

"I live every day with one thought my father gave me. He said, 'Larivieres never have much money, but I gave you a good name, and you will give that to your kids' the former solicitor said. "Somewhere along the line, I'll see him again, and the name is gone. I destroyed my father's name by giving it to these clowns."

Lariviere v. Solomon Court Papers

Lariviere v. Solomon Depositions

Lariviere v. Solomon Transcripts

January 23rd

Is this a case of being fair, or is it a case of heaping more on Manzi? On January 23rd, President Joe Aiello of the 65-member Police Patrolmen's Union filed a grievance with the city, seeking 11½ hours of contractual time off for Christmas Eve and New Year's Eve. Aiello argued that since City Hall employees had those days off, the officers should also receive holiday compensation.

However, after reviewing the grievance, Manzi denied the patrolmen's request, stating that the city could not afford the additional expense of time-off compensation for holiday days not included in the patrolmen's contract.

When the union received the mayor's denial in March, they contacted their representative at the Massachusetts COPS

Coalition, who then filed an appeal demanding arbitration. In the appeal, the Union stated, "The [patrolmen] deems this time off to be an unfair labor practice for failing to negotiate in good faith additional benefits to certain employees and unions while omitting the same benefit to members of the [patrolmen]."

They further argued that it had been a "past practice" for the last 14 years for the patrolmen to receive contractual pay for these specific days.

"Certain collective bargaining units have that holiday, and [patrolmen] don't," Manzi told the *Eagle-Tribune,* "It's a matter of the city not being able to afford to grant [paid time off] beyond the benefits of the existing contract."

One union, AFSCME A, commonly called the "clerk's union," has these days off contractually written into their agreement. This union comprises secretaries, clerks, and administrative assistants from City Hall and the police station.

Due to the absence of support staff, the mayor gave department heads and non-union employees Christmas Eve off and closed City Hall early on New Year's Eve.

"With all the support personnel gone, I did give a couple of administrative personnel time off because they would have had no one in their office," Manzi explained.

The mayor countered the patrolmen's argument by highlighting that their negotiations resulted in benefits other unions did not enjoy.

"It's the way negotiations go," Manzi said. "The contract we reached with them was eminently fair. I don't think there's any hardship in the contract. It treats them quite well."

The 2007-2008 financial crisis was considered the most severe worldwide economic downturn since the Great Depression.

"Cities and towns are going to be seeking a lot more [from unions] in future contracts," Manzi said of towns and cities facing unprecedented financial constraints. "Even in areas where we've been justifiably generous in the past, cities and towns can't afford this now. Taxpayers can't afford it."

January 31st

Four months after putting Solomon on paid administrative leave, Mayor Manzi, in consultation with the city solicitor,

2008

decided Solomon's fate. On January 31st, Manzi issued a formal letter to Solomon, notifying him of an upcoming civil service disciplinary hearing. Scheduled to occur in the weeks ahead, the hearing aimed to address serious allegations, including the mismanagement and/or improper use of federal grant funds, along with other misconduct. Mayor Manzi outlined that the possible consequences of the hearing could range from a formal reprimand to termination of Solomon's employment.

In a statement released to the local newspaper, Mayor Manzi underscored the gravity of the situation, stating: "As Chief of Police, Joseph Solomon bears ultimate responsibility for the proper administration and execution of public safety grants, as well as the lawful and effective management of the Police Department as a whole."

February 19th

In a setting that mirrored his previous hearing 10 months earlier — with the same hearing officer, the same room, and many of the same key figures — Solomon once again faced scrutiny, this time over an expanded slate of allegations. Detailed in an eleven-page document released to the media as part of an agreement with Solomon's legal team, the new charges were presented ahead of, per Solomon's request, a closed-door hearing scheduled for February 19th.

The allegations spanned a broad spectrum of misconduct, including:

- Violations of conflict-of-interest laws.
- Improper sharing of personnel information.
- Misuse of municipal property for personal benefit
- Abusive behavior.
- Mismanagement of an investigation.
- Employing municipal resources to hire private Counsel.
- Mishandling grant funds, and
- Failing to fulfill essential leadership responsibilities.

The breadth of the accusations suggested that Mayor Manzi was intent on exhausting all avenues to hold Solomon accountable.

The hearing unfolded with the procedural rigor of a civil trial. Both sides delivered opening and closing statements, submitted evidence and documentation, and called witnesses to support their arguments. Presiding over the proceedings was hearing officer Michael Marks. He handled the case with formal precision.

Counsel for Solomon was his steadfast attorney, Andrew Gambaccini, and John Vigliotti, a lawyer affiliated with a police chiefs association. On the city's side, Solicitor Peter McQuillan and outside counsel David Grunebaum led the case against the chief.

The hearing spanned seven days over two months. The city presented 58 exhibits, and Solomon introduced 25. Methuen called nine witnesses during the proceedings, while Solomon had four witnesses and testified on his own behalf.

March

Deputy Chief Joe Alaimo announced his retirement on February 10th, effective March 1st. He cited personal reasons and a desire to explore new opportunities. The announcement came at a pivotal time — just over a week after Manzi issued the disciplinary hearing notice to Solomon and a little over a week before Solomon's hearing began.

"Certainly, it's been trying on me the last year and a half," Alaimo told reporters when asked if the MPD controversies influenced his decision. He showed gratitude for his career. "Overall, I've had an excellent career. The police department has given me everything I have."

Critics, however, speculated about the timing and motives behind his departure. Some viewed it as an attempt to step away before further fallout ensued. Others believed it stemmed from frustration over being passed over for the chief's position — again — for a subordinate. As deputy chief, Alaimo would have traditionally been the next in line for the role. However, considering he was among those who benefited from the misappropriation of grant funds, it was understandable that Manzi chose Captain Kathy Lavigne who was both qualified and uninvolved in the scandal.

2008

April

Mayor Manzi awoke on the morning of April 16th, probably relieved that Solomon's hearing was finally over and fate would soon decide the outcome. I am sure he was hoping the drama surrounding the police department would subside for a while.

You know the saying, "Death and taxes are the two certainties in life"? In Methuen, however, there is a third — drama in local government. By the end of that day, Officer Joseph Aiello would file a complaint in the United States District Court in Boston against Mayor Manzi, Acting Chief Lavigne, Captain Thomas Fram, and the City of Methuen.

Aiello's Court Complaint

Aiello, the Patrolmen Union president and a close Solomon ally, filed the complaint asserting that his removal from the detective division in January was retaliation for the union's decision not to endorse Manzi in the previous election and because Aiello was cooperating with an FBI investigation into Manzi concerning bribery.

One of the items detailed in Aiello's complaint was that during union contract negotiations the previous August, Manzi told Aiello he expected the union's endorsement in the upcoming election. Aiello further claimed that Manzi, borrowing a line from *"The Godfather,"* warned he would "come after" those responsible if an endorsement didn't materialize. Despite the lack of endorsement, Manzi won the election by a 2-1 margin.

When the *Globe* contacted the FBI office at the time of their story, the agency said they could neither confirm nor deny an investigation into Mayor Manzi. The FBI also stated they cannot comment on ongoing cases except when public records, such as search warrants, exist. In this instance, they were unaware of any public records on Manzi. At the time of Aiello's trial, Manzi had not faced any charges, and the Assistant U.S. Attorney confirmed that the case had been closed.

Aiello's removal from the detective division did not affect his base salary. Still, it cost him a stipend, the opportunity to earn overtime by appearing in court as a witness, and the prestige of being a detective. The previous September, the Essex County

District Attorney's office took the unusual step of contacting the defense attorneys, to which Aiello was the main witness, with a signed "Brady list" affidavit. Prosecutor's offices and police departments nationwide compile and maintain their own Giglio or Brady list. The name comes from two landmark U.S. Supreme Court cases, *Brady v. Maryland* (1963) and *Giglio v. United States* (1972), which established the legal precedent that prosecutors must disclose exculpatory evidence (evidence that could help the defendant) and evidence that could impeach the credibility of prosecution witnesses to the defense, respectively. It includes law enforcement officers who have committed acts of untruthfulness, have criminal convictions, issues of candor, or other actions that call their credibility into question. Putting a "Brady cop" on the witness stand could jeopardize a conviction due to the potential for witness impeachment.

This affidavit stated that as an MPD detective in 2005, Aiello had pleaded guilty to tampering with public records. This incident occurred while Aiello was on leave from the MPD and involved forging the title of a motorcycle he had sold at his shop.

In Aiello's case, he pleaded guilty to a crime of moral turpitude, and the District Attorney's office became aware of it in 2007 when a defense lawyer filed a motion to compel the DA to disclose his record. The judge in that case approved the motion, revealing the conviction to the District Attorney's office, which had been unaware of its existence until that point.

At the time of the Brady disclosure, Aiello's attorney astonishingly stated that his client's history did not inhibit him from performing his current duties.

"He is fully able to testify and carry out all of his other police duties," the attorney said. "Joe [Aiello] has the full confidence of the Chief and the District Attorney. It's really not that big of a deal."

Could the fact that an MPD detective could not testify in court, becoming an impotent detective, be why the department removed Aiello from the detective's division? January would be the logical time to make such a move. The election was over, and Solomon, who had previously protected Aiello, was on leave and unable to intervene.

Manzi was quoted by *The Boston Globe* saying the lawsuit was "frivolous and without merit." In another interview, he was even more direct.

"If there were quid pro quo, I wouldn't have given a contract before the endorsement." When the reporter asked about the timing of the lawsuit – filed the day after Solomon's hearing concluded – Manzi remarked, "The two are clearly linked. His close political sponsor has always been Joseph Solomon.

"Look at the time frames involved and look who's pulling the strings here. There has been a continuing attempt since [Solomon was put on leave] to intimidate me, to blackmail me, to use political coercion to get me to change my official actions, and to misuse federal law enforcement to achieve the goal of restoring Joe Solomon to the job of Chief of Police." Aiello's attorney, however, dismissed the claims as "sheer coincidence."

The lawsuit sought to have Aiello reinstated to his position as a detective, along with back pay and damages. By the time of the trial, his lawyer estimated $21,148 in lost wages.

May

Hearing Officer Marks issued his report on Solomon's disciplinary proceedings to Manzi on May 5, 2008. In it, he chastised Solomon for portraying himself as the victim and attempting to save himself by "impugning the reputation of others."

Marks consolidated the nine allegations against Solomon into four primary charges: Abuse of Office, Abuse and Intimidation of Police Officers, Mismanagement of the Weed & Seed Grant, and Loss of Confidence. These charges encapsulated the core of the city's claims against Solomon and shaped the hearing's contentious narrative.

The Abuse of Office charge encompassed five of the nine allegations against Solomon, each addressing serious misconduct that questioned his ethical judgment and adherence to established protocols.

2008

Conflict of Interest Regarding Sergeant Phillips

This charge centered on Solomon's alleged interference in an investigation led by Sergeant Phillips concerning the theft of a tractor connected to Solomon's ex-brother-in-law. The accusation suggested improper involvement in a case with personal ties. The hearing officer found this charge to be proven.

Disclosure of Confidential Information to Personal Attorneys

The City alleged that Solomon violated privacy laws, Methuen ordinances, and MPD regulations by sharing confidential disciplinary letters — documents detailing recommended discipline for MPD officers — with his private attorneys. The hearing officer deemed the charge proven and ruled the action violated departmental integrity and privacy protections.

Preferential Surveillance of a Relative's Home

The city claimed Solomon misused MPD resources via unwarranted security details and equipment for his sister, Mary Ellen Kalil, and her husband, Sam.

This allegation suggested favoritism and improperly using departmental assets for personal benefit.

The city contended that between 2004 and 2005, MPD officers conducted 280 "property checks" at the Kalil residence. Additionally, they claimed that MPD installed a surveillance camera in the Kalils' driveway and connected it to a video recorder inside their home. The hearing officer found this charge to be proven.

Ethics and Procurement Violations Concerning the Marine Unit

The city brought two counts against Solomon related to his dealings with Merrimac Marine, a business owned by the Kalils. These charges alleged violations of ethics rules and state procurement laws due to the MPD's business relationship with the company.

2008

In March 2006, the MPD sought to purchase a second boat for the department — a smaller 16-foot aluminum vessel with a 25 HP motor designed to navigate the shallower areas of the river that the department's larger boat could not access. Solomon submitted a purchase order to the mayor's office. The mayor's executive assistant, Lisa Alaimo – the wife of Deputy Chief Alaimo – approved the PO. The purchasing agent and the auditor's office then processed the order.

The MPD officially purchased the boat three months later for a total cost of $6,770. However, in violation of state procurement laws, only a single bid was solicited — Merrimac Marine. The hearing officer found this charge to be proven.

Interference with a Counterfeiting Investigation Involving Detective Flanagan

This allegation centered on Solomon's directive for an MPD detective to provide investigative materials from an active counterfeiting case to an external investigator, raising concerns about improper interference in law enforcement operations.

Retired MPD Detective Walter Flanagan recounted Solomon summoned him to a June 2002 meeting with Solomon, Joseph Alaimo, Alaimo's father, Mike Alaimo, and Lieutenant Michael Wnek. The senior Alaimo, a retired MPD lieutenant, owned Eagle Investigation. During the meeting, Joseph Alaimo instructed Flanagan to disclose "everything" he knew about the counterfeiting investigation he had conducted in January 2001.

Flanagan found the request highly unusual, as no one had ever asked him to share sensitive case information with a private investigator. The meeting atmosphere felt less like a professional discussion and more like an "ambush," with an interrogative tone that left him uneasy. Following the encounter, Flanagan alerted the Secret Service and later handed over a videotape capturing the suspects passing counterfeit money.

These five allegations collectively underscored what the city viewed as systemic abuse of Solomon's authority for personal and professional advantage, forming the foundation of the Abuse of Office charge. However, the hearing officer found this charge not to be proven.

2008

The Intimidation of Police Officers charge contained two of the nine counts:

The Roll Call Room Incident

This charge stemmed from an evening when Solomon entered the station and discovered patrol officers watching a football game instead of being on patrol. The hearing officer found this charge to be proven.

Discipline of Sergeant Phillips

During the same evening, Sergeant Phillips made remarks to several officers. While some described his comments as characteristic of his usual behavior, others claimed he intimidated them. In response, Solomon placed Phillips on administrative leave, confiscated his gun and badge, and ordered a fitness-for-duty examination pending the outcome of an internal investigation.

Whether Solomon's actions were a justified response to Phillips' behavior or a form of retaliation for Phillips' refusal to exclude Solomon's ex-brother-in-law from a prior investigation remains a matter of debate. The hearing officer found this charge to be proven.

The final two charges filed against Solomon each consisted of a single count:

Despite the City's negotiations and appeals, federal authorities ultimately demanded repayment of $170,000 due to insufficient documentation for overtime worked by superior officers and Solomon's secretary. The hearing officer found this charge to be proven.

Loss of Confidence

One charge against Solomon fell under a broad "catch-all" category. Mayor Manzi asserted that his loss of confidence in Solomon resulted from an "evolving process" that culminated in the Methuen Square incident. The charge further alleged falsehoods and blackmail attempts and claimed that the MPD had developed a poor reputation among other law enforcement

2008

agencies under Solomon's leadership. The hearing officer found this charge to be proven.

The hearing officer recommended that Mayor Manzi terminate Solomon's employment. As mayor, Manzi had the discretion to follow this recommendation or impose any appropriate disciplinary action. At the same time, Solomon retained the right to appeal any decision to the Civil Service Commission.

In his decision letter to Solomon, Mayor Manzi wrote, "You have utterly failed in general to provide the leadership necessary for promoting and maintaining the morale of an effective law enforcement entity." With this, Manzi proceeded to terminate Solomon's employment.

The day after Manzi fired Solomon, the police department swiftly moved to clear out his belongings. They snapped the padlock on his locker using a pair of bolt cutters. What they found inside left everyone — those present and those who later heard about it — baffled, raising more questions than answers.

Inside the locker, officers discovered a dent puller, a bag of marijuana, five knives (including a double-edged one), four pistols, ammunition, three booking photos, a hacksaw, a crack pipe, a bong water pipe, two keys, two IDs, an accident reconstruction report, a bag of clothes, four floppy computer disks, two baseball bats, two blue cylinders, nunchucks, tools in an evidence bag, white gloves, two sneakers in separate evidence bags, another pair of sneakers, photographs, three pornographic magazines, two VHS tapes related to unspecified rape investigations, a tire iron, four articles of clothing, a funnel, a hickory stick, an AM/FM cassette radio, a Black & Decker skill saw, a socket and five screwdrivers, an envelope containing five photographs, a box of plastic bags, a homemade club, a change purse containing $17.05, and a Valentine's Day card.

MPD Inventory Sheet

The unusual assortment of items found in Solomon's locker years after the city promoted him to chief raised immediate concerns. At the MPD, officers typically used their lockers to store uniforms and personal belongings. Discovering such a varied — and potentially incriminating — collection was highly irregular. Acting swiftly, Acting Chief

2008

Lavigne had each item inventoried, photographed, and videotaped before launching an investigation into the origin and intended purpose of the stored materials.

That evening, Solomon's attorneys released a statement to the *Eagle-Tribune* in which Solomon denied any recent association with the locker's contents. He asserted that he had not opened it since his swearing-in as chief more than five years earlier.

> "Most of the items mentioned as being in my personal locker are not my personal property. My recollection is that many of these items constitute evidence in cases closed long ago,"

Solomon further stated:

> "At the time that these cases concluded, it was not unusual for such evidence to be stored in an officer's locker at various times. Illicit magazines were evidence in a particularly gruesome sexual assault case."

In the same *Eagle-Tribune* article, the Acting Chief, Kathy Lavigne, refuted Solomon's claim by explaining that storing evidence in department lockers was against MPD policy. She clarified that the department had both temporary and long-term evidence storage rooms, emphasizing that the locker room and the evidence room were entirely separate areas, making it impossible to confuse one for the other.

Chief Lavigne contacted District Attorney Jonathan Blodgett's office, which determined that Solomon had not broken any laws. A spokesperson for the office stated, "All the cases are closed, so it has no impact [on the cases]."

This was the first warning sign of Methuen's evidence crisis. Rather than ordering a full audit, city leaders shrugged. That choice set the stage for what would surface 15 years later — that the evidence room had never once been audited, even as its custodian himself was arrested.

In law enforcement, evidence is paramount. It ranges from an officer's observations for a speeding ticket to a bloody handprint crucial in prosecuting a murder trial. Evidence is the bedrock of justice, ensuring due process for the defendant and the plaintiff.

2008

The Founding Fathers recognized its significance, embedding it in the Constitution via the Bill of Rights and reaffirming it in the 14th Amendment, guaranteeing due process across all states.

Discovering improperly stored evidence from numerous cases raises concerns about potential violations of defendants' civil rights. This mishandling of evidence has compromised the chain of custody — a critical component of due process — casting doubt on whether Solomon handled each item correctly. Chief Lavigne's clarification of department policy underscores the imperative of maintaining strict standards in evidence handling.

In pursuing justice, meticulous care in preserving and presenting evidence is essential. Upholding the integrity of the legal system hinges on adherence to rigorous protocols, ensuring justice is served and the rights of all parties involved are protected.

The absence of a credible explanation for Solomon's possession of these items and the lack of proper documentation or logs raises troubling questions about his conduct. At best, it suggests negligence; at worst, it implies misconduct. He broke the chain of custody if he failed to sign the evidence out. If he never logged the evidence, that amounts to dereliction of duty.

As chief, Solomon had after-hours access to the evidence room. Unfortunately, that room lacked adequate security and monitoring, creating an environment where anyone could manipulate, remove or substitute evidence without detection. This situation, combined with Solomon's authority, cast a shadow over the integrity of law enforcement and the pillars of justice. Such failures erode public trust and undermine the fundamental principles upon which the legal system stands.

Even more troubling is the decision by District Attorney Jonathan Blodgett's office not to demand a full audit of the evidence room. If Solomon's improper possession of evidence was not cause for concern, the failure to order an audit only added fuel to the fire.

In 2023, Mayor Neil Perry, Police Chief Scott McNamara, City Council Vice Chair Joel Faretra, and other City Councilors publicly acknowledged dysfunction within the MPD's evidence room, underscoring the gravity of the situation. The Council Chair's statement — that the MPD had not conducted a comprehensive audit in decades, if ever — speaks volumes about the negligence that persisted under Solomon's leadership.

2008

July

In the second month after Solomon's departure from the MPD, Mayor Manzi explored the possibility of rehiring Shaun Cronin to the police force. Cronin was a former MPD officer who had previously sued Solomon for interfering with his efforts to secure a job with another law enforcement agency. In an interview with the *Eagle-Tribune*, Manzi stated it was "very likely" that the city would reinstate Cronin. "We are currently looking into that possibility and working out some legal language between counsels that would make that a very distinct possibility," he said.

The catalyst for these discussions was an internal Lawrence Police memo filed with the court after the city was released from Cronin's lawsuit. Manzi confirmed that Cronin's lawyer had provided the municipality with "some documents" that significantly impacted his decision. However, Manzi declined to elaborate on the specific contents of the documents, only mentioning his intention to avoid "some potential liability for the City."

Solomon's testimony indicated that he never spoke to the Lawrence Police Department about Cronin's background. However, an internal memo written by Captain Molchan contradicted this, stating that Solomon had told him that Cronin had "too many issues." Solomon recounted an incident where he was in traffic near Cronin, who had pulled over a driver. Despite hearing Cronin radioing that he was in a fight with the driver, Solomon saw no signs of a battle and concluded that Cronin was "just looking for medals and recognition."

Recall that Cronin had been disciplined three times during his 17 years with the MPD: once for abuse of sick leave, once for an incident involving a family member, and once for filing a false report. Given these past disciplinary actions, if Solomon witnessed the incident with Cronin, it raises the question of why he did not investigate further, at the very least for untruthfulness.

When contacted by the newspaper, Cronin's lawyer, Sharon Meyers, confirmed that the city would be bringing Cronin back, though neither she nor the city could specify the timing. Manzi noted that the City was working on some Civil Service issues and would need to finalize a "prospective legal agreement." The agreement stipulated that the city would not owe Cronin back pay in exchange for his reinstatement.

Cronin did not participate in the interview but, through his lawyer, expressed that he was "looking forward to resuming his position."

August

In the second month following Chief Solomon's departure from the MPD, the department organized a high-stakes training exercise focused on school safety — one of the most critical scenarios law enforcement personnel may face. According to the *Eagle-Tribune*, on August 19, at Methuen High School, officers participated in a simulated active shooter drill designed to be as realistic as possible. The goal: train officers to respond swiftly and effectively to an active shooter situation while minimizing risks to bystanders and themselves.

During the pre-exercise briefing, trainers emphasized the importance of restraint, instructing participants to avoid unnecessary aggression.

Officer Ron Valliere was assigned the role of the suspect. His instructions were clear: sit on a teacher's desk with a simulated firearm visible in his pocket, then, upon the officers' arrival, stand, raise his hands, and follow all commands.

Officer Kevin Dzioba was the first to enter the classroom. Valliere stood and complied. Dzioba ordered him to place his hands on his head and kneel. But as Valliere began to do so, he suddenly heard footsteps charging from behind.

"While attempting to get on my knees, I heard from behind someone running towards me at full sprint," Valliere wrote in a department memo. "I hit the floor hard and then felt this person kneel into my back. He slammed my head onto the ground and wrenched my arms with extreme force, causing excruciating pain as I yelled, 'It's just a [expletive] training scenario."

Lieutenant Frank Korn immediately halted the drill by firing the air horn. Valliere, whose back had been to the approaching officer, didn't know who had tackled him until the scenario ended — it was Sergeant Larry Phillips. Both men had been wearing helmets and protective gear; Phillips, too, was unaware of Valliere's identity at the time of the takedown.

According to Valliere's memo, Phillips left the scene without acknowledging what had happened or participating in the post-exercise debriefing.

Later that evening, Valliere, suffering from pain in his neck, back, shoulders, and left arm, sought medical treatment at a hospital. Phillips later attempted to check on Valliere but was unable to reach him directly and instead left a message with Valliere's wife.

Acting Chief Lavigne told the *Eagle-Tribune* that Valliere was out on "injured in the line of duty" (ILD) status and receiving medical care, but was expected to return soon. When asked about Phillips, Lavigne said he remained on duty and believed the incident was accidental, noting, "These things do happen. It's the type of work we do."

However, the matter escalated when union president Aiello filed a grievance on Valliere's behalf. Valliere alleged that Phillips' actions were not accidental but "an excessive and blatant personal attack on me with the intent to cause me harm and intimidate."

In response, Chief Lavigne hired private investigator Michael Healy to conduct an independent inquiry. In a 13-page report dated September 23, Healy interviewed all nine officers present during the drill, including Valliere and Phillips. He found a consistent theme in the interviews: Phillips and Valliere had a history of mutual distrust and animosity.

Phillips told Healy that he had not intended to injure Valliere. He and three other officers had entered the room, saw Dzioba giving commands, and moved in. Phillips used his left hand to push Valliere down and reached for his hands to apply handcuffs.

In his post-incident memo, Valliere wrote that all role players had been "advised not to show any signs of aggression." During Healy's investigation, several officers confirmed that while trainers had advised against aggression, they had not explicitly prohibited the use of force.

The incident occurred amid internal strife within the department, with tensions still lingering between supporters of former Chief Solomon and those outside his inner circle. While officers largely agreed on the sequence of events, they disagreed on the intent and appropriateness of Phillips' actions.

Officer Dzioba, closest to the encounter, defended Phillips, calling the takedown "quick and stealth — that's how we are

2008

trained." He added, "If you don't want to get hurt, go bag groceries." Lieutenant Korn, by contrast, said he told Phillips afterward that such force was excessive and that "300-pound tackles were not needed."

Accounts of Valliere's condition immediately following the takedown also varied. Some officers reported he appeared injured, while others saw no signs of distress. Korn recalled Valliere standing up and moving his arms and torso as if stretching. Lieutenant Michael Wnek similarly noted that Valliere showed no visible signs of injury and was later seen carrying a box downstairs.

Healy also addressed Valliere's decision to pursue a criminal complaint against Phillips in Lawrence District Court. In his report, Healy criticized the action as premature and based on "flimsy evidentiary documentation," suggesting the matter should have been handled internally.

Ultimately, Healy concluded that Phillips had not committed any misconduct. "I find no fault in his actions," he wrote.

Officer Valliere remained on ILD status with no scheduled return to duty.

September

In their second September meeting, the City Council voted to approve a transfer of funds from the City's reserves to the police department's personnel budget. To avoid a conflict of interest, Councilor John Cronin, father of the to-be-reinstated officer, left the room during the discussion and vote. This funding would ensure that the Methuen Police Department would not have to terminate one of the three hired recruits to accommodate Shaun Cronin's return to the force.

Although Cronin successfully achieved his goal of returning to the police department, his lawsuit against former Chief Solomon and Deputy Chief Alaimo was still ongoing. Lawrence Superior Court held the summary judgment hearing on June 25th. More than three months later, on October 6th, Judge John T. Lu ruled that neither Solomon nor Alaimo made "reckless statements" about Cronin, dismissing all claims against them.

Meanwhile, as the City Council moved forward with Cronin's reinstatement, Solomon was preparing for another hearing, this time with the Department of Workforce Development, to secure unemployment benefits. It took a month for the hearing officer to release her decision, which coincidentally came in the same week Solomon's appeal to the Civil Service Commission began.

In the report, review examiner Phyllis Desharnais ruled that Solomon was entitled to unemployment benefits retroactive to his termination on May 10th. The hearing resembled a mini-appeal of his firing, with Desharnais concluding that the city could not prove that Solomon had purposely mismanaged federal grants, obstructed police work to prevent an investigation or arrest of a relative, intentionally directed business to his sister's marine business, or acted irrationally when reprimanding officers for watching a football game instead of patrolling the streets.

Mayor Manzi responded to the ruling by stating that they would appeal the decision, asserting,

> *"Unemployment benefits are for people who lose their job through no fault of their own, not people who are fired for cause."*

He expressed frustration with the system, calling the report another example of why people were dissatisfied with the process. It is unclear whether the city followed through with an appeal.

October

October 7th was a quintessential New England fall day — mildly warm with clear skies. It was the kind of day that naturally filled you with a sense of hope. It was also the day after Solomon had won a victory in the Cronin case.

On that day, the offices of the Civil Service Commissioners in Boston became the focal point as Solomon exercised his right to appeal his termination. All those who had participated in Solomon's disciplinary hearing in January gathered once more, prepared to revisit the events of that contentious process. The previous hearing had been merely a dress rehearsal for Solomon — this was the actual performance.

Newly appointed commissioner Paul Stein oversaw the meeting. Stein's background included managing his own law practice and serving as Deputy Chief of the Insurance Division

2008

under Attorney General James Shannon. In an interesting twist of fate, Commissioner Stein's appointment to the commission occurred almost simultaneously with Solomon filing his appeal.

The hearing stretched across 18 days of testimony over 20 weeks, concluding on February 24th of the following year. At least eleven witnesses testified, and lawyers submitted 160 pieces of evidence. Commissioner Stein's decision wouldn't be delivered until July 29, 2010 — just over two years after Solomon filed his appeal and more than three years after his termination.

The prolonged duration of the proceedings was so substantial that it prompted Massachusetts State Senator Arthur Broadhurst, a Methuen native, to file legislation requiring the Civil Service Commission to conduct its hearings on consecutive days, similar to the court system. He condemned the current process as "inefficient," arguing, "It delays the process. It's unfair to both parties and especially unfair to the taxpayers who are funding a system that operates in such an inefficient manner."

Unlike the previous proceeding, this inquiry was open to the public, a decision agreed upon by both parties after the *Eagle-Tribune* requested transparency.

The court addressed procedural matters on the opening day of the hearing, which concluded before lunch. Since it was a Friday, both parties agreed to reconvene the following Tuesday afternoon. The hearings would continue every Tuesday and Thursday, at least until the end of the month.

One of the key issues discussed on the first day was Solicitor McQuillan's notes from the interviews he conducted during his investigation into Solomon the previous January. These interviews, held with MPD personnel, had formed the basis for the charges against Solomon. However, McQuillan objected to releasing the notes, citing confidentiality agreements with the interviewees. Several had strongly insisted on anonymity due to fears of retaliation by Solomon. One stated, "I don't want my name involved, I don't want to testify, but I will provide information."

The Commissioner appeared inclined to allow Solomon's lawyers to review only the names of those interviewed — nothing more. A final ruling on the matter would be made at a later date. This decision was puzzling, as it seemed the only outcome would be to give Solomon more names to add to his potential revenge list.

In their opening statements, Solomon's team described Methuen's political culture as "one of the most toxic political environments" imaginable, portraying his firing as a move driven by political gain. Lawyer Gambaccini said this would be "marvelous political theater, if not for a man's career hanging in the balance."

The city began presenting its case with Mayor Manzi as its first witness. Manzi covered a range of topics over his five hours on the stand, including his account of the Alaimo phone call, which involved the "Speech A" or "Speech B" scenario.

Manzi also elaborated on Solomon's letter following their September 13, 2007, meeting to discuss the discipline of four officers involved in the "football game incident" at the police station. In response, Solomon penned a letter to Manzi summarizing their conversation:

> "At this meeting, you informed me you did not want any disciplinary actions taken before the election due to your feeling that it would negatively impact your re-election bid. You further stated you needed peace and quiet for two months and then, after the election, I could take whatever actions were justified and you would then support my decisions."
>
> "Regardless of the above, I cannot ignore my responsibility as Chief of Police to investigate allegations of wrongdoing. The officers who have allegations against them have the right to know the outcome of the investigation once they are completed, which is outlined in our professional standards policy. Additionally, these types of investigations wear on officers' minds and delaying the outcome only causes more stress."
>
> "Therefore, the following professional standards investigations have been completed and submitted to me. I have just concluded my review of the findings and thus am required to take appropriate action or report the findings and/or forward the investigations to your office for action."

2008

Manzi's testimony depicted Solomon's letter as a "complete falsehood" and a blatant attempt at "blackmail." He firmly denied asking Solomon to defer discipline or mentioning anything related to the election during their discussion of disciplinary actions. Upon completion of Manzi's testimony, the hearing was concluded for the day.

The hearing continued a week later, and retired MPD detective Walter "Gus" Flanagan testified on behalf of the City. He recounted details from a counterfeiting investigation he conducted in 2001–2002 and a subsequent meeting in 2002 involving Solomon, Deputy Chief Joseph Alaimo, Lieutenant Wnek, and Michael Alaimo, a private investigator, a civilian and who also happened to be Deputy Chief Alaimo's father.

According to Flanagan, Deputy Chief Alaimo ordered him to disclose "everything" he knew about the case to Michael Alaimo. According to the *Eagle-Tribune*, Flanagan recalled that Solomon and Lieutenant Wnek were present at the meeting but just "sat there" and "said nothing." Flanagan described the experience as intimidating, explaining that he felt like a criminal being interrogated rather than a detective working on an investigation.

On the same hearing day, additional witnesses for the City – MPD Sergeant Phillips and Lieutenant Wnek testified before the commission. They recounted the events surrounding a football game and the disciplinary actions that followed. Sergeant Phillips also testified about installing a camera at the property of Solomon's sister and participating in an investigation involving Solomon's ex-brother-in-law for theft.

At the prior hearing on October 30 — the sixth day of proceedings — the city called resident Michael Neve as a witness. Neve, a longtime friend of Manzi, Solomon and Alaimo, testified about his involvement in the Manzi bribery investigation. Neve's family owned a restaurant in the city square and lived seven houses down from Solomon's sister and brother-in-law. Neve was the "informant" Solomon had refused to identify in the previous hearing.

Neve recounted an incident from around 2002 when he offered then-Councilor Manzi a $15,000 bribe while seeking assistance to build a home on his parents' property after the Zoning Board denied his variance request. Neve asked Manzi, "What do I do now?" and proposed bribes if Manzi could help secure the variance. According to Neve, Manzi refused, saying he could not assist.

In 2007, Neve again sought a variance, appealing to the Zoning Board that winter. In February, he encountered Manzi on the road and followed him until Manzi stopped at a credit union. The two men chatted, during which Neve asked if Manzi had "done his homework." Neve later explained to the Commission that the phrase referred to Manzi potentially advocating on his behalf to gain favorable consideration for his project. Manzi, in turn, asked if Neve had spoken to neighbors and gathered support from abutters.

As their conversation ended, Manzi got into his car, rolled down the window, and joked, "Don't forget the satchel," before smirking. Neve testified that he interpreted the comment as a joke and reiterated that he never gave any money to Manzi.

Months later, during a conversation between Neve and Solomon, the topic of Manzi arose as Solomon and Manzi's disputes peaked. Solomon, angry and fearful of losing his job, asked about the satchel comment when Neve mentioned it. After hearing the story, Solomon reportedly became excited, saying, "We could use this." Neve testified that he told Solomon the matter was inconsequential and that he did not understand what he intended to "use."

Less than a week later, two FBI agents arrived at Neve's door, asking if this was the property where he gave the bribe to Manzi. Neve recounted that he told the agents there had never been any payment to Manzi.

On the seventh day of the hearing, held on November 6, the City's purchasing director, Joanne Ouellette, took the stand. She explained the procurement procedures and the requirements of state procurement law as they pertained to the city's purchase of a boat for the police department. According to the law, city officials could not award any municipal purchase exceeding $5,000 through a sole-source agreement. Instead, cities and towns must solicit bids from at least three vendors to ensure compliance.

Despite these requirements, when the MPD decided to purchase a boat for $6,770, they obtained only one quote. That was from Merrimac Marine, the business owned by Solomon's sister and brother-in-law — the pair linked to prior incidents involving the surveillance camera and property checks.

2008

Lawyers asked Ouellette why she issued a purchase order despite the absence of three required quotes. She explained, "I was told to stay out of the police [department]," a directive she attributed to Mayor Pollard. However, Solomon's attorney pointed out that Pollard's mayoral tenure had ended three months before the boat purchase. When asked if she informed Pollard's successor, Mayor Manzi, about this directive, Ouellette replied, "No."

The next witness later in the day was City Solicitor Peter McQuillan, who had the unusual dual role of lawyer for the defense and witness for the defense. He testified as to Solomon's disclosure in 2002 to Mayor Pollard about his familial relations with Merrimac Marine's owners, as per the ethics laws. McQuillan stated that the disclosure was regarding "repairs and maintenance of a boat then owned by the police department, period." Solomon should have made a new disclosure to Manzi for the boat purchase but never did.

On the tenth day of the hearings, Melanson Heath & Company auditors John Sullivan and Scott McIntire, took the stand. Sullivan, a specialist in fraud and forensic audits, testified before the commissioners that MPD superior officers — Solomon, McCarthy, Alaimo, Mahoney, Havey, and Secretary Giarusso — failed to maintain adequate records of the overtime they worked under the Weed and Seed Grant program.

Although the auditors did not find evidence of criminal activity or any explicitly inappropriate conduct, they concluded that the lack of sufficient timekeeping records violated the grant's requirements.

2009

January 6	Day 13 of *Solomon v. Methuen* before Civil Service Commission.
January 8	Day 14 of *Solomon v. Methuen* before Civil Service Commission.
January 20	Day 15 of *Solomon v. Methuen* before Civil Service Commission.
January 21	David Dumont files a bypass appeal with the Civil Service Commission.
January 22	Day 16 of *Solomon v. Methuen* before Civil Service Commission.
January 23	Day 17 of *Solomon v. Methuen* before Civil Service Commission.
February 7	Nicholas Milone files a bypass appeal with the Civil Service Commission.
February 10	Day 18 of *Solomon v. Methuen* before Civil Service Commission.
February 12	Day 19 of *Solomon v. Methuen* before Civil Service Commission.
February 23	Day 20 of *Solomon v. Methuen* before Civil Service Commission.
February 24	Day 21 of *Solomon v. Methuen* before Civil Service Commission.
March 12	Day 22 of *Solomon v. Methuen* before Civil Service Commission.
March 14	Mayor William Manzi holds annual St. Patrick's Day fundraiser.
April 9	Day 23 of *Solomon v. Methuen* before Civil Service Commission.
May 22	Patrick Waldron files a bypass appeal with the Civil Service Commission.
June 1	Charles Sciaccia files a bypass appeal with the Civil Service Commission.
July 2	Civil Service Commission opens an investigation into the Methuen Police Department reserve officer hiring process.

2009

July 9	Civil Service Commission issues a "Modified Interim Order" regarding the bypass appeals of Dumont, Milone, Waldron, and Sciaccia.
July 22	Arbitration hearing held to determine whether Officer Joseph Aiello's injury occurred in the line of duty.
July 31	Day 24 of *Solomon v. Methuen* before Civil Service Commission.
August 3	Civil Service hearing for Dumont, Milone, Waldron, and Sciaccia.
August 11	Fulya (Metin) Capanelli voluntarily surrenders her New York State insurance agent license in lieu of disciplinary proceedings.
August 19	Officer Ron Valliere accuses Sergeant Larry Phillips of assaulting him during training.
August 20	Civil Service Commission releases formal findings and orders regarding the City's 2008 reserve police hiring process.
August 25	City of Methuen files suit against the Civil Service Commission seeking to overturn its decision reinstating Chief Joseph Solomon.
August 28	Solomon's daughter is sued in connection with a hit-and-run accident.
September 11	Herbert Stacy files a bypass appeal with the Civil Service Commission.
September 17-19	Launch of the anonymous blog Methuen Police Secrets, featuring initial posts titled: "Sgt. Bully," Captain Fram's Private Chest of Overtime," "Lt.Perjurer" & "When will it end"
September 18	Methuen Police Secrets blog post: "Methuen Chief to 'work things out' with Patrolmen's Union"
September 19	Methuen Police Secrets blog post: "breaking News – Do not Speak to the Press or Anyone Else"
September 29	Methuen Police Secrets blog post; "Violation of the 1st Amendment to the US Constitution."
October 4	Methuen Police Secrets blog post: "Freedom of Speech"
	Methuen Police Secrets blog post: "New Blog Administrator"
October 6	Methuen Police Secrets blog post: "As the World Turns or As the Cruiser Rocks?

2009

	Methuen Police Secrets blog post: "I Know Nothing.... I See Nothing... I Can't Any Question! I Must ask Mayor Moneybags for the Answers"
October 7	Methuen Police Secrets blog post: "I Struck a Chord with: As the Worlds Turns or as the Cruiser Rocks"
October 13	Methuen Police Secrets blog post: "Who am I?"
October 23	Methuen Police Secrets blog post: "Who am I Continued?"
October 27	Methuen Police Secrets blog post: BREAKING NEWS... BREAKING NEWS...BREAJING NEWS...BREAKING NEWS
October 29	Methuen Police Secrets blog post: This is HOT, HOT, HOT... Mayor 'Moneybags' Manzi loses Big One."
	Methuen Police Secrets blog post: "This Just In... Read All About It..."
	Methuen Police Secrets blog post: "WARNING Hazardous to your Health"
	Methuen Police Secrets blog post: "Chief Surrounds Herself with another Questionable Appointment!"
November 1	Methuen Police Secrets blog post: "Salvo Grand Jury in Full Swing"
November 6	Methuen Police Secrets blog post: "A Call to Action," "Salvo Grand Jury Hears Testimony," "Violation of the 1st Amendment to the U.S. Constitution - 2nd Offense," and "The Kiss of Death"

January

The new year brought a series of hearings at the Civil Service Commission for Solomon, beginning on January 6th. Acting Chief Kathy Lavigne testified on behalf of the city, addressing several issues, including the Manzi bribery investigation. Lavigne was one of three individuals who met with the district attorney and the FBI regarding the matter.

During her testimony, Lavigne described the FBI's keen interest in Solomon's account of a $15,000 bribe involving a satchel. Solomon had reportedly enlisted the informant, Michael Neve, to wear a wire for the FBI and secretly record Mayor Manzi. However, Neve ultimately refused to cooperate.

The investigation took a turn three months later when a FOX 25 TV reporter approached Manzi about the bribery allegations —

claims he stated he had never heard of before. The reporter's questions raised a critical question: who leaked the story to the media?

Suspicion naturally fell on the three people who had attended the confidential meeting with the FBI. Among them, Lavigne's name surfaced most frequently. Some speculated that she might have been the leak, given her possible motive and opportunity. However, Solomon, who also attended the meeting, had his own motives. With his established media contacts and an interest in publicly and politically damaging Manzi's reputation, he too could have been responsible for the leak.

The question of who was behind the leak added another layer of intrigue to an already complex situation. As the hearings progressed, tensions rose, and both parties continued to navigate a minefield of political maneuvers, accusations and personal vendettas.

On the stand, Lavigne firmly denied being the source. She testified that she had kept the meeting confidential, only learning of the media's involvement when an astonished and irate Manzi called her after being approached by the reporter. According to Manzi, the reporter claimed Lavigne was aware of the bribery allegations.

At this point, the Commissioner interrupted Lavigne's testimony to ask whether she had any idea who might have leaked the story. Lavigne claimed that she believed the matter had been kept relatively secret, implying no knowledge of how the information had reached the press.

For the record, the issue of who leaked the story to the FOX 25 reporter would surface during the 2010 civil lawsuit brought by Officer Joseph Aiello against the City of Methuen, Manzi, Chief Lavigne, and Captain Thomas Fram. During the jury trial, the City called the FOX 25 reporter to testify. Under oath, the reporter confirmed that Joseph Solomon was the individual who had leaked the story.

With Acting Chief Lavigne's testimony concluded, it was time for Solomon to call his witnesses. First on the stand was his longtime colleague and former police partner, Joe Alaimo.

Alaimo's testimony spanned a range of topics, including his role in procuring the MPD's new patrol boat and various meetings with Mayor Manzi. During one such meeting after Manzi placed

2009

Solomon on leave, Alaimo recalled Manzi allegedly saying, "This is all the midget's fault," referring to Solomon. Later in the conversation, Alaimo claimed Manzi added, "I hate Joe Solomon."

When questioned about these remarks following the hearing by an *Eagle-Tribune* reporter, Manzi, who is noticeably taller than Solomon, denied remembering them. He admitted that he and Solomon had engaged in "spirited" discussions that may have occasionally crossed the line but insisted he couldn't imagine personalizing the conflict to such a degree. "I honestly don't recall calling him a midget or saying I hated him," Manzi stated. "That's something I think I would remember."

Regarding the purchasing agent's claim that superiors instructed her to avoid police purchasing decisions, Kelly, who oversaw the purchasing department, testified that this was the first time he had heard of such a directive — learning of it only during the court proceedings. After Kelly spoke, the hearing wrapped up for the week.

When the hearing resumed the following week, Solomon called retired MPD Lieutenant Mike Alaimo to testify. Alaimo spoke about the infamous "speech A or speech B" telephone call and the Flanagan counterfeiting investigation. The remainder of the January hearing dates saw limited testimony from various officers, many of whom were within Solomon's inner circle.

Later that day, Tom Kelly, the city's auditor, took the stand as a witness for Solomon. He detailed the extensive work he and his team undertook to compile records for the Department of Justice as part of the grant investigation. He explained that one of the challenges stemmed from the misalignment of fiscal years: the federal fiscal year runs from October 1st to September 30th, while Methuen's fiscal year runs from July 1st to June 30th. While Kelly presented this as a complicating factor, it's hard not to question the issue's significance — after all, differences in fiscal calendars are not uncommon and shouldn't have posed an insurmountable obstacle.

An impactful testimony came on February 10th, when Samuel Kalil, Solomon's brother-in-law and owner of Merrimac Marine, took the stand in support of Solomon. Kalil described purchasing his home at auction a decade earlier, detailing its dilapidated condition and history as a hangout for drug addicts. Even after

2009

renovations and moving in, Kalil testified, he still observed a "constant flow" of drug activity on the street. "It is a quiet spot, so they try to take advantage of that," he stated.

Kalils' account contrasted sharply with testimony from other officers. For example, Lt. Wnek, testifying for the City, characterized the area as quiet and uneventful from a policing perspective. Meanwhile, Officer Fleming, speaking on Solomon's behalf, described the neighborhood as plagued by drug activity.

Lawyers also questioned Kalil about his marine business dealings with the police department. Pollard had previously directed Solomon to delegate these dealings to Deputy Chief Joe Alaimo to avoid a conflict of interest. However, Alaimo relied on Sergeant Mike Havey and other marine unit officers to manage interactions with Merrimac Marine. It's worth noting that Havey is Kalil's first cousin who stated the familial connection without further examination — another apparent conflict of interest the Commissioner only briefly acknowledged.

Kalil also recounted his interactions with the MPD regarding their boat. During Chief MacDougall's tenure, MPD tried to use Merrimac Marine to purchase a specific boat for the department. When his business didn't carry the desired model, Kalil suggested other dealers and the department eventually acquired the boat from a dealer in Medford, Massachusetts. Initially, the MPD had the boat serviced in Medford but later switched to Merrimac Marine to avoid the time and risk associated with towing the vessel.

Kalil testified that he prioritized the MPD boat at his shop, directing his staff to treat it as if it were his own. His technicians even performed on-site river repairs and, in some instances, provided services free of charge. Notably, preferential treatment and free services from vendors violated state ethics rules, which mandated that municipalities could not receive benefits unavailable to the general public. Despite this ethical concern, no one raised this issue during other hearings or forums.

Following Samuel Kalils' testimony, Solomon was to take the stand. However, citing illness and medical advice from his physician, he could not attend the hearing. In his absence, Officer Joseph Aiello, a loyal subordinate and close friend of Solomon, was called as the next witness.

2009

Aiello's testimony covered a range of topics, including two phone calls he had with Mayor Manzi that the FBI recorded as part of their investigation into the bribery allegations brought forward by Solomon. Aiello recounted that after the Patrolmen's Union unanimously voted on October 1, 2007, to abstain from endorsing either candidate in the upcoming mayoral election, he called Manzi while seated in an FBI vehicle. The FBI was recording the call as part of their probe into the bribery claims Solomon had reported just a week earlier.

During the call, Aiello testified, Manzi used frequent profanity and expressed anger over the union's decision not to endorse him. According to Aiello, Manzi allegedly wanted to meet Aiello behind the Searles Building (City Hall). Aiello recalled Manzi saying, "When I shoot at or come after someone, I get them between the eyes."

As the hearing continued, efforts were underway to obtain the FBI recordings of these conversations, but the agency was reportedly unwilling to release them. The FBI is notorious for withholding evidence or documentation in cases where their investigation's status — ongoing or closed — remains unverified.

Solomon's attorneys maintained that the FBI investigation was ongoing, while City officials asserted the FBI informed them it had been closed.

Aiello also testified about events following the patrolmen's contract finalization in 2007. He said the mayor had expected the union's endorsement as a goodwill gesture. When Aiello, acting as the union president, failed to deliver that endorsement, Manzi allegedly instructed Chief Lavigne and Captain Fram to demote Aiello from the detective's division as retaliation. Aiello had since filed a lawsuit against Lavigne, Fram, and the City over the incident.

That evening, when the *Eagle-Tribune* questioned Mayor Manzi about the phone call with Aiello, he reiterated that he had no issue with the union's decision to refrain from endorsing any candidate. However, he expressed frustration over what he described as false statements about him to the union and later published in the media.

"These accusations are orchestrated by Solomon," Manzi told reporters.

2009

> *"Look who's pulling the strings here. There has been a continued attempt since September 28 to intimidate me, blackmail me, use political coercion to influence my official actions, and misuse federal law enforcement to achieve the goal of reinstating Joe Solomon as police chief."*

The final witness to take the stand was Solomon. He testified over two days, addressing every topic discussed during the hearing.

Solomon recounted to the Commissioner how his friendship with Manzi — predating their employment with the city — began to deteriorate when Manzi suspended him over the COPS grant controversy. Despite this, Solomon claimed the two had been working on mending their relationship in the aftermath. He even attended one of Manzi's political fundraisers, bringing his parents along. Solomon said he was "shocked" when Manzi placed him on paid leave and initiated an investigation against him. At the time, Solomon stated he wasn't worried about losing his job, believing that while there might be repercussions for going to the FBI, Manzi would never go so far as to dismiss him. Solomon speculated that political tensions had escalated, and when Manzi discovered he had gone to the FBI, it caused Manzi to "go off the deep end," leading to his suspension.

During cross-examination, City lawyers contested Solomon's claim that he hadn't realized his job was at risk. They argued that the signs had been apparent for some time: the controversies surrounding his leadership, the night of the Patriots football game incident, the city council's no-confidence vote, the reduction in his salary, his suspension over the COPS grant, and the ongoing investigation into the Weed and Seed grant. Solomon countered, saying, "To me, controversy means people are out there fighting."

When questioned about the alleged bribery involving Manzi, Solomon maintained that the FBI investigation was still active and that he continued to work closely with the agency. He firmly believed that his decision to report the alleged bribery was the primary reason for his firing.

Solomon described the night his long-time friend, Michael Neve, disclosed the bribery allegation. He painted a vivid picture of Neve, his friend of 30 years, as visibly agitated, sweating, and upset while recounting the events. "I asked him, 'Are you sure this is exactly what it is?'" Solomon recalled. "I could not believe that after all these years of helping each other out, Manzi was asking him to pay. I was beside myself."

After meeting with the district attorney and the FBI, Solomon said he began cooperating with the federal investigation. The new alliance included frequent communication, sometimes speaking with FBI agents three to five times a day, exchanging emails, meeting at various locations around the Merrimack Valley, conducting inquiries, and talking with individuals on the agents' behalf.

Another topic Solomon addressed during his testimony was the incident on the night of the football game. He admitted raising his voice, possibly using profanity, and using hand gestures to emphasize his disappointment to his officers. Following the incident, he asked the officers to write reports detailing what had transpired that evening.

However, those reports painted a different picture, describing Solomon as being on a tirade that night — contradicting his account on the stand. When questioned by the Commissioner, Solomon was asked if anyone present that evening could corroborate his version of events.

In response, Solomon expressed skepticism about the authenticity of the reports, arguing the officers wrote the accounts after Mayor Manzi placed him on leave. "My personal belief is that they did not physically write those reports," he told the Commissioner.

Once Solomon concluded his testimony before Commissioner Stein, the witness portion of the hearing officially came to a close. Given the prominent role the Weed & Seed Grant controversy played throughout the proceedings, Stein inquired about the status of the Department of Justice's demand for repayment — now approaching two years since the initial demand letter.

The city solicitor responded, stating that the city had yet to repay the DOJ and continued to receive demand letters, the most recent arriving in December. The solicitor added that the city remained hopeful for mitigation efforts to persuade the DOJ to reduce the amount owed.

Additional procedural hearings occurred among the lawyers and Commissioner Stein in March and April. During one of these meetings, Solomon's attorney, Andrew Gambaccini, sought to introduce a new piece of evidence: a recording of a song performed at Mayor Manzi's 2008 St. Patrick's Day fundraiser. He argued that the song was central to their defense, demonstrating that Manzi's actions were politically motivated.

The song, performed by State Representative Barbara L'Italien, was part of the traditional roast-style entertainment. Known for her preference for singing over telling jokes, L'Italien incorporated the ongoing conflict between Manzi and Solomon into her lyrics:

> *I have lived in Methuen since I was a tyke*
> *Wanted to be mayor before I wanted a bike*
> *Now I am running the city, living my dream*
> *I order Kraunelis, get my coffee with cream*

♪ *I am Mayor Bill Manzi, Mayor Manzi I'm yours,*
I am the king of Methuen for three terms and no more

> *Came to office in 2006*
> *Took over from Pollard, had lots to fix*
> *She left me a police unit filled with dissent*
> *And a chief who couldn't say*
> *How the money was spent*

♪ *I am Mayor Bill Manzi, Mayor Manzi I'm yours,*
I am the king of Methuen for three terms and no more

> *Now I am trying to fire a chief who won't go*
> *And a city attorney who wouldn't take no*
> *I wish they would listen and play by the rules*
> *Take the buyout like Joe from the schools*

♪ *I am Mayor Bill Manzi, Mayor Manzi I'm yours,*
I am the king of Methuen for three terms and no more

> *The Tribune's front page covers my sins*
> *Runs the photo of me and my many chins*
> *Baddour is there always getting good press*
> *He'll drop a dime telling on the rest*

2009

♪ *I am Mayor Bill Manzi, Mayor Manzi I'm yours,*
I am the king of Methuen for three terms and no more

Now I am glad you came to my St. Pat's feast
Giving me money for my campaign chest
Now I think I can win, but I may lose
I will go back to my store
Selling my booze

♪ *I am Mayor Bill Manzi, Mayor Manzi I'm yours,*
I am the king of Methuen for three terms and no more

While Gambaccini complimented L'Italien's voice, he criticized the appropriateness of a state representative singing about an ongoing employment matter. He assured Commissioner Stein that he would submit a copy of the recording before the end of the month. Stein reserved judgment on whether he would admit the song as evidence.

When contacted by the *Eagle-Tribune* about Solomon's legal team attempting to use her performance in his defense, L'Italien dismissed the notion: "If that's the best they've got to defend themselves, boy are they in trouble."

At the 2009 St. Patrick's fundraiser, L'Italien performed another song, this time having someone hold up a sign reading "Political Satire" during her performance.

The attorneys had until the end of July to submit their final briefs, outlining how they believed the Commission should rule.

Once the lawyers turned in their briefs, Commissioner Stein cautioned the lawyers that there was no definitive timeline for a decision. "I would love to give you an estimate, but I know it would not be accurate." While acknowledging that this case was unusually long and complex, Stein emphasized that termination cases take priority.

Solomon's hearing generated 3,500 pages of transcripts and numerous exhibits the Commission must review. Stein stressed that the process would take time, as he must carefully consider every detail to produce a well-reasoned decision.

And now, we wait.

2009

July 2nd

We can learn behaviors through attrition — when those in authority consistently bend the rules, this behavior becomes normalized. Over time, it fosters an acceptance of a distorted sense of propriety. This statement reflects the culture of the MPD at the time and would only get exponentially worse as the years went on.

To become a police officer in Massachusetts, candidates must take the annual Civil Service exam. The state places newbies on an eligibility list ranked by their passing test scores. When a city or town seeks to hire new officers, it requests this list from the state. Priority is given to disabled veterans and veterans who score at least 70 on the test, followed by candidates with the highest overall scores. Municipalities may also request tailored lists to address specific needs, such as candidates who reside in the community, all-female lists, or minority lists. While other classifications can affect an individual's ranking, we will skip those details to keep it simple.

In Methuen, the police department periodically called for the eligibility list to replenish its roster of reserve officers. Reserve officers are permitted to work road details, and when a vacancy arises in the regular patrol force, the highest-ranking reserve officer is placed into the police academy. Upon graduation, officials swear in the reserves as permanent patrol officers. In July 2008, the city requested the eligibility list and began the process of selecting 10 permanent reserve officers. Civil Service provided a list of 41 candidates, with two disabled veterans at the top and four other veterans scattered throughout the rankings. Standard rules required the city to contact all on the list to see if they would accept an appointment if selected. Twenty-five of the 41 contacted on the list indicated they would serve if appointed.

Protocol stipulated that the city should select twice the number of candidates needed, plus one, in ranked order, to move on to the next hiring process step. These candidates were provided with background check paperwork to complete. If any failed to return the forms or did not pass the background checks, the city could proceed to the next eligible candidates on the list.

By September 2008, after going through the initial list and failing to reach the required 21 candidates, the city requested

2009

additional names from Civil Service, who then provided 36 more names for consideration. Methuen officials picked eight of the ten selected reserve officers from the second list.

Following the interviews, two of the four selected reserves from the initial list had familial ties to current city employees. William Kannan, the son of City Councilor Jennifer Kannan and Matthew Jajuga, brother of MPD Lieutenant James Jajuga Jr. and son of former state senator James Jajuga Sr. Five of the eight individuals chosen from the second list also had familial ties. These included Katie D'Agata, the niece of Chief Lavigne; Luis Felix, D'Agata's fiancé; Kristopher Haggar, the nephew of Captain Randy Haggar; Brian Henrick, a relative of a school committee member; and Ronald Bonanno, a nephew of City Councilor Larry Giordano.

After being notified by the City that they had been bypassed, four candidates — Patrick Waldron, Charles Sciacca, David Dumont, and Nicholas Milone — exercised their right to appeal to the Civil Service Commission. Faced with multiple appeals from the same municipality, the Commission launched an investigation on July 2, 2009, to review the city's process of selecting reserve officers during 2008 and 2009.

In its review and subsequent hearing on August 3rd, the Civil Service Commission determined that the City's selection process for twelve reserve police officers in 2008 and 2009 was fundamentally flawed. The Commission found that the City repeatedly flouted civil service laws and rules throughout the process.

One key conclusion was that there were never fewer than 21 individuals from the original eligibility list willing to accept appointments. Therefore, the City had no justification for requesting a second list. The Commission highlighted compelling circumstantial evidence suggesting that the City sought the second list primarily to appoint five candidates with personal or familial connections. The Commission also raised significant concerns about the interview process. Chief Lavigne and her four captains conducted the interviews while the detective division handled the background checks. To avoid conflicts of interest, Lavigne refrained from participating

Civil Service Investigation Report

in the interviews or evaluations of her niece and her niece's fiancé and disclosed these relationships verbally to the mayor. However, she did not provide the written disclosure required by law. The Commission emphasized that, under conflict-of-interest laws, Chief Lavigne should have fully recused herself from the selection process to avoid the perception of bias against other candidates.

Additionally, one of the appellants bypassed by the City was a disabled veteran whose status would have placed them above all other candidates on the eligibility list. Civil service law mandates that when bypassing a candidate, the City must immediately notify the State Human Resources Department of its reasons, which it failed to do.

As a result of these findings, the Commission ruled to rescind the second list issued to the city. The commission directed Methuen to restart the hiring process, adhering strictly to the original list and civil service regulations.

The reserve officer debacle was not the first instance of the city manipulating the system to hire relatives or those with political connections, and it most certainly would not be the last.

July 22nd

Arbitrators met with the Methuen Patrolmen's Union and the city concerning a grievance filed by Officer Joseph Aiello. The grievance sought to re-classify an alleged injury he sustained on March 19, 2008, as Injured in the Line of Duty (ILD).

According to the *Eagle-Tribune*, March 19th was the day Acting Police Chief Lavigne called Aiello on his cell phone while he was off duty. The call concerned a simple question that is well within the rights of a police chief to ask of their subordinates. She simply wanted to question him about the nature of the time off Aiello had been granted to attend the Massachusetts Coalition of Police president's dinner earlier in March.

Instead of answering her question, Aiello, feeling harassed, hung up and contacted the union lawyer for guidance. The lawyer advised him to inform the chief that all communications should go through the lawyer moving forward. At the time, Aiello, also the union president, relayed this message to Lavigne.

As a side note, Aiello's behavior seemed unusual for a union president. In my 22 years as a trooper and union member, I've never encountered a union leader who would respond in such a manner. Union presidents typically thrive on confrontation; they are anything but timid and often see themselves as the most significant presence in the room. Aiello's reaction immediately raised an eyebrow.

According to union documents, Lavigne reacted strongly to Aiello's statement, responding, "No, I am going to call you, and I am going to look into this." This exchange reportedly upset Aiello significantly. Feeling stressed and overwhelmed, Aiello experienced a rapid heartbeat, prompting his mother to call 911. EMTs transported Aiello to the hospital, where he was treated for chest discomfort and described by the doctor as "very shaky, having palpitations." He continued to experience chest pain, but doctors expected him to recover within a week following a follow-up with his personal physician.

Aiello subsequently requested ILD status from March 19 to March 28, which would have entitled him to paid leave and indemnification of his medical expenses. He claimed that the phone call from Lavigne constituted interrogation and harassment, which triggered high blood pressure and related complications. Aiello further asserted that, by answering the phone and discussing work-related matters with the Chief, he had effectively "returned to duty."

Lavigne denied the ILD status request, prompting Aiello to file a grievance. This action led to arbitration, but the hearing did not occur until July 22, 2009. During the arbitration, both Aiello and the City presented their arguments. The arbitrator ultimately ruled in favor of the City, denying Aiello's request for ILD status. While the arbitrator acknowledged that Lavigne caused or at least exacerbated Aiello's injury with the phone call, they concluded that answering the phone did not constitute returning to duty.

For context, the phone call occurred between the second and third days of a significant hearing involving Solomon at City Hall, overseen by hearing officer Marks, and two weeks after Deputy Chief Alaimo's retirement.

September

September 17th, a date that many overlook, is Constitution Day — a time that Congress had set aside five years earlier to

2009

encourage citizens to honor and learn about the United States Constitution. One Methuen resident found a unique way to mark the occasion, exercising their First Amendment right to free speech. This is the day the "Methuen Police Blotter" blog came to life.

Initially penned by an anonymous writer identifying as "John Doe, Methuen Police Officer," the blog offered its perspective on MPD officers and happenings. Over time, ownership of the blog shifted to "John W. Wilson," a self-proclaimed Methuen resident who asserts having no connection to local government or politics.

One of the blog's inaugural posts, titled "When Will This End," wastes no time clarifying its stance. The post reads:

"There has been a significant amount of stress, pressure, and manipulation exerted on the fine men and women at the Methuen Police Department by Mayor Manzi and his administration at the PD. The time has come to reject this dictatorship form of leadership that Mayor Manzi has brought to the City of Methuen and the Methuen Police Department.

The vote of 'No Confidence' in Chief Lavigne taken by the Methuen Police Patrolmen's union is the first step to standing up to this regime.

The cover-ups and abuses of the system by Chief Lavigne and Captain Fram need to be exposed."

The blog author harbored strong grievances against Mayor Manzi, Chief Lavigne, and Captain Fram, positioning the post as a pointed critique of their leadership and actions within the Methuen Police Department.

In the days that followed, the blog's tone grew increasingly combative, with the writer escalating their criticism and expanding their focus to include additional members of the Methuen Police Department. At times, as many as four posts appeared in a single day, each more pointed than the last.

Over 50 days, the blog churned out 26 posts, each more inflammatory than the last. While Mayor Manzi, Chief Lavigne, and Captain Fram remained the principal targets, the blogger's focus soon extended to Sergeant Larry Phillips and Lieutenant Michael Wnek, who became regular subjects of scathing attacks.

The author spared no topics. Accusations ranged from infidelity and domestic violence to unwarranted overtime, assaults, cover-ups, perjury, alcoholism and bullying. The posts were rife with insinuations — whether grounded in fact or entirely speculative — relentlessly hurling allegations designed to provoke outrage and tarnish reputations.

Suspicions lingered for years about the true identity behind the blog's vitriol. It wasn't until a 2011 court case that the mystery was finally unraveled. During his testimony, Sergeant Larry Phillips revealed that multiple senior officers within the MPD had been informed by the Essex County District Attorney's Office in September 2010 about the findings of their investigation.

According to Phillips, the DA's office identified Solomon as the sole financier and sponsor of the *Methuen Police Blotter*. This revelation shed new light on the blog's origins and its agenda, exposing a deeper connection to the controversies it so aggressively chronicled.

November

The controversy surrounding the August 2008 school training exercise — and the excessive force complaint filed by Officer Ron Valliere against Sergeant Larry Phillips — did not fade easily. It persisted even after a court magistrate dismissed the criminal complaint. And it continued despite the internal investigation's conclusion that Phillips had not used excessive force during the drill. Through the Patrolmen's Union, Valliere brought the matter before an arbitrator, Robert Canavan, arguing that Phillips' actions were a "blatant, personal attack."

Since the August 19, 2008, incident, Valliere had been out of work for 66 weeks, collecting $1,078 per week under his In the Line of Duty (ILD) injury status. The arbitrator heard testimony from officers involved in the training that day and, like the initial investigation, found conflicting perspectives on whether Phillips had used excessive force. After reviewing the testimony and interviews, Canavan ultimately ruled that Phillips had not acted inappropriately, denying Valliere's grievance.

In his determination, Canavan noted that Phillips did not know the individual he was restraining was Valliere, as his face and head were covered by protective gear. He also pointed out that the training exercise was specifically designed to simulate a real-life school shooting scenario and that Lieutenant Korn had not instructed officers to avoid physical contact. The training was intended to be *"intense and realistic."*

Canavan also referenced Valliere's ongoing medical issues. Valliere had undergone arthroscopic surgery on his shoulder the previous February and was scheduled for another procedure. Canavan cited medical reports indicating that Valliere continued to experience pain, struggled with daily activities, and had difficulty sleeping. However, he also highlighted a discrepancy in Valliere's claims. In a doctor's report, Valliere stated that he suffered from knee pain and was unable to stoop, squat, or kneel without discomfort, despite MRI scans showing no significant abnormalities. Notably, this was the first recorded mention of any knee injury in the year-long dispute.

2010

July 29	The Massachusetts Civil Service Commission releases its decision ordering the reinstatement of former Police Chief Joseph Solomon.
August 16	Sean Fountain submits a letter to the City notifying that he intends to file a lawsuit on behalf of his son.
August 25	The City of Methuen files an appeal challenging the Civil Service Commission's decision to reinstate Solomon.
September 7	The City files a motion to stay enforcement of the Commission's decision.
September 30	Judge Murtagh denies the City's motion, clearing the way for Solomon's reinstatement.
October 1	Joseph Solomon returns as Chief of the Methuen Police Department.
November 15	Second day of jury trial in *Joseph Aiello v. Mayor William Manzi et al*.
November 16	Third day of *Aiello v. Manzi et al* trial.
November 17	Fourth day of *Aiello v. Manzi et al* trial.
November 19	Fifth day of *Aiello v. Manzi et al* trial.
November 22	Jury deliberations conclude with a hung jury; no verdict is reached.

July

Six hundred fifty-three days. That's how long the case drifted in limbo — beginning with Solomon's first hearing on October 14, 2008, and concluding only when the Civil Service Commission cast its final vote on July 29, 2010. In between lay 23 hearing days stretched across half a year, followed by an agonizing 476-day wait for Commissioner Paul Stein to deliver his decision.

That day, the temperature in Methuen soared to 90 degrees, but by sunset, it wasn't just the heat making the city feel scorched. The long-awaited ruling ignited a firestorm of debate, frustration, and uncertainty, leaving city officials and residents bracing for what would come next.

There's an old saying that government is not a speedboat but an ocean liner. In the case of the Massachusetts Civil Service Commission, however, it operates more like a rowboat. How can

2010

such a prolonged process be fair to either party? And how can a commissioner deliver a just decision when the details of the case are no longer fresh in their mind?

Commissioner Paul Stein's 125-page decision may have been exhaustive in length, but in our view, it was unmistakably biased, unbalanced, and deliberately one-sided. When held up against the other 13 reports Stein authored in 2010, the contrast is striking. We extended our analysis to include all 78 reports issued by the commission that year — and only one stood out as a glaring anomaly: the Solomon report. Authored by Stein, it is the lone outlier in an otherwise consistent body of work by the Commission.

On page 7 of Solomon's report, Stein begins summarizing the witnesses, categorizing them into three groups: Methuen Municipal Officials, Methuen Police Department Personnel, and Other Witnesses. While these are logical classifications, Stein fails to distinguish between Appellant (Solomon) Witnesses and Respondent (City) Witnesses, leaving the reader to determine who testified for whom.

Stein's Decision

A review of the 78 decisions issued by the Civil Service Commission in 2010 reveals that:

- 60 cases categorized witnesses by appellant and respondent,
- 8 cases listed no witnesses, and
- 10 cases presented them in a simple comma-separated list.

Only one decision, Solomon's, used this atypical classification, further setting it apart from standard Commission practices.

In the 60 Civil Service decisions of 2010, witness names are typically followed by their title or other descriptor. However, in Solomon's case, each witness is given an extensive paragraph or more.

For example, Stein describes Mayor William Manzi as follows:

> *"The present Mayor of Methuen, William M. Manzi, III, was elected to his first term as Mayor in November 2005*

> *and assumed office in January 2006. Prior to becoming Mayor, he served as a city councilor and as City Council Chair. He was re-elected to a second term as Mayor in November 2007, opposed in that election by Kathleen Corey Rahme, then a member of the Methuen City Council and one of two council members who testified before the Commission. His family owns a liquor store in Methuen Square. Mayor Manzi is a man of commanding stature, nuanced, loquacious and colorful speaking skills, and a mildly brusque demeanor — an acumen certainly consistent with survival in the 'robust' political environment of Methuen, as Mayor Manzi, among others, described it."*

Later in the decision he wrote that Manzi demonstrates "skills at verbal gymnastics."

While this biography is detailed, much of the information — such as his family's liquor store ownership, his stature, and his speaking style — is irrelevant to the appeal and inconsistent with standard Civil Service Commission practices.

Stein's portrayal of Solomon is notably detailed, extending beyond his professional qualifications to emphasize his character and demeanor. Unlike his treatment of Mayor Manzi, which was more succinct and procedural, Stein's depiction of Solomon presents a layered narrative — one that acknowledges his mistakes but ultimately frames him as a sincere and dedicated public servant.

> *"Solomon was present throughout the hearing and testified over the final two days. He is a polite, highly focused and passionate man of medium height and build. He carries much pride about his career, his law enforcement colleagues, and his record of service with Methuen. As a party with a huge stake in the outcome of these appeals, his testimony necessarily must be scrutinized together with the other evidence in the record, both consistent and contradictory, and with his potential bias in mind. Overall, his responsiveness to questions on direct and cross-examination and by this Commissioner, and his demeanor, as witness and observer, appeared*

> *sincere and truthful. He acknowledged he had made mistakes and, in hindsight, would have done things differently. Despite the pressure of his career on the line, he was calm, courteous and respectful. He never displayed animus against those who opposed him or criticized him during the hearings, including during some tough cross-examination."*

In a typical Civil Service Decision, total witness lists take up less than a page, yet in this case, ten pages of the report are devoted to extensive character portrayals of 25 witnesses.

Using newspaper accounts from the time of the hearings, we were able to reconstruct which witnesses were called by each side — and in doing so, we noticed a peculiar pattern in their descriptions.

Analyzing the keywords related to truth, credibility, memory and demeanor, we found that every one of Solomon's witnesses had language in their bios referencing some or all of these themes. In contrast, Stein described none of the city's witnesses in such terms. As an example:

Solomon's witness:

> *"Randy Haggar – MPD Captain with 15-years of service on the MPD. Another dedicated, knowledgeable and impressive law enforcement professional. He is a credible witness with a good memory. His rapid rise through the ranks (taking the civil service test for captain as a sergeant and scoring first on the list) is consistent with his convincing demeanor as a witness before the Commission (sincere, good eye contact and responsive)."*

Methuen's witness:

> *"Thomas J. Kelly has been Methuen's City Accountant, aka City Auditor, since 1990. Prior to 1990, he held other administrative posts for the (then) Town of Methuen. The City Auditor, also appointed by the Methuen City Council, supervises Methuen's financial operations, including "budgeting, financial forecasting, revenue projections [and] handling all grants" to assure that expenditures*

> *comply with Methuen's municipal procedures as well as all laws regarding appropriation, purchasing and expenditure of municipal funds, including the conflict of interest and bidding laws, G.Lc.30B and G.L.c.268A. The City Auditor oversees daily operation of the Purchasing Department, but the staff of the Purchasing Department, including the Purchasing Agent, are hired by and directly responsible to the mayor."*

This selective emphasis suggests an intentional framing of witness credibility, subtly reinforcing a narrative about one side's reliability over the other. This pattern is yet another deviation from standard Civil Service Commission decisions, where witness descriptions are typically just titles rather than editorialized.

The Commission's procedural history asserts that a total of twenty-seven witnesses testified: eleven called by the City, fifteen called by Solomon, plus Solomon himself. Yet when one turns to the "Summary of Witnesses" section later in the decision, the count does not match. Only twenty-six individuals are actually profiled. Moreover, Solomon is not set apart under a distinct "Appellant" heading, as one might expect from the procedural math, but rather is folded into the list of Methuen Police Department personnel.

This mismatch creates an unresolved question: did the Commission inadvertently double-count Solomon in its opening arithmetic, or was one of Solomon's supposed fifteen witnesses omitted altogether from the narrative summaries? The decision never clarifies. Either explanation is problematic. A clerical miscount in a case of this magnitude raises doubts about the Commission's care in documenting its own proceedings. An omitted witness would be even more serious, suggesting the record presented to the public was incomplete.

In either scenario, the numbers simply do not add up. This discrepancy illustrates yet another irregularity in how Solomon's case was handled — an inconsistency that, while perhaps minor in isolation, fits a broader pattern of procedural anomalies, unexplained deviations, and questionable judgment that characterized the Commission's treatment of this appeal.

It would be remiss not to acknowledge that this was likely one of the most complex hearings the Civil Service Commission had conducted in quite some time, if ever. While most hearings typically last a single day — three at most in exceptional cases — Solomon's case far exceeded this norm.

The extended duration and depth of the proceedings may account for some deviations from standard practices. Still, they do not fully explain the irregular structuring, extensive witness characterizations and selective language choices reflected in the decision. These anomalies distinguish this case from typical Commission rulings and warrant closer scrutiny.

The abnormalities also raise a critical question: Why assign such a high-stakes, intricate case to the Commission's least experienced member — someone with only four months on the job? Given the complexity and significance of this hearing, one would reasonably expect a more seasoned commissioner to oversee the proceedings. This decision introduces yet another layer of irregularity to an already unconventional proceeding.

As for the charges, Stein found that only two were partially substantiated, while the petitioners failed to prove the rest. Below is Stein's rationale for each count:

Conflict of Interest Regarding Sergeant Phillips

Commissioner Stein found this charge to be proven in part, acknowledging that Solomon should have recused himself from the Sergeant Phillips investigation earlier than he did.

In his ruling, Stein stated:

> *"Chief Solomon likely knew all the facts that prompted his recusal, and he would have been prudent to distance himself from the Sgt. Phillips investigation sooner than he did. Chief Solomon's briefly delayed recusal, however, in this one unique and isolated situation, falls far short of proving the purported level of serious ethical misconduct upon which Methuen based its decision to discharge Chief Solomon. Indeed, as noted below, as to every other alleged ethical impropriety lodged against him, Chief Solomon fully acquitted himself and credibly showed himself to be a person who, in fact, took his ethical responsibilities seriously and, save for this one slip, hewed to them consistently."*

2010

Despite Stein's attempt to downplay the conflict of interest, the circumstances surrounding Solomon's delayed recusal raise serious concerns. His claim that he did not learn about his ex-brother-in-law, James Caron's grand jury subpoena until he arrived home that evening seems highly improbable, given the gravity of the situation. Notably, the brother-in-law was ultimately charged with two counts of receiving stolen property — coincidentally, just months after Solomon's termination.

Commissioner Stein briefly acknowledged the arrest, stating, "There was no evidence that anything came of this inquiry although the ex-brother-in-law was later charged with an undisclosed offense at some point in 2008." However, it seems unlikely that Stein was unaware that the charge was directly related to the original offense that Sergeant Phillips had sought to pursue. If the city had provided this crucial information, it would have further substantiated their case against Solomon.

This aspect of the case underscores a recurring theme in the Stein's findings — while acknowledging lapses in judgment or procedural missteps by Solomon, the wording by Stein throughout his decision consistently suggests blatant bias.

Disclosure of Confidential Information to Personal Attorneys

Commissioner Stein partially upheld the findings of the city-level hearing, determining that while the charge against Solomon had merit, it was not entirely as the city had alleged.

Stein addressed the matter in his ruling, stating:

> "*Methuen erroneously assumed that Chief Solomon included copies of MPD personnel and investigative files; the substantial evidence established that the letters, and the letters alone, were what Chief Solomon sent to his attorneys. Nevertheless, there is sufficient sensitive personnel information in the letters themselves to make these disclosures problematic. Chief Solomon credibly acknowledged his mistake and promised he would 'recalibrate' his decision and not repeat the error in the future. Moreover, Chief Solomon's actions were clearly a reaction to the unique political forces inside and outside*

> the MPD that were then plotting his imminent removal. The fact that the only recipients of the information were legal counsel, with whom Chief Solomon had attorney-client relationships that required them to keep the information confidential, is a key distinction here. Thus, I view the disclosure as materially different from sharing information with a politician or member of the general public."

Despite partially affirming the charge, Stein effectively gave Solomon a pass — accepting his admission of a "mistake" and his promise not to repeat it as sufficient justification. His leniency toward Solomon starkly contrasted the intense scrutiny and skepticism applied to testimony from those who had challenged the chief's actions.

Ethics and Procurement Violations Concerning the Marine Unit

Lawyers proved this charge in the city-level hearing, but the Commissioner Stein found it unproven.

Stein stated in his report:

> "...Upon becoming Police Chief, Solomon was proactive in disclosing the family relationship with Merrimac Marine and fully complied with the ethics laws by obtaining Mayor Pollard's approval to continue the MPD's relationship with Merrimac Marine. Further, although not ethically required, he took himself out of the loop by delegating all future business dealings with Merrimac Marine to Deputy Chief Alaimo, including the purchase of the second Marine Unit boat."

Stein further concluded:

> "Chief Solomon did not personally participate in the procurement process involving the second Marine Unit boat, which was handled entirely by Dep. Chief Alaimo, Capt. McCarthy, and Sgt. Havey. While complete and effective delegation of the matter may relieve Chief Solomon of conflict-of-interest problems, he could, in

> *theory, still be held responsible for wrongdoing by a subordinate acting pursuant to that delegation. Here, however, I find no wrongdoing has been proven on the part of any of the MPD superior officers involved in the purchase, much less vicarious liability on Chief Solomon's part for any alleged procurement errors or omissions."*

While delegating a conflicted matter remedies the ethical concern, it also creates a separate issue, as outlined on the Massachusetts Ethics Commission website under self-dealing and nepotism:

> *"A public employee may not participate in any particular matter in which he or a member of his immediate family (parents, children, siblings, spouse, and spouse's parents, children, and siblings) has a financial interest... Participation includes discussing as well as voting on a matter and delegating a matter to someone else."*

This standard suggests that Solomon was wrong in delegating the procurement process to Deputy Chief Alaimo, mainly when one of the officers involved had a blood relation to Mr. Kalil of Merrimac Marine.

The proper procedure should have been to delegate the matter to the city's purchasing office, not internal MPD personnel. Protocol should have limited the MPD's role to providing specifications for the needed equipment, which the purchasing agent would then use to obtain three competing bids, ensuring compliance with procurement laws and avoiding conflicts of interest.

Keeping the process entirely within MPD allowed for the manipulation of bids, ensuring that a preferred vendor could be awarded the contract under questionable circumstances — at the very least giving the appearance of a conflict.

Further underscoring this concern is the testimony of City Auditor Mr. Kelly before the Commissioner Stein. He claimed he had only recently learned of the supposed directive excluding the city's purchasing agent from police-related purchases. However, this assertion strains credibility, given that Kelly served as the city's purchasing agent before becoming auditor. With his extensive knowledge of procurement regulations, he should have immediately recognized the absence of the legally required two additional bids when the purchase order crossed his desk — yet he still personally authorized the payment, a clear violation of Massachusetts procurement laws.

Kelly further told Commissioner Stein that obtaining and documenting multiple bids was merely "a minor informality." As a former purchasing agent, he knew full well that this was not a trivial oversight but a blatant disregard for the law. Despite this, Stein memorialized Kelly's statement as fact in his decision — when, in reality, it was demonstrably false.

As discussed earlier in this chapter, Commissioner Stein's descriptions of the hearing's witnesses appear skewed in favor of those aligned with Solomon. Consider his neutral description of the purchasing agent:

> "Joanne Ouellette is Methuen's Purchasing Agent, a position she has held for approximately ten years."

Now compare this to Stein's portrayal of former Mayor Pollard:

> "Mayor Manzi's predecessor, Sharon Pollard, served three terms as Mayor from January 2000 to January 2006. She also represented Methuen in the Massachusetts Senate from 1976 to 1982. She displayed a good memory for events dating back to her tenure as Mayor and credibly testified only to what she recalled."

Many sources we interviewed expressed the same view: former Mayor Pollard and Solomon had a mutually beneficial relationship — she elevated and protected him politically, while he served as her enforcer. While direct proof of this quid pro quo arrangement remains elusive, circumstantial evidence strongly points in that direction.

Ouellette's testimony is particularly revealing. Unlike Pollard, who had a clear motive to shape the narrative in her favor, Ouellette had no reason to fabricate her account. Her claim that superiors directed staff to circumvent procurement laws is telling.

Furthermore, her continued adherence to this directive even after Mayor Manzi took office suggests that the practice was deeply entrenched. Manzi, a close ally of both Pollard and Solomon, would have had little incentive to challenge the existing system — so why would the purchasing agent defy a directive simply because the name on the mayor's office door had changed?

This suggests that the "hands-off" approach to Methuen Police Department purchases was not an isolated irregularity but a long-standing practice. It was deliberately maintained to allow insular decision-making within the department, bypassing standard procurement oversight and controls.

Preferential Surveillance of a Relative's Home

This charge was proven in the city-level hearing, but the Commissioner Stein found it unproven.

Stein stated in his report:

> *"As to the surveillance camera, the evidence established that the idea (which cost Methuen nothing and lasted only a month) came from others in the MPD. Chief Solomon had nothing to do with ordering it, installing it, or removing it. In sum, the activity on Kalil's street was nothing other than routine police work. Moreover, this unsubstantiated charge was based upon events that had occurred during Chief Solomon's tenure in the Pollard Administration, years before he was summarily placed on leave. The Commission has been clear that it frowns on an appointing authority's deliberate attempt to justify discipline by 'piling on' marginal charges, such as this one."*

Stein's reasoning, however, overlooks key concerns. While others may have suggested the surveillance camera, the commissioner must consider the chain of command and authority within the MPD. Even if Solomon did not personally order, install, or remove the camera, it is unlikely that such an action would have occurred without his awareness or tacit approval — especially given his close relationship with key figures in the department. Solomon's claim that he only became aware of the installed camera during a visit seems contrived. On the other hand, if he was truly as unaware as he claims, it raises serious questions about his competence and oversight as Chief.

Furthermore, the Commission's dismissal of this charge as merely part of a "piling on" strategy ignores the broader pattern of questionable actions under Solomon's leadership. The issue is not solely about the surveillance camera but whether the MPD used it appropriately and whether its deployment served a legitimate law enforcement purpose — or if it was another example of the MPD's insular decision-making under Solomon's command.

Once again, Stein portrayed a witness favorable to Solomon in glowing terms — this time, Samuel Kalil, who testified regarding the surveillance and Merrimac Marine:

> "...Mr. Kalil's demeanor was very convincing. He maintained good eye contact and came across as sincere, both in direct testimony and cross. He demonstrated very good powers of observation and a clear memory for many events. Nothing about his testimony suggested that he gave it any slant because of his personal relationship with the Solomon family or his business relationship with the MPD."

Stein's description emphasizes Kalil's supposed credibility and preemptively dismisses any concerns about his objectivity — despite explicit conflicts of interest.

Another factor to consider is that subsequent investigations and historical aerial photography confirm that Kalil's property has long been, and continues to be, used for storing boats as part of their business. Could this be the real reason for the heightened security measures? And that's without even addressing whether the city correctly zoned the property for commercial boat storage.

Interference with a Counterfeiting Investigation Involving Detective Flanagan

The city did not prove this charge in the city-level hearing overseen by Hearing Officer Marks, Manzi pursued the charge with the Civil Service Commission, which also found it unproven.

2010

Commissioner Stein characterized the allegation as yet another instance of Methuen's questionable tactics, stating:

"This charge was another example of Methuen's questionably motivated 'piling on' a stale and dubious claim, this one dating back to June 2002, which predates Solomon's tenure as Police Chief, even as Acting Chief, which he did not assume until October 2002.

The allegation centered on the claim that Solomon ordered then-Detective Walter "Gus" Flanagan to compromise a criminal investigation by handing over investigatory materials to former MPD Lieutenant Mike Alaimo, who was working as a private detective for a defense attorney.

Stein dismissed this charge, stating that it was primarily based on the testimony of Flanagan and Lieutenant Wnek, both of whom harbored longstanding disdain for Solomon. In contrast, Stein found that:

> *"The substantial credible evidence of all other witnesses, corroborated by official court records, disproves Mr. Flanagan's version of the events."*

This ruling reflects a broader theme in the Commission's handling of the case, where particular witness testimonies were deemed unreliable due to perceived bias. In contrast, the Commission accepted others without challenge, often without requiring substantive documentation to support their claims.

What Commissioner Stein failed to consider is that while Solomon was not yet chief and Alaimo was not yet deputy chief at the time of the alleged incident, both still outranked Detective Flanagan and were able to order him to turn over investigatory materials. Their official titles at the time were irrelevant to the power dynamics at play — his superior officers would expect him to follow orders.

Additionally, Stein could not have known that Flanagan probably could not have grieved the issue with Chief MacDougall. Given that Solomon had the ear of Mayor Pollard while MacDougall did not, it is plausible that Flanagan had little recourse and may have felt that raising concerns would be futile — or even detrimental to his position.

2010

With Solomon's close ties to Mayor Pollard, the political dynamics within the department likely created an environment where Flanagan's options were severely limited – whether it was coincidence or otherwise, it is worth noting that it was only six months after the meeting that MacDougall retired to make way for Solomon to become Chief.

Stein's descriptions of Flanagan, Joe Alaimo, and Mike Alaimo reveal a clear pattern: while he goes out of his way to emphasize the credibility of those aligned with Solomon, he subtly (or not so subtly) undermines those who might challenge him.

Consider Stein's portrayal of Mike Alaimo:

> *"...He is a highly credible, professional law enforcement officer who took pride in having maintained good relations with 'all the men I worked with,' including long-standing friendships with both Mayor Manzi and Solomon. Lt. Wnek said both he and Solomon 'would go through brick walls for Mike Alaimo.' The fact that members of Mike Alaimo's family had careers with Methuen (among them, his son [Joseph Alaimo] as Deputy Police Chief, and daughter-in-law [Lisa Alaimo], as the mayor's administrative assistant), and the history of his own contractual relationship with the Methuen School Department, made his testimony (not all of which was favorable or flattering to either Solomon or Mayor Manzi) all the more credible."*

Here, Stein not only calls Mike Alaimo "highly credible" but frames his deep personal and professional ties within Methuen — including direct connections to Solomon and Manzi — as factors that enhance his credibility rather than potential conflicts of interest. He even bolsters this impression with a glowing character endorsement from Lieutenant Wnek.

Compare this to his treatment of Joseph Alaimo:

> *"He began as a patrol officer and worked his way up the ranks to become Deputy Chief in 2002, appointed by former Mayor Pollard. His interests, in many ways, were closely allied with Chief Solomon. I have weighed Joseph Alaimo's testimony with this in mind. Substantial other*

> *evidence that corroborated much of his testimony leads me to find those parts of it credible."*

While Stein acknowledges that others corroborate much of Joseph Alaimo's testimony, he immediately qualifies his credibility by noting that Alaimo's interests were "closely allied" with Solomon. This disclaimer signals skepticism — something conspicuously absent from his discussion of Mike Alaimo despite their similarly close ties to key figures in the city.

Now contrast this with his portrayal of Walter Flanagan:

> *"... Mr. Flanagan's credibility is principally addressed later in the context of the conflicting evidence involved in his testimony. It is noted, here, however, that Mr. Flanagan did not hide his disdain for some of his superiors at the MPD, including Chief Solomon and Deputy Chief Alaimo. ('I really didn't like the way he [Solomon] conducted himself' when he first joined the MPD. As to Deputy Chief Alaimo: 'He didn't like me, and I didn't like him.') He implied Solomon and Alaimo tried to frame him and have him fired because 'they're desperate people."*

Rather than clearly assessing Flanagan's credibility, Stein frames him as someone who openly expressed "disdain" for his superiors and suggests that personal grievances taint his testimony. Unlike Kalil or Mike Alaimo, Stein does not emphasize Flanagan's ability to recall details, maintain composure, or testify objectively. Instead, his description primes the reader to view Flanagan's testimony as emotionally driven and self-serving.

The Roll Call Room Incident

Officials upheld this charge at the city-level hearing, yet the Commissioner Stein ultimately found it unproven.

The football game incident dominated the hearings, consuming more time than any other topic. Similarly, Stein's decision devoted ten pages to dissecting the event.

Stein opined in his report:

> "Witnesses to the ensuing five-minute encounter gave somewhat different versions of what occurred. I find Solomon's testimony to be a plausible, thorough, and consistent recollection of events; the versions given by Lt. Wnek and Sgt. Phillips, along with the unsworn hearsay statements of the five officers (none of whom testified before the Commission), suffer from selective memory and inconsistency. Similarly, I discount Officer Aiello's selective memory of events, which I infer is a natural result of his interest as union president to steer clear of statements that put a member in jeopardy of discipline or undermine his own credibility for earlier asking for more patrol manpower.
>
> "Officers Bistany, DeLeon, and Moore also wrote 'unofficial' memoranda focusing mainly on critiques of Solomon during the 'roll call' encounter, which Lt. Wnek said they were afraid to include in an official report sent through the chain of command. None of these three officers testified before the Commission, and Solomon did not see these memoranda in the ordinary course. They appear to have been forwarded to the City Solicitor, possibly before Solomon was placed on administrative leave in late September 2007 and first came to Solomon's attention in the course of the Mayoral-level hearing on his termination in February 2008. I am not convinced that the uncorroborated hearsay opinions and conclusions in these officers' unofficial statements, which have never been subjected to cross-examination, have sufficient indicia of reliability to be worthy of independent weight."

Stein's analysis suggests that he accepted Solomon's claim that someone fabricated the officers' unofficial reports. While three officers did not testify in person, the two who did were ranking officers. Notably, when Stein directly asked Solomon if anyone could corroborate his version of events against the five officers' accounts, Solomon did not answer. Instead, he deflected, arguing that he did not believe the officers had physically written the reports.

Others have alleged that Solomon knew before arriving at the station that night that the grand jury had subpoenaed his ex-brother-in-law and Sergeant Phillips. Still others have said that Officer Aiello called Solomon to tip him off about the officers watching the football game. Aiello was the union president representing three of the five officers involved that night — yet those three bypassed their union and submitted their reports directly to the city solicitor. Why? We can speculate that it was because they knew Aiello would never allow those reports to see the light of day.

Discipline of Sergeant Phillips

Commissioner Stein ultimately found this charge unproven, contradicting the city's position that Solomon had improperly disciplined Sergeant Phillips for his actions on the night of the football game incident.

In his ruling, Stein stated:

> *"Kara Lapides credibly persuaded Capt. Lavigne (and Officers McMenamon and Aiello), as well as this Commissioner, that she was, indeed, 'intimidated' and placed in 'fear' of Sgt. Phillips as a result of his conduct on August 24, 2007, and at other times. That information alone would have been sufficient to initiate an investigation that, depending on how the facts developed, very likely could have led to stiff discipline. Sgt. Phillips' reputation as a 'bully' added credence to Solomon's concern that action needed to be taken to protect one of his employees from unlawful harassment (which could become a source of liability to the MPD and Methuen). Putting Sgt. Phillips on administrative leave does seem somewhat precipitous, but I am not about to second-guess Solomon's sense of the urgency of the situation, especially when his judgment was confirmed by Capt. Guy and, eventually, by psychologist Jeff Zeizel, who recommended further counseling of Sgt. Phillips for anger management. While the Commission does not have the merits of the misconduct before it, and will not take sides on the underlying controversy, Methuen's position that Solomon should be disciplined for abusing a perpetrator of alleged harassment, rather than support his decision to take*

> *measures to protect the rights of the alleged victim, or even conduct a plenary hearing, is hard to square with basic merit principles."*

The allegations against Phillips stemmed from a remark he allegedly made to Lapides about being "one of the privileged" to receive overtime, which she claimed made her feel intimidated and fearful. Later that evening, Phillips exchanged words and gestures — flipping his middle finger — with Lapides' boyfriend, Officer Thomas McMenamon, and another officer. Commissioner Stein acknowledged that Phillips' gesture was "discourteous and unbecoming behavior for a superior officer," but also concluded that "the banter of the exchange, however, infers that both patrol officers brushed it off as harmless."

However, Stein's analysis overlooked a key inconsistency: the exchange between Phillips and Lapides occurred before the interaction between Phillips and McMenamon. If Lapides had genuinely felt fearful, logic suggests she would have immediately sought out her boyfriend, who was in another room with Aiello discussing union business, to express her concern. Yet, when McMenamon later interacted with Phillips, giving him the finger, McMenamon's demeanor suggested he did not hold any animosity against Phillips — he treated the interaction as a joke rather than confronting Phillips in defense of Lapides.

This discrepancy raises serious questions about the validity of Lapides' claim of intimidation and whether Solomon's actions were truly justified. Stein's ruling appeared to benefit Solomon from the doubt while disregarding inconsistencies in the testimony that might have pointed to a different conclusion.

Mismanagement of the Weed & Seed Grant

Lawyers established the mismanagement of the Weed & Seed (W&S) Grant in the city-level hearing, and the Civil Service Commission found it partially proven.

Commissioner Stein acknowledged that there was one legitimate criticism of Solomon's handling of the grant, stating:

> *"He did, appropriately and immediately, rectify the lack of documentation for superior officer overtime on a*

> *prospective basis, once it came to his attention in 2006. He was less effective, however, in marshalling the case for overturning the $170,000 demand for reimbursement and can be held accountable for taking, at times, an overly personal, defensive approach to the ongoing investigation, presumably out of concern for his own self-preservation and potential personal liability ... This critique can only go so far, as the 'robust' political climate in Methuen was not primarily of his making, it was not conducive to a fully collaborative and trusting working relationship with other Methuen officials, some of whom were openly hostile to him, and who had marginalized him long before the details behind DOJ's claim became fully known."*

Stein also noted that the grant application implicitly acknowledged that W&S coordinators would need to work beyond the allotted four grant hours per week but that these extra hours would be considered part of their existing city salary.

In his testimony, Joseph Alaimo told Stein that he and Solomon put in many unpaid hours:

"We did more work" and put in "many hours that [he] wasn't compensated for."

Regarding Solomon, he stated:

"The man lived down there ... 18 hours a day easily."

Solomon's testimony echoed these sentiments. Stein accepted this, stating:

> *"This testimony might seem mere hyperbole, but for the fact that both men showed genuine pride for the W&S program that came through clearly in their testimony and demeanor; I have no doubt they chose to work many hours on W&S for which they received no MPD or W&S grant pay."*

However, a fundamental contradiction arises here:

As a commissioner, one would expect a reliance on documentation and verifiable records rather than the words and demeanor of two men whose lack of documentation was at the heart of the $170,000 grant repayment demand. Accepting testimony based on pride and sentiment rather than clear records raises serious concerns about the evidentiary standards applied in this decision.

An examination of time-keeping practices for the W&S revealed that the MPD used a record-keeping software called PRO-IV. This system had a password-protected payroll section, accessible only to Sergeants and above for entering payroll data.

However, conflicting testimony emerged regarding whether anyone could remotely access the software. Melanson & Heath, the auditors, testified that both the city's IT staff and Microsystems, the software vendor, told them remote access was not possible. In contrast, Solomon and Captain Randy Haggar testified that remote access was possible based on personal knowledge and both had laptops that enabled them to access the system remotely.

Commissioner Stein weighed these testimonies, ultimately siding with Solomon and Haggar:

"The clear evidence leads me to credit the direct testimony of Haggar and Solomon on this point."

This ruling is remarkable, considering the Civil Service Commission's mission statement describes it as an "independent, neutral appellate tribunal and investigative entity." Instead of relying on the testimony of two certified CPAs from a private auditing firm — who had direct conversations with the software owner and the city's IT personnel — the commissioner accepted the unverified claims of two individuals with a clear personal stake in the outcome. No demonstration or technical verification was required, making this decision highly questionable.

During the hearing, significant discussion arose regarding PRO-IV's limitations in documenting detailed officer shift duties. Due to this, MPD officials kept paper records for patrol officers' grant-funded shifts.

However, Solomon testified that while patrol officer records were maintained, ranking officers' records were not. Instead, MPD officials basically placed superior officers on an honor system, responsible for self-reporting their hours. Solomon defended this practice, stating:

> "I would be insulted by any suggestion that one of my 'high-level' command staff 'can't be trusted' to put their

> *[own] hours in and take seriously their duty to sign off on the [weekly] payroll."*

This lack of oversight created an environment where their bosses trusted superior officers to report their own time without verification. Given that the $170,000 grant repayment demand stemmed from poor documentation, this approach raises serious concerns about financial accountability and administrative oversight within the MPD's handling of grant funds.

Loss of Confidence

Lawyers proved this charge at the city-level hearing, but the Commissioner Stein found this to be not proven.

> *"The independent evidence of the charge consisted mainly of Mayor Manzi's contention that he lost confidence in Solomon through an 'evolving process ... there was testimony from three witnesses (Lt. Michael Wnek, Sgt. Larry Phillips and former Det. Walter 'Gus' Flanagan), who disparaged Solomon's ability. ... Arrayed against this slim evidence is the resounding formal endorsement of the MPD superior officers' union (sergeants, lieutenants and captains), as well as testimony of numerous other current and former MPD officers, of all ranks, the gist of which was that most members just 'want to do their jobs' and it was, rather, the intrusion of politicians into the affairs of the MPD that 'split' the department. I conclude that it was not Solomon's performance that led to a 'loss of confidence,' but, rather, his failure to bend to the prevailing political winds of those who were already pre-disposed against him."*

Commissioner Stein concluded his decision with the following epilogue:

> *"I conclude that the Commission is justified to exercise its authority to set aside the discharge of Solomon and to modify the discipline to an appropriate remedial sanction, which is determined to be a suspension for a period of 12 months, measured from the date of his discharge in May*

2008. Save for this period of suspension, Solomon shall be fully reinstated to his position as Methuen's full-time tenured Police Chief without loss of any other pay or benefits. This modification takes into account Methuen's own prior selection of a 3-day suspension imposed by Mayor Manzi for poor judgment in administration of the COPS/HSOP grant, as well as all of the facts as found from the evidence presented to the Commission, including without, limitation, the findings about the narrow scope of Solomon's personal responsibility and other relevant facts concerning the W/S grant; the findings about Solomon's only other two isolated instances of poor judgment, involving what were principally procedural errors in his handling of discipline arising out of the August 24, 2007 incidents. It has considered Methuen's improper overreaching, by "piling on" a number of dubious and stale charges without merit which Solomon was obliged to defend, and which prolonged the appeal, as well as the overarching undue and improper influence that political and personal motives played in every facet of this case, especially in Solomon's unjustified summary removal from office and subsequent decision to discharge him. The modification is also specifically designed to represent a meaningful, remedial level of discipline that reinforces, to Solomon and to all other similarly situated civil service personnel in high office, the importance of maintaining an exemplary standard of public service commensurate with that high station, as well as to give assurance to Methuen and its citizens that Solomon will strive with all his being to deliver on this obligation upon his return to duty. This discipline is, as the civil service law intends, remedial. Just as Methuen must take care to comply with its obligations under civil service law in the future, Solomon must see his reinstatement as admonition to correct [his] inadequate performance, on pain of further discipline in the future."

At the Civil Service Commission's July 29th meeting, the full Commission held two votes on Stein's decision. The first vote, to dismiss Solomon's appeal of the initial city-level hearing and

2010

uphold a three-day suspension related to the COPS grant, passed unanimously. The City prevailed on that one.

The second vote addressed the charges from the second city-level hearing. The Commission voted to allow Solomon's appeal in part, modifying his discipline to a one-year suspension. The decision passed with a 4-1 vote. Notably, the lone dissenting commissioner agreed with the overall ruling but believed city officials should have limited the suspension to 30 days rather than one year.

The ruling mandated that city officials reinstate Solomon as Methuen's Police Chief by October 1, 2010. Additionally, the city must compensate him for all wages accrued beyond the one-year suspension, unless a settlement — such as a buyout — can be negotiated between Solomon and the city to reach an alternative resolution.

After the Commission made the decision public, Manzi issued the following statement:

> "The Massachusetts Civil Service Commission's ruling in the case of Joseph Solomon v. the City of Methuen is lengthy and currently under review by the City's legal counsel. While we are disappointed by the Commission's decision to reinstate Mr. Solomon as Chief of Police, two key points must be emphasized.
>
> "First, the Commission fully upheld my initial three-day suspension of Mr. Solomon for the misallocation of the COPS Grant, which resulted in a taxpayer back charge of over $20,000 for the City of Methuen.
>
> "Second, although the Commission overturned the City's decision to terminate Mr. Solomon, they did find sufficient wrongdoing to impose a significant penalty: a one-year unpaid suspension. While this penalty is severe, it is less than the termination we sought. Additionally, the mismanagement of grant funds by the Methuen Police Department resulted in a taxpayer back charge exceeding $170,000."

In a pointed remark aimed at Commissioner Stein, Manzi added, "I would like to return the 'compliment' of the Commissioner and say that he has demonstrated great skill at 'verbal gymnastics.'"

2010

City Solicitor Peter McQuillan also spoke to the media, expressing dissatisfaction with the ruling. "The evidence does not support the decision," he said. "The termination should have been upheld."

In a conversation with *Eagle-Tribune* reporters, Manzi criticized Stein's ruling, claiming it highlighted the flaws within the Civil Service system. He pointed to the lengthy and costly process, which included 23 days of hearings over six months. He noted that Stein had imposed his own disciplinary approach instead of upholding the City's. "The City clearly demonstrated both sufficient facts for the discipline we imposed and the need to move the department forward," Manzi added.

While Manzi did not rule out a reasonable settlement with Solomon, he refrained from commenting further on the matter, emphasizing that the civil service decision would not benefit the police department's future and would likely lead to continued uncertainty. Time would ultimately tell — but now that time has passed, Manzi's prediction proved almost Nostradamus-like in its accuracy.

When reporters approached Chief Lavigne for comment, she appeared upset and offered little response. However, when asked about the impact Solomon's return might have on the department — especially with some officers having testified against him — Lavigne replied, "It could be very difficult."

At Solomon's home in Methuen, supporters gathered in celebration, even though Solomon was absent. Festive balloons and signs adorned the property, including one enormous banner reading "Welcome Back Chief!" Later, others arrived, offering hugs, including Joseph Alaimo.

Solomon released a statement through his attorney, expressing his eagerness to return to work. "I am anxious to return to work, advance the interests of Methuen and its Police Department, and heal any rifts caused by this process," he said.

He continued,

> "This experience has been humbling, and I have learned much about myself — not only as a person but also as a police officer and a chief of police. The time spent reflecting on the past, present, and future has only strengthened my resolve to serve the Methuen community

2010

and lead the Methuen Police Department to the best of my abilities."

Stein's Decision-Making Style and the Solomon Outlier

When Consistency Breaks, Truth Emerges

Most people will never read a Civil Service Commission ruling. They are meant to be background noise — dry, technical, and predictable. In fact, their predictability is their strength. A steady format reassures the public that the system is fair, impartial, and mechanical. Win or lose, you should at least know the same rules applied to you as to the person before you.

But in 2010, something strange happened.

Commissioner Paul Stein, a man who typically wrote rulings of nine or twelve pages, produced one that ran 125. It was verbose, defensive, and almost unrecognizable compared to his other work. And the case? None other than Joseph Solomon, the politically wired police chief of Methuen.

That is not coincidence. That is the investigative tell.

By holding Solomon's decision against the backdrop of Stein's dozens of other rulings, the pattern becomes impossible to ignore. A commissioner who had built his reputation on restraint suddenly wrote like an advocate. He abandoned his formula — then snapped right back to it in every decision that followed. Years later, when asked about it, Stein could not even defend his own words. At the mere mention of Solomon's name, he went silent and passed the call to a lawyer.

This isn't about word counts. It's about what the break in consistency reveals: a system bending itself around one man.

Stein's Normal Style: Predictable and Neutral

Paul Stein was nothing if not consistent. His decisions read like a template:
- Length: rarely more than 9–18 pages.
- Structure: procedural history, facts, law, analysis, conclusion.

- Tone: restrained, legalistic, impersonal.
- Credibility findings: brief, factual.
- Orders: clipped and directive, usually one line: "The appeal is denied."

Examples abound:
- *White v. Wareham Police Department* (2009): 9 pages, neutral testimony summary, straightforward denial.
- *Ung v. Lowell Police Department* (2009): 12 pages, restrained, formulaic.
- *Anderson v. Boston Police Department* (2010): 15 pages, factual chronology, detached tone.

These rulings were boilerplate in the best sense efficient, consistent, and immune to theatrics.

The Solomon Decision: A Stark Outlier

Then came Solomon v. Methuen Police Department.
- Length: 125 pages — eight times the norm.
- Structure: headings blurred fact, law, and commentary.
- Tone: unusually descriptive, adjective-laden, defensive: more like a legal brief than a ruling.
- Order: not crisp but qualified, including a peculiar wrinkle: delaying discipline to encourage settlement.

For anyone familiar with Stein's style, the shift was jarring. It wasn't subtle. It was seismic.

A bar chart of Stein's decisions makes the point visually: a flat cluster of rulings between 9 and 18 pages, then one massive spike — 125 pages. The spike belongs to Solomon. And Solomon alone.

The Investigative Tell: Pattern Shifts

- Before Solomon: concise, restrained, and predictable.
- During Solomon: sprawling, defensive, atypical.
- After Solomon: instant return to brevity and neutrality.

Temporary departures from a lifelong pattern do not happen by chance. In investigative work, when the ordinary breaks, you ask why.

2010

Silence Speaks

The irregularities did not end with the written word.

Years later, I tried to interview Stein about the decision. The moment I said "Solomon," the line went quiet.

"Hold on," Stein muttered. Moments later, the Commission's chief legal counsel — not Stein — was on the phone.

This was a case long closed, a public record, authored by a public official. And yet, Stein himself refused to discuss it.

Sometimes what a decision-maker will not say tells you far more than what he wrote.

Why the Difference Matters

Administrative law survives on consistency. Outliers of this magnitude are not accidents; they are signals. When a commissioner known for concise rulings suddenly produces a sprawling, defensive tome—and then immediately reverts to his old style — the only real question is why.

And when that commissioner cannot even speak his own words without a lawyer present, the answer becomes harder to deny: the system bent, the rules shifted, and justice was not blind.

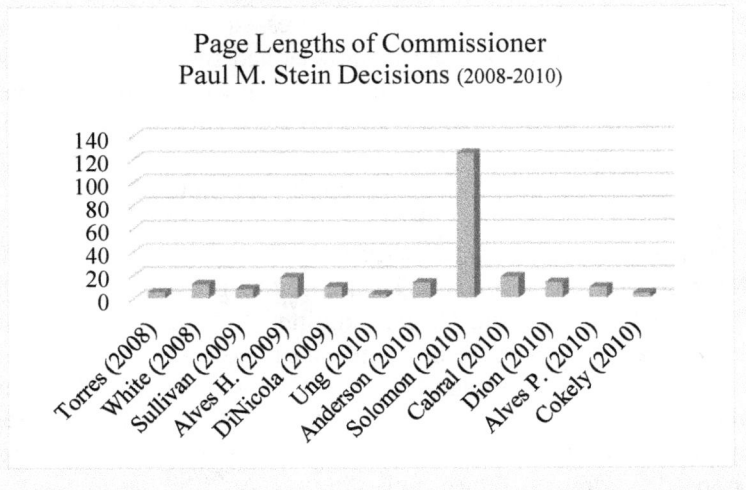

Page Lengths of Commissioner Paul M. Stein Decisions (2008-2010)

2010

August

News of the Civil Service Commission's ruling on Solomon spread rapidly throughout Methuen, sparking a wide range of reactions from residents and city officials. Speaking to the *Eagle-Tribune*, some welcomed the ruling, while others expressed deep reservations about its impact on the city and its police department.

One gentleman, a longtime supporter of Solomon and organizer of the "Friends of Chief Solomon" group, had mixed feelings about the outcome. Having led rallies supporting the embattled chief, he acknowledged the situation's complexity. "It would be nice to see Solomon come back," he said, "but there's been so much damage — damage that can't be undone."

City Council Vice Chair Jeanne Pappalardo echoed similar concerns, emphasizing the financial toll the case had taken. "I don't think there's a winner in any of this," she stated. "The biggest loser in Methuen is the taxpayer."

Manzi and McQuillan announced their intention to appeal the Civil Service Commission's ruling in Superior Court within the 30-day deadline. Additionally, they planned to seek a stay on Solomon's return to work until the courts resolved the appeal process.

City Council Chair Jack Cronin expressed optimism about the city's chances on appeal but acknowledged that the legal battle could drag on for another 18 months. Meanwhile, Councilor Pat Uliano took a starkly different stance. "We would be pretty stupid to spend one more penny on an appeal that has no chance of winning," she stated bluntly. "This is the end. It's done. It's finished."

Discussions of a potential settlement also divided city officials and residents. While personally opposed to giving Solomon any financial compensation, Cronin admitted that he had a duty to consider all options in the best interest of taxpayers.

Residents voiced similar concerns. One woman worried about the financial strain, stating that as a taxpayer, she was frustrated by the mounting costs with no clear resolution in sight. Another opposed Solomon's return, believing it would be detrimental to the city, but she also dismissed the idea of a buyout. "The city doesn't have any money," she said.

City Councilor Joyce Campagnone captured the growing frustration among Methuen's residents.

> "It's time to move on. The people in the community just feel enough is enough. How much can this community afford to pay out on court cases?"

September

As the October 1st deadline for Solomon's return as Chief of Police approached, the city did act swiftly, filing a petition for Judicial Review to overturn the Civil Service Commission's decision to reinstate him. The Lawrence Superior Court, with its own slow-moving timeline, was tasked with handling the review. With less than a month left before Solomon could potentially return to the police department, the city requested a stay on the enforcement of the Commission's decision, aiming to prevent Solomon from resuming his duties until the "Appeal of the Appeal" could be heard in court.

The situation came down to the wire. It wasn't until the day before Solomon's scheduled return that Justice Thomas Murtagh issued his ruling. You might recall Judge Murtagh from his involvement in Officer Cronin's lawsuit against Solomon and Alaimo and Solomon's ongoing civil case against the city. While Cronin's case concluded earlier this year, Solomon's legal battles continue to wind through the courts.

Regarding the city's plea for a stay on enforcement, the judge outlined that the Methuen officials needed to meet three criteria to succeed. First, they must demonstrate a likelihood of success on the merits of their case. Second, they must prove that denying the injunction would result in irreparable harm. Third, the city must show that, given their likelihood of success on the merits, the risk of irreparable harm to the city outweighs any potential damage to Solomon if the court grants the injunction. Moreover, because this is a matter that involves governmental action, the city must consider the risk of damage to the public interest.

Judge Murtaugh looked at the first hurdle — the likelihood of success on the merits. The only evidence the court had before it was the 125-page decision of the Commission. The judge noted that he could not consider any of the testimony transcripts and exhibits introduced during the hearing, only the Civil Service Commission decision. He thought, at least on the face of it, the Commission decision was a thorough and thoughtful consideration of the evidence presented by the parties.

The city argument to the court was there was no substantial evidence to support the Commission's decision to reverse Solomon's termination. Again, the Court assessed the city's claim solely based on the Commission's decision and found that the decision was internally consistent, logically coherent, free of any legal misconceptions, and aligned with the statutory authority granted to the Commission. Furthermore, the judge determined that the conclusions reached by the Commission were rationally based on the evidence and the findings of fact.

The second challenge for the city was to prove that denying the injunction would result in irreparable harm. While the judge acknowledged that Solomon's return might cause some disruption within the police department, particularly in repositioning key command positions, the court concluded that, as law enforcement professionals, the staff would continue to fulfill their duties despite dissatisfaction with Solomon's return. Consequently, the court determined that there would be no irreparable harm.

The third criterion was the balance of harm. The judge found that the disruption to the city caused by Solomon's return would not outweigh the harm to Solomon if the city did not reinstate him.

After evaluating these three criteria, the court denied the City's request for a stay of the Civil Service Commission's order to reinstate Solomon as Chief of the Methuen Police.

October

The following day, Solomon reported to the police station and called a meeting with all the staff under his command. He assured them that there would be no animosity and promised that, moving forward, the department would work together rather than against one another.

Solomon's reinstatement horrified the rank and file, though, in truth, not entirely surprised. They had long been aware of

2010

Solomon's significant influence — an influence now glaringly apparent to the community as well. His return signaled a troubling shift that seemed to bolster his authority even further, making him appear almost omnipotent within the department.

The lingering question on everyone's mind was not if retaliation from Solomon would occur, but when.

Although Solomon has resumed his role as Chief, the City's plea for judicial review was still ongoing despite the slim chance of success.

Upon resuming his position under the civil service ruling, the city paid Solomon $199,000 in back wages. However, Solomon disputed that amount, claiming that, according to his calculations, the city still owed him more. Unable to reach an agreement, he filed a civil lawsuit to have a judge determine the correct amount.

November

Just over six weeks after Methuen reinstated Solomon as police chief, Aiello's civil trial against the City of Methuen began in Boston — where Aiello is suing because he was removed from the detectives' division not long after the city put Solomon on leave.

During the four-day proceeding in November 2010, lawyers gave the 10-member jury a snapshot of the ongoing controversies involving Solomon, the mayor, the Methuen Police Department and the FBI. Among the evidence was a recorded phone call between Aiello and Manzi, in which Manzi unleashed a barrage of profanity while chastising Aiello. The FBI had contested the inclusion of this call, arguing that they held the inherent right to keep such recordings confidential, mainly to ensure future cooperation with subjects. However, Judge Robert Collings disagreed, ruling that the FBI's investigative privilege was not absolute and that the jury's need to hear the recording outweighed the claim of privilege.

Acting Captain Thomas Fram, Aiello's supervisor at the time of his transfer, testified that the MPD based their decision to remove Aiello from the detective's bureau based on Aiello's criminal conviction, him not being "a good fit" and lacking aggressiveness. Acting Chief Lavigne concurred with Fram's recommendation to transfer Aiello out and ordered the action to take place.

2010

The First Assistant in Jonathan Blodgett's District Attorney's office, Jack Dawley, took the stand and testified that while he had no issue with Aiello working as a detective, he was concerned about Aiello serving as a witness in court. "Drug cases are tough enough," Dawley stated. "We didn't need our chief investigator, our lead guy, being impeached."

When Lieutenant Michael Pappalardo, a long-time Solomon supporter, testified for the plaintiff, he recounted a December 2007 meeting with Solomon, Captain Lavigne, and a state police officer. During the meeting, they discussed allegations that Manzi had accepted a bribe and was involved in narcotics use. However, while on the stand, Pappalardo did not elaborate on the claims of drug use, and he declined to comment further when approached by reporters outside the courtroom.

Taking the stand, Aiello testified that after the election, Manzi was furious that the patrolmen's union had chosen not to endorse him or his opponent. According to Aiello, Manzi angrily told him, "He wanted me to meet him behind City Hall to go settle the matter."

Solomon appeared as a witness for Aiello's defense, testifying that he listened to a telephone conversation where Manzi had physically threatened Aiello — an accusation Manzi has consistently denied.

Retired Deputy Chief Joseph Alaimo testified for Aiello; he recalled speaking with Manzi about this threat. Alaimo stated that, while he never saw Manzi as a "tough guy," he knew Aiello had some fighting skills. He told the mayor, "This man will hurt you."

The infamous FBI tapes, which both Aiello and Solomon referenced in Solomon's 2008 city-level hearing and again in the 2009 Civil Service hearing, were alleged to contain threats made by Mayor Manzi. However, nobody could substantiate these claims because the FBI refused to release the recordings. As a result, during the Civil Service hearings, Commissioner Stein accepted the men's testimony at face value, assuming the threats had occurred.

When the jury in this case listened to the profanity-laced phone conversation between Aiello and Manzi, they did not hear Manzi issuing threats of violence. Instead, they heard Aiello attempting to bait Manzi and even challenging him to a fight — directly

2010

contradicting the sworn testimony of Aiello, Solomon and Alaimo, who had all asserted that Manzi had made threats. It also conflicted with Aiello and Solomon's testimony in both prior hearings.

Despite the evident contradiction, neither Aiello nor Solomon was ever held accountable for lying under oath — an omission that defies logic and raises serious questions about the integrity of the proceedings.

In his closing arguments, McQuillan told the jury, "This is a simple case about two supervisory police officers [Chief Lavigne and Captain Fram] who made a routine decision." He emphasized to the jurors that the mayor learned about the FBI investigation from a reporter two weeks after the transfer.

Countering the solicitor's argument, Aiello's attorney, Hillary Schwab, asserted that Manzi was aware of the investigation, and the evidence proved it. She asked the jurors to "picture another world, a parallel universe," where her client did not cooperate with the FBI and his union had endorsed the mayor. "There is no way Mr. Aiello would have been removed if he had shown himself to be a Manzi supporter," she argued.

Schwab further hypothesized that Acting Chief Lavigne and Acting Captain Fram had conspired with the mayor to "get rid of Mr. Aiello." In return, the MPD rewarded them with permanent promotions.

In her final appeal to the jury, Schwab urged the panel to deliver a guilty verdict, insisting they should "send a message" that superiors bullying employees should not be tolerated and that employers should not exploit their workers to advance their own careers. She further alleged that Manzi, Lavigne, and Fram had lied under oath during their testimonies.

After closing statements, the jury, armed with 18 questions to answer and 32 pages of jury instructions, sequestered themselves for deliberations to determine whether Mayor Manzi transferred Aiello out of the detective division as retaliation.

On the second day of deliberations, the jury found themselves hopelessly deadlocked, forcing Judge Collings to declare a mistrial due to a hung jury. The following month, the judge ordered both parties to go into mediation to reach a settlement. If mediation failed, the court would schedule a new trial to begin on May 2, 2011.

2010

A new trial was unnecessary as the parties settled, awarding Aiello $15,000 and "costs incurred to date of the judgment." However, the interpretation of "costs incurred" became a significant point of dispute. McQuillan maintained that the settlement did not include attorney's fees while Aiello's legal team argued otherwise. With three lawyers representing him and over $250,000 in legal fees, Aiello also sought compensation for litigation expenses and interest on the judgment. The matter would ultimately need a judge's ruling to resolve.

To avoid a potential judgment surpassing $300,000, McQuillan brokered another settlement for a total of $120,000, which included the initial $15,000. After securing a 6-2 vote in favor from the City Council, the court approved the settlement, closing yet another chapter in the ongoing saga of the MPD.

Aiello v. Manzi Court Papers

Aiello v. Manzi Depositions

Aiello v. Manzi Transcripts

Among the court documents was a single sheet from the New Hampshire Courts, dated January of this year. It recorded the *annulment* of Aiello's conviction for tampering with a public document. Under New Hampshire law, that annulment means the conviction is treated as if it never occurred, allowing Aiello to legally state that he has no criminal record for that offense.

However, there is an important caveat. As a police officer, Aiello is held to a higher standard than an ordinary citizen. While the annulment clears the conviction in a legal sense, it does not erase its impact on professional accountability. Internal affairs files, licensing reviews, and public records of misconduct can still reference the incident — meaning the conviction remains relevant in the context of law enforcement scrutiny and career consequences.

Annulment

2011

January 31	Sergeant Larry Phillips files a federal civil rights lawsuit against the City of Methuen, Police Chief Joseph Solomon, Captain Kathy Lavigne, Captain Randy Haggar, Officer Michael Pappalardo, Officer Joseph Aiello, and Officer Ronald Valliere.
March 7	The City files a motion to dismiss Phillips' lawsuit.
April 5	Judgment is entered in *Joseph Aiello v. City of Methuen*.
April 20	Final judgment issued in *Aiello v. City of Methuen*.
May 5	Solomon files a federal lawsuit against former Mayor William Manzi and the City, alleging unconstitutional and retaliatory conduct.
June 6	Former City employee Fulya Metin (Capanelli) files for bankruptcy protection.
October 5	The City Council votes to settle with Metin for $250,000.
October 11	*Phillips v. City of Methuen* is dismissed.
December	Former City Solicitor Maurice Lariviere obtains a home equity loan to resolve his settlement obligation with Fulya Metin.
December 14	A non-jury trial is held in Solomon's lawsuit seeking lost wages from his period of removal.

January

At the start of the new year, the City of Methuen faced yet another legal battle. On January 31st, Sergeant Larry Phillips filed a lawsuit in the United States District Court, naming the City of Methuen, Solomon, Captain Randy Haggar, former Chief Katherine Lavigne, Officer Joseph Aiello, Officer Ronald Valliere, the Methuen Police Patrolmen's Association, and John Doe as defendants.

The lawsuit alleged that the city violated Phillips' civil rights due to his cooperation in a federal investigation involving an individual with political and familial ties to the Methuen Police Department. Phillips claimed that city officials and police department members had

Phillips v. Methuen, Solomon, et al Court Papers

retaliated against him for assisting federal authorities. He further accused them of improperly coordinating with law enforcement agencies in New Hampshire to gather damaging information against him, falsely accusing him of criminal and inappropriate behavior, and subjecting him to online harassment through internet blogs and chat rooms.

This lawsuit added another layer of controversy to an already embattled police department, further exposing the deep divisions and ongoing power struggles within Methuen law enforcement.

Sergeant Phillips' lawsuit detailed events that began with his assignment to a stolen tractor case in 2006. At the time, Captain Kris McCarthy instructed him not to investigate or file criminal charges against James Caron, the ex-brother-in-law of Solomon. Phillips suspected that these instructions had come directly from Solomon himself.

During his investigation, Phillips determined that Caron was directly involved in the theft and that there was sufficient evidence to charge him criminally. He reported his findings to his superiors, but on July 26, 2006, his immediate supervisor, Lieutenant Michael Wnek, relayed an order from McCarthy and Solomon: Caron was not to be charged — only the second suspect would face charges.

Recognizing that Solomon's involvement posed an apparent conflict of interest — and suspecting that he and other members of the Methuen Police Department would interfere with the case — Phillips contacted the FBI. After multiple meetings with federal agents, he agreed to serve as a cooperating witness in a broader criminal investigation into Solomon and other city officials. His information extended beyond the stolen tractor case, exposing other alleged illicit activities within the department. Ultimately, he agreed to testify before a grand jury regarding Solomon and others' effort to obstruct the investigation into Caron.

In August 2007, Phillips received a subpoena to testify before the grand jury. Following department regulations, he promptly informed his superiors. Shortly afterward, the football game incident at the police station unfolded, leading to his abrupt suspension. The next day, two Methuen Police Department lieutenants arrived at his home, informed him of his suspension, and ordered him to surrender his badge and firearm. Phillips claimed officials never gave an explanation for his suspension, denied his right to a hearing, and required him to undergo a psychological evaluation.

Three days after being placed on leave, Phillips testified before the grand jury. He later asserted that after learning of his testimony, Solomon and his command staff coordinated to discredit and intimidate him.

Two weeks after his grand jury appearance, the deputy chief of the Salem, New Hampshire, police informed Phillips that Methuen Lieutenant Michael Pappalardo had repeatedly traveled to Salem, attempting to gather damaging information about him. Pappalardo allegedly sought access to Phillips' records, including incident reports, log entries, and any documentation related to him or his home address — particularly any allegations of domestic violence.

Shortly thereafter, Solomon ordered Captain Katherine Lavigne to conduct an internal investigation into Phillips, centering on the alleged "harassment" of dispatcher Kara Lapides and two officers during the football game incident. Notably, Lavigne completed the investigation without interviewing Phillips. Solomon then used the findings as justification for disciplining him. However, after the city removed Solomon as police chief, MPD overturned the disciplinary recommendation against Phillips, and expunged all references to the investigation from Phillips' personnel file.

After serving 30 days on leave and obtaining medical clearance, Phillips was allowed to return to work. However, upon his return, he discovered that Solomon had ordered Haggar to change the passwords on his work computer, effectively blocking his access to files and investigative reports.

Phillips further alleged that union president Joseph Aiello repeatedly filed frivolous grievances against him to harass and intimidate him. One such grievance — discussed in an earlier chapter — stemmed from an incident on August 19, 2008, when Officer Ronald Valliere accused Phillips of intentionally assaulting him during a training exercise. Valliere and Aiello then attempted to pursue criminal charges against Phillips through the Patrolmen's Union, but the Clerk Magistrate at Lawrence District Court ultimately rejected their case.

What puzzles the author is why Aiello, as a union representative, was assisting Valliere in seeking criminal charges against another Methuen officer for a training-related accident. Not only does this action clearly overstep the bounds of union reach, but it is also a violation of Massachusetts law. As usual, Solomon's henchmen don't so much as even get a sideward glance for breaking the law. And where was the Superior Officers' Union defending Phillips in all this?

Phillips also contended that Captain Haggar actively solicited letters and complaints from other Methuen officers against him after the Valliere incident, allegedly encouraging them to fabricate misconduct allegations.

A key element of Phillips' case involved the Methuen Police Blotter blog, which lawyers introduced as evidence in court. Many posts targeted Phillips, accusing him of alcoholism, sexual harassment, threatening co-workers, and spousal abuse. While the blog remains online, no one has posted any entries since November 6, 2009.

Phillips' lawsuit outlined fourteen counts against multiple defendants, including federal and state claims. The federal claims included two counts of due process violations, two counts of conspiracy, supervisory liability, and Monell liability. The state claims encompassed violations of the Massachusetts Civil Rights Act, conspiracy under the same act, intentional infliction of emotional distress, loss of consortium, negligence, conscious pain and suffering, slander, and libel.

Phillips sought a jury trial and $750,000 in damages, citing stress and other health issues resulting from the alleged actions against him.

Solomon's attorney, Andrew Gambaccini, dismissed the lawsuit as "exceedingly stale." He added,

> *"Any individual with a couple hundred bucks for a filing fee and a few pieces of paper can put together a complaint and file it based upon any kind of grievance, no matter how slight or imagined."*

On March 7th, the City filed a motion to dismiss, urging the judge to consider several factors: failure to state a claim, the complaint being time-barred, lack of a valid legal basis for relief, failure to allege an underlying constitutional violation, and the complaint not meeting the standard for Monell liability.

2011

Judge Joseph Tauro sided with the City and granted the motion to dismiss without prejudice, meaning the court temporarily dismissed the case, but Phillips retained the option to refile it later.

Although Phillips' attorney vowed to appeal the decision in the lower courts, there is no evidence that they followed through. Solomon secured another courtroom victory — on procedural grounds, not merit.

Reflections: The Fragility of Justice

Justice does not collapse with a bang. It collapses quietly, when the integrity of evidence is eroded piece by piece.

The Phillips retaliation case laid bare the danger. When a sergeant investigating a crime tied to Solomon's family was sidelined, it wasn't just office politics — it was the manipulation of the very evidence system meant to protect the public. When contraband, drugs, and files were later discovered in lockers where they didn't belong, it sent an even clearer message: evidence was not sacred. It was expendable.

Once the chain of custody breaks, every prosecution that follows is tainted. A single piece of compromised evidence can topple a case. And when officers see their leaders bending rules for convenience or revenge, the culture shifts. Integrity becomes optional.

Prosecutors bear responsibility too. In Methuen, they looked the other way. By failing to demand audits or enforce standards, they normalized misconduct. And once misconduct is normalized, it spreads.

The fragility of justice is this: it does not require a grand conspiracy to fail. All it takes is indifference. Methuen proved how quickly that indifference corrodes faith in both the police and the courts.

May

Solomon was still unsatisfied after having regained his badge, job, and $199,000 in back pay. On May 5th, he filed a federal

2011

lawsuit against Mayor Manzi and the City of Methuen, alleging unconstitutional and retaliatory actions. He claimed his termination had been unlawful, arguing that it violated his First Amendment rights. According to the lawsuit, his dismissal was a direct result of appealing a suspension, filing a lawsuit against the City, and participating in a federal investigation involving Manzi.

Solomon sought a jury trial and various forms of relief, including back pay, front pay, treble damages, compensation for emotional distress, punitive damages, attorney's fees, court costs, and any other remedies deemed appropriate by the Court.

His attorney, Robert Sulman, told *Eagle-Tribune* reporter that he had to file the lawsuit that day, as it marked the third anniversary of Solomon's termination — the deadline set by the statute of limitations. Sulman claimed his client had no desire to pursue legal action but was forced to do so because the City was appealing the Civil Service decision, and the contract lawsuit remained unresolved. "He was hoping this would all blow over and get resolved," Sulman explained, emphasizing that the situation was not of Solomon's making.

Solomon v. Manzi Court Court Papers

Other than the lawsuit, Solomon's first year back as police chief was largely uneventful for both him and the Methuen Police Department.

Meanwhile, Manzi's tenure — marked by his long-standing battle with Solomon — ended in January due to term limits. With City Councilor Stephen Zanni set to take over the mayor's office, Solomon launched an aggressive campaign seemingly to extract as much money from the city as possible for himself, his family and his allies. At the same time, he worked to elevate his public profile, actively seeking recognition and accolades.

2012

	Solomon and Alaimo go to work for Alaimo's father Michael at Eagle Investigations (EIS) to help revitalize the business
January 2	Stephen Zanni sworn in as Methuen Mayor
January 24	City Council approves settlement for Fulya lawsuit
March 13	Judge orders City to pay Solomon $49k in lost wages
April 2	Zanni proposes a settlement with Solomon
April 11	Methuen files an appeal to Solomon's lost wages court decision
April 13	Solomon also files an appeal to the lost wages court decision
May 17	Aiello v. Methuen appeal hearing
June	Methuen files counterclaim to Solomon's federal lawsuit
June 12	MPD stops both Zanni and McQuillan for speeding – letting both go without tickets
July 26	Aiello v. Methuen appeal denied
	Judgement in City of Methuen v. Civil Service Commission 'appeal of appeal'
September 19	Patrolmen's Union signs employment contract for 2011 to 2014
November 11	Demonstration held at Methuen school debuting a school shooter detection system
November 14	Judgement in Solomon lost wage appeal
December 7	Methuen files an appeal to Solomon's lost wages court decision
December 12	Solomon files an appeal to his lost wages court decision

The exact date remains unclear, but according to published reports, Solomon reunited with his former police partner, Joseph Alaimo, in 2012 to work at Eagle Investigations, Inc. (EIS). Founded in 1997 by retired Methuen Police Lieutenant Michael Alaimo — Joseph's father — EIS and its division, Eagle Security, had begun to decline by 2012. In response, Alaimo and Solomon stepped in to assist Michael in revitalizing the business. Two years later, they assumed ownership, expanding operations to include training and consulting services while continuing investigative and security work.

2012

According to the EIS website, Alaimo and Solomon are listed as the company's owners and operators, with Alaimo serving as Chief Executive Officer (CEO) and Solomon as Chief Financial Officer (CFO). Their office is conveniently located just around the corner from Solomon's residence and minutes from the police station.

Massachusetts conflict of interest laws includes an "after-hours restriction" clause, prohibiting municipal employees from holding outside employment that conflicts with their public duties. As Chief of Police, Solomon was contractually required to be available 24/7, creating a direct violation of this law.

Although he claimed to have filed a disclosure with the Methuen City Clerk in March 2016 regarding his role at EIS, this came four years late and failed to meet legal requirements. The filing only referenced a client of EIS — Jeanne D'Arc Bank — for security services, rather than the business itself. As such, it did not grant him the legal right to hold both positions. Even if it had, the situation raised serious concerns about whether he could effectively manage two full-time roles without compromising the quality or integrity of either.

EIS's services further complicated the ethical concerns surrounding Solomon's involvement, particularly its firearm training classes for civilians seeking a license to carry in Massachusetts. State law requires individuals to complete such training before applying for a license through their local police department, where the police chief holds discretionary authority over approvals. This created a clear conflict of interest, as Solomon, in his role as Chief of Police, ultimately oversaw the issuance of licenses. Even if he delegated this authority to a subordinate, he retained final decision-making power, raising significant ethical red flags.

Additional concerns stemmed from EIS's offerings, including Active Shooter Training, Crisis Response Training, and School Threat Assessments. To provide these services, Alaimo and Solomon needed specialized training and certification — funded by the City of Methuen. This raised ethical issues, as it suggested that taxpayer resources had been used to enhance a private business for their personal financial gain.

From the outset, the lines between Solomon's public duties and private business interests were blurred, particularly in regard to

2012

EIS employees. Several Methuen Police Department officers, including Joseph Aiello and Ron Valliere, also held positions with EIS — both of whom remain employed there to this day. This dual employment further deepened concerns about conflicts of interest, as it intertwined a private enterprise with the public responsibilities of law enforcement officials.

January

Mayor Stephen Zanni was sworn into office on January 2 at the historic Nevins Library auditorium. In his inaugural address, he expressed gratitude for the city's opportunities and pledged to make decisions with future generations in mind.

> *"If we make decisions and act with these future generations in mind at all times, then our discord will be minor and our mutual accomplishments plentiful. This will be the test of our success together."*

In hindsight, these words stood in stark contrast to what ultimately transpired. During his tenure — particularly in its final years — the handling of the Methuen Police Department was anything but forward-thinking. At best, it reflected incompetence; at worst, it veered into outright corruption.

Like most new administrations, Zanni inherited unresolved issues from his predecessors. One such issue was the lawsuit filed by former city solicitor's secretary Fulya (Metin) Capanelli, a case that had lingered since the tenure of former Mayor Manzi and the previous city council — of which Zanni himself was a member.

Her litigation against Maurice Lariviere, Joseph Solomon, Joseph Alaimo, and the City of Methuen took an additional three years to reach trial, following the case of *Lariviere v. Solomon and Alaimo*.

In October 2011, on the eve of trial, all parties reached a settlement. Lariviere resolved his portion by taking out a home equity loan to pay Fulya $75,000 in December 2011. However, the City's portion required city council approval. Despite receiving the agreement in early October, the council failed to act before their term ended in December, likely due to election-year politics or an inability to reach a consensus. The decision was thus left to the newly elected council in January 2012.

That same month, the city council received a $33,000 bill from the outside law firm representing the city. Given the complexity of Fulya's lawsuit, the city had retained outside counsel to defend the city, Solomon, and Alaimo. Over seven years, the legal fees had ballooned to an astonishing $442,835. The additional bill prompted the new council to scrutinize the mounting costs and reconsider the pending settlement. By the end of January, facing concerns that going to trial could cost as much as $1.5 million, the council reluctantly approved the agreement. Shortly thereafter, Fulya received a $250,000 settlement check from the city, finally bringing the matter to a close.

A brief update on Fulya following her return to New York: Before July 2008, she secured a job as an agent for GEICO Insurance. However, she later attempted to exploit the company's "cash-for-quote" incentive program by posing as a potential customer seeking insurance quotes. Her scheme was discovered, and GEICO reported her to the New York State Insurance Department for potential violations of insurance law. To avoid formal charges and disciplinary action, Fulya agreed to surrender her insurance licenses in lieu of a hearing and any penalties.

On June 6, 2011, Fulya filed for Chapter 7 bankruptcy. At the time, her total assets amounted to just $16,926 — including $3 in cash, $48 in her bank account, and a Jeep with 120,000 miles on it — while her debts stood at $27,685.

An analysis of her financial obligations showed that her debt was fairly evenly split among credit cards, collection agencies, and department stores such as Macy's and Bloomingdale's, with a smaller portion attributed to medical expenses.

However, her financial situation changed dramatically following the settlement with the city and Lariviere. While she incurred an additional $132,000 in legal and IRS fees, she ultimately walked away debt-free, retaining just over $173,000 from the $375,000 settlement.

Sadly, Maurice Lariviere passed away in 2015 from frontotemporal dementia.

2012

March

2012 proved to be another year of lawsuits surrounding Joseph Solomon, continuing to cast a shadow over the city.

On March 13th, Superior Court Judge Thomas Murtagh once again ruled in Solomon's favor, this time in a case involving the City Council's decision to cut his and Joseph Alaimo's pay after their contracts expired in 2007.

A non-jury trial was held the previous December, during which Solomon testified that his lost compensation amounted to nearly $150,000. This total included lost wages, the loss of a take-home vehicle, a clothing allowance, and accrued interest.

In his decision, Judge Murtagh ruled that the city was required to provide written notice and a hearing before reducing Solomon's pay.

As a result, Murtagh's ruling allowed Solomon to recover the difference between what he should have been paid and what he actually received. However, the court deducted $76,474 that Solomon earned from teaching while he was not working for the city, as well as $11,619 in unemployment benefits. The final amount the city owed Solomon in back pay was approximately $49,000. Additionally, the ruling required the city to restore Solomon's annual salary to its pre-cut level of $129,811, plus cost-of-living adjustments, raising it to $161,226.

Mayor Zanni, who had been a member of the City Council at the time of the pay cut, expressed his disappointment with the ruling. He told reporters that while the city had believed it was on solid legal ground, the issue ultimately came down to a procedural misstep, rather than the pay cut itself.

Following the ruling, Solomon released a statement:

> *"I am grateful that the judge conducted a fair trial and that, in deciding complex issues, he upheld the rule of law and the provisions of my contract, which were fairly negotiated and unfairly terminated. For me, the bottom line is that I receive at the very least the same compensation and benefits as the Fire Chief and those which were provided to former Chief Lavigne."*

At the next City Council meeting, the two police unions weighed in on the ruling. Patrolmen's Union President Thomas McMenamon, a close ally of Solomon, urged councilors to drop the remaining court cases involving the chief. "We need to move forward," McMenamon said, emphasizing it was time to stop giving newspapers more material to write about.

Echoing his sentiments, Superior Officers' Union President Frank Korn also called for an end to the legal battles, stating that both the city and the police department needed to move forward, and that everyone was looking for closure.

At the same meeting, City Solicitor McQuillan recommended appealing the decision, but city councilors lacked enthusiasm for this option. Several councilors voiced on the floor that they would not support an appeal. "We've got to put this to bed," said Councilor Michael Condon. "The more you prolong it, the more the taxpayers pay and the more the attorneys make. It's time to move forward and bring fresh air into Methuen. The air is just too stale. It's time to just move on." Councilor Sean Fountain added, "How many times are we going to lose this case before we get the hint?"

The question of who would make the final decision on the appeal — whether it was the mayor or the council — remained a point of contention. The solicitor argued that the decision rested with the mayor, while the mayor asserted it was the council's prerogative. "It's like playing 'Hot Potato' as a kid," said Fountain. "They're scared to leave it in their hands because they're afraid of the heat." He added, "No one is stepping up to the plate."

April

It was a blustery, rainy Monday in Methuen, but that did not deter Zanni from attempting to resolve five years' worth of lawsuits between the City and Solomon. On April 2nd, he sent a settlement offer to Solomon, hoping to bring the matter to a close.

As it was the initial step in negotiations, Zanni would not disclose the amount offered but assured the public that he was not looking to impose a significant financial burden on the city. He hoped that both parties could reach a mutual understanding by the following week.

2012

Solomon confirmed receiving the offer but declined to discuss the details.

If the sides reached no settlement, the city had until mid-April to appeal the Superior Court ruling regarding the restoration of Solomon's pay cut.

To preserve the city's rights and because he believed Murtagh's decision contained serious legal inconsistencies, McQuillan filed an appeal challenging the restoration of Solomon's wages just one day before the April 12th deadline.

The following day, the final day before the deadline expired, Solomon's lawyers filed an appeal. Solomon told reporters that since the city had filed its appeal, he had no choice but to preserve his rights and do the same, though he had hoped it wouldn't come to this. In his appeal, Solomon sought an additional amount between $60,000 and $100,000 that had not been awarded to him by the judge.

Meanwhile, settlement talks continued.

The *Eagle-Tribune* featured a section in its daily newspaper called "Sound Off," where readers could call a dedicated phone number and leave short, recorded messages about current issues. One such message, appearing in the April 24th edition, captured the sentiment of the citizenry regarding the ongoing situation:

"Can't Methuen Police Chief Joe Solomon get enough? He wants more money. How do you sue someone to keep your job if they want to get rid of you? Solomon is costing Methuen millions of dollars, and he still wants more. He gets his job back, he gets a raise, and yet he wants more. This has to stop."

Solomon submitted a counteroffer to Zanni in the last week of April. However, neither side would disclose the details of Solomon's proposal. Zanni remained hopeful they could meet and agree to resolve the three ongoing lawsuits.

May

Like the cast of a bad sitcom that refused to die, the Solomon-City ensemble once again convened in the courtroom — this time at Lawrence Superior Court — for yet another hearing. This session, presided over by Judge Robert Cornetta, centered on arguing the Civil Service Commission's 2010 decision.

2012

Coverage of the hearing appeared in the *Eagle-Tribune*, where a reporter summarized the arguments from both sides.

On one side sat Solicitor McQuillan, joined by David Grunbaum, a private labor attorney hired by the city. Together, they pressed the case for reinstating Solomon's firing. Their argument was blunt: the Civil Service Commission had "simply missed the boat," riddling its decision with errors and omissions. McQuillan insisted the Commission had overstepped its authority by reducing a termination to a suspension, basing its ruling on an "error of law" unsupported by substantial evidence.

At the heart of his case was one charge — Solomon's mishandling of two public safety grants, a failure McQuillan said had cost the city and its taxpayers $200,000. He pointed to physical evidence, including a Department of Justice investigative report, which, he argued, the Commission had "disregarded" in overturning the termination. "They have to account for all the credible evidence on the record, and they did not do that," McQuillan asserted.

In closing, he went further, questioning why Solomon had not appealed the one-year suspension — especially given Solomon's history of contesting every ruling that failed to go his way.

Solomon's attorney, Andrew Gambaccini, countered with scorn. McQuillan's arguments, he said, were "laughable." The Commission's decision, while "unduly harsh" on a personal level, and was, in his view, "bulletproof" from a legal one.

Outside the courtroom, Gambaccini doubled down: "From the beginning, it's been a waste of everyone's time. There is simply no basis to challenge the Commission's decision."

June

Looking back, it seemed inevitable — negotiations for a settlement between Solomon and the city broke down around the first week of June, impacting a meeting on the 19th with a federal judge to discuss the talks. Mayor Zanni acknowledged that a resolution before the court date was unlikely "unless, of course, [Solomon] comes in with another proposal that's near the direction I'm looking at."

The two had met privately five or six times before talks fell apart. "I was hopeful that a meeting of the minds could be

2012

achieved through good-faith negotiations," Solomon said in a carefully worded statement designed to cast himself in a favorable light.

> *"On Tuesday, I heard through my lawyer that there would be no settlement. Then on Wednesday, the mayor told me there was no reason to continue to negotiate. The mayor's statement stunned me, as I had thought the settlement talks were productive, and we seemed close to reaching an agreement to present to City Council."*

He further claimed that he had made significant concessions since his initial offer.

> *"Unfortunately, it now appears that additional costs on both sides will be incurred, and potential damages increased,"* he said. *"It is unfortunate, but I will continue to work hard each and every day to protect our citizens and rebuild a professional law enforcement agency within budget constraints."*

As expected, the two sides did not reach an agreement before the scheduled court appearance. In the days leading up to the meeting, the city filed counterclaims against Solomon, seeking reimbursement for the two mismanaged federal grants — funds that Methuen taxpayers had been forced to repay, totaling $195,795.85 in costs ultimately covered by Methuen taxpayers through tax increases. Solomon's attorney dismissed the counterclaims as a political stunt, calling them baseless.

On June 19th, both sides met at the federal courthouse in Boston for discussions before Chief Judge Mark Wolf. However, the hearing yielded no progress, prompting the judge to order both parties to return the following week.

Zanni did an interview on July 2nd with the *Eagle-Tribune* to commemorate his first six months in office. The reporter asked about his campaign promise to resolve the city's costly legal battles with public employees – specifically, the ongoing lawsuits with Solomon.

2012

> "Good question. And I can tell you very frankly, we met [June 19] with federal Judge Wolf in his chambers. It was like mediation. He ended up stating to us, 'Go out, seek a number that you think would be beneficial to both [Solomon] and the city.' We went out, we discussed it. I came back with a number. He came back with another. The judge then turned around and said to us, 'Here is a number based on all the different lawsuits in federal court, what it could take. This is the number I'd like you to agree to. Would you please write the number on a piece of paper? Next to it, put a yes or a no.' We then went out to our own separate chambers, came back to the judge. The judge looked at mine. He said, 'You're in agreement.' I said, 'Yes, Your Honor, I agree with the number that you think because of what you mentioned with all the lawsuits.' The other party did not agree. So, at that point, we're going forward with the scheduling of the court."

This interview would come back to haunt Zanni the following week.

July

After reading Zanni's interview in the *Eagle-Tribune*, Solomon wasted no time contacting his legal team. On July 11th, one of his attorneys, Joseph Sulman, filed a motion seeking severe sanctions against the City, citing "gratuitous and detailed disclosures to the media."

Sulman argued that Zanni "understood the expectation of confidentiality and willfully ignored it." He further stated,

> "The circumstances and extent of the City's disclosure of confidential information warrant the imposition of severe sanctions. Based on the sophistication of the attorneys and parties involved, it should have been known by all, including Zanni, that the court trusted the parties to keep these discussions confidential. Zanni betrayed that trust with his public statements."

The motion also sought monetary compensation for Solomon, covering attorney fees incurred for the conference with Judge

Wolf and the cost of drafting the sanctions motion and any related court appearances.

Sulman accused the city of deliberately damaging Solomon's reputation in the eyes of Methuen residents. "This is the type of reputational harm that [Solomon] alleges has been caused by the City's political and personal attacks since 2007," he wrote.

In response, Methuen filed a motion urging the court to reject Solomon's request. McQuillan dismissed the sanctions filing as "vexatious and frivolous," arguing that it was an attempt to pressure the city into a settlement. He described it as "retaliation that actually constitutes a form of coercion meant to intimidate the City."

Public frustration over the ongoing legal battle was evident in the *Eagle-Tribune*'s Sound Off section, where one resident voiced exasperation.

> "*Methuen Police Chief Joe Solomon needs to rein in his lawyer. Once again, we have to listen to and read about what his lawyer seems to think the mayor and the City of Methuen are doing against his client. He must be really racking up the billable hours. I read the article about the court date and found nothing wrong with it. No monetary amount was mentioned — so what's the problem?*
>
> "*Chief Solomon, get a grip and get over yourself! Good or bad, you got your job back, and that's more than a lot of people who have lost theirs. Most people who are fired don't get a second chance. Just do your job and stop the nonsense. We're all getting sick of hearing about it, never mind the cost that taxpayers are being hit with. Enough already!*"

July 15th

The *Eagle-Tribune* received an anonymous tip alleging that two city officials had been pulled over for speeding, but officers let them go without even a warning.

Following up on the tip, the newspaper submitted a public records request to the Methuen Police Department. In response, Solomon released two internal memos detailing the incidents.

According to the first memo, the MPD had conducted a citywide speeding crackdown on June 12th, resulting in officers stopping over 500 motorists who were either warned or ticketed. However, just weeks before this enforcement effort, Zanni and McQuillan had been pulled over for speeding — yet neither received a citation nor a formal warning.

The first memo described an incident involving Zanni. Officer Jeff Torrisi had stopped Zanni on Pelham Street for driving 41 mph in a 35-mph zone. Upon recognizing the mayor, Torrisi rolled down his window, apologized, and informed Zanni that he had been about to stop him for speeding — before ultimately letting him go.

The second memo the *Eagle-Tribune* received was written by Sergeant Randy Haggar, and recounted a similar episode on Milk Street. Two traffic enforcement officers believed they had clocked a vehicle traveling 46 mph in a 30-mph zone. Haggar pulled the car over and discovered the driver was Solicitor McQuillan, who explained he was running late for court. Haggar wrote, "I felt it was in the best interest of the police department to utilize my discretion and terminate the stop and allow Mr. McQuillan to go on his way. It was strictly my decision and not that of the officers present."

This episode was a textbook example of Solomon's media manipulation. The evidence suggests that Solomon or someone within his inner circle planted the anonymous tip — it seemed to be part of a calculated effort to discredit the mayor and solicitor in the public eye. Over the next decade, Solomon would refine and master this tactic, leveraging the media as a weapon to serve his interests.

July 26th

The long-awaited day had arrived — the final determination in Solomon's Civil Service case, the appeal of the appeal. As expected, the wheels of justice had turned at their usual glacial pace; it had taken 19 months from the initial filing for a ruling on the judicial review to be issued.

And just as Judge Murtaugh had predicted, the city's chances of success were slim.

On July 26, 2012, Justice Robert Cornetta denied the city's motion for judgment on the pleadings and upheld the Civil Service Commission's ruling. Once again, Solomon prevailed.

2012

The sheer amount of time, money, and effort poured into the legal battles surrounding Solomon over the past seven years was nothing short of staggering.

At last, the city seemed to have reached the same conclusion. Rather than pursuing another appeal, officials opted to return to the negotiating table to get a final settlement — that would end the lawsuits once and for all. Solomon, for his part, appeared open to the idea.

Yet, despite both sides expressing a willingness to talk, no formal offer or meeting materialized until November, when Zanni finally extended the first olive branch.

December

In mid-December, seven new patrol officers were sworn into the Methuen Police Department, bringing the total to 67 — the highest in the city's history. Among them were several with deep local ties: Kara (Lapides) McMenamon, a former MPD dispatcher and wife of Detective Thomas McMenamon; Kenneth Pilz, son of MPD officer Richard Pilz; and William Kannan, son of Methuen City Council Chair Jennifer Kannan.

However, McMenamon's appointment raised questions. The *Eagle-Tribune* reported that while MPD listed her as a reserve officer since 2010, her name did not appear on the official reserve list compiled by then-Mayor Manzi — a list that the city created after the Civil Service Commission invalidated the 2009 version. Neither her maiden nor married name was found in those records, leaving the timing of her appointment unclear.

Kannan's inclusion on the force was less mysterious — his name appeared on the 2009 and 2010 candidate lists. However, given that his mother was City Council Chair while Solomon was engaged in settlement talks and civil litigation, the timing of his hiring, while not overtly suspect, certainly raised eyebrows.

By Christmas, settlement negotiations remained stalled. Solomon dismissed Zanni's latest offer as "too low, like not even in the ballpark."

Tensions escalated further as Solomon demanded $198,179, he claimed were owed from past judgments, plus interest. While the city had paid him $199,000 upon his 2010 return to duty, he argued that they had failed to include interest on that back pay.

2012

Additionally, he asserted that he was still owed money from the ruling in his pay-cut case, along with accumulated interest.

No longer willing to roll these funds into settlement discussions, Solomon accused the City of acting in bad faith by using the unpaid amount as leverage in the federal case.

"I've been overly patient, considering this goes back to 2007," he said, adding that each week the city delayed payment, his total owed increased by $900.

2013

January 7	City Council fails to reappoint City Solicitor Peter McQuillan
February 22	Solomon tells reporters that he and Zanni have reached a consensus on the terms of settlement
	Zanni denies there is a consensus
February 6	Council Chair Sean Fountain announce that there are four finalists for city solicitor position
February 26	Solomon and the City meet with federal judge to explore resolutions
March 20	MPTC Director Dan Zivkocich sends out letter with requirements for intermittent officers
March 26	City Council conducts public interviews with two finalists for city solicitor position
March 28	City Council vote on settlement with Solomon for federal lawsuit
March 29	Lawrence Mayor William Lantigua send letter to Methuen City Council about D'Agostino
April 1	City Council vote to not hire either solicitor candidate and use outside law firm for legal department
April 6	City pays judgement of $100,001 to Solomon
	Solomon teaches an EIS class for police entrance exam prep

January

The first Methuen City Council meeting in January set the stage for several key actions. The council unanimously elected Sean Fountain as chair and Michael Condon as vice chair. Additionally, as required in odd-numbered years, they voted on the two-year contract renewals for three key city employees: the city auditor, city solicitor and council clerk.

The council reappointed the clerk and auditor without debate. However, City Solicitor Peter McQuillan, who had served for five years, faced a more contentious decision. In a narrow 5-4 vote, the council opted not to renew his contract.

While council members gave no official explanation at the meeting, several councilors later told the *Eagle-Tribune* that their concerns centered on McQuillan's handling of two high-profile lawsuits involving Solomon and former City Solicitor Maurice

Lariviere. Others speculated that the move was a strategic play to strengthen Solomon's position in settlement negotiations — a theory that, in hindsight, appears increasingly plausible.

The councilors who voted against McQuillan's reappointment were Sean Fountain, Jennifer Kannan, Lisa Ferry, Jeanne Pappalardo and Tom Ciulla. Those favoring retaining him included Michael Condon, Ron Marsan, Jamie Atkinson and Joyce Campagnone.

Following the vote, McQuillan addressed the council, thanking his supporters and assuring the body that he would continue fulfilling his duties until the city hired a replacement ensure a smooth transition.

Within three days, the council posted the city solicitor job opening, which remained open for two weeks and received twelve applications. City officials formed a search committee to review candidates, comprising four councilors — Fountain, Kannan, Ciulla, and Ferry — along with two local attorneys, Bryan Chase and former State Representative Arthur Broadhurst.

February

As the upcoming federal court hearing loomed, Zanni made one final settlement offer for Solomon to consider. The two then met to discuss the details.

Shortly after, Solomon told the press that he and Zanni had met on February 22nd and reached a consensus on the terms. However, Zanni had a different take, clarifying that while the two sides had made progress, no finalized agreement existed.

"I would say we got closer," Zanni told the *Eagle-Tribune*. "There's no signed document. I shook his hand. We are getting closer, but I didn't agree to anything."

When a reporter reached out to Solomon for his response to Zanni's denial, he was indignant. "That's inaccurate because I sat in the room and shook the man's hand. I don't understand how he could say that."

The City and Solomon's legal teams returned to the federal courthouse the following Tuesday for a two-hour closed-door meeting with the judge to explore possible resolutions. While discussions were reportedly productive, they did not result in an

2013

agreement. The trial would proceed as scheduled if lawyers did not reach a settlement before June.

Meanwhile, the search for a new city solicitor was ongoing. After two meetings, the search committee narrowed the applicant pool to four finalists — but not without controversy. Both meetings allegedly failed to comply with the state's Open Meeting Law, which requires at least 48 hours' advance public notice. The group even held a meeting in the private office of a committee member.

Further scrutiny arose when committee chair Sean Fountain disclosed that he intended for the full Council to interview the four finalists in executive session and publicly release only the final two names before the vote. When a reporter pointed out this could also violate Open Meeting Law, Fountain quickly backtracked. "If that's the case, then that's what we'll do. I have no problem being open," he said.

Initially, Fountain announced on February 6th that the search committee had selected four finalists. He later retracted this statement after the Attorney General's office informed him that once the search committee chose finalists, city officials cannot legally conduct further interviews in closed-door sessions. To justify another executive session, Fountain cited the absence of a counselor at the last meeting, stating, "We want to give him the courtesy of having his input."

By the last week of February, the search committee named its four finalists: Richard D'Agostino, William Faraci, Robin Stein, and Kerry Anderson, all of whom had municipal law experience. However, Stein and Anderson withdrew from consideration within days, leaving only two candidates.

Some councilors had mixed feelings about proceeding with just two finalists. Councilors Pappalardo and Marsan argued that restarting the search was in the city's best interest. Councilors Ciulla and Condon felt it would be unfair to the remaining applicants. Meanwhile, Councilor Jamie Atkinson suggested a third option — reappointing McQuillan.

Ultimately, the council voted to continue the process and interview the two finalists.

2013

March

On the evening of March 26, citizens of Methuen and neighboring towns tuned in to witness the latest episode in the ongoing drama of Methuen's government. This time, the City Council conducted public interviews with the two finalists for the solicitor's position. In true Methuen fashion, the cast of characters did not disappoint, delivering both intrigue during the interviews and controversy in the aftermath.

William Faraci, a 35-year veteran assistant solicitor for the neighboring City of Haverhill, told the Council that his extensive experience serving under five consecutive mayors had prepared him well. He assured them that getting up to speed in Methuen would not be difficult. Faraci explained that he left Haverhill when the city eliminated his position for budgetary reasons.

Richard D'Agostino's interview, scheduled from 6:30 to 7:15 p.m., was far more contentious. A key point of scrutiny was his departure from his previous role as assistant city solicitor for Lawrence — he was fired in April 2012 after returning from a 16-month medical leave due to stress.

D'Agostino claimed an overwhelming caseload caused his medical leave — more than 20 cases in six weeks. "I received no support; it was a physical impossibility to do what I did. And I cried out for help ... Stress has never been something that has knocked me out of the ring," he asserted.

He didn't mention that, unlike Methuen's solicitor office which had only one support staff, the Lawrence solicitor's office had two other assistant solicitors, a solicitor and additional support staff.

He claimed the city fired him for refusing to cooperate with a "corrupt mayor." That man was William "Willie" Lantigua, one of Lawrence's most controversial leaders. D'Agostino insisted that standing up to corruption had cost him his job and maintained that his record remained impeccable.

Midway through the interview, Atkinson questioned D'Agostino about a letter the council had received that morning from Lawrence District Court Clerk Andrew Gradzewicz, who had rescinded his recommendation of D'Agostino's candidacy without explanation. Caught off guard, D'Agostino responded, "This is news to me."

2013

Unbeknownst to him, outgoing solicitor McQuillan was watching the proceedings from home and reacted immediately. In a moment of impulse, he texted D'Agostino, "That's a lie — he tried to contact Gradzewicz today!!!!"

It wasn't until after the interview that D'Agostino saw the message. The next day was a frenzy. Not only did D'Agostino contact the council to accuse McQuillan of interfering in the search process, but Lantigua also sent a letter to the council, accusing D'Agostino of lying about his dismissal from Lawrence.

"I think it is unprofessional and unethical conduct as a municipal employee," D'Agostino told the *Eagle-Tribune* of McQuillan's actions. "You want to say the process is tainted? Boy, there's a lot of taint here. He's injected himself into the process." He called for a Council investigation and threatened to report McQuillan to the Massachusetts Bar.

McQuillan admitted to sending the text but denied any attempt to sabotage the interview. "That is an absolute, outright lie. I would never do that to anyone," he said.

Lantigua, whom D'Agostino had not only politically supported but also represented as a private attorney at one point, was displeased with how D'Agostino responded to questions during his interview. In his letter to the Methuen City Council, Lantigua emphasized that the city did not fire D'Agostino; rather, Lawrence and D'Agostino had mutually parted ways after settling his workers' compensation claim following 16 months of leave. Lantigua, citing "decorum," refused to address D'Agostino's allegations of a "corrupt mayor."

Lantigua's Letter

For context, Lantigua had been the subject of a grand jury investigation. While at least one member of his administration was convicted and sentenced to jail, Lantigua emerged unscathed from the investigation. There is a reason that Methuen is often called "Lawrence with Trees."

D'Agostino's political career began at age 23 when he ran for office in Lawrence. His first candidacy was for the Lawrence School Committee in 1977, where he lost to future Mayor Stephen Zanni. He later served as Alderman of Engineering from 1981 to 1985 and ran unsuccessfully for State Representative in 1984. In

1987, he secured what some considered a patronage position as director of the small City of Lawrence Municipal Airport, a role he held until 1992 despite having no airfield experience. During his tenure there, he studied for and passed the Massachusetts Bar.

March 28th

Nearly a year after negotiations began, the City and Solomon finally hammered out a settlement for the federal lawsuit. Under the agreement, the City would pay Solomon $100,001 and cover his legal expenses from that suit. In return, Solomon would drop his federal lawsuit against the City.

The settlement required approval from the City Council, which convened on March 28th and voted in favor of the measure. A check for the full amount was issued on April 6th, leaving only one remaining legal dispute in play — the appeal over Solomon's back pay.

Methuen's Offer of Judgement

April

When the City Council convened for a meeting at City Hall — coincidentally on April Fool's Day — the agenda included a vote on appointing a solicitor. In discussions with reporters before the meeting, some councilors expressed concerns that the process had been tainted, while others referenced an investigation into the text message sent to D'Agostino. Councilor Jeanne Pappalardo told the *Eagle-Tribune* that while the outgoing solicitor's text had been inappropriate, she saw no need to involve the police.

Later that evening, the Council narrowly voted against D'Agostino's appointment, defeating it by a 5-4 margin, and took no action on a vote for William Faraci. With no viable alternative, the Council unanimously agreed to restart the search process from the beginning.

Eventually, McQuillan and the city parted ways, and the Council hired an outside law firm as a "temporary" solicitor until the city found a permanent replacement. It took until June 2014 — eighteen months after deciding not to renew McQuillan's contract — to finally appoint an in-house solicitor. Kerry Regan was selected for the role, becoming the first woman to lead Methuen's legal department.

Even though the Council did not hire him in either round — likely due to the controversy surrounding his time in Lawrence — this would not be the last that Methuen sees of D'Agostino.

April 6th

As Solomon and Alaimo settled into reviving Eagle Investigation Services for Alaimo Sr. and themselves, one of their first actions was to revamp the company's website. While their primary focus was on "security and private investigations," they also advertised additional services, including a "National Security Officer Certification Program" featuring courses in CPR and First Aid, effective communication, interviewing techniques, patrol methods, and other essential topics. They also offered Crisis Response Training and IED Identification Training.

One particular training seminar, led by Solomon himself, was titled "Massachusetts State Police & Municipal Police Entrance Exam 2013 Preparation Seminar." Initially scheduled for March 16th, it was postponed to April 6th and held in Haverhill, Massachusetts. The promotional material for the seminar read:

> *"This seminar will be presented by Chief Joseph E. Solomon. Chief Solomon has nearly three decades of experience as a police officer and has mastered the art of exam-taking during his career. He topped every promotional exam he took and rose through the ranks from patrolman to chief in just eight years. Solomon has mentored numerous officers who, as a result, have been promoted to and have held ranks as Police Lieutenants, Captains, Deputy Chiefs, Police Chiefs, and even Town Managers. His mentoring gave these officers the competitive edge that pushed them over the top. Officers he has mentored have attained these positions in multiple states, including Massachusetts, New Hampshire, Maine, and New Mexico."*

It was unclear how the Ethics Commission would view a sitting police chief profiting from a police exam prep seminar —

potentially training officers he might later have a role in hiring. It is worth noting that this appeared to be a one-time event and does not seem to have occurred on any other occasion.

2014

April	The City of Methuen discontinues the use of Massachusetts Civil Service for promotions within the Superior Officers' ranks.
April 22	The City Council votes to approve the final settlement agreement with former Police Chief Joseph Solomon, including the terms of his personal employment contract.
June	Kerry Regan is hired as Methuen's new City Solicitor.
July 27-Aug. 1	Chief Solomon, Officer Joseph Aiello, Officer Kevin Mahoney, and Officer John Walsh attend the National School Safety Conference in Orlando, Florida. (July 28-Aug 1)
	During the conference, Chief Solomon receives the *Innovation in School Safety and Security, Crisis Management, and Intervention Award*.
October 23-29	Solomon attends the International Association of Chiefs of Police (IACP) Conference in Orlando, Florida.
November 3	Integrity Testing administers a captain's promotional assessment for the Methuen Police Department. Officer Frank Korn ranks first, and Officer Greg Gallant ranks second.
December 14	While off-duty, Chief Solomon initiates a traffic stop on Interstate 495 and arrests a woman for assault and battery.

When the MPD needed to fill a position in the upper ranks, candidates were required to take a promotional exam through Civil Service. In 2013, Civil Service sanctioned using "sole assessment centers," where a private company would conduct multiple evaluations instead of a traditional multiple-choice written test. These evaluations included interviews, job-related simulations, and psychological assessments to rank candidates for promotion.

Assessment centers had been in use for several years across the state to hire chiefs and deputy chiefs of both police and fire departments, and the system generally worked well. These centers tested candidates on the knowledge and practical skills required for the job rather than rewarding those who were good at taking written exams.

However, when Civil Service began using assessment centers for all promotional exams, the process became more vulnerable to misuse. While the hiring of chiefs and deputy chiefs tended to draw public attention and scrutiny, police departments typically handled promotions to upper ranks internally — so the moves often went unnoticed by the public until after the fact.

For instance, consider a hypothetical scenario involving a sexual assault detective who had repeatedly failed the standard civil service sergeant promotional exam but maintained a close relationship with the chief. When a sergeant position became available, the chief arranged for an assessment center to oversee the promotional process. Before the exam, representatives from the assessment company met with the chief to determine the criteria for evaluating candidates, as each department's needs varied. Conveniently, when officials administered the assessment, it was heavily focused on sexual assault topics and scenarios, which directly favored the detective's specialized experience.

In April 2014, Methuen adopted the assessment method and selected a newly formed company, Integrity Testing, to oversee the sergeants' promotional exams. Two of Solomon's contemporaries founded this company — retired Tewksbury Police Chief Alfred Donovan and retired North Andover and Wareham Police Chief Richard Stanley. Notably, in 2006, Donovan had been hired to investigate Solomon for abuse of power. His favorable report secured Solomon's loyalty, positioning Donovan as the department's preferred investigator for internal matters — and now, for promotional assessments as well.

Given Solomon's close ties to Donovan and Stanley, the abrupt shift from traditional promotional exams to using assessment centers warranted, at minimum, closer scrutiny.

Perhaps because police chiefs tend to be overachievers, they rarely retire to leisurely days on the golf course, world travel or building model ships in bottles. Instead, many transitioned into the investigative business. Some diversified further, founding multiple companies focused on consulting, security work, assessment centers, seminars or representing the latest law enforcement gadgets. Rather than competing, they often intertwined their businesses, creating a web of overlapping partnerships.

A closer look at Solomon's network revealed the depth of these connections:

2014

Joseph Solomon

Solomon had partnered with Joseph Alaimo through Eagle Investigation Services (EIS), and over the years, their ventures had employed several current and former MPD personnel. He also co-owned a business, the International Association of School Resource Officers, with one of his subordinates at the MPD, Joseph Aiello. Their advisory council included retired Chief Richard Stanley of Integrity Testing. Solomon had also given seminars and served on the advisory board for the School Safety Advocacy Council, co-owned by then-Lieutenant Sean Burke of the Lawrence, Massachusetts Police Department and retired Fort Lauderdale police officer Curtis Lavarello.

Alfred Donovan

Retired Tewksbury Police Chief Alfred Donovan operated three companies:
- APD Management, which conducted internal investigations for the MPD;
- Police Assessment Center Training, where he partnered with retired Fitchburg Police Chief Robert DeMoura, who served as an Associate Assessor, and;
- Lastly, Donovan who co-owned Integrity Testing with Richard Stanley, the company hired to conduct Methuen's police promotional assessment testing. To further complicate matters, Solomon was employed as an assessor for them since they started.

Donovan also was an instructor for the Municipal Police Institute, which conducted training sessions for police departments, including the MPD.

Richard Stanley

Stanley proved equally prolific. In addition to co-owning Integrity Testing with Donovan, he:
- Ran his own investigative firm, RMS Associates;
- Created BOLO Mobile, a file-sharing app designed for law enforcement,
- Worked as a distributor for various law enforcement vendors, selling several of his products to the MPD; and

– Served on advisory councils for Solomon and Aiello's School Resource Officer program and Joseph Alaimo's Foundation for School Safety and Security.

This interconnected network highlighted their repeated violations of the state's conflict of interest laws.

The adage "you are the company you keep" aptly applied to Solomon and his close associates. Each carried their own controversies from their time on the force, with many of their actions following a shared playbook. Colleagues who had worked with these chiefs described them as quick-tempered micromanagers known for rewarding unwavering loyalty while harshly punishing any perceived disloyalty. Their leadership often embodied a "do as I say, not as I do" mindset, further underscoring the complexities of their management style.

Numerous controversies marred Stanley's law enforcement career, including a DUI and playing two towns against each other. One particularly notable case occurred in July 1992, when Stanley, driving a town-owned unmarked Crown Victoria cruiser, crashed into a railroad crossing gate in Reading, Massachusetts, after returning from a Northeastern Massachusetts Law Enforcement Council (NEMLEC) picnic.

Three witnesses, including a New Hampshire state trooper, reported seeing Stanley driving at high speed shortly before the crash. Around 10 p.m., a Reading police detective patrolling the area heard the collision and responded to the scene, finding Stanley staggering near his vehicle. The detective immediately noticed the strong smell of alcohol and suspected that Stanley had been drinking.

Since the department's breathalyzer was out of service, officers recorded Stanley's booking on video to document his behavior. As a former state trooper, I can say that the standard protocol in such cases would have been to transport the driver to another police station to administer the test. The decision to videotape the booking instead may have been a "courtesy" extended to a sitting police chief. If Stanley had taken the test, he likely would have failed; if he had refused, it would have resulted in an automatic license suspension for refusing to submit.

At trial, Stanley claimed that a carburetor issue that made his car accelerate unexpectedly caused the accident. He also argued that he had consumed only a couple of beers over a ten-hour party, disputing allegations of intoxication. Two mechanics testified to the alleged carburetor problem, and a party attendee vouched for Stanley's sobriety. Despite these defenses, the judge found him guilty of driving under the influence of alcohol. The court fined Stanley $300, revoked his driver's license for an undetermined period, and placed him on probation for one year.

The trial's outcome shocked many, including two North Andover selectmen who attended the proceedings — one was Sean Fountain Sr., father of Sean Fountain Jr., who would later become a Methuen City Councilor and intermittent police officer. Following a 3.5-hour executive session, the selectmen imposed several penalties on Stanley: a three-week suspension without pay, the forfeiture of 20 vacation days, and a requirement to write a public apology to the town's residents.

Although Stanley appealed the DUI verdict, he ultimately entered an Alford plea shortly before his jury trial in November. An Alford plea allowed him to accept the evidence against him without admitting guilt. In an agreement with the Middlesex District Attorney, the court sentenced Stanley to probation, a 45-day license suspension and mandatory enrollment in an alcohol education program.

One of Stanley's more notable controversies occurred as interim Chief of Police in Wareham, Massachusetts. In August 2009, he stepped in for the retiring chief while the town initiated civil service protocols to hire a permanent replacement. However, Stanley had no intention of relinquishing his role as Chief of Police in North Andover.

Though unconventional, he secured the approval of both North Andover and Wareham. He devised an unusual arrangement: working Monday through Thursday in North Andover, using Friday as a paid vacation day, and then serving as Wareham's interim chief from Friday through Sunday, including nights. Wareham provided him with a cruiser for the 90-mile commute. Despite initially claiming his interim role would last a year at most, Stanley remained in the position for 20 months, leaving both communities frustrated.

In April 2011, Stanley announced he would permanently transfer to Wareham, motivated by a financial incentive — a $166,000 annual salary, $30,000 more than he earned in North

2014

Andover. This maneuver foreshadowed similar controversial tactics later employed by Solomon.

The Civil Service Commission later investigated allegations that Stanley's appointment violated residency laws. Evidence showed conflicting claims regarding his compliance, including mileage logs revealing that he had driven 49,378 miles, nearly a thousand a week, in his town-owned vehicle over a single year. Despite procedural irregularities, Commissioner Paul M. Stein, the Commissioner in Solomon's hearing, ruled in Stanley's favor, allowing him to remain Wareham's police chief until he retired in 2013.

If there's one takeaway from our experience writing this book and investigating these cast of characters, it's this: while these scenarios may seem improbable and impossible, we've shown they were all too real.

Alfred Donovan's career in Tewksbury also had its share of controversy, but one case stood out. We learned of this case thanks to a victim's court complaint that was eventually settled out of court.

According to the complaint, in 2003, a young woman was sleeping on her mother's couch when her uncle, Neil McLaughlin – staying at the house due to marital issues – came home intoxicated, entered the room and sexually assaulted her.

The following day, the woman confided in her mother. Instead of immediately reporting the crime to the police, the mother requested that they discuss the matter with McLaughlin, Chief Al Donovan, and Donovan's wife, Katie, before taking any further steps. Notably, McLaughlin had recently started working as a police dispatcher under Donovan, who was married to his sister, Katie.

Following the meeting, the mother relayed that the group had decided to keep the matter "quietly within the family" to protect its reputation. McLaughlin promised to seek help and resign from his job at the police department. Shortly after, McLaughlin reportedly called the victim, his niece, to apologize. While she initially agreed to avoid involving the police — a bitter irony given Chief Donovan's role as a police chief — she began to have second thoughts as time passed.

As rumors spread over the following months, tensions escalated. The victim faced increasing pressure from her mother and

2014

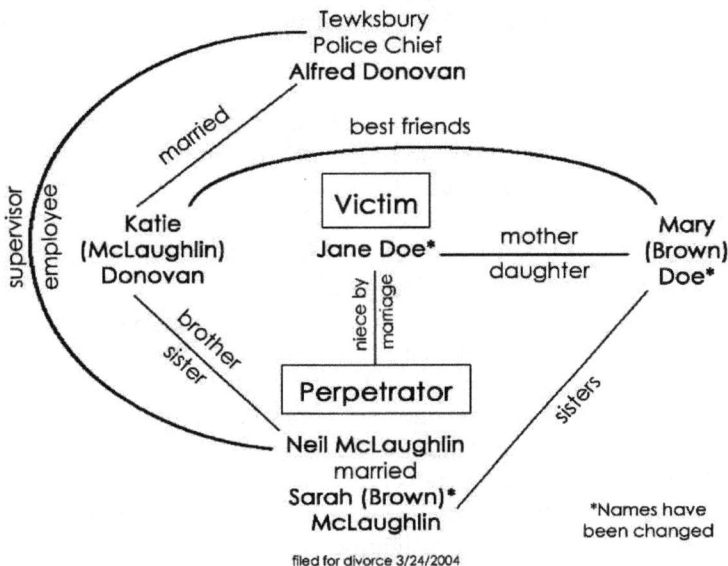

employees of the Tewksbury Police Department to remain silent, while McLaughlin publicly denied the assault ever happened. In December, the victim decided to come forward to file a police report. However, the ordeal took a toll, and she passed out after making the report, requiring hospitalization. Due to the conflict of interest, Tewksbury police turned the case over to the Middlesex County District Attorney's office. Unfortunately, the victim's mother screened the phone calls and failed to inform her daughter that the DA's office had been trying to reach her. With no response, the DA's office had no choice but to drop the case.

The situation reached a breaking point during a family gathering later that month. When McLaughlin denied the assault and questioned the victim's character, a heated argument broke out between the victim, her mother and two aunts. McLaughlin called the police, who then charged the victim with assault and battery. The next day, Donovan escalated the situation further when he arrested the victim at the daycare center where she worked, adding two additional counts of assault and battery and two charges of mayhem. The public arrest cost the victim her job.

Distressed by the victim's treatment, the mother took matters into her own hands. She secretly recorded a phone conversation with McLaughlin, during which he admitted to the assault, stating, "I did it." When Donovan learned of the recording, he allegedly threatened to arrest the mother if she played or distributed the tape.

The tide finally turned when the District Attorney dropped the charges against the victim and reopened the assault case against McLaughlin. A grand jury indicted him, and the case proceeded to trial in July 2007.

At trial, Tewksbury Detective Lieutenant Dennis Peterson testified that during his investigation, McLaughlin admitted to kissing the victim, fondling her breasts and putting his hands down her pants. Peterson also stated that he informed Donovan of these admissions. However, when Donovan took the stand, he contradicted Peterson's testimony, claiming Peterson never told him such details. According to Donovan, Peterson only described the incident as more of a "pass" than a sexual assault.

This stark contradiction had significant consequences. After Peterson completed his investigation, Donovan removed him from the detective unit, a move widely viewed as retaliatory. The situation came to a head after Peterson's testimony in court. Following Donovan's sworn statement that directly conflicted with his own, Peterson decided to retire from the force.

The jury did not find McLaughlin guilty of rape, but did find him guilty of indecent assault and battery and assault with intent to rape. He received a sentence of two and a half years in one of the state's house of corrections.

April 22nd

It had been a year since the last settlement between the city and Solomon, yet one final lawsuit remained unresolved between the sides. This case centered on the pay cut enacted by the 2007 City Council. Although a judge had awarded Solomon back pay, the City had appealed the decision. To reach a resolution, Zanni held multiple meetings to negotiate a financial figure acceptable to both parties. Simultaneously, discussions were underway regarding Solomon's new employment contract.

What some might dismiss as coincidence, others could reasonably view as a deliberate maneuver. A review of Zanni's campaign contributions reveals a distinct shift in support from the

2014

MPD. From Zanni's first mayoral run in 2011 through early 2014, his campaign had received virtually no donations from anyone affiliated with the MPD. That changed abruptly in March 2014 — a non-election year and, notably, the same month that final settlement discussions between Zanni and Solomon were underway.

Between March and December of that year, Zanni's campaign reported 15 separate donations from Methuen police personnel, primarily from superior officers closely aligned with Solomon, totaling $2,290 — half of which came in March alone. Among the contributions were $250 each from Solomon and his longtime ally, Alaimo, though those particular donations weren't made until September.

By the April 22nd City Council meeting, Zanni placed both the back pay resolution and Solomon's new contract on the Council's agenda for a vote.

During his presentation to the Council, Zanni highlighted key aspects of the agreement. Solomon's position would remain protected under Civil Service, but future police chiefs would not have that designation. The city set the settlement at $195,000, with the condition that Solomon release the City from all outstanding claims, including those related to emotional distress, severance pay, or wrongful termination.

The employment contract, set for a three-year term, included a four percent cost-of-living increase spread over its duration. Addressing concerns about the lack of detail in Solomon's previous contract, the new agreement explicitly outlined his duties and required an annual job evaluation. The Council unanimously approved both the settlement and the contract.

With this latest $195,000 settlement — alongside the $199,000 he received upon his return to the job in 2010, and the $100,001 settlement he secured in 2013 — Solomon's total payout from the city reached $494,353.

While some applauded Solomon for receiving what they viewed as his "due," far more believed the city should have fired him and that Solomon was guilty of most, if not all, of the charges brought against him by Manzi, the former mayor. In hindsight, the majority was more than likely correct. Unfortunately, the biggest losers in this ordeal were Methuen taxpayers.

2014

With the financial burdens of his legal settlements and contract dispute no longer hanging over Solomon — and now that Solomon and Joseph Alaimo were the sole owners of EIS — Solomon appeared to set out on a calculated path to extract as much as possible from the City of Methuen. The evidence suggests that it was retribution, driven by a deep sense of grievance over what he believed the City had done to him and his family.

July

In July 2014, Joseph Solomon was awarded the "Innovation in School Safety and Security, Crisis Mitigation, and Intervention Award" by the School Safety Advocacy Council (SSAC) at its annual National School Safety Conference, held at the Walt Disney World Swan and Dolphin Resort in Orlando, Florida. Given Solomon's usual eagerness to issue press releases, promote himself on social media, and highlight the Methuen Police Department's activities, it was uncharacteristic that the only reference to this award appeared years later in a 2018 *Boston Voyager* magazine article profiling Solomon, Joseph Alaimo, and their company, Eagle Investigation Services (EIS).

Curious, I set out to determine whether the award was legitimate or simply a piece of promotional padding inserted to enhance the article's portrayal of Solomon and Alaimo's business ventures.

Solomon Award

A copy of the award certificate was eventually found attached to a 2015 contract between EIS and a local college for security services. Notably, the certificate was not made out to the City of Methuen or the MPD, but to "Joseph Solomon – Eagle Investigation Services, Inc."

That clarified the lack of publicity — but it raised more serious concerns.

The trip itself, which cost Methuen taxpayers $7,658, had been authorized for four city officials to attend the school safety conference. If Solomon's true purpose for attending was to promote and represent his private company rather than the department, then this wasn't merely poor judgment — it was a calculated abuse of public trust. He submitted travel, hotel, and meal reimbursements under the guise of professional development, only to accept an award in the name of his private business.

That's not innovation, that's deception. And the fact that no one questioned or flagged this at the time points to a deeper, systemic failure in oversight and accountability.

Fall

According to Methuen's vendor reports, Integrity Testing was paid at the beginning of the year with two checks totaling $9,800 for assessment testing, apparently for sergeant and lieutenant promotions. Then, in October, Donovan's investigative company was paid another $9,800 for assessment testing for captain promotions.

Just doing a little math, Donovan and Stanley received $19,600 for conducting assessments. The current cost per officer to take a written civil service promotional exam is $150. They could have had 131 officers take written exams for the cost they paid out in assessments!

Granted, the promotional lists are good for three years, but for just under $20,000, they only promoted three sergeants in 2014, one of which was Solomon's stalwart supporter, Joseph Aiello.

November

Solomon was known as a micromanager; there was hardly anything in the police department that he was not involved with in one way or another. After returning as Chief of Police, he took a particular interest in school safety, immersing himself in that aspect of police work — an area he was also incorporating into his other business ventures.

During his tenure, Solomon was notably progressive in the realm of technology. He launched an MPD website and blog well before the city had its own online presence. Striving to be a leader in law enforcement innovation, he sought to implement the latest advancements in police technology, positioning the MPD as an early adopter of cutting-edge tools. So, when the opportunity arose to merge his interests in technology and school safety, he seized it.

In 2012, officials selected one of Methuen's schools as a test site for a new system designed to detect gunfire and instantly alert police to the exact location of a shooting – the first system of its kind to be installed in the United States.

Shooter Detection Systems (SDS), a company based in Rowley, Massachusetts, provided and installed the $90,000 system at no cost. In exchange, the MPD provided officers and materials for two years of testing and training.

A live demonstration took place at the undisclosed school on November 11, 2014, drawing dignitaries and media representatives.

The ensuing media frenzy benefitted Solomon, giving him something he relished — being at the center of public attention. He was extensively quoted in print, appeared on local and national television and featured in multiple YouTube videos discussing the product.

Hoping to expand the system citywide, the Superintendent of Schools sought grant funding to install it in the four remaining school buildings.

Notably, two company representatives were retired Boston Police Chief Ed Davis and retired North Andover and Wareham Police Chief Richard Stanley — Solomon's longtime friend and an MPD vendor. This marked the first of many products the MPD would acquire or purchase through companies affiliated with Stanley.

That no one questioned — other than in hushed tones — the conflicts of interest surrounding Solomon and Stanley remain remarkable.

December

It is customary for police chiefs to be issued an unmarked take-home cruiser for both official and personal use. Solomon was no exception, the city provided him with an SUV.

This synopsis draws from Solomon's official police report, recounting the afternoon of December 14, as he drove home from a jewelry store in Andover.

2014

Solomon noticed an SUV ahead. From behind, through its tinted windows, he claimed to see the rear-seat passenger, an adult woman, aggressively shaking someone next to her. When the SUV merged onto the highway, Solomon followed.

He later reported seeing a small figure, possibly a child, pop up beside the woman before she violently shook them. Then, with what he described as a "full windup," she struck the figure in the head, twice. That's when he hit the lights and siren.

After pulling the SUV over on the shoulder of I-495, Solomon approached the male driver, identified himself, and explained what he believed he had seen. At the passenger side, he asked the woman to step out. Only then did he get a clear view: the figure was a young boy, his cheek red and cut — an injury Solomon believed matched the impact of a ring or knuckle.

Leading the woman to the guardrail, Solomon again identified himself as a Methuen officer. She quickly broke down. Crying, she said her son was nonverbal and only responded to physical discipline. She admitted to losing control but added that she, too, had been raised with force and "turned out fine." She described the toll of raising two children with special needs, paying $100,000 in tuition, and feeling helpless after being asked to leave their son's skating lesson earlier that day.

Trying to calm her, Solomon asked, "What happened today that brought you to this point?"

As the woman explained, her husband repeatedly exited the vehicle despite being ordered back inside. At one point, he shouted through the window that no assault had taken place.

Solomon called for backup. When Methuen officers Sirois and Sergeant Delano arrived, Solomon deferred to Delano, who had more recent patrol experience. Delano recommended arresting the woman for domestic assault and battery. Solomon agreed. She was handcuffed and taken to the station. Child Protective Services (CPS) was contacted, and the child was photographed. The mother was booked and placed in a holding cell.

But according to the family's court testimony, the encounter unfolded very differently.

Their day, they said, began at St. Patrick's Church in Lawrence for religious education, followed by skating lessons at Phillips Academy. Their younger son — who had autism — kept collapsing on the ice and eventually had to be removed from the

2014

rink. On the way back to the car, he fell again. Unable to carry him, the mother leaned him against a wall until the father arrived. They noticed a small cut but didn't think much of it.

Driving home to Haverhill, the mother sat in the back with the boy to stop him from unbuckling his seatbelt while their other son sat upfront with the father. They noticed a blue SUV weaving behind them. As it sped up and flashed dashboard lights, they pulled over.

They said a man in plain clothes, Solomon, rushed to the rear door and yanked it open so forcefully they thought it would break. Without identifying himself, he allegedly shouted, "Get out of the car!" repeatedly. The mother exited, confused and frightened, only to be berated as a "bad woman" and "bad mother." When she tried to show him, her son was unharmed, Solomon ordered her to step back. At one point, she stumbled and hit the guardrail, injuring her leg.

When backup arrived, she was allegedly handcuffed roughly and placed in a cruiser. Her injuries, she later claimed, worsened during the arrest. She was taken to the station, photographed, and held in a cell. CPS allowed the children to go home later that night, pending follow-up.

She was released without bail.

The two versions of the story couldn't be further apart, and one key question hovered over the whole case: could Solomon, from his angle and through the SUV's tinted windows, have actually seen what he claimed?

Solomon, with a long history of temper flare-ups during traffic stops, had a duty to act on suspected abuse. But critics questioned whether his response was appropriate, or overzealous.

The Department of Children and Families (DCF) launched an investigation. After interviewing teachers, doctors, and others involved in the child's care, DCF found no evidence of abuse or neglect.

Still, the District Attorney pressed charges. Over the next year, the case saw multiple delays. The mother, reportedly suffering from PTSD and public humiliation, waited for closure. Finally, on the day of trial, the Commonwealth dropped the charges, stating that pursuing them was not in the child's best interest.

But the ordeal wasn't over.

2014

The family sued Solomon in federal court, alleging excessive force. That case was dismissed under qualified immunity. That is a legal doctrine that protects government workers from civil lawsuits for actions taken while performing their official duties.

A state tort suit followed, including claims of malicious prosecution and emotional distress. Nearly three years after the arrest, the parties reached a settlement. The trial was canceled.

< Redacted >
v. Solomon
Court Papers

Whether Solomon saw a real act of abuse or misread a moment through darkened glass, his decision set off a chain of events that forever altered the family's life and left lingering questions about his judgment and restraint.

Temper

Solomon's temper tantrums, tirades, and acts of brutality, witnessed firsthand by many, spanned decades. As far back as the 1990s, when he was just a sergeant, former Chief Bruce MacDougall publicly referred to him as a "rogue cop," a quote later published in the *Eagle-Tribune*, Solomon went ballistic. He demanded an apology. The timing of MacDougall's subsequent retirement suggests Solomon's influence.

We've already covered two notable incidents in this book where Solomon lost his temper: the night of the football game at the police station in 2007, and the 2014 traffic stop when he pulled over a mother on the highway.

During testimony, Solomon claimed he remained calm during the traffic stop and admitted he may have lost his cool the night of the football game. His demeanor on the stand was convincing — to a judge. But for those who dealt with him regularly, his temper was no secret.

We heard and read numerous accounts, some verified, others not, of Solomon "pulling nutties." Of the ones we could corroborate, we've compiled a few that reveal how he operated outside the public spotlight. Some might accuse us of "piling on" by including these short anecdotes, but we believe they show a side of the chief that the public rarely saw — one that provides

2014

essential context for understanding his behavior and leadership style.

Shortly after becoming chief in August 2003, Solomon went out to dinner at a local restaurant. At some point during the meal, he asked to speak with the owner to complain that his fish dinner didn't taste right. According to those present, the conversation quickly escalated — mostly on Solomon's side. Incredibly, he then got on his police radio and called for a cruiser to be dispatched to the restaurant to collect the remaining fish and have it tested. Unfortunately for the Chief, the remnants of his dinner had already been scraped into the dishwasher, leaving nothing left to test.

Another well-known incident — though the year remains unclear — involved Solomon passing an officer in a cruiser traveling in the opposite direction. It's unknown whether the officer saw Solomon, but one thing was certain: the officer did not acknowledge him. Solomon took this as a personal slight and immediately demanded, over the radio, to know the officer's identity. Later that day, he issued a memo stating that any officer who passed a superior without acknowledging them would face disciplinary action. Behind his back, officers mockingly referred to it as the "wave rule."

In 2017, officers responded to a devastating accident involving a mother and her six-year-old child. The child was ejected from the vehicle, run over by a van, and tragically killed. The responding officers did everything they could — assisting the child, securing the scene, and helping both drivers. It was, by any standard, one of the most traumatic calls an officer could face.

When Solomon arrived, his focus was not on the tragedy. Instead, he reportedly "lost it" over the fact that some officers were not wearing their hats. As a former state trooper, I can say with certainty: the last thing on an officer's mind at a fatal accident scene is putting on a uniform hat. CPR and trauma care are not compatible with dress-code formalities. Respect and solemnity define these moments — not starched uniforms.

On another occasion, an officer was assigned to a street-paving detail when Solomon's sister arrived, insisting on being allowed through despite a posted detour. The officer calmly explained that driving over the freshly laid asphalt would cause damage, but she refused to comply. Instead, she called her brother. Solomon

2014

responded by berating the officer for how he had "treated" his sister. Whether there were formal repercussions remains unknown, but the verbal lashing was remembered.

Back in 2003 MacDougall called Solomon a "rogue cop," in my opinion, MacDougall was 100 percent right.

2015

January 7	Police Chief Joseph Solomon joins the Board of Directors of both *The Psychological Center, Inc.* and *Debbie's Treasure Chest*, two local nonprofit organizations.
January 28	Former City Council Chair Sean Fountain, acting on behalf of his son, files a lawsuit against the City of Methuen.
January 29	Ryan Dorgan files a bypass appeal with the Massachusetts Civil Service Commission against the City.
	Chief Solomon signs a contract with Northern Essex Community College (NECC) to launch the Methuen Police Academy.
	Eagle Investigative Services, Inc. (EIS), operated by Michael Alaimo Sr., submits a $1.5 million security services bid to NECC.
February 1	Brandon Cote files a bypass appeal with Civil Service against the City.
February 25	Mayor Stephen Zanni is honored with the *Anti-Bullying Award* at the national Bullying Prevention Conference, held February 24–27.
	Michael Phillips also files a bypass appeal with Civil Service.
March 4	Stephen Dwinells files a Civil Service bypass appeal against the City.
March 12	EIS, Inc. is officially awarded the NECC security contract.
May 1-3	Chief Solomon and Officer Joseph Aiello attend *Municipal Police Training Committee (MPTC)* Active Shooter Response Training in Randolph, Massachusetts.
May 13	Solomon's long-running lawsuit over lost wages is dismissed or settled.
May 18-21	Solomon and Aiello return to Randolph for additional MPTC training.
June 26	The first graduating class of the Methuen Police Academy completes training.
July 9	The Civil Service Commission rules in favor of Michael Phillips, finding the City acted negligently in bypassing his promotion.
July 12	Sergeant Tod Himmer and Lieutenant Michael Wnek respond to a call reporting a man entering a bar with a firearm in his waistband.

2015

July 26-31	Chief Solomon, Aiello, Sergeant Kris McCarthy, and Mayor Zanni attend the *National School Safety Conference* in Las Vegas, Nevada (conference held July 27–31).
August 3	Thomas Fleming, who had been consulting for the police academy, is formally hired as its Director.
October 29	Day 1 of the disciplinary hearing for Sergeant Himmer and Lieutenant Wnek.
November 9-10	Integrity Testing conducts promotional assessment tests for the rank of Police Sergeant.
November 19	Day 2 of the hearing for Himmer and Wnek.

January

In mid-2014, police departments across the state grappled with enrollment backlogs at police academies. In response, a group of Merrimack Valley police chiefs approached Northern Essex Community College (NECC) with a proposal to establish a new academy at its Haverhill campus. To lead the project, NECC hired Thomas Fleming, a former Lowell police officer and former director of the Lowell Police Academy, as a consultant to handle logistics and lay the foundation for the academy. Notably, this decision came despite recent headlines surrounding Fleming's early retirement and the scandal that led to his departure.

Sergeant Thomas Fleming was placed on paid administrative leave from the Lowell Police Department (LPD) on July 3, 2014, after allegations surfaced that he had brought an electronic device into a promotional exam with the intent to cheat. A three-member board of inquiry interviewed Fleming and other sergeants who had taken the exam. During the investigation, the panel determined that Fleming had perjured himself during their inquiry. Before the panel reached any conclusions regarding the cheating allegations or potential disciplinary action for his dishonesty, Fleming retired two weeks later, effectively avoiding any formal ruling.

Government should not permit this practice of retiring to evade consequences, particularly in law enforcement. First, it fosters a "do as I say, not as I do" mentality, creating a perception of hypocrisy. Second, officials should never abandon an investigation simply because an individual files for retirement.

2015

Officials should withhold retirement until the issue is thoroughly investigated and resolved.

Only a few weeks after his retirement, Fleming began working at NECC.

On January 28, 2015, Solomon formalized the police academy initiative by agreeing, on behalf of the Methuen Police Department, to a contract with NECC and the MPD to establish the academy on a biannual schedule. NECC would oversee the academy's daily operations, while an advisory board — comprising Merrimack Valley police chiefs appointed by the college president — would provide oversight and technical guidance.

NECC/MPD Police Academy Contract

Solomon would serve as the chairman of the board. As part of the MPD contribution, Solomon agreed to provide a full-time instructor at no cost to the college or the academy. Additionally, the MPD decided to provide access to their firearms range, or an alternative facility, for training purposes and to supply academy uniforms for both the MPD instructor and the academy director. Despite the city solicitor reviewing the contract and its value exceeding the $50,000 threshold, it was never presented to the Methuen City Council for approval nor signed by the mayor, as required by the city charter. Despite the regional composition of the advisory board, the academy was named the Northern Essex Community College/Methuen Police Academy. Why NECC singled out Methuen among the other towns remains unclear, but Solomon's prominent role in the academy's development positioned him as a key figure in its leadership hierarchy.

NECC/EIS Security Contract

One day after the school finalized the police academy contract, Solomon and Alaimo's company, EIS, submitted a bid to manage security operations at NECC's Haverhill and Lawrence campuses. The $15.8 million bid proposed a five-year contract with two optional two-year extensions. Despite receiving lower bids from other companies, NECC awarded the contract to EIS a few weeks later. This decision further blurred the lines between Solomon's private business interests and his public role, raising concerns that the contract was a deliberate favor in exchange for his efforts to bring the academy to NECC.

Another notable example of a conflict of interest involved a recruit in the academy's first class — a reserve officer for the MPD, the son of an MPD sergeant, and an EIS security guard at NECC. This situation underscored the entanglement of Solomon's professional and personal interests.

Within weeks of finalizing the academy's contract, the first class of 46 recruits — including ten destined for the MPD — began an intensive 25-week daily curriculum. Their training spanned a broad range of subjects, including constitutional law, community policing, domestic violence, victim's rights, firearms training, and other crucial courses designed to prepare them for careers in law enforcement.

Following the successful graduation of the first class, NECC hired Fleming as the permanent director of its police academy in August. Just a couple of years later, yet another controversy overshadowed Fleming's tenure as director, casting a dark cloud over his legacy.

As a side note, Solomon's entanglement with the Academy and EIS's contract with Northern Essex College was one of the topics covered by *Eagle-Tribune* reporter Keith Eddings's three-part exposé in 2019. The newspaper ultimately shelved the investigation after pressure from Solomon's camp.

February

Another school safety conference was scheduled for February, spanning four days in Orlando, Florida. For this event, Solomon was accompanied by Aiello and Zanni.

Zanni's attendance raised some eyebrows, as Solomon had nominated him for the School Safety Advocacy Council's 2015 National Bullying Prevention Award. It was a surprising choice, considering that Zanni, during his time as a city councilor, had previously cast a vote of no confidence in Solomon, supported reducing his salary, advocated for removing his position from civil service, and opposed him during contract negotiations. Despite

2015

their contentious past, Solomon now put Zanni forward for national recognition.

As expected, there were two conflicting perspectives. Solomon's supporters claimed he was simply recognizing Zanni's contributions. Detractors saw it as a calculated move — an ego-boosting tactic to secure Zanni's loyalty. Time would prove the skeptics right, as for the remainder of his mayoral term, Zanni appeared to view Solomon as someone who could do no wrong.

A Facebook post by the Methuen Police on March 1st appeared to quote sections of Zanni's nomination letter for the anti-bullying award, highlighting Zanni's 36-year career in education — as a teacher, then as a school administrator, and later as an elected school committee member. Notably, none of these roles occurred in Methuen; they were in Hudson, New Hampshire, and in nearby Lawrence, respectively. However, as Methuen's mayor, he automatically served as chair of the Methuen School Committee. The letter also praised Zanni's commitment to strengthening public education and school safety, asserting that his efforts benefited Methuen's children by fostering a positive attitude and discouraging bullying.

The post further stated that Zanni had been dedicated to the safety and security of Methuen's schools, consistently advocating for improved methods and tactics. It credited him with authorizing a public-private partnership between the school department, the police department, and a private contractor to enhance school security. The result of three years of research and development was installing a state-of-the-art automatic shot detection system in one of Methuen's schools.

Additionally, the release highlighted Zanni's leadership in working directly with Methuen's youth, creating positive learning and sports environments. He had volunteered as a coach for youth and high school athletics and served on the Methuen Youth Commission.

Solomon also credited Zanni as the driving force behind the installation of artificial turf at the city's football stadium and the design of modern, safe field house and clubhouse facilities for both male and female student-athletes. According to the letter, Zanni carefully crafted each of these initiatives to promote positive interactions with youth, build self-esteem, and reduce violence and bullying.

2015

Zanni was recognized by the School Safety Advocacy Council for his efforts as a positive role model for children and an innovator in education and safety — becoming the first mayor ever to receive the award.

While Solomon peripherally mentioned bullying as a byproduct of other initiatives, the nomination seemed like a significant stretch for a national Bullying Prevention award — giving more weight to the dissenters' theory than the supporters.

April

The MPD had maintained a well-staffed permanent reserve police roster. However, after exhausting its reserves, Solomon requested the current Civil Service list. By January 2015, the city had hired 26 new reserve officers.

When filling a vacancy, the city was required to select the candidate with the highest-ranking score on the list, prioritizing the most qualified applicant based on test results. Officials intended this process to ensure that police departments made appointments based on merit rather than favoritism. However, the city retained the authority to bypass a candidate for a stated reason.

Ryan Dorgan was one such candidate bypassed for a reserve position. In Dorgan's bypass letter, the city cited his prior employment history, driving record, allegations that he had contacted town officials to exert political influence over the hiring process, and a custody event involving his minor child. The letter also referenced a school employee, whom Dorgan had listed as a reference, as the individual who had allegedly approached officials on his behalf. However, upon learning of the claim, the referenced individual contacted the mayor's office to refute it.

Dorgan's Civil Service Hearing

Within a week of issuing the initial bypass letter, the city sent a second letter omitting the claim of political interference. Despite this, Dorgan appealed to the Civil Service Commission, contesting the city's decision.

As Dorgan's April 13th hearing date approached, three additional bypassed candidates had filed appeals. Around the same time, Dorgan and the city reached a proposed settlement: in exchange for withdrawing his appeal, the city would request that Civil Service place Dorgan at the top of Methuen's list, guaranteeing him at least one additional consideration for appointment.

The Civil Service Commission rejected the settlement, as the city did not offer similar consideration to the three other candidates with pending appeals. At that time, the commission decided to take no action on Dorgan's initial bypass until they heard the other appeals and requested additional information regarding the reasons for the bypass.

The three other bypassed candidates were Stephen Dwinells, Brandon Cote, and Michael Phillips.

One allegation common to all four appeals was that MPD officials bypassed them in favor of candidates related to various MPD or city employees. Below is the civil service test ranking of the candidates mentioned in the appeals:

Dwinells' Civil Service Hearing

- 10th, Joseph Aiello, son of Officer Joseph Aiello
- 11th, Stephen Dwinells (bypassed)
- 12th, Brandon Cote (bypassed)
- 21st, Mark Parolisi, stepbrother-in-law of Captain Kris McCarthy
- 22nd, Ryan Dorgan (bypassed)
- 22nd, Michael Havey, son of Officer Michael Havey
- 23rd, Justin Antoon, son of a city employee
- 23rd, Michael Phillips (bypassed)
- 24th, Joseph Alaimo, son of retired Deputy Chief Joseph Alaimo
- 27th, Patrick Fleming, son of Officer Walter Fleming

Over the next few months, each candidate had their appeal hearings before the Civil Service Commission. During these

2015

Cote's Civil Service Hearing

hearings, testimony revealed that MPD officials severely bent conflict-of-interest laws in several instances.

Captain Kris McCarthy, whose wife's stepbrother was among the selected candidates, was typically responsible for supervising the background investigations of each applicant. While he assigned this duty to a subordinate, ethics laws prohibit individuals with a conflict of interest from participating in matters involving family members — including delegating those matters to others. Additionally, McCarthy inserted himself into the process when he and Detective Tom McMenamon met with candidate Stephen Dwinells before his formal interview to request his social media usernames and passwords.

Phillip's Civil Service Hearing

Solomon testified at the civil service hearing, that he had a personal friendship with two selected candidates, Joseph Aiello Jr. and Joseph Alaimo Jr., and had attended family events at their homes, including holiday parties, birthday celebrations, and high school graduations. While personal friendships do not violate ethics rules, these relationships create a clear "appearance of a conflict." The same concern applied to three other selected candidates, whose fathers were part of Solomon's close circle within the MPD

After completing all background checks and formal interviews, Solomon convened a panel composed of more members from his inner circle — Captain Randy Haggar, Officer Tom McMenamon, and Lieutenants Michael Pappalardo and Kevin Mahoney — to review the applicants and determine which candidates the department would recommend to the mayor for appointment.

The Civil Service Commission reviewed why the city bypassed the four candidates.

Cote scored a 99 on his test and had excellent references, a high credit score, no criminal record, and no adverse driving history. The City cited his current employment at the Washington, D.C. Police Department, arguing that Cote appeared "noncommittal to accepting the position" in Methuen. The panel also noted that his interview responses were "sometimes vague and not very well thought out."

In the end, Methuen appointed 26 permanent reserve officers — 18 of whom ranked below Cote on the civil service list. The commissioner noted in the report that one of those candidates had a notably poor driving history, including payment defaults, license suspensions, and bad credit — the exact opposite of Cote's strong credentials. Despite this, the Commission found no evidence of personal or political bias in Cote's bypass. It deemed the decision justifiable, citing the interviewers' uncertainty about his commitment to the role — even after Cote explicitly stated his willingness to return to Methuen to serve.

Methuen's reliance on this flimsy rationale for bypassing a highly qualified candidate underscores the extent to which officials manipulated the hiring process to secure appointments for friends and family.

Dwinells also scored a 99, was a military veteran with no criminal record, but had several driving citations and a poor credit history. The city justified his bypass by citing weak interview responses and two social media posts — one allegedly racially insensitive and another showing him on a boat, wearing a pirate hat and holding a beer.

During the hearing, Dwinells explained that the post in question was not racially motivated; it had been shared by a fellow Marine, an African American, who knew Dwinells was a fan of Jay-Z and had posted about one of the artist's songs. Despite this explanation, the Commission upheld the bypass, stating that "police are held to a higher standard of conduct and such material does not meet that standard." They also pointed to Dwinells' poor interview performance, which resulted in lower scores than any of the selected candidates, as a justified reason for his exclusion — despite his veteran status, which should have granted him preference over less qualified candidates.

Michael Phillips' bypass was far more complex. He scored a 95 on his test, had no criminal record, no driving citations, and a positive credit report. All his references and neighbors spoke highly of him. However, the city's reason for bypassing him was troubling:

"Mr. Phillips showed a lack of discretion in his response to the drunk driving scenario question. He stated he would arrest his mother and father. The answer appears insincere and sounds like Mr. Phillips is trying to respond in the way he thinks the panel wants him to respond."

During the interview process, officials asked each candidate a standard scenario-based question:

"You are on duty and are called to a motor vehicle crash on Howe Street. You arrive to find a single vehicle off the road in a culvert. The operator is standing outside the vehicle, smelling of alcohol and appearing unsteady on his feet. How would you handle this situation?"

Officials then asked candidates variations of the same scenario – one where the intoxicated driver was a police officer from Salem, N.H., whom they knew personally, and another where the driver was a close family member.

Asking this type of question should never be allowed — it places candidates in a Kobayashi Maru scenario, a no-win situation. If I say I wouldn't make the arrest, I admit to breaking the law and violating ethical standards. If I say I would, the panel assumes I'm being disingenuous, merely telling them what they want to hear. Either way, there's no correct answer.

Beyond that, the premise itself is flawed. Regardless of whether the individual is family, allowing someone to evade legal consequences due to personal connections clearly violates both the law and ethical standards. Any system that rewards candidates for suggesting they would compromise their integrity is deeply problematic and raises serious concerns about the hiring process.

Captain Randy Haggar testified that he was looking for candidates who could "justify their decision" and "stay the ground in making the arrest or not making the arrest" even when panelists pressured them about their choice. He emphasized that the question was not about whether an applicant would arrest friends but about their reasoning and discretion.

Lieutenant Michael Pappalardo explained that he sought "bearing, honesty, and how quickly the person can think on their feet," adding that he did not want a simple "yes or no" response but an explanation of how and why the candidate would justify their decision. When asked whether he believed candidates who claimed they would arrest a family member, Pappalardo stated, "To be quite frank, I just don't believe them."

When asked whether an applicant who responded, "I would contact a supervisor because it would be a conflict of interest," provided a strong or weak answer, Pappalardo replied, "Myself personally, I think that's a cop-out answer — you don't want to make a decision."

Of the eight candidates ranked below Phillips that the department hired, six explicitly stated they would arrest a stranger in the first scenario but would not arrest a police officer they knew or a family member. Another candidate said they would arrest both. Interviewer notes on most candidates who refused to arrest a friend or family member included comments such as "knows discretion."

After Phillips filed his appeal, Solomon directed Sergeant Smith to investigate Phillips' personnel file at the Lawrence Police Department following allegations that Phillips was involved in a questionable incident. The file contained only generic information, and members of the Lawrence Auxiliary spoke highly of Phillips. The Commission viewed this post-appeal inquiry as Solomon's "fishing expedition" to justify the retroactive bypass.

In its ruling, the Commission expressed deep concerns about the hiring process related to Phillips. First, it found the MPD's decision to obtain Phillips' personnel file after he had already appealed to be "chilling."

The Commission noted that the city had:

- Conducted a background investigation that found no negative issues,
- Bypassed Phillips for reasons unrelated to that investigation, and
- Notified him of these reasons, upon which he based his appeal.

For the city to re-open his background investigation — without his knowledge — after he had filed an appeal was deemed inappropriate and cast doubt over the entire selection process.

Second, the Commission found that the city had "turned the process upside down" by awarding higher points to candidates willing to engage in conduct unbecoming of a police officer — potentially even illegal — while penalizing candidates like

Phillips, whose answers aligned with the high ethical standards expected of law enforcement officers.

Additionally, the Commission criticized the city for failing to take extra steps to ensure fairness, given the number of selected candidates with personal or familial ties to city and police department employees, including Solomon himself. It was particularly troubling that Phillips' bypass letter stated he "showed a lack of discretion" for indicating that he would apply the same standard to a drunk-driving family member as he would to a stranger. This was not a clerical error — several panelists praised candidates willing to apply different standards based on personal relationships, citing their "understanding of discretion."

The Commission carefully reviewed and re-reviewed the testimony of interview panelists who attempted to frame the scenario to assess a candidate's honesty. However, the Commission found no valid justification for awarding the highest points to candidates who openly admitted they would apply one set of rules to strangers and another to friends and family.

Equally troubling was the testimony that a police officer choosing to call a supervisor to remove themselves from a potential conflict of interest was considered a "cop-out."

As a result, the Commission ruled in favor of Phillips' appeal. The remedy required that his name be placed on all future certifications for the position of Methuen Reserve Police Officer until he was either appointed or bypassed again. Furthermore, if Phillips were ever appointed, he would receive a civil service seniority date retroactive to the same date as those appointed during this selection cycle.

Ryan Dorgan, the original appellant, had his hearing before the Commission. As previously stated, Dorgan's bypass letter cited his prior employment history, driving record, allegations that he attempted to exert political influence over the hiring process by contacting town officials, and a custody dispute involving his minor child.

While the Commission found that the city had justifiable reasons to bypass Dorgan based on his employment history and driving record, it also noted an inconsistency: the city had hired at least one candidate who ranked below Dorgan and had a comparable, if not worse, driving record. While this discrepancy did not alter Dorgan's situation, it raised concerns about the city's hiring practices. As the Commission observed:

"It is not clear how the candidate with the same or worse driving record than Mr. Dorgan poses any less of a safety or liability concern to the City than Mr. Dorgan."

However, the Commission took exception to the other two reasons cited for Dorgan's bypass.

First, regarding the child custody dispute, the Commission noted that this incident occurred after Dorgan's background check and interview, meaning he had no opportunity to explain his side of the story. This omission undermined the city's ability to conduct a reasonably thorough review.

For four years, Dorgan and the child's mother had followed voluntary custodial arrangements without any police or court involvement. However, just before Solomon and the interview panel convened to select the candidates, the mother reported to the MPD that Dorgan had failed to return the child at the agreed-upon time. She believed custody would revert to her on Wednesday, while Dorgan maintained that the agreed-upon return date was Thursday.

During the hearing, it emerged that the child's grandfather was Sergeant Michael Havey of the Methuen Police Department — a known ally of Solomon. Officials did not include this detail in the official hearing report. Notably, Havey had served in the MPD's marine unit when the department purchased a boat from his first cousin, Samuel Kalil, Solomon's brother-in-law.

Further complicating matters, Havey's son was one of the candidates competing for a reserve officer position alongside Dorgan. The two men were tied for 22nd place in the rankings. Not only was he the son of Sergeant Havey, but he was also an employee of Solomon's private company, EIS, working as a security guard at Northern Essex Community College.

Was there animosity between the Havey family and Dorgan over the child custody dispute? Or was this a convenient pretext used to justify Dorgan's bypass?

The city also cited Dorgan's alleged attempts to exert political influence by contacting "numerous individuals," including town officials, to advocate on his behalf. However, one of the officials in the bypass letter had already informed the mayor that this claim was false. When investigators asked Solomon to provide the names of the "numerous" individuals Dorgan had supposedly contacted, he could not name a single one.

Ultimately, the Commission denied Dorgan's appeal based solely on his employment and driving history.

October

A call was received by the MPD at 4:27 p.m. on July 12 regarding a suspicious male entering a bar with a possible firearm in his waistband.

According to a report by the *Eagle-Tribune*, Sergeant Tod Himmer, Officer Joseph Rynne, and another patrol officer responded to the call. Upon meeting with the caller — who wished to remain anonymous — he described seeing a man arrive in the parking lot. Before entering the bar, the man removed a security shirt and adjusted his t-shirt, revealing a gun in a holster. Finding the man's behavior suspicious and believing he might already be under the influence, the caller contacted the police.

Officers Rynne and the other officer entered the bar and found the man seated with a half-filled glass of beer in front of him. After agreeing to step outside with the officers, the man explained that he was a security guard with a valid firearm license. He had just finished work and had stopped for a drink. After speaking with him for several minutes, the officers determined that he showed no signs of impairment.

Himmer used his personal cell phone to call his shift supervisor, Lieutenant Michael Wnek, who also used his personal phone, to discuss the situation. As a precautionary measure, they decided to impound the man's .357 handgun, ammunition, holster, and license to carry. In his official report, Wnek later wrote, "The temporary inconvenience of securing the firearm was outweighed by the risk to public safety for inaction." Notably, Massachusetts state law does not prohibit licensed individuals from carrying a firearm into a bar unless intoxicated.

Upon confiscating the loaded weapon, Himmer informed the man that the licensing authority — Chief Joseph Solomon or his designee — would decide if and when the department would return the property.

When Solomon arrived at the station the following morning and learned of the seizure, he had an outburst and immediately ordered

2015

the property returned to the man. Some later speculated that the 69-year-old man was a friend of Mayor Zanni. The only apparent connection was that the mayor's son and the man's son had played high school football together.

Wnek and Himmer did not escape repercussions from the incident. Solomon launched an internal investigation, enlisting his associate, Al Donovan, to conduct it. Three weeks later, the investigation concluded. In his report, Donovan questioned Himmer's actions that night, noting that as a representative of the police department, the Fourth Amendment of the U.S. Constitution and Article 14 of the Massachusetts Bill of Rights bound the officer by prohibiting the seizure of property without proper legal justification. Donovan further opined that, during his 30-year career, he had "witnessed many police officers stopping off at a local public or liquor-serving establishment after their respective shifts, having a few beers before going home, and a great deal of them carrying a concealed weapon." He added, "It is difficult to believe an off-duty Methuen police officer would have been treated the same way under similar circumstances."

Citing Donovan's findings, Solomon suspended Wnek and Himmer for violating department rules of professional conduct and using personal, non-recorded phones to discuss police business that evening. He determined that they had participated in the "improper seizure" of a "lawfully possessed handgun." Solomon issued Wnek a five-day unpaid suspension and Himmer a three-day unpaid suspension. The two men contested their suspensions through their superior officers' union, successfully securing a hearing scheduled for October 29.

Hearing Officer Darren Klein oversaw the hearing took place at City Hall in the Great Hall. Klein was a lawyer and shareholder at KP Law, formerly known as Koppelman and Paige – significant because KP Law had long served as the city's contracted legal counsel. He even acted as the sole legal advisor when Methuen lacked a city solicitor in 2013. As a legal representative of the city, the firm held an inherent loyalty to its client, creating a direct conflict of interest that should have disqualified Klein from serving as the hearing officer.

Donovan's testimony regarding his investigation mainly consumed the three-hour hearing. The *Eagle-Tribune* later reported that attorneys Nolan and Parroni, representing the union, aggressively questioned Donovan about whether he believed it was acceptable to carry a loaded, concealed weapon while consuming alcohol in a bar. Donovan repeatedly stated that the practice was "lawful." When attorney Parroni asked, "Is it stupid for someone to consume alcohol while carrying a loaded weapon?" Donovan responded, "It's a lawful decision... I don't impose my will on other people." The line of questioning escalated, with Donovan distinguishing between simply having a drink and being intoxicated or impaired. Later, growing defensive, Donovan snapped at attorney Nolan, saying, "I don't like that you are trying to put words in my mouth."

Both attorneys also pressed Donovan to disclose the amount the city had paid his company for the investigation, the report, and his testimony. However, Hearing Officer Klein stopped the questioning, deeming it irrelevant. Challenging Klein, Attorney Nolan argued, "How can you say it's irrelevant if you don't even know the answer? If he's paid an exorbitant amount of money, we are entitled to that information." A review of city invoices from July 2016 to January 2017 showed six payments to Donovan totaling $9,668, though it was unclear how much of that amount pertained to this case.

The hearing was recessed and reconvened on November 19th, with Solomon scheduled to testify. No additional newspaper articles covering the hearing were published. Ultimately, Wnek and Himmer entered into a resolution agreement, both retiring on July 4, 2017.

2016

	Police Chief Joseph Solomon is named to the Executive Board of the Massachusetts Chiefs of Police Association.
January 28	The Patrolmen's Union signs a new employment contract covering 2014–2017.
February 1	Solomon's daughter is hired as a clerk in the City Assessor's Office.
	City Solicitor Kerry Jenness submits her resignation.
	Officers Ferreira, Valliere, McMenamon, and Smith are promoted without formal City Council approval.
February 21-24	Solomon, Officer Joseph Aiello, Sergeant Kris McCarthy, Mayor Stephen Zanni, and Lieutenant Kevin Mahoney attend the *National Conference on Bullying* in Orlando, Florida. On February 22–24, they deliver a seminar titled *"Police Response to Students with Spectrum Disorders."*
February 29	Kerry Jenness officially departs as City Solicitor.
March 31	Solomon files a long-overdue financial disclosure with the City Clerk concerning his involvement in Eagle Investigative Services, Inc. (EIS), four years late.
April 28	Solomon, Joseph Alaimo, and Aiello, representing EIS, operate a booth at *MASSBUYS* at Gillette Stadium and present *"How to Survive an Active Shooter Incident."*
May 18-19	Solomon attends the Massachusetts Major City Chiefs Retreat.
June 12-17	Solomon, McCarthy, and McMenamon attend the *Taser Axon Conference.*
June 23	Councilor Sean Fountain receives his final paycheck from the City Council.
June 30	Fountain signs a conditional offer of employment to serve as an intermittent officer with the Methuen Police Department.
July 1	Fountain's official start date with MPD.
July 5	Fountain receives legal guidance on how to file ethics disclosures.
July 5-7	Solomon travels to Washington, D.C., for a White House meeting on the opioid crisis.
July 7	Fountain receives a formal attorney opinion allowing him to work MPD details.

2016

July 8	Fountain signs and submits his financial disclosure and exemption form.
July 11	The City Council votes to approve a Home Rule Petition for Fountain's employment.
July 12	Solomon signs off on Fountain's disclosure form.
July 24-30	Solomon, Aiello, and Valliere attend the *National School Safety Conference* in Orlando, Florida (conference dates: July 25–29).
August 1	HR Director Anne Randazzo questions Solomon's appointment of Matthew Despins as a full-time intermittent officer despite not being Civil Service certified.
	During a regular City Council meeting, Councilor Thomas Ciulla unexpectedly nominates Richard D'Agostino as City Solicitor. The motion is halted by a Charter Objection.
August 2	Fountain posts a public notice calling for a special August 4 City Council meeting to vote on D'Agostino's appointment.
August 4	The City Council holds a special meeting and votes to hire D'Agostino as City Solicitor.
August 15-17	Solomon travels again to Washington, D.C., for a White House meeting.
October 14-19	Solomon, Captain Randy Haggar, Mahoney, and McCarthy attend the *International Association of Chiefs of Police (IACP) Conference* in San Diego, California (conference dates: October 15–18).
October 17	The City Council retroactively confirms the promotions of Ferreira, Valliere, McMenamon, and Smith from earlier in the year.
November 9-13	Solomon and Aiello attend the *School Safety Leadership Conference* in Palm Springs, California (event held November 10–11).
November 29-December 3	Solomon and McMenamon attend the *Massachusetts Police Accreditation Conference* in Falmouth, Massachusetts.
December 6	Solomon's niece-in-law is hired as head clerk in the City's Water Department.

February

After serving for just 18 months, City Solicitor Kerry Regan (now Jenness) submitted her resignation to City Council Chair Sean Fountain on February 1st. Her final day in office had been January 31st.

According to the *Eagle-Tribune*, her brief resignation letter expressed gratitude to Fountain for "the opportunity." She also stated, "I look forward to assisting this transition with the guidance of the council."

Neither Regan nor city officials gave an official reason for her departure. However, if we believe the City Hall rumor mill — renowned for its accuracy — her decision was prompted by a council member's directive to "mind her own business."

Following her resignation, the council reverted to using an outside law firm, KP Law, until city leaders appointed a new solicitor.

Promotions

That morning, Regan submitted her resignation; that evening, promotions took place.

Promoting friends and family had long been a tradition in Methuen's government, and the MPD had refined the practice into an art form.

According to a post on MPD's Facebook page, a swearing-in ceremony was held at Sanborn Hall in the police station to recognize the promotions of Officers Eric Ferreira, Ronald Valliere, and Thomas McMenamon Jr. to Sergeant and Sergeant Stephen Smith's advancement to Lieutenant. Three of the four promoted officers had been longtime loyalists to Solomon.

MPD's Facebook posts from that evening indicated that Mayor Stephen Zanni presided over the swearing-in, congratulating the officers before an audience of friends, family, and fellow officers. However, in hindsight, this may have been a serious blunder by the administration. In Massachusetts, judges, court or city clerks, notaries or justices of the peace must administer oaths or affirmations of office. Zanni, who held none of these titles, lacked the legal authority to conduct the swearing-in, raising concerns about the event's validity.

MPD Facebook Post

Compounding the issue, the Methuen city charter mandated that all superior officer appointments — ranked Sergeant or above — be made by the mayor and confirmed by a full city council majority vote. Yet, city records revealed that the council was not presented with the promotions until the October 17th meeting — eight months after the swearing-in ceremony. This delay constituted a second major procedural violation, further undermining the legitimacy of the promotions.

The lingering question was: why the delay? Had the Mayor and Chief believed they could bypass the Council entirely, only to be caught and forced to rectify the situation? The circumstances suggest an attempt to sidestep proper procedures, with efforts made to correct the oversight only after discovery.

The October meeting included Chair Fountain, Vice Chair Atkinson, Councilors George Kazanjian, James Jajuga, Jennifer Kannan, Ron Marsan, Tom Ciulla and Lynn Vidler, while Lisa Ferry was absent. The sparse audience included Lieutenant Greg Gallant, the four officers, and Joe Aiello.

With Solomon attending a conference, Gallant took the podium to present the biographies of each candidate. The council then held a single vote to appoint all four officers simultaneously. Fountain asked if there was any discussion, but he received none, so he proceeded with the vote. The outcome: four votes in favor, four abstentions, and one absence.

In the video of the meeting, if you turn up the speaker volume, Councilor Kazanjian can be heard saying, "It can't get through," to which Chair Fountain softly says to someone, "That right? Okay." Fountain then shifts into his authoritative chairman voice and announces, "Congratulations, gentlemen," prompting applause from the chamber.

The abstentions were due to conflicts of interest — Jajuga, Vidler, and Kannan each had family members in the MPD, while Fountain served as an intermittent officer within the department.

Following the vote, the council congratulated the officers and posed for photographs. But in doing so, they overlooked — or ignored — a critical detail: council approval required five affirmative votes, not four. Kazanjian knew it, and so did Councilor Marsan, who had leaned over to Fountain right after the vote and whispered something. Fountain responded, "It's a confirmation appointment anyway," before his voice trailed into inaudibility. Moments

Meeting Video

2016

later, the officers approached for handshakes, cutting the exchange short.

Despite this apparent sleight of hand, the promotions went through — the third major procedural error in the process.

The audacity of the situation was staggering. First, Zanni, who lacked legal authority, administered the swearing-in. Then, the officers were promoted without the required council approval. Finally, the council voted invalidly, allowing the appointments to stand.

Adding another layer of complexity, newly appointed or promoted officers were required to sign their oath, which the City Clerk recorded. Upon request, we obtained copies of these oaths, revealing that the officers had signed them on February 1st — the swearing-in day – not the day of confirmation. Anne Drouin, the then-Assistant City Clerk, had signed as the administering official.

Drouin's signature raised more questions. Had Zanni's performance merely been for show and Drouin swore them in earlier in the day? Why the assistant clerk, as City Clerk had traditionally administered the oath? It may be that nothing unethical took place, but the procedural irregularities raise questions.

March

Meanwhile, the March 7th City Council agenda included a motion to begin the search for a new city solicitor. However, as soon as officials raised the matter during the meeting, Councilor James Jajuga moved to table the search, with Councilor Jennifer Kannan seconding the motion. Council held zero discussion on why they were delaying the hiring process. They only voted, resulting in a 5-4 decision in favor of tabling the motion.

A few days later, the *Eagle-Tribune* reported that councilors had differing opinions on how to proceed with hiring a solicitor. Councilor Jamie Atkinson expressed surprise that his fellow councilors tabled the motion, noting that some of the councilors who voted in favor had previously stated that the process should begin as soon as possible. Typically, hiring a solicitor takes 60 to 90 days from advertising to final selection.

Fountain explained that if council had not tabled the motion, he would have voted against it. Before deciding, he wanted to evaluate how the outside law firm functioned as an alternative to an in-house solicitor.

Kannan justified the decision to table the motion by pointing out that, under city rules, if council had voted down the motion, it could not be reintroduced for a full year. Tabling it, however, kept the option open for reconsideration.

For those observing from the sidelines, the argument for hiring an outside law firm — such as cost savings from having specialized attorneys in one firm and avoiding expenses like pensions and health insurance — had some merit. However, having an in-house solicitor remained the more practical choice for handling day-to-day legal matters. Relying on an external firm could delay timely legal advice required by department heads, boards and commissions.

Then, there was the political element — why were some council members so determined to retain the outside law firm? In particular, why was Council Chair Sean Fountain so adamant?

During the previous November election, Fountain campaigned to outsource the legal department. Could this have influenced the former solicitor's decision to resign only months after Fountain's re-election? The timing certainly raised questions.

July

Despite his roles on Methuen City Council, as a North Andover firefighter and a deputy in the Essex County Sheriff's Department, Fountain formally joined the ranks of the MPD as a part-time intermittent police officer on July 1, 2016 – at Solomon's invitation and with Zanni's blessing.

This course of action posed several challenges. Firstly, a provision in the Methuen City Charter prohibited elected officials from being employed by the city for one year after leaving office. Secondly, it was not permissible for an individual to receive more than one income from the city simultaneously.

Zanni's Letter to Fountain

2016

Advisory Letter from KP Law

To tackle the initial challenge, Fountain, having already started his employment for a week, sought guidance from through the Mayor's chief-of-staff to the outside law firm KP Law. They in turn instructed him to submit a disclosure and request an exemption from the city council to continue in the position. Additionally, the lawyer advised Fountain to exclusively handle police details associated with non-city work, such as those requested by utility companies, with payment made directly from those companies to Fountain rather than through the city.

On that same day, Solomon sent a letter to Mayor Zanni claiming that while Fountain served on the City Council, he would only work private detail shifts — and that "he will not receive any checks from the city treasury that originated from city funds." But that statement directly conflicted with guidance from KP Law. By December, a concern was raised with the Ethics Commission regarding Fountain's employment with the MPD. In a letter sent to Fountain at that time, Ethics, relying on information provided by Fountain were satisfied that the matter did not require any further action on their part.

Ethics Letter from Fountain

Solomon knew full well how the detail system worked: outside companies would pay the city for the officer's time, and the city — not the company — would then cut a check to the officer. No city employee could legally be a "subcontractor" paid directly by an outside business. The city set the detail rates, added an administrative fee, and ran everything through a separate revolving account dedicated to officer detail payments. These checks were completely separate from an officer's regular salary and didn't count toward pension benefits. But they were still paid by the city — from a fund managed by the city — not by private contractors.

Just four days later, during a City Council vote on whether to approve Fountain's financial disclosure and exemption, city officials told the council that Fountain would be paid directly by the contractors — even though that wasn't true.

2016

The Massachusetts Ethics Commission clearly outlines this type of situation as a conflict of interest. One of their examples states: "A police officer may not work as a paid private security guard in the town where he serves because the demands of his private employment would conflict with his duties as a police officer." They further emphasize that "municipal employees may not be paid by outside people or organizations in matters where the city or town has an interest — because municipalities are entitled to the undivided loyalty of their employees."

Additionally, city officials told the Council that Fountain would forgo his council stipend from that point onward – which he did.

Solomon signed off on the disclosure the next day, certifying: "I have received a disclosure under G.L. c. 268A, § 20(b) from a municipal employee who seeks to provide personal services to my municipal agency, identified above. I certify that no employee of my agency is available to perform the services described above as part of his or her regular duties."

While this might have provided a temporary solution for a lack of officers to fulfill details, historically, there were other avenues to address such shortages, including utilizing police from neighboring towns, neighboring out-of-state officers, sheriff's departments, state police, and University of Massachusetts Police.

As 2016 unfolded, Solomon became aware that Fountain's contract with the sheriff's department expired at the end of the year. Fountain began exploring other career options, seeking a role that would allow him to be home more consistently to care for a family member in need. Transitioning to a full-time police officer seemed the ideal solution, providing a stable job and the flexibility to support his family. Recognizing this, Solomon saw an opportunity to assist Fountain in making this career change and gain his loyalty and gratitude. Consequently, Solomon offered, and Fountain accepted an offer to become a full-time "permanent intermittent" police officer.

The term "permanent intermittent police officer" presents an intriguing paradox. "Permanent" conveys stability and continuity, while "intermittent" suggests irregularity and inconsistency. When combined, these opposing concepts create a contradictory and unconventional phrase — implying someone consistently inconsistent or permanently irregular in their role. This unique designation underscores the unconventional nature of such a position, raising questions about its purpose and practicality within law enforcement structures.

July 6th

In the years leading up to 2015, the opioid crisis had escalated into a full-blown epidemic across both the city and the state. The situation had grown so severe that, in November 2014, MPD personnel underwent training on the administration of Narcan to reverse drug overdoses. According to an article in the *Eagle-Tribune*, overdose statistics in Methuen had risen at an alarming rate. While the city recorded just two overdoses in February 2014, that number had surged to 14 by the following February. Drug addiction was yet another area of policing in which Solomon had taken a deep and personal interest.

Solomon had drawn inspiration from The ANGEL Program, an initiative launched in June 2015 by the police chief in Gloucester, Massachusetts. The program prioritized helping people with a substance use disorder rather than arresting them. Under this initiative, individuals seeking assistance could walk into the Gloucester police station, and instead of being placed in a holding cell, they were connected to a recovery center. Interestingly, Gloucester city officials fired the police chief the following year after he lied to investigators about potential relationships with several women. He was also dishonest about the status of his city-issued cell phone, which he wiped clean before turning it over to his attorney.

On July 18, 2015, Solomon publicly introduced his version of the concept — the Methuen Outreach Initiative. His plan involved hiring two outreach coordinators who would work alongside officers to go door-to-door, engaging with known drug addicts and their families. Their mission was to provide support, resources, and guidance to help individuals combat addiction.

> *"Methuen police officers are committed to assisting those who suffer from the disease of addiction. We become police officers to help people, not to simply arrest people because they have an illness," Solomon stated in a press release announcing the program. "We are a proactive*

> *police department, and while we will continue to aggressively pursue drug dealers and traffickers, we believe there is tremendous potential in tapping recovery centers and providing educational resources to streamline the process of getting a person into a long-term recovery program."*

Solomon fully immersed himself in the fight against opioid addiction. The previous year, he joined the Psychological Center, Inc. board. At the beginning of 2015, the chief became a member of the Executive Advisory Board for the Police Assisted Addiction and Recovery Initiative (PAARI). Then, on July 5, 2015, he traveled to Washington, D.C., along with 16 other police chiefs, for a meeting at the White House with the Obama Administration officials to discuss funding for programs aimed at combating opioid addiction.

August

After five months of relying on an outside law firm instead of an in-house city solicitor, City Council Chair Sean Fountain had a change of heart. At the August 1st regular council meeting, he cited the firm's high monthly legal bills, telling his fellow councilors that the arrangement was unsustainable and that they needed to fix the situation.

A lengthy discussion followed until Councilor Tom Ciulla, a strong proponent of hiring an in-house solicitor, had his turn to speak. In a surprising move, he motioned to appoint Richard D'Agostino — the candidate from three years prior — as interim city solicitor. He then called for a second, which Councilor Ron Marsan provided.

Questions immediately arose about whether they could even vote on a motion that had not been listed on the agenda. With no legal representation present to provide an opinion, Chair Fountain asserted that it was a "privileged motion from the floor" and that the council act upon it.

Sensing that the situation was spiraling out of control, Kannan invoked a "charter objection," halting all discussion. Under council rules, a charter objection postpones a matter until the next meeting, whether regular or special. However, if more than one

2016

councilor joins the objection, council can only address the matter at the next regular meeting. Councilor Lisa Ferry obliged and stood in objection, ensuring the delay.

Despite the two councilors objecting, Fountain scheduled a special meeting three days later to address the matter. The council remained deeply divided over the push to hire an interim solicitor. Detractors argued that rushing to appoint a predetermined candidate without reviewing a resume or conducting any vetting was a "disservice to the council and to the city department heads."

Proponents, however, focused on potential cost savings, as D'Agostino would not be receiving benefits. Notably, he also would not be receiving a contract. This unusual decision left councilors voting without even knowing the terms of his compensation, as no negotiations with D'Agostino had yet taken place.

That night, the council voted 5-4 to hire D'Agostino, securing his appointment by a narrow majority.

The abrupt push to hire D'Agostino appeared to be a political maneuver, particularly given the lack of prior discussion, making it seem orchestrated. Several factors at the time may have influenced this decision — one being Fountain's lawsuit against the city. He had filed the suit on behalf of his minor son, who had sustained an injury on city property during an afternoon program.

The lawsuit raised a troubling ethical issue. Fountain had repeatedly voted on hiring legal representation for the city while simultaneously suing it. Since the city solicitor — or the outside law firm — reported directly to the council, with Fountain serving as its chair, a clear conflict of interest emerged. How could Fountain justify voting on the entity responsible for defending the city against his lawsuit?

2017

January 5	Officer Sean Fountain is cleared to patrol unsupervised.
February 12	Lieutenant Gregory Gallant is promoted to Captain.
February 16	Police Chief Joseph Solomon signs a five-year employment contract with Mayor Stephen Zanni.
February 21	The City Council approves Solomon's contract and votes on litigation related to *Fountain v. Methuen*.
February 28-March 4	Solomon, Officer Joseph Aiello, and Lieutenant Kevin Mahoney attend the *National Conference on Bullying* in Orlando, Florida (event held March 1–3).
March 6	Gallant is formally promoted to Captain.
March 13	Solomon and Aiello, representing Eagle Investigative Services, Inc. (EIS), and the Foundation for School Safety, operate a booth and present *"Crisis Response Training"* at Gillette Stadium.
March 24	Solomon receives the *First Amendment Award* from *The Valley Patriot* for his support of body cameras and release of public information.
March 28	Solomon and former Deputy Chief Joseph Alaimo are sworn in as Essex County Deputy Sheriffs.
April 2-7	Solomon, Sergeant Kris McCarthy, Gina Scanlon, and Derek Licata attend the *SMILE Conference* in Long Beach, California.
April 8	The City Council approves a Home Rule Petition for Fountain.
April 19-20	Integrity Testing conducts assessment tests for the ranks of Police Lieutenant (April 19) and Police Captain (April 20).
April 24-25	Aiello and Officer Ronald Valliere attend Active Shooter Training in Rockland, Massachusetts.
April 26	Solomon and Aiello, as employees of EIS and the Foundation for School Safety, present *"Surviving an Active Intruder Incident"* at *MASSBUYS* at Gillette Stadium.
May	Mayor Zanni begins contract negotiations with all city unions.
May 2	Solomon's brother-in-law begins work as a laborer in the Department of Public Works (DPW).
May 5	The City issues a $10,000 check to Fountain's son as part of a legal settlement.
May 31-June 1	Solomon and Valliere attend the *Massachusetts Major City Chiefs Conference* in Falmouth, Massachusetts.

2017

June 2-5	Solomon and Valliere attend the *Major City Chiefs Retreat* in Falmouth.
June 4-22	Solomon attends the *Senior Management Institute for Police* hosted by the Police Executive Research Forum (PERF).
June 8	Solomon and Aiello form a new business entity, *International Association of School Resource Officers, Inc.* (not registered as a charitable nonprofit).
July 1	Fountain begins work as a "permanent intermittent" officer at the Methuen Police Department (MPD).
Abt. July 3	Solomon attends an undisclosed conference lasting six days.
July 10	With Zanni's approval, Solomon expands the number of Captains on the police force from three to five.
	The City Council approves the promotions of Lieutenants James Jajuga Jr. and Kevin Mahoney to Captain, Sergeant Joseph Aiello to Lieutenant and Officer Ronald Valliere to Sergeant
July 4	Sergeant Tod Himmer & Lieutenant Michael Wnwk retire.
July 17	A woman whom Solomon had pulled over in 2014 for suspected child abuse files a federal civil rights lawsuit.
July 22-30	Mahoney, McMenamon, Aiello, Havey Sr., Valliere, and Solomon attend the *National School Safety Conference* in Las Vegas (event held July 24–28).
July 27	Aiello is awarded the *School Safety Award* at the Las Vegas conference.
August 1	Governor Charlie Baker signs the Home Rule Petition for Fountain.
	The deadline passes to pull nomination papers for Mayor; James Jajuga Sr. is running unopposed.
August 7	City Council approves a Home Rule Petition for Jamie Atkinson to serve as a junior accountant in the MPD.
August 8-10	Solomon, Officer Michael Pappalardo, and McCarthy attend the *PERF Conference* in Washington, D.C.
August 12	Fountain retires from the North Andover Fire Department.
August 20-24	Solomon, Mahoney, McCarthy, and Gallant attend the *International Association of Chiefs of Police (IACP) Conference* in Philadelphia, Pennsylvania (conference held August 21–24).
August 31	The Superior Officers' Union contract is signed by Zanni and Gallant.
September 6	Solomon emails the Patrolmen's Union president with proposed contract language related to base pay.

2017

September 18	City Council approves police union contracts using the "Rule of Necessity."
	Solomon changes Fountain's badge number from I29 to P162.
September 29	Solomon delivers an EIS-sponsored workshop titled *"How to Survive an Active Shooter/Violent Intruder Incident."*
November	Solomon, as an EIS employee, presents *"Surviving an Active Killer Crisis Response"* at The Massachusetts Department of Fire Services.
November	Solomon, as an EIS employee, presents *"Surviving an Active Killer Crisis Response"* at The Massachusetts Operational Services Division.
November 16	The Massachusetts Ethics Commission initiates a preliminary inquiry into Thomas Fleming of the Methuen Police Academy for a possible conflict of interest.
November 26	Solomon transfers Fountain into the Criminal Investigation Bureau (CIB).
December 12	The woman from the 2014 traffic stop files a second federal civil rights lawsuit against Solomon.
December 13	Governor Baker signs the Home Rule Petition for Jamie Atkinson.
October 18	Solomon's lawsuit with the mother he pulled over in 2014 is settled out of court.
December 26	Gallant's son begins work as a laborer at the DPW.
	Jamie Atkinson starts as a junior accountant in the MPD.

The following memo was sent out from Solomon: "Effective January 5, 2017, at 1630 hours, the following temporary assignment will take effect: Intermittent Officer Sean Fountain had completed the Field Training Officer Program and was now eligible to work by himself on patrol." This development had occurred just over six months after Fountain had begun working at the MPD. At that point, Fountain had started performing patrols. It raised questions about the initial plan only to undertake private details.

A home rule petition had been necessary for Fountain to transition to full-time employment. This petition had required approval from the city council, the state legislature and the governor to waive the one-year rule for Fountain's employment as a 'permanent intermittent' police officer with the police department. Ideally, the city would have completed this process before his start date in July, but legal procedures were Solomon's forte when he was focused on achieving a goal.

February

With everything falling into place — a supportive mayor, a favorable council, and good public relations — the time was ripe for Solomon to set the next phase of his plan in motion: employment contracts.

Solomon's contract with the city was due to expire, prompting negotiations with the mayor beginning in early 2017. It didn't take long for both parties to sign the ten-page document and present it for council approval at their February 21st meeting.

This contract would be from March 1, 2017, to February 28, 2022. Right out of the gate the contract was already at odds with the city charter, which mandates that department heads' contracts be for three years, not five.

The contract presented an intriguing blend of items, beginning with a change in Solomon's title: Chief of Police, Emergency Management Director, and Harbor Master. While the first two roles were self-explanatory, the inclusion of Harbor Master raised eyebrows. The designation seemed perplexing given that Methuen is inland and lacks a harbor, with the closest one being in Newburyport about 18 miles away. Methuen also lacks a public dock or marina, featuring only a single boat ramp on the Merrimack River. Despite the newly created position, the document failed to specify any duties for the harbormaster role.

The first section of the contract outlines the duties of the police chief, all of which appear reasonable for the role: overseeing the department's operations, managing the budget, supervising weapons, equipment, and communications, organizing training programs, handling disciplinary matters, managing staffing, and any other duties reasonably assigned by the mayor.

The second section of the contract addresses the work hours, specifying that the chief's responsibilities entail a 24 hour-a-day, seven day-per-week schedule. It acknowledges that

Solomon's 2017 Employment Contract

2017

Solomon's Payroll Records

city official may call the Chief to respond to emergencies any time of day, night or week. It further states that the Chief agrees to devote the time and energy reasonably necessary. However, Solomon's commitments to his private business divide his time and loyalty, which may not align entirely with the expectation of round-the-clock availability for the City of Methuen.

Sections four, five, seven and eight of the contracts appear to be standard additions, covering indemnification for professional liability, dues for professional associations, protocol in the event of the chief's death during his term of employment, and discipline or discharge. These clauses are typically included in contracts across various professions to manage legal risks, maintain professional affiliations, and outline procedures for unexpected circumstances.

Section six of the contract addresses professional development, a crucial aspect for any police chief to stay abreast of the latest innovations and trends in law enforcement. However, as demonstrated in previous chapters, Solomon appears to have exploited this section for maximum personal gain. The contract stipulates that he will be permitted to attend various training conferences organized by reputable associations such as the Massachusetts Major Cities Chiefs, New England and International Chiefs of Police Association, and the three School Safety Advocacy Council conferences, with the city covering all associated expenses. Additionally, Solomon was entitled to budget and expense coverage for short courses, institutes, and seminars that he deemed necessary for his professional development. While professional development is essential, this section's generous terms may suggest exploiting resources for personal benefit.

Section nine of the contract outlines Solomon's compensation. According to Massachusetts law, police chiefs in departments with 30 or more permanent, full-time police officers must receive a base rate of compensation that is not less than two times the highest annual compensation rate of a permanent, full-time police officer in the department. In Solomon's contract, the ratio is 2.5 times the highest-paid permanent police officer until June 30,

2017

2017, and then increases to 2.6 times from July 1, 2017, until the city and Solomon agree on a new contract.

Additionally, Solomon built into the contract to receive the maximum of the following benefits: sick, vacation, personal, and bereavement days, holiday pay, longevity pay, educational incentive pay/Quinn Bill, uniform and cleaning allowance, health and life insurance, contractual time, training/seminar compensation time, hazard duty pay, and other benefits, as well as retirement buyback benefits including educational incentive/Quinn incentive, equivalent to those received by regular police officers of any rank in the city as of the execution date of the contract.

In addition to his salary and other ancillary monetary benefits, Solomon's contract granted him a "night differential" — typically an extra percentage of an employee's base rate for working a less desirable shift, usually at night.

Solomon earned an additional $366.39 per week in night differential pay. Annually, as a contract 24/7 employee, he was making an extra $19,052.28 per year for a shift he rarely worked.

As previously outlined, Solomon was entitled to receive the highest benefits of any MPD officer on the rolls. While the contract did not explicitly state this clause, Solomon took advantage of a provision in the patrolmen's contract that allowed officers, in addition to their annual longevity payment, to exercise an "additional" longevity stipend equal to 15 percent of their base weekly pay. The city paid this stipend to officers weekly for up to 52 weeks, but once an officer opted for it, they permanently forfeited their annual longevity payment. Consequently, only officers planning to retire or leave the department within the year typically chose this option.

In 2018, two officers utilized the additional longevity option — so Solomon also claimed his 15 percent. In addition to his base pay, he applied the 15 percent increase to his night differential and college incentive. These three components added an extra $840.34 per week, amounting to a staggering $43,697.43 annually.

For 2018 his earnings broke down as follows:

Base Earnings:
- Regular Pay: $158,769.00 annually
- Night Differential: $19,052.28 annually

2017

- College Incentive: $39,692.12 annually
- Regular Pay 15%: $31,895.87 annually
- Night Differential 15%: $3,827.59 annually
- College Incentive 15%: $7,973.97 annually

Total Base Compensation: $261,210.83

Additional Earnings:
- Longevity Payment – $21,893.00
- Clothing Allowance – $600.00
- Holiday Pay – $9122.67
- College Holiday Pay – $2,280.67
- End-of-Year Sick Buyback – $7,948.08
- Fitness Stipend – $1,200.00
- End-of-Year Sick Pay – $8,759.15
- 12/27/18: Cleaning Allowance – $1,000.00
- 11/29/18: Tech Compensation – $1,000.00
- Additional Cleaning Allowance – $1,100.00

Total Additional Earnings: $53,803.57

Total Base & Additional: **$315,014.40**

Comparative Analysis

To put these earnings into perspective, here is a 2018 statistical comparison of police salaries and department sizes:

Category	Boston	Methuen	Massachusetts State Police
Total Pay (Commissioner/Chief)	$319,319.93	$315,014.40	$200,602.69
Sworn Police Officers	2,144	98	2,500
Civilian Employees	569	16	611
Stations/Precincts/Barracks	11	1	39
Population Served	692,048	50,597	6.88 million
Department Budget	$395,000,000	$12,876,124	$388,575,833
Geographic Area	48.4 sq. miles	23.1 sq. miles	10,544 sq. miles
Crime Rate (per 100,000)	622.45	86.83	338.11
Homicide Rate (per 100,000)	8.06	0	1.97

This data highlights the striking disparity between Solomon's compensation and the scale of the Methuen Police Department compared to larger agencies, including the Boston Police Department and Massachusetts State Police.

Section ten of Solomon's contract pertains to providing a motor vehicle for the chief's use. The city was obligated to supply a police vehicle for the chief's professional and personal use, as he was on-call in case of emergencies.

However, it appears that the city provided Solomon not just one but two vehicles. The second vehicle, referred to as the 'red' one, was allegedly used by Solomon when he wished to smoke cigars. During snowstorms, he and the highway superintendent, who also served as one of his intermittent officers, would reportedly drive around 'inspecting' snow plowing operations while smoking cigars. Massachusetts General Law prohibits smoking in all state and municipal vehicles.

The remainder of the contract appears to be standard language that outlines terms and conditions beneficial to Solomon and the city.

Chairman Atkinson presented the contract by title at the city council meeting on February 21st. It was motioned to accept, seconded, and passed unanimously without discussion. The vote comprised five yes votes from councilors Tom Ciulla, Lisa Yarid-Ferry, George Kazanjian, Ron Marsan, and Jamie Atkinson. Three councilors abstained due to their relatives working under Solomon: Jajuga, Kannan and Vidler. Additionally, Fountain abstained from voting due to his employment with the MPD.

Fountain v. Methuen

As soon as councilors adjourned their meeting, the council reconvened in session to discuss the pending lawsuit, Fountain v. City of Methuen, which Fountain had filed on behalf of his minor son.

The incident had occurred in 2009 before voters elected Fountain to the council, but the lawsuit was not filed in court until 2015 – after his election. During an after-school program at one of the city's schools, the child had suffered a severe leg injury after cutting himself on a protruding bolt, requiring 38 stitches.

In 2016, when an *Eagle-Tribune* reporter questioned Fountain about a potential conflict of interest — or at least the appearance of one — given that he had voted to appoint the city solicitor on

2017

multiple occasions since filing the lawsuit, Fountain defended his actions. "My attorney filed that [lawsuit], and I disclosed it," he stated. "I filed on behalf of my son. He was a minor at the time. I have not been part of any negotiation. My attorney has been handling that."

However, the claim that he was not involved in the lawsuit negotiations seemed unlikely — at least until his son reached adulthood at the end of 2015. In what may have been just a coincidence, City Solicitor Kerry Regan submitted her resignation a little over a month after his son's birthday.

Notably, in the year and a half following his son's 18th birthday, Fountain never amended the lawsuit to reflect the son as the plaintiff; instead, it remained filed under Sean Fountain's name.

The executive session proved to be productive, as the two sides reached a settlement, and a few months later, the city issued a check for $10,000.

March

Following the retirement of Captain Kathy Lavigne — whether voluntary or quietly forced remains unclear — the Methuen Police Department initiated promotional assessments to identify her successor. Lieutenant Greg Gallant, a dependable ally of Chief Joseph Solomon, placed second in the evaluation, finishing behind Lieutenant Frank Korn. In keeping with demonstrated approach, he bypassed the top-ranked candidate and advanced Gallant instead.

On March 6th, Mayor Stephen Zanni and Solomon presented Gallant's nomination to the City Council. Present that evening were Chair Jamie Atkinson, Vice Chair George Kazanjian, and Councilors Ferry, Fountain, Jajuga, Kannan, Marsan, and Vidler. Councilor Tom Ciulla was absent.

Roughly forty minutes into the session, the council reached Gallant's appointment. A motion was made and seconded. Atkinson opened the floor for discussion, but no councilor spoke. When the vote was called, the result was telling: four votes in favor, four abstentions.

The silence in the chamber broke with a muttered "Oh God." Atkinson, visibly unsettled, turned to the clerk and asked, "What do we have to do?" The room grew uneasy. Mayor Zanni interjected, "You can't get it passed, there's nothing left." Fountain recalled, "We did the same thing last time." Off-camera, other voices added: "You need five votes." "Oh shit!"

A roll call was taken, but the tally remained unchanged: four in favor, four abstentions. The motion failed.

At that point, councilors shifted away from open deliberation and into strategy. Councilor Kannan raised the possibility of invoking the "Rule of Necessity," a rarely used maneuver for situations where recusals prevent a quorum. City Solicitor Rick D'Agostino hesitated, explaining that he would need additional time to research. Atkinson pressed on whether abstentions could be treated as non-votes rather than no-votes. D'Agostino, however, confirmed that the city charter required five affirmative votes. With that, Councilor Marsan called for a five-minute recess.

The camera feed shifted to a neutral view of a flag and window, but the microphones remained live. What followed was a revealing glimpse into how city business was actually conducted.

Zanni's voice led the discussion: "Is there any way we can get this done?"

D'Agostino began to caution that the rules were fixed in the charter, but Zanni cut him off: "Make it a necessity." The conversation turned to other strategies. Kazanjian suggested that if one councilor left the room, the math would change. "Then it's 4 to 3." Fountain agreed: "Right."

The group latched onto the idea. "If someone leaves the room, it's a majority of the room," Fountain reasoned. Marsan added that the vote could be reconsidered with seven members instead of eight. Though hesitant, D'Agostino eventually conceded, "I'm going to say we can probably get away with that."

Zanni summarized the plan: "He left. He is going to leave permanently. They are going to reconsider their vote — now they can vote. He's gone. If you go on to new business then go back to reconsider, you have a 4–3 vote. He's gone from the meeting."

We later heard Atkinson's voice off-camera, outlining the plan to someone out of view. When the meeting resumed, the council quickly moved through the remaining appointments before Councilor Marsan introduced a motion to reconsider Gallant's appointment.

During the subsequent roll call, the outcome shifted: four votes in favor, three abstentions. With Fountain's calculated absence removing the possibility of a tie, the motion appeared to pass as if legally valid. In truth, however, the vote remained invalid, as the city charter required five affirmative votes for approval.

Captured in the hot-mic recording was Zanni's remark: "Who's gonna appeal?" It laid bare the underlying mindset — compliance with the rules was secondary to achieving the desired outcome. The council had openly conspired to circumvent the charter, forcing through an appointment that had initially failed. In doing so, they betrayed the trust of taxpayers and the community they were sworn to serve.

This episode revealed several critical dynamics at play. The manipulation of the process showed that loyalty outweighed merit. Despite Korn's higher score in the assessment, Gallant's ties to Solomon ensured his advancement. The council's maneuvering demonstrated a culture where rules were obstacles to be navigated, not principles to be upheld. And the unanimous vote recorded that night created an illusion of legitimacy — masking the fact that the appointment had only been salvaged through deliberate subversion.

Meeting Video

The question lingered: why go to such lengths for Greg Gallant?

Part of the answer lay in the Methuen Police Department's transition in 2014 from civil service exams to an assessment center model. The first captain's assessment under this system drew only two applicants: Korn and Gallant. Korn placed first, Gallant second. Yet no captain promotion occurred for three years — until this meeting. Was it simply that Korn, though the higher-ranked candidate, was not part of Solomon's inner circle? Or were there truly no vacancies until now? If the latter, then why did Solomon hold the assessment at all?

Adding further context, Korn had served as president of the Superior Officers Union until early that year, when Gallant assumed the role. With Solomon's own lucrative contract tied to the terms of union negotiations, having a loyal ally like Gallant at the union helm strengthened his bargaining position and, ultimately, his financial interests.

Thus, Gallant's contested appointment as captain was not an isolated decision — it was a move with far-reaching implications.

2017

It represented the intersection of patronage, political maneuvering, and financial gain, and it would prove to be a pivotal moment in events yet to unfold.

April

Like Gallant's promotion, Methuen politics thrived on a culture of favors and exemptions — a system where rules bent easily for insiders, while ordinary residents were expected to play by the book. A clear example came with Councilor Sean Fountain's home rule petition, which surfaced on the City Council agenda for April 8th. The petition sought to sidestep the city charter's mandatory one-year "cooling-off" period, a safeguard designed to prevent elected officials from immediately converting political office into city employment. Fountain's request was straightforward: to bypass that restriction so he could serve as an intermittent police officer with the Methuen Police Department.

The Council voted 6–1 to adopt an Emergency Preamble (EPA), a procedural move that allowed them to bypass the standard two-meeting requirement and pass the measure in a single vote at a single session. Under both the Methuen City Charter and Massachusetts General Law:

> *"No measure shall be passed finally on the date on which it is introduced, except in cases of special emergency involving the health or safety of the people or their property."*

From a personal and professional standpoint, it's difficult to see how Fountain's early employment with the MPD qualified as any kind of emergency.

Following the passage of the EPA, Chair Atkinson proceeded to read the resolution number — TR-17-17 — but notably omitted reading the full title aloud: "Resolution Submitting a Home Rule Petition for the Purposes of Waiving Certain Provisions of Methuen Home Rule Charter: Article 2, Section 2-5." This section

Fountain's Home Rule Petition

explicitly states that no sitting City Councilor may hold another paid position within the city government and that former councilors must wait one year after leaving office before accepting a paid city appointment — unless returning to a previously held position.

Atkinson's failure to read the resolution's title aloud breached council protocol and served to obscure the resolution's true purpose from the viewing public – whether it was deliberate is unknown. The act of waiving the cooling-off period for an elected official — particularly one like Fountain, a firefighter who had never served as a police officer and was over the age limit for new police hires — was bound to raise serious concerns among Methuen taxpayers.

After the routine motion to accept and a second, the resolution passed unanimously — seven votes in favor, none opposed, and no discussion whatsoever. The city then forwarded the petition to the State House for further action.

Beyond the procedural issues, the move created the strong suggestion of a quid pro quo. This action unfolded during ongoing contract negotiations involving Solomon and upcoming police union contracts, casting doubts over the council's motivations.

At this juncture, it seems clear to me that Solomon wielded a level of influence over the City Council that made it impossible for the body to make objective decisions.

It is worth noting that Councilor Lynn Vidler was absent from this meeting — perhaps a prudent decision, given the controversial nature of the proceedings.

May

Councilor James Atkinson

In the fiscal year 2018 Methuen budget, a new junior accountant position, paying $64,951, was quietly added to the police department roster. At the May 30, 2017, budget workshop, Solomon justified the need for this role, explaining that he handled

2017

the department's finances and required someone with expertise in financial management and public administration to take over those responsibilities. At that time — and ever since — no other city department besides the schools had a dedicated "accountant."

Two days later, the city council approved the entire city budget during a meeting that lasted a mere 12½ minutes. Passing the whole budget without opening the document or discussing its contents — an unprecedented departure from standard practice. Historically, the council had meticulously reviewed each department's budget line by line, deliberating over potential cuts before voting on each department's personal service and other expense categories and then approving the budget. A process that took several nights to accomplish.

The new police department accountant position was posted on the city's website and at City Hall for just one week. James "Jamie" Atkinson, the sitting council chair, was the sole applicant. Atkinson's resume listed five years as a cell phone salesman and a decade as a real estate agent. He held a Bachelor of Arts in Communications and Media Studies, and a master's degree in business administration, but his resume did not include any accounting or business experience.

One of the department captains interviewed Atkinson, after which Solomon and the mayor offered him the position. When questioned by the local newspaper, Atkinson stated that the job "seemed like a good opportunity and right up [his] alley." Solomon defended the hire, saying Atkinson "has the background" and "more degrees than we would have required" for the job. Notably, there was no evidence that Atkinson ever worked in accounting or a related field.

As with Fountain, Atkinson required a legislative exemption to bypass the city charter's one-year cooling-off period for council members seeking employment with the city. A Home Rule petition was filed and placed on the city council's August 7 agenda. That evening, the council voted 6–1 in favor of the petition, with Councilor Ciulla casting the sole opposing vote. Atkinson and Fountain abstained and left the room during the vote.

City Solicitor D'Agostino opined no conflict of interest existed until the legislature acted on the petition. If the legislature declined the petition, the city would rescind the job offer. However, if

2017

approved, Atkinson would be required to abstain from voting on police-related matters.

As the petition progressed through the Legislature, the Senate introduced an amendment requiring Atkinson to resign from the council before starting the job. The House and Senate approved the measure, and Governor Baker signed it into law on December 13, 2017.

When exemptions become the rule, the law itself loses meaning. Every exception carved out for insiders widened the gap between the public and their government, reinforcing the belief that the system served power — not the people.

July

With two councilors now seemingly beholden to him, Solomon shifted his focus to the rest of the council. To ensure his proposals passed smoothly, he would need a majority, five out of nine votes — or preferably a supermajority of the council under his influence. A supermajority means a proposal needs more than just half the votes to pass — it requires a higher level of support, in this case six votes. In a democracy, supermajority rules can protect minority rights by making it harder for a simple majority to make significant changes.

Solomon's quickest and most effective way to achieve this was by leveraging the police department to offer promotions to the family members of councilors employed by the MPD.

With the MPD's departure from using State Civil Service promotional exams and eligibility lists for superior officers, the city adopted a private alternative: Donovan and Stanley's assessment center, Integrity Testing. This shift granted Solomon significantly greater flexibility in influencing promotional outcomes. Unlike the standardized and regulated civil service process, officials could more easily shape assessment center results to align with internal preferences — allowing Solomon to steer promotions to serve his broader agenda.

The beneficiaries included Vidler's husband, Dan O'Connell, a patrol officer; Jajuga's son, James Jr., a lieutenant; and Kannan's son, William, a patrol officer.

2017

Councilor Jennifer Kannan

Sometime between January and September 2017, Solomon assigned Kannan's son William to the elite detectives' unit — a coveted position that Solomon could grant or revoke at his discretion. Being elevated from patrol officer to detective brought substantial benefits: increased pay, the privilege of wearing street clothes, potential access to a take-home vehicle, and the prestige associated with the position. For many, it was a career-defining opportunity that sets them apart from their peers.

Councilors James Jajuga, Sr. and Lynn Vidler

On July 10, 2017, the city council considered promotions for two veteran officers: James Jajuga, Jr., a 16-year MPD veteran, for Captain, and Vidler's husband Dan O'Connell, a 12-year veteran, for Sergeant. That same day, with Zanni's approval, Solomon increased the number of MPD captains from three to five. The move facilitated the promotions of Jajuga Jr. and one other lieutenant.

That evening, the council also approved the promotion of three officers from Solomon's inner circle: Lieutenant Kevin Mahoney to Captain, Sergeant Joseph Aiello to Lieutenant, and Officer Ron Valliere to Sergeant.

Addressing the council and the mayor, Solomon attributed the promotions to the city's growth, stating, "With how much our city has grown over the past few years, it has required us to create more positions and move some people up in rank, and I really appreciate that we've had all this support." He praised the newly promoted officers for their initiative and described their advancements as "well-deserved."

Due to conflicts of interest stemming from their family member's employment with the MPD, Councilors Jajuga, Fountain, Kannan, and Vidler abstained from voting on any police appointments that evening. The remaining councilors unanimously approved the promotions.

Dressed in suits, the newly promoted officers sat prominently in the front row of the council chambers, receiving a standing ovation from the council and some audience members. A formal

2017

pinning ceremony followed later that evening at the police station.

Solomon solidified favor with four council members by orchestrating these promotions and leveraging Fountain's sporadic council votes, even if their conflicts of interest precluded them from casting votes on police appointments. This left three council votes still in play, keeping the balance of power within reach.

Solomon further consolidated power over the city council through Atkinson's appointment and his broader strategy. By leveraging conflicts of interest and legislative loopholes, he limited the council's ability to influence police department matters — or did he?

Conventions

Conventions and trade shows provide professionals with important opportunities to refine their skills, stay current on industry trends, and explore emerging tools and technologies that can enhance their effectiveness. Law enforcement is no exception. Each year, numerous policing and public safety conferences take place across the country in major destinations such as Las Vegas, Miami, Reno, Atlantic City, and Palm Springs. These events often focus on timely topics including school safety, use of force, social media, crisis response, and anti-bullying strategies.

Solomon had a particular enthusiasm for these events — so much so that his employment contract guaranteed city-funded attendance at multiple annual conferences. These included the Massachusetts Major Cities Chiefs Association, the training conferences of both the New England and International Associations of Chiefs of Police, and all three annual conferences hosted by the School Safety Advocacy Council (SSAC).

While professional development is undeniably important, concerns arise when such travel becomes excessive — especially during a time of fiscal crisis or when it appears to serve personal rather than professional interests.

In just 2017 and 2018, Solomon attended at least 19 separate conferences at the city's expense. Each trip required hotel stays and, in most cases, airfare. Over those two years, Solomon spent a total of 108 days away from Methuen — an average of 54 days per year, equating to nearly 11 full workweeks annually, or roughly one-fifth of the working year. Although not all receipts were available, verified travel expenses during that time totaled $28,465.39.

Solomon rarely traveled alone. He was often accompanied by at least one member of his command staff — typically Joseph Aiello — and, on many occasions, by multiple colleagues and even their spouses. Collectively, his accompanying staff logged an additional 208 days away from the city over two years, costing Methuen taxpayers at least another $76,027.04.

And that's not the whole story. The absence of senior staff members triggered "out-of-grade" pay for subordinate personnel temporarily filling their roles. On one notable trip, four of the department's five captains accompanied Solomon. According to reports, the chief even instructed them to park their city-issued vehicles behind the station to avoid drawing attention to their prolonged absence.

One example highlights the majority of the questionable nature of these trips: the National School Safety Conference & Exposition, held at the Hard Rock Hotel and Casino in Las Vegas from July 24–28, 2017. On the morning of July 22 — two days before the conference began — Solomon, his wife, newly promoted Captain Kevin Mahoney and his guest, Sergeant Thomas McMenamon, newly promoted Lieutenant Joseph Aiello, Sergeant Michael Havey Sr., newly promoted Lieutenant Ron Valliere, and Valliere's wife boarded a flight from Boston to Las Vegas.

Several issues emerge upon examining the details of this trip. While Solomon, Aiello, and Mahoney — who were senior staff overseeing the school resource officer (SRO) program — had a clear connection to the conference, the remaining officers did not. Ironically, Sergeant McManamon's wife, an actual SRO, did not attend. The entire group arrived two days before the event began, with the city covering hotel accommodations for all six officers and their guests, along with the standard $40-per-day meal allowance for each officer during this pre-conference period.

It is common for conferences to open with limited programming on the first day — typically a late afternoon exhibitor showcase followed by an evening networking event. Similarly, the final day

2017

of most conventions often end around noon to accommodate same-day travel for attendees.

A review of Solomon's travel records from 2017 and 2018 reveals a consistent pattern: he routinely arrived one to two days before an out-of-state conference began. His departure date, however, varied widely — sometimes leaving on the final day, other times a day or even two days after the event had ended.

For the 2017 National School Safety Conference in Las Vegas, Solomon's hotel receipt ends on July 28 — the day the conference officially concluded. The receipt includes a handwritten total that matches the amount for which he was reimbursed, though the hotel folio lists a scheduled checkout date of July 29. He also claimed one fewer day of per diem meal allowance compared to the rest of the group. Due to the absence of the return flight information in city records, it is unclear whether Solomon and his wife left early or remained in Las Vegas beyond the date covered by his reimbursement.

The rest of the group, however, did extend their stay by an additional night, departing on the evening of July 29 — well after the conference had ended at noon on July 28. Rather than taking a red-eye flight back to Boston that night, they waited until 9:30 p.m. the following day. This gave them a full day and a half of leisure time after the conference had concluded, all at taxpayer expense. When combined with their early arrival, the group effectively received three and a half days of city-funded vacation time in Las Vegas — alongside their invited guests.

The travel and hotel expenses associated with the 2017 Las Vegas conference were only the tip of the iceberg. Social media activity from the period reveals a deeper, more troubling narrative — one that suggests a significant overlap between public responsibilities and private business interests, particularly involving Solomon and Aiello.

As previously noted, Solomon was a business partner in EIS alongside Joe Alaimo, and both Ron Valliere and Joseph Aiello — who attended the conference in question — were employed by EIS either during or following their time with the Methuen Police Department. Adding to the ethical concerns, Solomon and Aiello had, within the two months leading up to the conference, established a new private entity: the New England Association of School Resource Officers, Inc. (NEASRO). The pair would go on to rebrand the organization as the International Association of School Resource Officers (IASRO) in September 2018.

In May 2017, two months before the Las Vegas event, the SSAC began promoting the upcoming conference through posts on both their official and personal social media accounts. Several of these posts featured NEASRO by name and even highlighted its logo. One such post read:

"The School Safety Advocacy Council is pleased to support and welcome the NEASRO... We welcome their board to the National School Safety Conference in Las Vegas, July 24–28, 2017."

This public acknowledgment raises red flags. While the City of Methuen was footing the bill for Solomon and Aiello to attend the event as municipal employees, the conference simultaneously spotlighted their private organization. The blending of official travel with promotion of personal business ventures represents a serious conflict of interest and calls into question the appropriate use of taxpayer funds.

The second day of the conference opened with a formal ceremony and the presentation of the National School Safety Awards. Both Solomon and Aiello received awards during the event. Immediately following the ceremony, the SSAC posted a congratulatory message on social media:

"Congrats to the New England School Resource Officers Assoc. SSAC is your partner and looks forward to our future!"

This message left little room for interpretation — there was a clear and public alignment between SSAC and NEASRO, the privately owned business of Solomon and Aiello. The implication was unmistakable: city funds were being used to support and promote their personal business interests under the guise of professional development.

To the public back in Methuen, however, the story was presented quite differently. Shortly after receiving his award, Solomon posted a close-up of it on the official Methuen Police Department Twitter account, which read:

> "Presented to Chief Joseph Solomon, Chief of Police (Methuen, MA) for your outstanding dedication to keeping students, staff, and schools safe."

2017

While this was a legitimate award presented to a public official attending a professional event, the handling of a second award later that day raised more serious concerns.

That evening, another tweet was posted from the MPD's official Twitter account. It featured a photo of Aiello holding an award beside the SSAC Executive Director Curt Lavarello, accompanied by a caption that read:

Solomon's Award

> *"Congrats Lt. @JAiello 4 receiving @SSAC9111 award 4 outstanding contributions to #SchoolSafetynationwide #Methuen @NEASROinfo @cityofmethuen"*

This post raised several red flags. First, Solomon used the MPD's official social media to tag and promote @NEASROinfo — the Twitter account for his and Aiello's privately owned business — effectively using a city platform for private business promotion. Second, a close-up of the award itself revealed that Aiello was not the actual recipient. The award, labeled the "Presidential Citation Award," was issued to the *New England Association of School Resource Officers* — not to Aiello personally. The reason cited: "outstanding contributions to the 2017 National School Safety Conference and [unintelligible]-wide School Safety." This recognition was awarded to a private business that had only been formally formed and registered with the Massachusetts Secretary of State a mere 47 days prior to receiving the honor. It struck us as particularly odd that Solomon and Aiello's business opened its doors just over a month before they received the award — well before they had accomplished anything that could reasonably justify such recognition. Even more questionable was the fact that there hadn't been sufficient time to follow any standard nomination, review, or vetting process typically required for such honors.

Upon returning to Massachusetts, Solomon leveraged the public relations firm retained by the MPD to issue a joint press release with Mayor Zanni regarding Aiello's award. The release, which was subsequently picked up by several media outlets, misleadingly stated in its opening paragraph that "Lt. Joseph Aiello was awarded the 2017 National School Safety Award,"

2017

implying that he had received the conference's top individual honor.

The press release included a glowing quote from Zanni, expressing pride in Aiello's achievement and celebrating his presence on Methuen's police force. This was followed by two paragraphs outlining Aiello's education, credentials, and professional background. Solomon himself was quoted as saying:

> "Lt. Aiello's decade of school safety training and experience has elevated him to a nationally recognized expert in school safety and security. His vision and knowledge make him a sought-after lecturer and trainer, and his dedication to school safety is a major asset to the City of Methuen."

However, the facts tell a different story. The award in question was not granted to Aiello personally, but to the *New England Association of School Resource Officers* (NEASRO) — the privately owned business he co-founded with Solomon just weeks before the conference. This deliberate reframing appears to have been a strategic move to enhance Aiello's professional reputation, using city resources and public trust to build credibility that could later be leveraged for the private venture's marketing and membership recruitment.

NEASRO's Award

Indeed, additional context reinforces the connection. On NEASRO's (now IASRO's) membership page, under the sign-up form, it reads:

"Regular Member – in partnership with the School Safety Advocacy Council, membership is free for the first year."

This language directly reflects the "partner" reference made in SSAC's earlier congratulatory tweet, which had raised initial concerns about the blending of private and public interests.

It is also worth noting that Sean Burke, president of the SSAC, is a retired police lieutenant from the neighboring city of Lawrence, Massachusetts. Burke's personal ties to both Solomon and Aiello add yet another layer of concern. His home is located in such close proximity that his front windows overlook the headquarters of EIS, while his backyard borders Solomon's

2017

property. These intertwined personal, professional, and geographic relationships further obscure the boundaries between public duty and private enterprise. As late as the 2019 National School Safety Conference, SSAC and the IASRO — Solomon and Aiello's rebranded organization — continued to publicly promote their "partnership."

One final observation regarding the 2017 SSAC conference: despite Solomon's well-known fondness for public recognition, it is notably curious that the press release — and all related media coverage at the time — omits any mention of the award he personally received. Aside from Solomon's own tweet immediately following the ceremony, there appears to be no formal acknowledgment of the recognition, which was ostensibly awarded to the Methuen Police Department. Given his tendency to highlight accolades, the absence of any public emphasis on this particular award raises questions about why it was downplayed or omitted altogether.

A year later, in May 2018, at the SSAC's School Safety Leadership Academy — where both Solomon and Aiello were featured speakers — Solomon received yet another honor. The event, with travel and expenses again funded by the City of Methuen, included a presentation of a plaque recognizing the Methuen Police Department's contributions to school safety awareness.

"Nothing is more important than the safety of our children," Solomon said during the ceremony.

This marked Solomon's fourth award from the School Safety Advocacy Council — two linked directly to his private ventures (EIS and IASRO) and two ostensibly tied to his public role with the Methuen Police Department. When adding in Mayor Zanni's earlier 2015 award, Methuen had, by that point, received five SSAC honors.

It raises an obvious and pressing question: how does a city of fewer than 50,000 residents, attending a national conference with more than 1,400 participants and a far broader membership base, walk away with such an outsized share of the accolades?

The optics become even more questionable when considering that Solomon had recently joined the SSAC as a member of its advisory council. This most recent award, presented while he was an insider in the very organization bestowing it, blurs the lines between merit-based recognition and strategic self-promotion. It suggests the potential use of public office and public funds to elevate private stature under the guise of professional achievement.

Since 2013, Solomon and his subordinate, Aiello, had regularly presented seminars at national conferences — most frequently at events hosted by the SSAC. Among the topics they covered were Law Enforcement Response to Students on the Spectrum, Law Enforcement, Schools & Community Partnership, The Role of Social Media in Cyberbullying, Developing Your School Safety Protocol, and Responding to Social Media and Its Impact on Campus.

What remains unclear is the capacity in which these presentations were delivered. Were Solomon and Aiello acting as representatives of the City of Methuen in their official roles, or were they leveraging these appearances to promote their private ventures — EIS and the IASRO? Or, perhaps, all of the above?

Social media posts from EIS and IASRO during that period suggest that some presentations were credited directly to their private enterprises, even though they were publicly funded by the City of Methuen. For example, a March 7, 2018 post on EIS Inc.'s Facebook page read:

> *"Presenting at the School Safety Advocacy Council National #Bullying Prevention Conference. Presenting on Law Enforcement Response to Students on the Spectrum Disorder. Joe Solomon JD Pinski Joe Aiello."*

Even more telling was a December 7, 2018 Facebook post from the Executive Director of SSAC:

> *"SSAC is pleased to have Mr. Joe Aiello, Executive Director of the International Association of School Resource Officers, about to speak at the National School Safety Leadership Academy here in Palm Springs, CA. Joe will address community partnership that focus on school safety."*

This deeply problematic overlap between public duty and private enterprise blurred ethical boundaries to such a degree that it became nearly impossible to discern whether these efforts were truly in service to the City of Methuen, or if they were thinly veiled promotional opportunities for Solomon and Aiello's personal business ventures. The lack of transparency and the conflicting narratives surrounding their dual roles raised serious questions — and legitimate concerns — about the appropriate use of public resources.

Reimbursement

In city government the procurement process contains many checks and balances. In Methuen city government, that has not always been their strong point.

While reviewing Solomon's travel and reimbursement records, a number of red flags emerged. Until 2020, the City of Methuen did not issue departmental credit cards, no petty cash accounts, no procurement cards. That meant officials like Solomon often used their personal credit cards for city-related expenses: flights, hotels, meals, even coffee for meetings. They would then submit receipts for reimbursement.

On paper, the system seemed harmless. In practice, it created an unchecked loophole, one that blurred the lines between public funds and private gain.

In 2011, Solomon submitted just $1,265 in reimbursements. By 2017, that figure had skyrocketed to $48,623, a staggering increase of nearly 3,750 percent. And it wasn't just for his own travel. Solomon regularly paid for other officers' expenses, whether or not he was on the trip. The city reimbursed all of it, no questions asked.

This method of spending, routed through a personal credit card, came with an added perk rarely reflected in a city ledger: cash-back rewards. With typical credit card incentives averaging around two percent, Solomon likely pocketed nearly $1,000 in personal rewards, earned entirely off taxpayer-funded purchases. Was it legal? Technically. Ethical? Absolutely not.

And that may not be where it ended.

As we've documented elsewhere in this book, Solomon frequently blurred the lines between his public role and private business ventures. According to records reviewed by our team, there is reason to believe he may have been reimbursed twice for

2017

certain expenses — once by the city and again by his private consulting firm, EIS.

Unlike ordinary income, payments from EIS were categorized as reimbursements. That meant they were tax-free to Solomon — and tax-deductible for EIS. If true, a single $10,000 expense could, in theory, yield a triple benefit: reimbursed by the city, reimbursed again by EIS, and written off as a business expense. Lending further credence to this theory, we found hotel receipts submitted to the city bearing the return address for EIS.

We cannot definitively prove that double reimbursement occurred. But as any seasoned fraud investigator will tell you: evidence points the way. And what we found was compelling enough to refer the matter to the IRS Criminal Investigation Division (IRS-CI). Members of our investigative team, myself included, were interviewed several times. Yet more than a year later, the IRS has taken no public action. Still, we remain hopeful the paper trail won't be ignored forever.

Even absent confirmation of double-dipping, the sheer volume of Solomon's reimbursements — paired with personal financial gain, questionable vendor relationships, and zero oversight — reveals a larger pattern: a public servant who found ways to profit from the very city he was sworn to protect.

By 2019, the state stepped in. A Chief Administration and Finance Officer (CAFO) was appointed to bring order to the city's finances. One of the first moves? Shut down the reimbursement abuse. The following year, Solomon's expenses dropped to just $4,000, a fraction of what they once were. The faucet had finally been turned off.

As a fraud examiner, Solomon's reimbursements raise glaring red flags. One in particular stands out: if, as the evidence indicates, he's collecting airline miles and credit card rewards, getting reimbursed by the city, and possibly by one or both of his businesses — all off the same receipt — and then using that same receipt as a tax write-off through the business? That's not just unethical. It's tax evasion, fraud, and perjury. These are the very kinds of financial crimes that brought down figures like Al Capone — when nothing else would stick.

Because in the end, it's not always the violent offenses that bring a man down. Sometimes, it's the quiet fraud he assumed no one was watching.

2017

August

The new fiscal year kicked off on July 1 — and with it came a quiet but controversial milestone: it was Fountain's first official day as a full-time intermittent officer with the Methuen Police Department. The move should have raised eyebrows, especially since the home rule petition meant to authorize his employment hadn't even cleared the State House. It would be another month before it passed the Legislature and reached the governor's desk for a signature.

Many mistakenly believed the petition retroactively legitimized Fountain's employment. It didn't. All it did was waive a provision in the City Charter requiring former city councilors to wait one full year after leaving office before taking a paid position with the city. The problem? Fountain had been paid for details – through the City, as an intermittent officer since 2016.

Despite the petition still awaiting approval, Chief Solomon went ahead and bumped Fountain's pay grade — from intermittent to *master patrolman*. The promotion didn't just defy logic; it violated the union's collective bargaining agreement and gave Fountain a salary he hadn't earned. Technically, he still wasn't even authorized to wear the badge.

Once the petition was finally signed into law, Solomon wasted no time. Fountain was suddenly credited with 16 days of sick leave and 40.5 days of "contractual time" — allegedly to cover "unpaid hours" worked before the law took effect. It was a creative stretch of policy that handed Fountain benefits far beyond what any average city employee could expect.

Then, in rapid succession: Solomon issued a personnel order formally naming Fountain a full-time intermittent officer. Three days later, Fountain clocked out of his firefighter job in North Andover — for good.

At the end of August, the *Eagle-Tribune* ran a story on the home rule petition. Solomon told the reporter that Fountain's appointment as "permanent intermittent" was the first of its kind in the department's history. At that time, the MPD employed 70 patrol officers, 23 reserve officers, and 20 intermittent officers. Reserve officers were selected from the civil service list and were awaiting full-time appointments and academy placement. Of the 20 intermittent officers, three were working full-time. However,

2017

Solomon categorically denied that any of them were "permanent." He described most intermittent officers as part-time workers, typically covering for full-time officers on leave. He added that city council usually reappointed the officers every three years — an exception he claimed Fountain would not require, thanks to the home rule petition.

In the same article, City Solicitor D'Agostino referenced the Acts of 1945, which established Methuen's unique legislation for an intermittent police force. He stated that the "intent was for permanency," asserting that "no one is really temporary" on the police force. He argued that all intermittent officers should be considered permanent intermittent officers.

Solomon disagreed. He claimed his interpretation of the Acts differed and maintained that Fountain's case was unique. He asserted he would continue reappointing other intermittent officers every three years unless otherwise directed.

As previously mentioned in this book, *The Acts of 1945* clearly stated in its opening paragraph that an intermittent officer could not be used unless no regular or reserve officers were available.

Anyone who had carefully read the law would have recognized that the full-time employment of Fountain and the three other intermittent officers directly violated its provisions. At the time, reserve officers — already selected through civil service — were available and actively waiting for full-time appointments.

The law also outlined specific steps that must be followed when employing an intermittent officer. First, the appointing authority was required to contact the director of civil service to certify that no permanent or reserve civil service officers were available to fill the vacancy. Additionally, if an intermittent officer were to fill such a vacancy, the appointment could not exceed a total of thirty days.

No requisition had been made to the director of civil service. Had there been one, the director would have undoubtedly informed Solomon that the city was required to use reserve officers before resorting to intermittent officers — and that no intermittent officer could serve for more than thirty consecutive days. By 2017, however, three full-time intermittent officers had already served for several years and would continue to do so.

Nowhere in the Acts of 1945 was there any mention of three-year reappointments, as Solomon claimed. D'Agostino came closer to interpreting the statute correctly when he referred to the word "permanent" in the context of the "permanent intermittent police force." However, his interpretation incorrectly suggested that "permanent" applied to the officer's position rather than to the structure of the force itself.

It was baffling that no one in Human Resources flagged the improper use of intermittent officers – especially given that the HR Director also served as Assistant Solicitor. D'Agostino may have only skimmed the Acts of 1945 when responding to the *Eagle-Tribune*, either choosing not to read the acts or failing to read them thoroughly.

Just five weeks later, Solomon issued another personnel order. Effective September 18, he changed Fountain's badge number from I29 to P162. The "I" denoted Intermittent, while the "P" signified Patrol — a designation reserved for full-time, academy-trained civil service officers. So, what was Solomon doing reclassifying Fountain as a patrolman, bypassing the formal requirements tied to that title?

September

With his employment contract secured, Solomon set his sights on negotiating the agreements with the Superior Officers Union and the Patrolmen's Union. If managed shrewdly, these negotiations could potentially yield significant financial gains for him.

During the preceding spring and summer, the Methuen Superior Officers Association and the city met to negotiate a new labor contract. Representing the superior officers were Captain Greg Gallant, who served as President, and Lieutenant Joseph Aiello, who acted as Vice President. On the city's side, the negotiating team included Zanni, D'Agostino, Assistant City Solicitor/Human Resources Manager Anne Randazzo, and inexplicitly Chief Solomon himself. City officials made feeble attempts to justify Solomon's involvement by claiming he was merely offering "police expertise," but this rationale demonstrated a troubling ignorance of Massachusetts General Laws. Chapter 268A, Section 19 clearly states that all municipal employees are to be excluded from participating in matters in which they have a direct financial

2017

interest — precisely the situation Solomon put himself in, as the negotiations directly affected his future salary.

Unless Solomon had submitted a full written disclosure and received explicit written authorization from his appointing authority, Mayor Zanni, his participation in the negotiations was a clear violation of the law. The City later confirmed there was no disclosure. This made his involvement not only illegal and ethically indefensible, but also a telling indication of Solomon's blatant disregard for legal principles.

More strikingly, two attorneys were present — Randazzo and D'Agostino — both of whom, by virtue of their positions and legal expertise, had a professional and ethical duty to flag this clear violation. Their failure to act not only enabled Solomon's unlawful participation but also raises serious questions about their own judgment, accountability, and complicity.

It's also important to note that every state, county, and municipal employee in Massachusetts is required to complete an online ethics training program administered by the State Ethics Commission — both upon hire and every two years thereafter, since 2008. Given this mandatory training, every individual present during those negotiations should have been fully aware of the legal and ethical implications of Solomon's involvement — especially Solomon himself.

In 2017, every city union was at the bargaining table. Mayor Zanni, facing mounting pressure to keep the budget in check, proposed a modest cost-of-living increase: 0 percent for fiscal year 2018, followed by 2 percent raises in each of the next two years, a pattern known in union circles as "0-2-2." It became the standard offer for all contracts, including the Superior Officers Union. And on paper, the union accepted it.

Base pay, not the percentage raises, was the real prize for the Superior Officers. That's what the Union set its sights on.

Unlike most of the city's unions, the police union's salaries are not a static number. They are built in layers, starting with base pay, then stacked with incentives: night shift differentials, rank differentials, holiday pay, uniform allowances, education bonuses, longevity pay, even a stipend for wearing their

Superior Officers' Union Contract

2017

bulletproof vests. All of which was calculated as a percentage of base pay. So, when you manipulate the base, everything else balloons.

And that's exactly what they did.

Patrolmen Union Contract

As negotiations progressed, the Superior Officers Union successfully secured a change in how base pay was calculated in discussions with Zanni. Under this new arrangement, the contract would now incorporate holiday compensation, uniform allowances and the protective vest stipend by rolling it into the base pay. This adjustment — later referred to as "artificial base pay" by the Inspector General's Office — folded the previously separate bonuses into base salary, dramatically inflating overall compensation and future retirement calculations.

The numbers climbed fast. If a sergeant's base pay was inflated, so was the lieutenant's — since theirs was calculated as a percentage of the sergeant's. Then the captain's rose, pegged to the new lieutenant figure. Each step up the chain was like climbing a staircase built on quicksand.

The union didn't stop there.

They proposed a new formula for holiday pay: not just 1.5 times base pay, but 1.5 times artificial base pay plus education incentives. And then, incredibly, they wanted that inflated holiday pay amount added back into base pay for future calculations. This wasn't a raise. It was a financial black hole.

Some members of the city's bargaining team raised concerns. "Where's the cost analysis?" some asked. But Zanni didn't want to slow things down. Instead, he ordered Solomon — yes, the very man whose salary would skyrocket from these changes — to draft the new language for one of the sections himself.

Then came a flood of last-minute additions. The uniform allowance jumped from $1,800 to $2,400 and was rolled into base pay. A new Narcan/hazardous duty stipend? Added to base pay. Specialty pay for detectives and school resource officers? They'd now be paid the next highest rank's base salary. A lieutenant working as a detective would earn captain's pay. Just like that.

And to ensure the language couldn't later be disputed, City Solicitor D'Agostino took the unusual step of asking the union

2017

president, Gallant, to write the final version of the contract along with Solomon's one clause. Incredulously, D'Agostino didn't even request a copy before it went to the council.

The union ratified the deal on August 30 and the final contract was given to the mayor's office for signature. Solomon returned it with a note claiming Zanni wanted one small revision to reflect the agreed 0-2-2 raises. Gallant made the change and handed it directly to the mayor.

Zanni signed it without reading a word.

The contract was then submitted to the city council clerk, just in time for the September 18, 2017 meeting. This was critical. It was an election year, and under state law, no increases in employee salaries could be approved in the final three months of a lame-duck term. September 18 was the council's last legal chance.

There was just one problem: they didn't have the votes.

Approving labor contracts required a two-thirds majority, six out of nine councilors. But five of them had direct conflicts of interest. Jajuga, Vidler, and Kannan had family members in the department. Fountain worked for the MPD. Atkinson had already been promised a job once his council term ended.

At a previous meeting, Councilor Kannan raised the question of whether the "Rule of Necessity" could be invoked — a seldom-used exception that allows disqualified officials to vote when too many conflicts prevent a quorum. At the time, the city solicitor gave a vague response, and no official opinion was issued, until this meeting.

According to the Massachusetts Ethics Commission, the Rule of Necessity is meant for rare situations when a board cannot legally conduct business because too many members are disqualified due to conflicts of interest. In such cases, otherwise ineligible members may temporarily participate, but only when it's legally essential, not just because the board wants to move forward.

Strict procedural steps must be followed:

- The board must publicly state the reason for invoking the rule, citing the conflict-related disqualifications.
- Each affected member must disclose the facts behind their disqualification on the public record.
- The board must demonstrate that action is legally required and that invoking the rule is the only option available.

2017

These safeguards are in place to ensure transparency and to prevent misuse of the rule as a matter of convenience.

At this particular meeting, Solicitor D'Agostino advised that the council could, in fact, invoke the Rule of Necessity. The council formally did so just before voting on the two police collective bargaining agreements.

Although the agreements were open for discussion, no councilor raised questions or sought input from the city auditor regarding potential budgetary impacts. Nor did the solicitor mention that he had not reviewed the agreements himself.

The council proceeded with a unanimous vote in favor of both CBAs.

Once the meeting adjourned, the council reconvened just 15 minutes later for a special session. Chairman Atkinson announced that, because all agreements needed to be passed by the end of the month, they would "do the second read today. We'll get it done now so councilors don't have to take time on another day."

But the city charter is clear:

"No measure shall be passed finally on the date on which it is introduced, except in cases of special emergency involving the health or safety of the people or their property."

No such emergency was declared, and the police agreements clearly did not meet this threshold — making the action a violation of the city charter.

Rather than correcting this procedural misstep, Solicitor D'Agostino instead focused on the so-called "lame-duck" rule, insisting the vote needed to occur before the end of the month.

The pay increases outlined in both contracts directly impacted Chief Solomon's salary and benefits — catapulting him into the ranks of the nation's highest-paid police chiefs.

By 2018, Solomon's total compensation, including benefits, reached $310,533.89. The following year, it climbed even higher to $326,707.

To put that into perspective: according to *The Business Journal's* ranking of the 20 highest-paid police chiefs in major U.S. cities, Solomon was just $39,000 shy of matching the salary of the Los Angeles Police Commissioner — the top spot on the list. And unlike many on that list, Solomon didn't lead a major metropolitan force.

2018

January	MPD begins participating in the development and testing of the BOLO Mobile app.
January 2	James Jajuga Sr. is sworn in as Mayor of Methuen.
March 2	Chief Joseph Solomon and Officer Joseph Aiello, as employees of Eagle Investigative Services (EIS), present *"Surviving the Active Killer, Crisis Response Training"* at Rhode Island College.
March 5-10	Solomon and Aiello attend the *National Conference on Bullying* in Reno, Nevada (conference held March 7–8) and present *"Law Enforcement Response to Students with Spectrum Disorder."*
March 6	The Superior Officers' Union files a class-action grievance with the City over the police contract.
March 19	Aiello and Officer David Gardner, representing MPD, conduct an Active Shooter Training session at St. Monica's Church.
March 24	Aiello and Gardner conduct a second Active Shooter Training session at St. Lucy's Church.
March 27-29	Solomon and Sergeant Ron Valliere attend the Massachusetts Police Accreditation Conference.
April 5	Mayor Jajuga sends letters to all police unions warning of layoffs if a resolution to contract issues is not reached.
April 17	Mayor Jajuga makes his first public disclosure about the growing controversy surrounding the police contracts.
April 24	Jajuga delivers his *State of the City* address.
May 1	Aiello and Officer Derek Licata, representing MPD, conduct an Active Shooter Training session at First Baptist Church.
May 2-5	Solomon and Aiello attend the *School Safety Leadership Academy* in Sarasota, Florida (event held May 3–4) and present *"Law Enforcement, Schools, and Community Partnership."*
May 2	Solomon and Aiello receive the *Award of Excellence* from the School Safety Advocacy Council.
May 9-10	Solomon, Aiello, and Alaimo, as EIS employees, participate in *MASSBUYS* at Gillette Stadium and present *"How to Survive an Active Killer/Violent Intruder Incident."*
May 17	The Massachusetts Ethics Commission finds Thomas Fleming guilty of violating conflict-of-interest laws during his time as director of the Methuen Police Academy.

2018

May 20-24	Solomon, Licata, Gina Scanlon, and Captain Gregory Gallant attend the *SMILE Conference* in Miami, Florida.
May 23-25	Solomon and Valliere attend the *Massachusetts Major Cities Chiefs Conference* in Falmouth, Massachusetts.
May 28-June 2	Solomon and Sergeant Kris McCarthy attend the joint conference of the *Major Cities Chiefs Association (MCCA), the New England Institute of Art (NEIA),* and *PERF* in Nashville, Tennessee (conference held May 29 – June 1).
June 13	The City Council eliminates the junior accountant position in the MPD as part of the FY2019 budget.
July 1	Jamie Atkinson is removed from her position at MPD and reassigned to the City Clerk's office.
July 18	The Superior Officers' Union signs a Memorandum of Understanding (MOU) with the City.
July 19	City Council votes to cut $1.8 million from the police personnel budget.
July 22-27	Solomon, Mahoney, Aiello, and Valliere attend the *National School Safety Conference* in Orlando, Florida (conference held July 23–27).
July 26	City Council tables the vote to ratify the Superior Officers' MOU.
August 2	Mayor Jajuga commits to pay the Superior Officers at the MOU rate without Council approval.
August 8	Jamie Atkinson is removed from the Clerk's office position.
August 13	The Patrolmen's Union board meets with Solomon.
August 18	Thomas Fleming resigns as Director of the Methuen Police Academy; Sergeant Dan O'Connell is named his successor.
August 20	Officer David Souther, President of the Patrolmen's Union, files three grievances with Solomon.
August 21	Souther is temporarily reassigned from the Detective Unit back to Patrol.
September 4	Solomon travels to Washington, D.C., to participate in a *Time Magazine* cover shoot for their "Guns in America" issue.
September 14	City Auditor Tom Kelly retires.
September 17	City Council meeting draws a large crowd of police officers and family members, all urging support for the Superior Officers' MOU and against department reorganization.
Sept. 18-20	Solomon attends the *Massachusetts Chiefs of Police Association (MOCPA) Conference* in Norwood, Massachusetts.
September 27	Intermittent Officer Matthew Despins files a lawsuit against the City.

2018

October 3-11	Solomon, Captain Randy Haggar, Mahoney, McCarthy, Gallant, and Aiello attend the *International Association of Chiefs of Police (IACP) & School Safety Active Shooter Conference* in Orlando, Florida.
November 7	Souther meets with Solomon to request reinstatement to the Detective Unit.
December 2-12	Solomon takes part in a 10-day trip to Israel, paid for by the Anti-Defamation League.
December 19	Officer Souther files a formal complaint with the Massachusetts Department of Labor.

January

On January 2, Mayor Zanni concluded his final term, and James P. Jajuga — former state trooper, state senator, Secretary of Public Safety, lobbyist, Methuen city councilor — took the stage at Methuen High School to be sworn in as Methuen's fifth mayor.

One of Jajuga's first actions as mayor was to appoint two of his former legislative aides to positions on the city payroll: one as Chief of Staff and the other as an administrative assistant.

Few expected any real change, as Jajuga had run unopposed throughout the mayoral race yet managed to raise $63,563 in campaign contributions for a position that paid only $80,000 annually. At least $5,850 of that amount came from police-related sources — along with an additional $200 from Solomon's close associate, Richard Stanley. Over the next two years, despite not seeking re-election and never facing an opponent, Jajuga collected another $95,904 in contributions during his single term in office — $20,525 of which, more than a fifth, came from police-related donors. Keep this in mind as you follow the events of 2018–2019.

Along with a new mayor, the majority of the city council was serving for the first time. In addition, the makeup of the council was markedly different from its predecessor — women held the majority for the first time, occupying five of the nine seats. Another first was the infusion of a younger generation into city leadership: four of the new councilors were under the age of 30. Historically, the council had been dominated by members aged 50 and older, with only the occasional representative in their 40s.

This new configuration signaled a clear message from residents at the ballot box — they were ready for change.

2018

Take Home Vehicle

Not long after settling into office, Mayor Jajuga began arriving at City Hall in a brand-new, blacked-out Chevy Tahoe. Traditionally, the city provided leased vehicles to Methuen mayors for use during their term — Mayor Zanni had driven a Jeep, and Mayor Pollard before him had used a Mercury Mountaineer. Jajuga's Tahoe, however, came from the police department fleet, much like the vehicle used by former Mayor Manzi — although, in Manzi's case, it had been an older Chevy Impala cruiser.

Massachusetts municipal vehicles, apart from unmarked police cars, are typically outfitted with distinctive blue municipal plates and display the city seal on the doors. Jajuga's Tahoe had neither, raising eyebrows around City Hall. Critics of Solomon claimed the vehicle was a gesture meant to curry favor with the new mayor. Supporters, however, defended the move, believing Solomon when he said a detective had requested the old mayor's Jeep, thinking it would attract less attention.

Solomon told the *Eagle-Tribune* that the Tahoe was simply an exchange for the Jeep and noted he would have allowed the mayor to use any vehicle from the department's fleet. "The mayor's the mayor — he gets a new car," Solomon said. As a veteran and former law enforcement officer, I can attest that real leaders prioritize their people. They'd give the better vehicle to someone on the front lines. Solomon's comment reveals his true view of leadership: to him, rank comes with privileges.

When asked by the *Eagle-Tribune* about the vehicle exchange, Mayor Jajuga claimed he was unaware of the arrangement. He said he simply received a call instructing him to return the Jeep and pick up the Tahoe. According to Jajuga, he never specifically requested the Tahoe — it was merely the vehicle provided to him by the police department. "Quite frankly, I didn't even question it," he said. "But I can tell you that... I feel it's appropriate for the mayor. I drive in all kinds of weather, and when something bad happens — during all the storms — I go out to the emergency operations center."

Despite Jajuga's explanation, the facts told a different story. The Tahoe had been purchased by the police department as one of four high-end vehicles acquired the previous October, each costing around $49,000. It was a four-wheel-drive SUV outfitted with tinted windows, running boards and a luxury package. If a detective had truly found the former mayor's Jeep to be more discreet, it raised an obvious question: why had Solomon authorized the purchase of the Tahoe in the first place?

It's worth noting that his son, MPD Captain James Jajuga Jr., also received an identical Chevy Tahoe in his capacity as a ranking officer.

March

Several months earlier, a disturbing incident at a Methuen church had deeply shaken its congregation. It was enough to prompt concern among parishioners and clergy. In coordination with another local church, the congregation reached out to the MPD, requesting guidance on how to respond to a worst-case scenario involving an active shooter — an increasingly common fear in places of worship across the country. The department trained all its officers to handle such situations as part of their standard tactical preparation.

In response, Officer Joe Aiello and another MPD officer organized and conducted two community sessions on March 19th and 24th. The presentations, titled "Active Shooter Response Training," were held inside the churches and attended by members of both congregations.

Programs like these — focused on preparedness and public safety — are broadly seen as a valuable service and something every municipality should strive to provide. In interviews with the *Eagle-Tribune*, Solomon emphasized that MPD had already conducted similar trainings at all of Methuen's public and private schools, the local Islamic center, and several nonprofit organizations. He also noted the department's interest in extending the training to local businesses but cited a lack of resources as a barrier.

At face value, Solomon's remarks seemed to reflect a commitment to public safety. But in hindsight, they appeared to echo a familiar pitch for EIS — the private company co-founded by Solomon and Alaimo. EIS listed "Active Shooter Response Training" as one of its core service offerings and actively marketed it to schools, businesses, and public agencies throughout New England.

Just three weeks before the Methuen church sessions, Solomon and Aiello had traveled to Rhode Island College to deliver a training session under the EIS banner titled "Surviving the Active Killer: Crisis Response Training." Records show that this was not a one-off event; Solomon and Aiello had conducted the same program on at least six separate occasions during 2017 and 2018 as representatives of their private company.

The close timing between the Rhode Island EIS event and the MPD-sponsored church sessions raised serious ethical concerns — especially given that the structure and content of the presentations were strikingly similar. As with their earlier school safety initiatives, Solomon and Aiello once again appeared to be leveraging their public positions to bolster the credibility and visibility of their private consulting venture. This overlap blurred the line between public service and personal gain, prompting questions about potential conflicts of interest, misuse of department resources, and the ethical integrity of their dual roles. While the community may have benefited from the training themselves, the motivations behind them — and the intertwining of official duties with private enterprise — suggested a troubling pattern that warranted closer scrutiny.

April

At the April 17th City Council meeting, Mayor Jajuga publicly acknowledged that the city was in trouble, serious financial trouble. And for the first time, he publicly named the culprit: the police union contracts. After weeks of tiptoeing around the issue, he now admitted the city would need an additional $1.2 million just to fund the terms of the agreements.

For a while, there had been no obvious signs of strain. The contracts had been cleverly structured to front-load a zero percent raise in the first fiscal year. But in preparing the budget for the upcoming fiscal year, the second year of the contract all the embedded perks, compounded bonuses, and artificially inflated base pay figures kicked in. That's when the real damage began.

Jajuga expressed frustration, recalling his time as a city councilor — back when he and his colleagues had voted to approve the very contracts now jeopardizing the city's finances. He recalled they were assured by officials that the deals were just a standard "0-2-2" raise structure and insisted they had no reason to question it. He then turned his criticism toward the prior administration, saying it failed to provide required financial impact statements. Without those, he argued, the council had no way to see the fiscal burden they were now shouldering.

But here's what Jajuga left out: every single councilor — himself included — had the power and opportunity to hit the brakes. They could've asked for a cost breakdown. They could've tabled the vote. They could've read the actual contract, 31 pages of fine print that would bind the city for years. Instead, they steamrolled it through during a lame-duck session, with no real scrutiny and no understanding of the long-term consequences.

To his credit, Jajuga didn't sugarcoat the mess. "I don't know what happened, I don't care what happened," he told the council. "It is my responsibility as the mayor of this city to fix this." He revealed he had already called on both police unions to return to the table for renegotiation.

Jajuga later told a *Boston Globe* reporter that it wasn't anyone in Methuen who first flagged the problem, it was the mayor of Haverhill. He had called Jajuga in alarm, saying his own police unions were eyeing Methuen's contract language and preparing to demand the same. A few days later, he called back again. The message was blunt: "You guys are in deep trouble." If another city could figure it out in days, why hadn't anyone in Methuen seen it coming?

Ethically, Jajuga had no business trying to fix the mess in the first place. His own son, Captain James Jajuga Jr., was one of the biggest beneficiaries of the sweetheart deal. Any attempt by the mayor to renegotiate the contract raised immediate conflict-of-interest concerns.

Still, Jajuga tried to make sense of what had happened. "It was the way the language was written," he said. "I can tell you, it was very craftily done. Very. It was very difficult. I don't know who did it, but whoever did it was a very bright, bright individual." It was a telling statement: a former state police officer, state senator, secretary of public safety, city councilor and now mayor, publicly admitting he couldn't understand the contract he had voted to approve.

Councilor Steve Saba wasn't satisfied with that explanation. He turned to City Auditor Tom Kelly, an employee of the council, not the mayor and asked a simple question: "How did this happen?"

Kelly's response only made things worse.

He explained he wasn't involved in negotiating these contracts, an odd departure from standard practice, since he had always been the one to provide financial analysis for collective bargaining agreements. When the finalized contracts were finally sent to him, Kelly said he immediately spotted red flags. He claimed that he brought his concerns to Mayor Zanni — who ignored them. Kelly said he also tried to warn two councilors, who likewise did nothing. The contract appeared on the following Monday's agenda. By then, the damage was already done.

But Kelly's answers rang hollow. If he had always been part of these negotiations, why was he left out now? And if he knew the contract was problematic, why didn't he notify the rest of the council, the very people who supervised him? Why didn't he speak up publicly at the council meeting when Mayor Zanni confidently assured everyone that the deal was just "0-2-2"?

To this day, Kelly has never publicly or privately explained his silence or named the two councilors that he warned to no avail.

Faced with a financial implosion, Jajuga sent a letter to the police unions on April 5th warning that the contract increases would force painful budget cuts. If they couldn't find a solution, layoffs would be the only option. Days later, his Chief of Staff, Paul Fahey, gave an interview to the *Eagle-Tribune* to explain the "enhanced benefits" buried in the contract.

They weren't small. On the patrol side, officers were receiving new technology stipends that started at $1,000 and rose to $3,000, plus "step raises" of up to $5,100 for veterans with over 30 years of service. And that was just the bottom of the pyramid.

Each rank up the ladder was pegged to the last: sergeants earned 134 percent of the top patrolman's base, lieutenants earned 118 percent of sergeants, and captains earned 118 percent of lieutenants — and Chief Solomon? His base salary was pegged at 260 percent of the highest-paid patrolman. Every dollar added at the bottom rippled upward like a tidal wave.

Solomon v. Kelly's interpretation of the Superior Officers' Contract

And yet the city had only calculated the minimum impact. They were still trying to decode the full financial scope — after the contracts were already in effect.

Union President Captain Greg Gallant confirmed they would listen to the mayor's concerns, but reiterated the deal was negotiated in good faith over months with the city's top brass, including the city solicitor, the chief of police, and the human resources director. When pressed, he offered no further comment and referred questions to the union attorney.

The following week, Mayor Jajuga delivered his "State of the City" address, marking his first 100 days in office. It didn't take long for him to address the elephant in the room — the police union contracts. He confirmed that both unions had agreed to meet, but warned residents that if the contracts weren't reworked, Methuen would be forced to slash services.

When reporters asked Chief Solomon for comment, he conveniently claimed he had taken a phone call during the portion of the speech where Jajuga addressed the contract crisis. He declined to discuss it, saying, "Whatever [Jajuga] chooses to speak about is his purview."

Police Innovations

As previously discussed, Solomon had demonstrated a longstanding passion for police technology and innovation. He took pride in positioning the MPD at the forefront of law enforcement trends — often striving to be the first in the state to acquire the latest gadgets and devices. This approach earned the MPD a reputation as an early adopter of cutting-edge tools.

There appeared to be no limit to the equipment the department accumulated — some of it standard, much of it excessive — including boats, bicycles, motorcycles, jet skis, ATVs, and even an RV outfitted as a mobile command center. The range of innovations Solomon pursued was extensive, including tasers, body cameras, license plate readers, drones, ballistic helmets, and even an underwater search-and-rescue vehicle.

2018

In 2020, an independent audit of the department raised concerns about this procurement strategy. While officers had been issued new and advanced equipment, much of it remained underused. At the same time, basic necessities — such as patrol cruisers — were aging and frequently in need of replacement.

Auditors commended the department's leadership for their enthusiasm for emerging technologies but criticized them for failing to thoroughly evaluate the practicality and necessity of such purchases. In some cases, this led to increased costs for training and maintenance. In others, the equipment proved impractical or ill-suited for the department's needs and was largely unused.

Interviews conducted during the audit revealed that Richard Stanley, a former police chief who had transitioned into a sales role, introduced many of these acquisitions. Officers reported that department leadership seemed more interested in the publicity and novelty of being early adopters than in whether the tools served a real operational purpose.

One prominent example was the MPD's participation in the 2016 pilot of BOLO Mobile — an app named after the police acronym for "Be On the Lookout." The program eventually evolved into the widely adopted BOLO app, which enabled law enforcement to instantly share information and photos of wanted or missing individuals. MPD formally implemented the app in May 2018, and over the next two years, Solomon became one of its most visible advocates. He provided endorsements on the company's websites and appeared in multiple media interviews. In one such FOX News segment — on a network that frequently featured Solomon — Stanley appeared alongside him, having become a part-owner of BOLO just two months earlier. The city purchased use of the app in March 2019 for $2,000.

The app was just the first example of Stanley representing a product later purchased by the city. Another involved dictation software designed to allow officers to compose reports verbally while in the field or driving. According to multiple officers interviewed by both the auditors and our firm, the software was cumbersome and largely ineffective. Many believed the purchase had more to do with Solomon supporting a friend than meeting the department's needs.

2018

Other acquisitions linked to Solomon's professional circle included a shooter detection system purchased in 2014 and the GPS Dart System acquired in 2016. In a FOX News segment on the latter, Solomon appeared in an interview while Sergeant Ron Valliere — a close colleague — demonstrated the system during a staged vehicle pursuit. In the segment, Valliere fired a GPS dart from his cruiser that successfully attached to a suspect vehicle. The concept aimed to reduce the dangers of high-speed pursuits by allowing officers to disengage and track suspects remotely.

However, results in practice were inconsistent. In one instance shown in the same interview, a dart failed to adhere to the target vehicle. Additional footage from a FOX affiliate in Atlanta showed two failed deployments that resulted in a crash. MPD officers reported that while the concept was promising, the technology frequently malfunctioned, with darts often failing to stick. Nonetheless, the city paid $15,550 for the system in 2019 — three years after its initial acquisition. The reason for the delayed payment remains unclear.

Ultimately, it was impossible to determine how many of the department's purchases resulted in commissions for Stanley, his company, or any other "friend of Solomon." Yet even a few such transactions represented a serious conflict of interest. While employed by Stanley's assessment firm, Solomon awarded contracts that directly benefited someone with whom he had a financial relationship.

Equally troubling was Solomon's blatant promotion of police-related products.

In Massachusetts, police chiefs and other public officials are subject to strict ethical, statutory, and policy constraints that significantly limit their ability to endorse commercial products. Such endorsements pose serious risks — including conflicts of interest, misuse of official authority, and violations of established ethics standards.

The first concern is the misuse of position. By publicly identifying himself as a police chief in news segments or promotional videos, Solomon leveraged his official role for private commercial gain, an action that may constitute a clear abuse of power.

The second issue is the appearance of a conflict of interest. Even if Solomon received no direct compensation, his endorsement alone raised red flags. Should the department later purchase or seek funding for the product he endorsed, his impartiality — and by extension, the integrity of the procurement process, could reasonably be called into question.

The Massachusetts Ethics Commission has consistently warned public officials against providing endorsements. Their advisories emphasize that such endorsements can unfairly influence the marketplace, create the perception of government approval of a private product or service, and erode public confidence in the integrity of government. Officials are expressly cautioned against using their titles, uniforms, badges, or department resources in connection with private promotional activity.

Solomon appeared to disregard these rules entirely. He repeatedly used Methuen Police Department personnel, equipment, and even the station itself to film promotional content for companies from which his department would later purchase products. Many of these segments were filmed in his office, with Solomon in uniform and the MPD logo prominently displayed behind him.

Some might argue that local news segments highlighting the department's new equipment don't count as endorsements. But in reality, they still constituted the use of public resources for promotional purposes. These appearances gave the featured companies an unfair advantage through free publicity, courtesy of the taxpayer, and served as informal advertising for Solomon's associates.

June

The newly seated Methuen City Council, reeling from the discovery of a $4 million overspend by the School Department and excessive raises within the police department, came under immediate pressure to reduce the fiscal year 2019 budget wherever possible. One of its cost-cutting measures was the elimination of funding for a recently created junior accountant position in the police department — a role held by former councilor Jamie Atkinson.

To retain his employment with the city, Atkinson, a member of the AFSCME union, invoked his seniority rights, commonly known as "bumping rights." Under the union's contract,

2018

qualifications were irrelevant; the employee with the least seniority was to be displaced. At the time, that employee was a clerk in the Parks and Recreation Department — ironically, the son of former Mayor William Manzi. However, for reasons not publicly explained, he was not the one bumped. Instead, the city moved down the seniority list and displaced the second-least senior employee: a principal clerk in the Treasurer/Tax Collector's office. City officials reassigned Atkinson to her role.

Sources inside City Hall later told a local reporter that the city had exercised some discretion in Atkinson's reassignment, basing the decision on job classification and his relative qualifications. On July 1st, when the new budget took effect, Jamie left the police station and began reporting to City Hall.

Around that time, a new voice had emerged in Methuen's local media landscape: Loop Weekly. Named after the local shopping plaza, The Loop, and playing on the phrase "keeping in the loop," the publication quickly established itself with a bold, investigative approach — starkly contrasting with Tom Duggan's Valley Patriot. While Loop Weekly's critical coverage of the Methuen Police Department made it difficult to attract advertisers, it ushered in a new era of transparency and accountability in local journalism.

Although not a Methuen native, Loop Weekly founder Tim Wood had moved to the city with his family in the summer of 2016. He quickly immersed himself in the city's politically charged atmosphere, where residents eagerly shared stories of Methuen's colorful history and ongoing drama. Despite being a newcomer, Wood embraced the community and hoped to make Methuen a long-term home for his family.

When news broke of Atkinson's reassignment, Loop Weekly and other local outlets reported on the situation, the public backlash was swift and intense, prompting Wood to dig deeper — particularly into a special Home Rule Petition that had authorized Atkinson's initial appointment.

The investigation uncovered a critical flaw. While Jamie had used union seniority to secure a role in the Treasurer's office, the Home Rule Petition that enabled his reemployment had included

Atkinson's Home Rule Petition

a specific condition: he could bypass the mandatory one-year cooling-off period only to serve as a junior accountant in the police department. By accepting a clerk position in another department, Atkinson had violated the very terms that had made his return to city employment legal.

Before publishing his findings, Wood consulted several municipal attorneys. Their consensus was clear: Atkinson would have needed a brand-new Home Rule Petition — requiring city council approval, followed by passage by the state legislature and the Governor — to take on a different role within city government legally. The attorneys also noted that, despite union provisions, state law superseded any contractual "bumping rights" under such circumstances.

After alerting city officials to these findings, Wood posted online that the officials appeared surprised by the petition's language — suggesting they had never reviewed it before reassigning Atkinson. In response, the city tasked Solicitor D'Agostino with reviewing the matter and recommending next steps.

The following morning, after just one month in the new position, Atkinson was terminated. City officials promptly reinstated the displaced employee.

But the matter didn't end there. On January 1, 2019, Solomon rehired Atkinson. With the City Council having defunded the junior accountant position, Solomon needed to place him elsewhere. Conveniently, the role of confidential secretary to the police chief had recently become vacant. That position was later expanded to include the duties of the department's records clerk. Atkinson remained in the role until shortly after Solomon's retirement in 2021.

In the aftermath, a coordinated campaign took shape — driven by Solomon's allies and supporters of mayoral candidate Neil Perry — focused on discrediting Wood and trying to force *Loop Weekly* out of business. Combined with the financial strain of the COVID-19 pandemic, the pressure became overwhelming. From the earlier incident of gasoline being poured into his car to this sustained smear campaign, the toll was too great. Wood and his family ultimately left Massachusetts — and have not looked back since.

The City Budget

By April 2018, Mayor Jim Jajuga had planned to finalize and submit his first city budget to the Council. Instead, he found himself teetering on a fiscal precipice — caught between the competing demands of the police department on one side and the school department on the other.

The school department had overspent its previous budget by $4 million and was now demanding an additional $10 million in funding. That alone would strain any municipal budget, but when combined with the inflated police contracts, it created a recipe for financial disaster.

As the first figures from the police contracts emerged, Jajuga scrambled to bring the unions back to the table. His objective was modest: align their salary increases with those accepted by other city unions, 0-2-2 percent over three years. The unions, however, showed little interest. The Patrolmen's Union agreed to one meeting. The Superior Officers? Their silence was deafening.

In June, the administration presented its proposed FY2019 city budget in a detailed, line-by-line spreadsheet. For each department, it listed actual prior-year expenditures, FY2018's adopted budget, department head requests, and the mayor's final recommendations. But there was a catch: under state law, the City Council could only cut funding, they had no authority to reallocate or add line items.

All eyes quickly turned to one section of the budget, police salaries. The numbers painted a stark picture:

Rank	FY2018 Personnel	FY2019 Requested (Solomon)
Chief	1	1
Captain	3	5
Lieutenant	7	7
Sergeant	12	12
Patrolmen	71	71

2018

	Chief	Captain	Lieutenant	Sergeant	Patrolmen
FY2015 Actual	$134,381	$309,634	$623,018	$1,065,191	$3,577,292
FY2016 Actual	$140,318	$327,342	$723,130	$1,033,697	$4,044,743
FY2017 Actual	$153,455	$355,922	$689,037	$1,050,471	$4,186,917
FY2018 Adopted	$158,769	$324,354	$657,531	$963,902	$4,377,955
FY2019 Solomon Requested Budget	$221,085	$775,748	$1,000,125	$1,115,55	$4,408,406
FY2019 Mayor's Budget	$185,43	$602,28	$703,35	$1,011,13	$4,306,97

Solomon defended his budget request, claiming it reflected his negotiating goals rather than what he actually expected to secure. The mayor slashed $700,000 from the initial request, yet even the revised figures were staggering.

Superior Officers' Union President Greg Gallant told the *Eagle-Tribune* he never presented Solomon's proposal to his membership. Still, he maintained that the union cared about the city's financial health. But as the standoff continued, it became clear that caring and compromising were two very different things.

Fueling the controversy was Solomon's request for two new captain positions — by far the rank with the most dramatic salary increases. One of those positions, perhaps not coincidentally, was earmarked for the mayor's son, James Jajuga Jr. Despite the conflict, the mayor approved the request. This would be the second time that Jajuga gave his son a significant monetary perk – the first was in 2017 with voting for the exorbitant superior officers' contract and now with a promotion.

It's remarkable — and troubling — how the conflict was allowed to play out so openly. Back in 2017, then-Councilor Jim Jajuga was well aware of his conflict of interest when voting on the controversial police contract that directly benefited his son. Despite this, City Solicitor D'Agostino erroneously advised that the Rule of Necessity could be invoked, and Jajuga took advantage of it — even though he wasn't legally required to vote. Fast-forward to his tenure as Mayor, and Jajuga made a deliberate decision to create a new captain's position — fully aware that the promotion would go to his son. What began as a questionable vote evolved into an outright act of self-dealing.

Solomon, who stood to gain significantly from the contract terms, repeatedly inserted himself into budget discussions under the pretense of his role as department head. In truth, his involvement represented a glaring conflict of interest. If the contracts remained intact, Solomon's total compensation was projected to reach a staggering $371,520.

When Attorney Gary Nolan, representing the Superior Officers' Union, learned that the city might not fully fund the contract, he issued a pointed warning to the City Council. In a May 31 letter, Nolan invoked Massachusetts wage laws and threatened triple damages if payments were withheld. "Any suggestion that the city was hoodwinked by so-called crafty language is not supported by the facts," he wrote. "This was a transparent agreement negotiated by both sides."

But "transparent" wasn't how the newly seated 2018 Council saw it. Having only been sworn in that January, most were blindsided by the financial tsunami about to engulf the city. Yet their shock only underscored a harsher truth: the real failure had occurred months earlier. The 2017 Council — which included several members still holding office — along with then-Councilor-turned-Mayor Jim Jajuga, had both the opportunity and the obligation to prevent the crisis. Instead, they did nothing. They rubber-stamped bloated contracts, failed to ask the hard questions, and ignored warning signs. Now, Jajuga — one of the architects of the problem — stood as mayor, scrambling to manage the chaos he helped create.

With a June 30 deadline looming, the Council slashed $1.3 million from the proposed budget, nearly half of it from one line item: captain salaries. Councilor Eunice Zeigler called it what it was — a message to the mayor: go back to the table and fix this mess.

Meanwhile, as the city's finances deteriorated, political contributions surged. As we stated previously, Jajuga raised over $63k pre-election, in the six months since he took office, Jajuga raised an additional $50,185 in campaign donations — nearly $11,000 of which came from police officers or their family members. That averaged $495 in contributions every single day, more than double his mayoral salary. Notably, the money dried up the moment Jajuga began publicly criticizing the police contracts.

The sudden stop in contributions wasn't just a political message — it foreshadowed the battles to come. Money had set the stage, but now the real fight would play out in budget negotiations where millions, not just campaign checks, were at stake.

Former Mayor Steve Zanni attempted to distance himself from the fallout, claiming he hadn't known the full cost of the contracts when he signed off on them. He shifted the blame to the negotiating team, particularly City Auditor Tom Kelly. But Kelly told a different story. He said he had warned Zanni and flagged concerns to two city councilors. Why he didn't inform the entire Council remains one of the great unanswered questions. As a direct employee of the Council, Kelly had a fiduciary duty to sound the alarm, and he didn't.

Unable to move money from the police budget to cover additional school costs, the Council rejected the proposed budget and returned it to the mayor. Their message was unambiguous: renegotiate and deliver a working, functioning budget for upcoming fiscal year 2019.

Two months had passed since Jajuga first sounded the alarm. Since then, only one formal meeting had taken place with the Patrolmen's Union, and just a couple of informal conversations with the Superior Officers. That was the extent of the progress.

Public confidence was unraveling. Residents couldn't tell who was stalling, Jajuga, the unions, or both. Councilors warned that approving a flawed budget without addressing union costs could leave the city legally exposed.

One thing was certain: Methuen couldn't meet the schools' needs, fund the police contracts as written, and remain solvent.

Reflections: Governance by Conflict

Methuen's budget crisis wasn't just about money — it was about conflicts of interest hiding in plain sight.

As a councilor, the mayor approved measures that directly benefited his own family. The police chief pushed budget,

2018

requests from which he personally stood to gain. And campaign donations flowed from those who stood to profit, drying up the moment resistance appeared.

This wasn't governance; it was self-dealing dressed up as public policy. Oversight bodies' rubber-stamped contracts, ignored warnings, and abdicated their duty to protect the public. By the time the truth surfaced, the damage had already been done.

The lesson is clear: corruption doesn't always wear a disguise. Sometimes it stands at the podium, cloaked not in secrecy but in procedure, relying on the confidence that no one will challenge it.

July

It wasn't until mid-July, after months of budget gridlock, political posturing, and growing public outrage, that the mayor's office and the Superior Officers' Union finally reached a supposed breakthrough.

The result was an eight-page Memorandum of Understanding (MOU), pitched as a compromise to correct the grossly inflated 2017 contract. On paper, the MOU promised savings for the city. In practice, it remained wildly generous, especially by the standards of ordinary taxpayers who were footing the bill.

The MOU

To illustrate the disparity, consider the case of a Methuen police captain:

Police Captain Salary Comparison
Pre-2017 Salary — $157,052
2017 "Stacked" Salary — $440,735
2018 MOU Proposed Salary — $191,460

Even after a 57 percent reduction from the inflated 2017 figure, the new salary was still nearly $35,000 higher than the original base — an increase of 22 percent. In any other setting, that might spark debate. In Methuen, it set off fireworks.

2018

Captain Greg Gallant, president of the union, made his position clear in an interview with the *Eagle-Tribune*: if the City Council rejected the MOU, the union would simply revert to the original contract, the one that triggered national headlines and threats of bankruptcy. He insisted the revised salaries could be implemented within the department's existing budget and urged the Council to do "the right thing."

Councilor Steve Saba didn't see it that way.

Before even seeing the document, Saba signaled resistance. Then after reviewing the MOU in full, his skepticism hardened into disgust. Responding to the *Eagle-Tribune* reporter, he called it "absolutely horrendous" and "very selfish," zeroing in on one particularly offensive clause: if the Council made *any* cuts to police personnel line items, the MOU would be void, automatically reinstating the original, exorbitant contract terms. In effect, the clause turned a budget negotiation into a hostage situation.

On July 19th, the Council gathered to approve the full FY2019 budget and, hopefully, move beyond the temporary 1/12th funding plan that had kept the city on fiscal life support. But with the Superior Officers' contract still unresolved and the MOU not even officially presented for a vote, the Council took a bold step.

They slashed $1.825 million from the police personnel budget.

This was not a random cut. The number was calculated to represent the cost, salaries and benefits included, of eliminating two captains, four lieutenants, and six sergeants from the department's upper ranks. They couldn't directly assign the cuts by law, but they made their intention unmistakable.

The backlash was immediate. Gallant accused the Council of violating the MOU and made it clear the union would not offer any more concessions. "We are absolutely unwilling to make further concessions that would result in us... not being compensated for the dangers of the job," he said.

Within two business days, the union filed a formal grievance, citing a breach of contract and seeking damages under the Massachusetts Wage Act. It was submitted to Solomon — who wasted no time forwarding it to the mayor's office, as per protocol.

But a curious question lingered: If the MOU had never been formally presented to or approved by the Council, could the city truly be said to have violated it?

That legal riddle loomed large over the next council meeting, held on July 26th. For two hours, the Council met in executive session with legal counsel, the city auditor, and the mayor's chief of staff. When they emerged, they took no public vote on the MOU. Instead, they tabled it, delaying any final decision.

A week later, Mayor Jajuga made a unilateral decision: the city would pay Superior Officers at the MOU rate — even without Council approval. Again, Jajuga made a decision that would benefit his son, regardless of ethics or integrity.

It was a gamble. The police budget had just been gutted by $1.8 million. And while the mayor claimed the cuts would be absorbed at the top, the reality was stark: it wouldn't be captains or lieutenants who got pink slips — it would be patrolmen. Early projections estimated 20 to 30 layoffs. Those at the bottom would pay the price to protect those at the top.

In the public's eye, the city's priorities were laid bare. It wasn't about safety. It wasn't about sustainability. It was about protecting rank, power, and the contracts that secured both.

August

The Methuen Police Academy Director, Thomas Fleming, the former Lowell police officer who retired before a formal investigation into a cheating scandal could be completed, became embroiled in yet another "issue."

Fleming played a pivotal role as a consultant in establishing the academy and was then hired by NECC to be the director, he then took on a second job with All Sports Heroes, a uniform and gear company owned by another former police officer.

It did not take too long for both of his roles to collide.

By the summer of 2014, Fleming had moved from part-time salaried employee at All Sports to earning commissions – 50 percent of the profit on each sale he facilitated. Within a month of securing his commission deal, NECC named him the director.

It was then that that Fleming, in his "consultant" capacity, urged the college to purchase gear for the new recruits, t-shirts, hats, pants, water bottles, and patrol bags from All Sports. The college agreed to the recommendation, placed the orders, and billed participating police departments for the cost of the gear. The ethical rub was Fleming was still on the All Sports payroll and earning a cut of the deal.

From 2015 to 2017, Fleming wore two hats, literally and figuratively. As academy director, he submitted purchase quotes and approved invoices for All Sports. As a company employee, he packed and delivered the boxes. Some invoices even listed him as the sales rep, while he also signed off as the buyer.

During that two-year period, Fleming made approximately $5,000 in commission from these sales. That was on top of his $65,000 NECC salary, plus his pension from the City of Lowell.

In the eyes of the Massachusetts Ethics Commission, this wasn't just messy, it was a clear violation of state law. As a public employee, Fleming was barred from participating in any matter where he, or a business he was affiliated with, had a financial interest.

In short: he wasn't allowed to double dip.

The Ethics Commission opened a formal inquiry in November 2017. Fleming was placed under oath in April 2018. Shortly afterward, he wrote to the NECC president admitting he had a financial interest in All Sports' business with the school. With the letter, he enclosed a personal check for $2,952, the amount he claimed he had earned from academy-related gear sales.

But NECC didn't deposit the check.

According to *the Eagle-Tribune*, the college returned the money after the ethics investigation concluded. A spokesperson refused to explain why. If the college didn't accept the reimbursement, how did it plan to recover the funds? And perhaps more curiously: Why did Fleming repay the college at all, when his commissions came from All Sports, not NECC?

Those questions were never answered.

Fleming admitted guilt to the Ethics Commission of two public ethics violations and was fined $5,000, yet Fleming wasn't fired. He resigned quietly eight days later, just after the scandal broke on August 19.

But the larger issue wasn't just what Fleming did, it was who allowed it to happen.

In the Matter of Thomas Fleming

2018

At the time, Solomon served as the official liaison between NECC and the academy. That made him directly responsible for overseeing operations. And yet, throughout this entire conflict-of-interest scandal, Solomon remained silent. No intervention. No inquiry. No corrective action.

Where was the oversight?

The vacuum of accountability became even more obvious when NECC needed someone to step in after Fleming's resignation. Solomon hand-picked Officer Dan O'Connell, a freshly minted sergeant who had only held the rank for six weeks. The appointment raised eyebrows for one reason: O'Connell was married to City Councilor Lynn Vidler.

The move reeked of political convenience. But to be fair, O'Connell was not necessarily part of "Team Solomon."

That fact alone didn't excuse the prior failure in leadership. If anything, it underscored it.

While Solomon may not have personally profited from Fleming's arrangement, his role as academy liaison meant he should have known and done something. Instead, he turned a blind eye. Given that All Sports was also a vendor for the MPD, Solomon would have been well aware of Fleming's involvement with the company.

And in a system where silence often equals consent, that silence spoke volumes.

September

After 39 years of service to the City of Methuen, City Auditor Tom Kelly announced his retirement. He departed amid two major crises: the unfolding Superior Officers contract debacle and the school department's overspending, which forced the City to borrow funds and triggered state oversight of its finances.

Kelly also left office without disclosing the names of the two city councilors he claimed to have warned about the exorbitant cost of the police contracts if they were approved. However, a clue may have emerged during a council meeting when a resident stated during public participation that Kelly had told him one of the councilors he warned was still serving while the other had been termed out. If that account is accurate, the likely candidates include Jennifer Kannan, Lynn Vidler or George Kazanjian all of whom served on the 2017 and now the 2018 City Council.

Upon retirement, the City Council reportedly gave Kelly a proverbial "golden parachute."

Police Speak Out

Over several months, headlines across the country reported that Methuen police captains were poised to earn more than $450,000 per year — a staggering figure in a city where the median household income in 2018 was just $72,631. The news reverberated through the community, prompting widespread backlash. The City Council, meanwhile, faced mounting pressure from the administration to restore funding to the police personnel budget to avoid laying off up to 50 patrol officers — not superior officers, but the department's front-line staff.

Public outrage took many forms. Demonstrators protested against the controversial MOU outside City Hall. Residents spoke out at council meetings — and so did members of the police department.

At the September 17 council meeting, the audience was packed with police officers and their families. One of the first speakers during the public participation segment was Gallant, president of the Superior Officers' Union. After reciting a brief biography highlighting his education and professional awards, Gallant turned to the heart of the issue: the contracts.

On that night's agenda, councilors had proposed a plan to reorganize the police department by reducing the number of superior officers — an effort to close the budget deficit exacerbated by the mayor's decision to pay superior officers according to the MOU's unapproved terms. Gallant responded to the plan bluntly, stating that the strategy was aimed at pressuring the union back to the bargaining table. "I am telling you — it won't," he declared. "We are not coming back to the table. We are going to stand strong."

Some of Gallant's other claims merited scrutiny. For example, he asserted, "We [the police] don't get involved with the political process." But that statement stood in stark contrast to the nearly $10,000 in campaign contributions made to Mayor Jajuga by

Methuen police officers and their family members. If that's not political involvement, what is?

Gallant also described the emotional toll the situation had taken on officers and their families, stating, "We should not have to deal with the death threats coming into the station." That's "threats," plural. If police personnel had indeed received multiple death threats, one would expect arrests, investigations or at least some form of press coverage. After all, the recipients of the threats were the police themselves — they had the means to act. In the absence of any evidence, Gallant's comment came across as exaggerated rhetoric aimed at winning public sympathy.

For nearly three hours, six ranking officers, two patrol officers, a wife and a mother-in-law addressed the City Council. The family members spoke of the sacrifices their loved ones had made. Conversely, nine residents voiced opposition to the high salaries — making clear that their criticism was directed not at the officers themselves but at the unsustainable terms of the contract.

Most of the ranking officers emphasized the scope of their responsibilities, arguing that they "don't just sit behind a desk," and spoke about the dangers they face and the demanding nature of their work.

One resident captured the public sentiment succinctly: "There is no price for risking your life, but we need to be paying what the city can afford."

At the start of the evening, as Gallant addressed the Council, one line stood out: "Integrity and honesty mean something to me." Hearing those words come out of his mouth made me laugh. Three and a half years later, I was assigned to interview Gallant as part of an internal investigation for the MPD. Beyond the most basic information — name, address, and so on — he refused to answer any substantive questions, instead repeatedly invoked his Fifth Amendment right against self-incrimination.

December

The mission of the Anti-Defamation League (ADL) has long been "to stop the defamation of the Jewish people and to secure justice and fair treatment to all." In alignment with this mission, the ADL has sponsored select groups of American law enforcement officials to attend its Leadership, Resilience, and

2018

Counter-Terrorism Seminar in Israel since 2004. According to the ADL's official website, the organization designed this intensive program to deepen participants' understanding of extremist and terrorist violence, mass casualty incidents, and strategies for fostering community resilience in the face of such threats.

In 2018, Solomon was among those invited to attend the seminar. The ADL fully funded the trip, which took place from December 2 to December 12. Participation in the program was by direct invitation from the ADL, according to multiple sources, highlighting the seminar's exclusive and selective nature.

As reported by *The Tufts Daily*, which covered the experience of their University Police Department Director who attended the previous year, the delegation engaged in an immersive, firsthand study of Israel's counterterrorism practices. The group received briefings and training sessions from senior commanders within the Israel National Police, the Israel Defense Forces, and Israeli intelligence agencies. These sessions explored tactical, strategic, and operational responses to terrorism, as well as the importance of resilience at both the institutional and community levels.

Curiously, aside from a brief and passing mention during a city council meeting that Solomon was in Israel, there was no formal media coverage or public announcement regarding his participation in the trip. This absence of communication was particularly striking given Solomon's well-known tendency to seek media attention and public visibility for departmental initiatives. In contrast to his usual practice of issuing press releases and engaging in media outreach, the silence surrounding this international training raised questions: Why was there no press release? Why the departure from his typical approach to public relations?

2019

January	The City begins the process of laying off 50 police officers due to a budget shortfall.
January 10	A resident is removed from a City Council meeting for "chuckling" during proceedings.
January 28-30	Email exchanges occur between Anne Randazzo (City HR Director), Chief of Staff Fahey, and Chief Solomon regarding Officer Sean Fountain's Civil Service status.
January 31	Officer Arthur Hardy is placed on administrative leave.
February	The planned layoffs of 50 police officers are cancelled after the City Council votes to restore funding.
February 1	The Massachusetts Inspector General issues findings on the 2017 City Council vote concerning police contracts, raising legal and ethical concerns
February 6	Solomon receives a public records request from journalist Tim Wood seeking Fountain's academy attendance records.
February 7	Solomon, representing PAARI (Police Assisted Addiction and Recovery Initiative), attends a meeting at the White House with five others to discuss the national drug epidemic.
February 14	Wood follows up with an email to Randazzo, Solomon, and Fahey requesting additional information on Fountain's academy records.
February 26-March 2	Solomon and Aiello attend the *School Safety Conference* in Jacksonville, Florida (conference held February 27 – March 1).
February 27	Numerous emails are exchanged between Randazzo, Solomon, and Captain Gallant regarding the handling of Wood's record request.
February 28	Gallant replies to Wood, advising him to contact the Municipal Police Training Committee (MPTC) directly for any documentation on Fountain's academy attendance.
March 6	Randazzo formally responds to Wood, stating that the City has no documentation confirming that Fountain ever attended a police academy.
	The Superior Officers' Union files a second class-action grievance with the City over the ongoing contract dispute.
April 24	The Superior Officers' Union files a formal demand for arbitration.

2019

May 2	Officer Arthur Hardy is suspended for 270 working days without pay following an internal investigation.
May 22-24	Solomon attends the *Massachusetts Major City Chiefs Conference* in Falmouth, Massachusetts.
June 25	Mayor James Jajuga announces that he will not seek re-election for a second term.
July 17-26	Solomon, Aiello, Valliere, and Mahoney attend the *National School Safety Conference* in Las Vegas, Nevada (conference held July 22–26).
September 16-19	Solomon attends the *Massachusetts Major Chiefs of Police Conference* in Norwood, Massachusetts.
September 26	The Methuen City Council sends a formal letter to the Massachusetts Ethics Commission regarding potential violations stemming from the 2017 Council vote on police contracts.
October 22	An arbitration hearing is held concerning the Superior Officers' Union contract dispute.
October 25-29	Solomon, Deputy Chief Randy Haggar, McCarthy, Mahoney, and Gallant attend the *International Association of Chiefs of Police (IACP) Conference* in Chicago, Illinois.
December 19	The Massachusetts Ethics Commission issues a *Public Education Letter* to former councilors Jamie Atkinson, Lynn Vidler, and James Jajuga, citing concerns over their roles in the 2017 police contract vote.

January

As the Methuen Police Department's budget edged deeper into deficit, threatening layoffs for more than 50 officers, city officials found themselves at a crossroads. On January 10th, the City Council summoned Solomon and the city auditor to explain the department's troubling fiscal year 2019 expenditures.

At a prior meeting, Solomon had warned the council that, without immediate financial support, cuts would be unavoidable — including the elimination of police details at events such as the city's Christmas and July 4th celebrations. The warning drew swift backlash, with some accusing him of using beloved holidays as leverage to preserve the salaries of his command staff. In response, Solomon revised his approach. Rather than focusing on the fallout of budget reductions, he shifted to emphasizing the

2019

department's value — spotlighting the essential services that, in his view, could not be compromised.

Notably, while he floated the idea of scaling back police presence at public gatherings, such as parades and tree lightings, Solomon did not reduce his own travel expenditures. City records show that in fiscal year 2019, the MPD spent at least $41,273 on travel for Solomon and several close associates.

Still, the council met his pivot from discussing cuts to highlighting departmental contributions with skepticism.

What followed was a lengthy speech that several attendees and viewers later described as a filibuster — a way, they felt, to divert attention away from the heart of the issue: the continued payment of superior officers at rates set by an unapproved Memorandum of Understanding (MOU). These unauthorized payments, made with the knowledge of both the chief and the mayor, were steadily draining the department's budget and contributing to what would eventually become a $1.8 million shortfall. The council faced an unenviable choice: either approve additional funding or initiate layoffs that would affect lower-ranking officers.

During Solomon's remarks, Councilor James McCarty briefly stepped out, prompting Solomon to pause and ask whether he should wait. Informed that the council expected no formal presentation and that they called on him primarily to answer questions, Solomon continued — but not before expressing his disapproval. He called McCarty's exit "extremely rude," claiming it was disrespectful not only to him but to the council and the public. With a renewed sense of urgency, he resumed his comments, comparing the department's budget to other city departments in an attempt to highlight disparities.

When McCarty returned and began asking questions, the tone of the meeting shifted. He asked the city auditor who was ultimately responsible for the overspending. The response was blunt: "The Chief."

Solomon objected, citing the city charter and pointing out that the mayor — not the chief — was the appointing authority, implying that fiscal responsibility lay elsewhere. However, the term "appointing authority" pertains strictly to hiring, firing, final discipline, and promotions — not to budgetary oversight. Looking to move the conversation along, McCarty quipped, "We can leave that to the lawyers." It seemed that whenever Solomon found himself cornered, he reached for the "appointing authority" defense — whether it applied or not.

Solomon pushed back. "Everyone keeps saying the Chief is responsible. I think we should all remember 2006 to 2010 and the significant financial impact on the city for violating my civil rights. The city has a finding against them," he said. "Every time that is said, it leads to retaliation complaints and is offensive to me."

McCarty declined to respond to the remarks and instead refocused on the need to resolve the budget crisis.

Later in the meeting, another interruption shifted the atmosphere. As Solomon spoke, he suddenly turned toward the audience. "I really don't appreciate that — whoever thinks that is funny," he said, responding to a faint chuckle he heard. "This is people's lives," he added, directing his frustration at a man seated nearby.

Chairwoman Jennifer Kannan intervened with her gavel, reminding everyone in the room, "There is no discussing with the audience. Anybody, please." Solomon continued, visibly upset. "If he is going to talk like that, can he be removed? He is talking about retaliation. I am trying to have a conversation," he said.

Meeting Video

Sergeant Shawn Moore, acting as sergeant-at-arms, approached the man — later identified as Ryan Dugan — and escorted him out of the chamber. Kannan called a brief recess, and the council asked technicians to pause the meeting's video feed.

What occurred during the recess remains a matter of debate. With no video footage, accounts diverged. Solomon and his supporters described one version of events; others, including Dugan and several attendees, offered a different perspective. As with many past disputes involving Solomon, the truth seemed to hinge on which account one chose to believe.

Police Report

The following week, Loop Weekly published further details, including interviews with Dugan and others present that evening. Dugan, a consistent critic of the city's handling of police contracts and a spokesperson for a

2019

local taxpayer group, had intended to speak during the public participation portion of the meeting.

That group had long called for greater financial transparency. It had urged Mayor Jajuga to stop issuing payments based on the unapproved MOU, arguing that the practice had prematurely exhausted the department's personnel budget. They had even considered legal action.

On the night of the incident, Dugan was seated beside fellow resident John Saba. According to Sergeant Moore's police report, Dugan was laughing and speaking loudly while Solomon was presenting, prompting concern that he was inciting the audience. Moore described Dugan as "boisterous" and "disruptive" and claimed Dugan had made a comment along the lines of "I'm here to rebel" before leaving voluntarily.

But this account was sharply disputed by those nearby. Several witnesses stated that the room was not full and described Dugan's reaction as a chuckle rather than a disruption. They claimed Moore approached aggressively and demanded Dugan "shut up," invoking the need for decorum. Witnesses also denied the report's description of mocking salutes or rebellious behavior, with Dugan pointing out that he was holding papers and a pen at the time — making such gestures improbable.

Saba in 2023 describing the Chuckle Incident (video)

Most who spoke out said Dugan had remained composed and had not voluntarily left but that Solomon asked Moore to remove him. Dugan later acknowledged that the chuckle may have been inappropriate but argued that it did not justify the police response.

Saba, concerned by the incident, requested a copy of the police report. After weeks of delay, he obtained it and was troubled by the discrepancies between its contents and what he had personally witnessed. He filed a formal complaint with the Attorney General's Office, then led by Maura Healey, who would later become governor. The office, however,

Dugan in 2023 talking about the Chuckle

redirected the complaint to the Methuen Police Department — the very agency under scrutiny.

You truly can't make this stuff up.

Pink Slips

The tug-of-war between the City Council and the mayor was escalating. The administration pushed to have $1.8 million reinstated into the police budget. The Council firmly refused. It had become clear to everyone — the standoff couldn't last forever.

In Massachusetts, it was illegal to deficit spend, and with four months remaining in the fiscal year, something had to give. For weeks, the mayor's only leverage had been the looming threat of layoffs. It had become a high-stakes game of chicken — and both sides were barreling toward each other. The question was: who would swerve first?

Jajuga swerved. On January 24th, the city initiated the layoff process. On the chopping block were 50 patrol officers. Because of Civil Service protections, the officers continued working until each had an individual hearing before the Civil Service Commission. Financial constraints were a legally valid reason for layoffs under Civil Service rules, allowing the cuts to be finalized by the end of February — unless the Council relented.

The fallout from losing half of the police force would have been devastating. Policing the city could not simply stop, officials would have been forced to gut other departments just to keep basic law enforcement afloat. Senior officers would be pulled from leadership roles to cover patrol shifts, leaving the department rudderless in a storm. But that wasn't even the worst of it. Methuen faced a very real threat: other cities and towns would swoop in and hire the laid-off officers almost immediately. And once Methuen's budget crisis passed, it wouldn't be a matter of simply rehiring them. The city would have to start from scratch — posting a civil service requisition, waiting for a list, interviewing candidates, conducting background checks, physicals, psychological evaluations, and sending recruits through the academy. That process alone would take a year and a half or more and cost the city at least a million dollars in taxpayer funds. The end result? A department flooded with rookies at the exact moment Methuen needed seasoned professionals. Public safety would suffer, and everyone knew it.

David Souther

At the first hint of criticism or dissent within Solomon's domain, the response was swift and unmistakable — a warning shot across the bow. One of Solomon's loyal enforcers would usually step in first — a sharp word, a subtle warning, a reminder to fall in line. If that didn't work, Solomon would make it personal. Retaliation wasn't random; it was methodical. He knew exactly how to apply pressure — not enough to break you, just enough to make you wish you'd backed off.

In Officer David Souther's case, it meant the chief stripping him of his position in the detective unit.

By this time, Souther was a seven-year veteran of the Methuen Police Department, assigned to the detective division. Watching former city councilor–turned-police officer Sean Fountain receive a patrolman's badge in place of an intermittent badge — and by fall 2017, a detective assignment — did not sit well with him. He knew Fountain wasn't qualified for the badge and lacked the training expected of a detective. Frankly, it would be hard to find anyone who believed Fountain's appointment was anything other than political favoritism.

According to his Massachusetts Department of Labor Relations paperwork, Souther brought his concerns to Patrolmen's Union President David Gardner, arguing that the move violated both civil service rules and basic standards. Gardner wasn't interested. He waved it off, citing the Home Rule Petition that was signed by the Governor.

But Souther read the petition. It exempted Fountain from the Methuen City Charter's one-year post-office employment ban, not from the training every other cop had to complete. It didn't waive civil service requirements. It didn't override common sense.

In his complaint he identified six full-time intermittent officers — hired in direct violation of the union contract and civil service law. At the time, twenty certified reserve candidates were waiting for legitimate hiring consideration. Solomon bypassed every single one of them.

2019

In December 2017, Souther was assigned a sexual assault case that had previously been handled by Fountain. When Fountain requested to review Souther's report, Souther refused. Fountain wasn't a certified sexual assault investigator — a fact confirmed by the state's MPTC training records. In fact, neither was Solomon. And under state law, the rule was clear: without certification, there was no access.

But instead of backing Souther, the department came after him.

Detective Sgt. Tom McMenamon challenged Souther's decision, arguing that Fountain, as a detective, was entitled to the report. Souther pushed back. He knew the rules. But it didn't matter.

Whispers started. Warnings were passed. "Back off Fountain, or you're out of detectives." Souther got the message.

In January 2018, the union held elections. The only contested position was president: Gardner versus Arthur Hardy. Gardner narrowly lost, and the union re-elected Souther to the union secretary post. But the political undercurrents got stronger. Several intermittent officers — including Matthew Despins, who also worked for Solomon at EIS, began pushing to join the union and vote.

Souther objected. These weren't civil service officers. They weren't eligible. He contacted union attorney Kareem Morgan, who declined to intervene. The intermittent officers were allowed in. They voted. And the balance shifted.

It didn't take a genius to see Solomon's fingerprints. Hardy was no friend to the chief — and Solomon had a long history of manipulating outcomes from the shadows.

On August 13, 2018, the union board met with Solomon to discuss several departmental issues affecting patrol officers. During the meeting, it was evident that Solomon was particularly irritated with Souther over his positions on certain issues. Exactly one week later, the union filed three grievances on behalf of three officers — actions that again seemed to provoke Solomon's ire.

The response was swift. The very next day, Sergeant McMenamon and Captain Randy Haggar informed Souther of a temporary reassignment to patrol.

The official reason? "Workforce shortage." Temporary. Six weeks.

2019

Two months later, in October, Souther asked for a meeting to discuss returning to detectives. Solomon acknowledged there were no complaints about his work. But he claimed to have received an informal report that Souther was "stirring up union issues."

Then came the clincher.

Solomon pointed to a command staff meeting on August 21, the day of Souther's reassignment. He said he had asked each division head to identify an officer to shift back to patrol. Everyone had a reason to retain their people, except the detective's unit. Their silence, Solomon claimed, was taken as a green light to move Souther.

He told Souther he'd likely be back in January. He never was.

On December 19, 2018, Souther filed a formal retaliation complaint with the Massachusetts Department of Labor Relations.

The city's response, filed January 29, 2019, rewrote the narrative.

They said Souther had been openly hostile toward Fountain. That Detectives McCarthy, Pappalardo, and McMenamon expressed concerns about morale. And most incredibly — they claimed Souther and Hardy had *requested* the patrol reassignment themselves.

Souther v. Methuen Papers

That last one broke the illusion. Souther had spent the better part of a year fighting irregular staffing. The idea that he'd voluntarily step out of detectives was fiction. He withdrew the complaint, realizing the process was a dead end.

And this wasn't Methuen's first round with this game.

But let's not forget a similar episode from earlier in the department's history — one that makes what happened to Officer Souther even more outrageous.

Years prior, Acting Chief Lavigne had removed Officer Joe Aiello from the detective division. The official reason? Aiello had a credibility problem. He'd been arrested on forgery charges — a direct threat to any officer's ability to testify in court. He later struck a deal, pleading guilty to a lesser included offense: tampering with a public document. It downgraded the felony to a misdemeanor. That plea deal saved his job — and more than that, it set the stage for a twisted reward.

Aiello turned around and sued the city, claiming his removal from detectives was retaliation for union involvement. The result? A $110,000 settlement — taxpayer-funded — despite the fact that Aiello's credibility issues were not only real but documented in a criminal case.

Compare that to Souther.

Souther didn't commit a crime. He didn't tamper with a public record or violate any oath. His only offense was speaking the truth: that Sean Fountain was unqualified to be a police officer, let alone a detective. That truth — inconvenient and politically dangerous — cost him his detective's badge. No lawsuit. No settlement. No redemption. Just silence.

The disparity in outcomes is difficult to ignore. One officer was rewarded after pleading guilty. Another was punished for telling the truth. The message was unmistakable: loyalty was rewarded, dissent was punished. For taxpayers, that meant whistleblowers were silenced, the truth was buried, and the cycle of corruption kept costing them more with each contract signed.

Reflections: The Danger of Fake Cops

The badge is more than metal. It is trust. It is the promise that the person wearing it has been trained, vetted, and prepared to wield power responsibly. When that promise is broken, the danger multiplies.

Sean Fountain's forged certification was not a paperwork glitch. It was a crisis. An untrained man was handed a badge, a gun, and the authority of the state — authority he had not earned. The danger was immediate, not theoretical. Every traffic stop, every call, every interaction carried the risk that he was unprepared for the responsibility he carried.

But the scandal was bigger than one man. It exposed a system where records could be forged, waivers backdated, and state oversight circumvented. If the process to certify officers can be gamed this easily, then the badge itself becomes meaningless.

2019

And once the public realizes the badge can be faked, the damage extends beyond safety. It strikes at faith. If the public cannot trust who is wearing the badge, then every legitimate officer is viewed with suspicion. Trust in law enforcement is not lost overnight — but it is lost forever once the public believes the badge itself is counterfeit.

February

From June 2018 through February 2019, a steady drumbeat of complaints made their way to the Massachusetts Office of the Inspector General (OIG). Phone calls, emails, and letters poured in, many from frustrated Methuen residents, others from concerned public officials. But they were all asking the same question:

How did a small city approve police contracts that promised captains some of the highest law enforcement salaries in the country?

In Massachusetts, it's rare for the watchdogs to bite. But this time, the OIG sank its teeth in.

To the shock of City Hall and the quiet relief of taxpayers, the OIG launched a formal investigation. The result was a blistering 17-page letter, dated February 1, 2019, sent to Mayor James Jajuga and the City Council.

What that letter described wasn't just fiscal mismanagement, it was a blueprint for how to fail the public trust.

17-page OIG Letter

The OIG didn't pull punches. They concluded that the former mayor and city council likely violated state law, ignored their city charter, and utterly failed their fiduciary duty to Methuen taxpayers. Their conduct in pushing through the superior officers' contract was, in the OIG's words, a "reckless disregard" for public accountability.

Key failures identified by the OIG:

Misuse of Rule of Necessity: The Council improperly invoked the rule without disclosing which members had conflicts — a violation of transparency laws.

2019

Ignored Resolution #4720: City law requires a financial impact statement before approving contracts. The Council ignored it.

Illegal Double Vote: The Council unlawfully voted to approve the contract twice in one day, a move the OIG flagged as procedurally invalid.

Unauthorized MOU Payments: Mayor Jajuga violated state law and the City Charter by paying officers under an unapproved Memorandum of Understanding (MOU).

Perhaps the most damning finding: some officials didn't understand the contract's financial impact, and those who did, approved it anyway.

The numbers were staggering. Under the 2017 contract, police captains stood to receive a 183.49 percent raise, boosting their base salaries to $432,295, not including overtime or paid details. That figure would have made Methuen's captains the highest-paid law enforcement officers in the country, out earning the police chiefs in New York, Los Angeles, Chicago, Boston, and even the Massachusetts State Police Colonel.

The OIG made their conclusion plain:

Paying those salaries would be a waste of public funds.

While the letter stopped short of recommending criminal charges, it was clear the OIG saw potential exposure. They urged the city to:

Seek legal counsel to assess the enforceability of the contract and MOU and to consult the State Ethics Commission on the Council's use of the Rule of Necessity.

For Methuen residents, the report was confirmation of what many had suspected all along: the 2017 contract wasn't just bloated, it was a betrayal.

Three days after the report's release, Mayor Jajuga made an announcement: he would rescind the unauthorized MOU pay rates granted to Superior Officers and invoke the "evergreen clause" from their prior 2014–2017 contract. Under that clause, the officers would temporarily revert to their previous contract's pay until a new contract could be negotiated.

Jajuga's Chief of Staff, Paul Fahey, told the *Eagle-Tribune* the move was designed to "bring the superiors back to the table."

One week after the OIG letter was made public, the Methuen City Council convened for a special session. The first item on the agenda: a request from the mayor's office to restore $1.5 million to the depleted police department budget.

Councilors debated how much of that request — if any — should be honored in light of the OIG's findings and Jajuga's move to halt MOU-based payments. In the end, the Council approved a reduced appropriation of $1.2 million, enough to avoid the threatened layoffs of 50 officers.

They also took care of unfinished business. In a move that should have happened long before, the City Council formally voted on the MOU. It was unanimously rejected, ending that chapter with at least some clarity.

Chief Solomon wasn't in attendance.

Instead, he was in Washington, D.C., attending a national summit on the opioid crisis hosted by Vice President Mike Pence. Solomon was representing Methuen as part of the Police Assisted Addiction and Recovery Initiative (PAARI), alongside hundreds of other law enforcement officials discussing national strategies.

Nolan's Letter

Back home, the Superior Officers' Union attorney Gary Nolan wasted no time. That same day, he sent a letter to the city, rejecting the OIG's conclusions outright. He dismissed the findings as merely "advisory" and "speculative," asserting that the OIG report had no bearing on the city's contractual obligations.

Nolan warned the city:

If Methuen failed to uphold the 2017 contract, as modified by the MOU, the union would pursue all legal remedies available, including triple damages and attorney's fees under state law.

For a department already drowning in mistrust and legal exposure, the message was clear:

The contract might have been reckless. But getting out of it wouldn't be easy.

And for the people of Methuen, there was little comfort in the fact that it took a state agency to finally say out loud what they'd known all along: they'd been sold out, not by outsiders, but by the very people they elected to protect them.

2019

Emails

Massachusetts General Law Chapter 66 grants the public the right to access most government records. While many assume that Public Records Requests (PRR) are primarily filed by news organizations, in reality, journalists account for only about 10 percent of total requests. The rest come from private citizens, advocacy groups, and researchers — people seeking transparency from their government.

On February 6, it was Tim Wood, a journalist from Methuen's *Loop Weekly*, who submitted a PRR request. Wood emailed Solomon with a simple inquiry: the date Officer Sean Fountain became a full-time employee and whether he had completed a full-time police academy, as required by state law. Under State regulations, Solomon had ten business days to respond.

He didn't need them.

Solomon replied promptly, but instead of providing the requested information, he deflected. "I cannot comment on personnel matters," he wrote. "All comments on those matters must come from Assistant Solicitor/Human Resource Director Anne Randazzo." He also claimed that the information was not "readily available" to him. The response raised an immediate question: Couldn't the chief comment, or wouldn't he?

As both an investigative reporter and a resident of Methuen, Wood was not easily discouraged. He responded, clarifying that he wasn't seeking sensitive personnel details — just a factual confirmation: Was Fountain hired full-time? Had he completed the necessary police academy training? Wood also informed Solomon that he had already submitted a parallel inquiry to the Massachusetts Police Training Committee (MPTC), the state agency responsible for certifying law enforcement training.

A week later, on Valentine's Day, Wood followed up — this time broadening his outreach. He copied not only Solomon but also Randazzo and Fahey, the mayor's chief of staff. In this message, Wood specifically requested any documentation the city might possess regarding Fountain's attendance at a full-time police academy, which is a requirement under MPTC regulations. He noted that the MPTC had no record of Fountain completing such training and asked if the city had anything that might clarify or resolve the discrepancy.

2019

Randazzo responded swiftly — not to Wood, but to Fahey. She asked if he wanted to meet to discuss the matter. Whether that meeting ever took place remains unknown, as there is no record confirming it.

By the ninth business day following Wood's updated request, a flurry of internal emails began circulating among Randazzo, Solomon, and Captain Greg Gallant. On the morning of the tenth business day, Gallant summarized the situation in an email to Solomon. He reiterated Wood's original questions and then added: "If we need to, we can have Anne reply that Sean didn't attend full-time academy. He attended reserve/intermittent police academy. If Tim wants the records, he can do a request to MPTC."

On the 19th business day after Wood's initial PRR submission — well past the statutory deadline — Randazzo finally responded. In her official reply, she stated in part: "The city has no documentation regarding attendance at a police academy ... We have requested documentation from the academy and a search is being conducted." Attached to her response was a spreadsheet listing Fountain as a police officer. Notably, the document assigned him a "Department Seniority" of 14th out of 67 officers and a "Civil Service Date" of August 29, 1999.

That date was highly revealing.

August 29, 1999, was not the date the Methuen Police Department hired Fountain as a police officer — it was the date he became a civil service firefighter. Under Massachusetts law, civil service seniority does not transfer between different job classifications; a firefighter cannot carry over years of service into a police position.

On February 23, 2017, it took just one hour and thirty-one minutes to daisy-chain an email in pursuit of a single, straightforward question: *"Can a Civil Service firefighter laterally transfer to a Civil Service police department?"*

In less than 92 minutes, Solomon received a definitive answer: *No*. Fountain could not transfer his civil service seniority from the fire department to the police department. The response from the state's Human Resources Division (HRD) was clear and unequivocal — there could be no crossover. Transfers were allowed only from fire to fire or police to police. There was no ambiguity.

2019

The email chain began with Solomon, who sent the inquiry to Donovan. Donovan then reached out to HRD. Once HRD responded, Donovan forwarded the answer back to Solomon, who passed it along to Fountain. Fountain replied with a single word: "Thanks."

From inquiry to final acknowledgment, the entire chain of communication — Solomon → Donovan → HRD → Donovan → Solomon → Fountain — unfolded in under an hour and a half, decisively closing the door on any hope of a lateral transfer.

Still, Solomon disregarded the rule and placed Fountain on the police civil service seniority list anyway.

As for the academy issue, Massachusetts law is clear. Any individual appointed to a full-time position within a municipal police department, in which they will exercise police powers, must complete a full-time police academy course approved by the MPTC before assuming those duties. The requirement is not optional, nor is it interchangeable with part-time or reserve training. Yet, according to the city's communications and the MPTC's records, there was no evidence that Fountain ever completed the full-time academy.

Not long after submitting his PRR requests, Wood began experiencing what appeared to be a campaign of harassment. Over a span of just four weeks, he was pulled over by Methuen police officers a staggering 12 times — an average of once every other day. Each encounter followed a similar pattern: Wood was stopped, made to wait on the side of the road for approximately 20 minutes, and then released without a ticket, warning, or any official record of the stop. It quickly became clear this wasn't routine traffic enforcement.

During one of these stops, an officer quietly offered an apology. Lowering his voice, he admitted the directive had come "from above" and confided that Wood was "in the doghouse." When pressed for more details, the officer wouldn't go further than saying, "Solomon's pissed about the PRR."

Soon, Wood began noticing cars parked outside his home for prolonged periods. When he approached one of the vehicles to confront the driver, the man identified himself as an off-duty police officer. He claimed to be a friend of Fountain and offered an unsolicited warning: "Lay off Fountain. He's a good cop with

2019

a lot of family issues. He doesn't deserve this." As far as threats went, it was veiled — but the message was clear.

The pressure didn't stop there. Wood's fledgling newspaper, *Loop Weekly*, began to suffer the consequences of coordinated efforts to undermine it. Several local advertisers, under apparent pressure, withdrew their support. The loss of revenue was immediate and damaging. Despite the financial strain, Wood persisted, pivoting from print journalism to podcasting. He began producing a hyperlocal audio show, covering Methuen's high school sports and community news — an effort to stay connected to his audience and continue holding power to account, albeit in a different format.

Eventually, Wood decided to drop the Fountain story. Not because the MPD silenced him and not because he had been intimidated into submission — but because larger, more consequential issues were surfacing. Chief among them was the brewing controversy over the Superior Officers' contract, a matter with far-reaching financial and political implications for the city. The story had grown beyond the qualifications of one officer. It was now about the integrity of the entire department, and the cost to the people of Methuen.

May

In Methuen, the rules weren't enforced equally — they were bent with precision and purpose. Favoritism wasn't a fluke, and retaliation wasn't random. These were deliberate tools of control, and under Solomon, few wielded them with more intent or effectiveness.

By 2018, another historic number emerged: 270 days. That was the length of the unpaid suspension imposed on Patrolmen's Union President Arthur Hardy for allegedly mishandling evidence. It was the second-longest suspension in Methuen Police Department history.

The longest? Solomon himself — suspended for 365 days in 2008 after mishandling federal grant funds.

Hardy's suspension came at a volatile time within the MPD — when thousands of dollars in pay for superior officers depended on the cohesion of the department's two police unions, and the controversial hiring of Officer Fountain relied on silence — the suspension of a union president should have warranted serious scrutiny. For anyone else, it would have. But not under Solomon.

Hardy's story had been years in the making. His relationship with Solomon was long marked by tension, mistrust, and mutual disdain. They had no personal connection. Hardy had no family members on the force, and offered Solomon no leverage — except the authority to write him up for even the most minor infraction, real or imagined. And Solomon did — again and again — hoping that the cumulative effect would eventually break him. But it didn't.

As demonstrated throughout this book, if you were in Solomon's good graces — or at the very least useful to him — you could get away with a lot. But for those on the outside, Solomon showed no restraint.

Years before, Solomon ordered Hardy to write an apology letter to the entire department — a disciplinary tactic usually reserved for schoolyard misconduct. It wasn't about accountability. It was humiliation, plain and simple.

And it didn't stop there.

In 2015, Hardy hit a pothole in the department parking lot, slicing a tire sidewall. Routine, right? Not in Solomon's Methuen. Hardy received a written reprimand.

Compare that with Lieutenant Ron Valliere, who struck a concrete barrier and caused $5,107 in vehicle damage. No write-up. No consequences. The difference? Valliere was in favor. Hardy wasn't.

Hardy's Tire Damage

Valliere's Accident Report

It gets better — the pothole Hardy hit? It was in a lot maintained by the city's Highway Department, run at the time by Clement "Jay" Bonanno — a long-time MPD intermittent officer and Solomon ally. The same pothole his friend didn't fix ended up on Hardy's disciplinary record.

Over the years, Hardy — and others like him — were written up for a range of alleged infractions. The MPD's disciplinary records resemble a catch-all list of vague and subjective charges, including conduct unbecoming, failure to follow orders, incompetence, harassment, neglect of duty, unprofessional conduct, lack of courtesy, and rudeness, among others. Some of these charges were substantiated; others were not. But for Solomon, securing a guilty finding wasn't always the point. It was just as effective to bog someone down in the disciplinary process — to "hem you up" and remind you who was in charge.

That same culture shaped the buildup to Hardy's suspension.

It began on August 1, 2018 when Hardy responded to a resident's report that someone may have fired shots into their home. Upon inspecting the damage, Hardy discovered what appeared to be bullet holes — not just at the initial address, but at a neighboring house as well.

At the second house, he noticed a metal fragment embedded in the siding. Not knowing if he was seeing the silver of insulation board or a bullet. Hardy asked the homeowner for a pair of needle-nosed pliers. He notified dispatch and requested detectives to respond. With the pliers, Hardy then extracted the object — possibly part of a bullet, possibly not.

The homeowner then handed Hardy a second object — a coppery piece of metal a neighbor had found weeks earlier. Hardy, believing it unrelated, held it in his hand while walking across the lawn. He accidentally dropped it when his hand hit his TASER holster. It disappeared into the grass.

Hardy, the homeowner and eventually the landscaper spent the next 15 to 20 minutes trying to recover the fragment, searching by hand, sweeping the area with a metal detector, and even running the mower over the spot again. But they had no luck.

After briefing the detectives on his findings, Hardy turned the investigation over to them. Back at the station, he documented the call in a report, which he completed the following morning.

As previously noted, Hardy had narrowly won the presidency of the Patrolmen's Union in January 2018, defeating David Gardner. The incident involving the bullet hole occurred just weeks before the pivotal August meeting between Hardy, fellow board members like Souther, and Solomon — ostensibly to discuss departmental and union matters. That meeting ended with Solomon visibly agitated. The following week, Hardy submitted three formal grievances on behalf of the patrol officers — further straining their already tense relationship.

2019

Nearly six weeks after Hardy responded to the bullet hole call — and three weeks after Hardy filed the grievances — Solomon sent Hardy a letter informing him that he was now under investigation.

The accusation: improper collection and preservation of evidence from the scene of the alleged shooting. To conduct the investigation, Solomon brought in his old pal, Al Donovan.

Internally, Donovan was known for delivering outcomes — not objectivity. His presence signaled that Solomon wanted Hardy gone.

Because Hardy was union president, Solomon had to tread carefully — the optics of retaliating against a union official required a layer of plausible deniability. Donovan, at least on paper, offered that. As an "impartial" investigator, his involvement lent the appearance of integrity. But for those familiar with how things worked, the outcome was never in question.

The 35-page report submitted by Donovan included Officer Hardy's first draft police report and a transcript of their interview. Most of Donovan's questions focused on Hardy's examination of a bullet hole and his handling of a metal fragment — an item that Hardy ultimately lost during the call.

Donovan concluded that Hardy had violated several Methuen Police Department policies, procedures, rules, and regulations. Specifically, he alleged that Hardy failed to properly recognize, collect, process, preserve, document, report, or secure evidence related to the case.

For anyone familiar with internal investigative reports, several troubling elements stood out — particularly in the interview transcript. Hardy told Donovan that the object handed to him by the homeowner looked like "just a piece of scrap copper or something." Despite that, Donovan repeatedly referred to the item in his report as a "bullet/casing fragment." This is a problematic characterization. Donovan never personally saw the object, nor is there any indication he obtained a description of it from the homeowner. He had no factual basis for identifying it as a bullet fragment — yet he did so throughout the report.

Donovan also emphasized that Hardy had turned off his body-worn camera (BWC) before the homeowner gave him the fragment — meaning that exchange wasn't captured on video. He cited this as a procedural failure. However, the department's BWC policy is clear:

> *"Officers will not disengage the BWC until the entire incident has been recorded or when further recording of the incident will not serve a proper police purpose."*

To support his claim that Hardy removed evidence before detectives arrived, Donovan included a timeline drawn from Hardy's BWC footage. But that timeline was suspiciously rearranged.

Here is the actual sequence of events:
   a. 3:46 – Bullet holes discovered at second house
   b. 4:17 – Hardy asks the homeowner if he has a pocketknife
   c. 4:35 – Hardy inserts the knife into holes in the house siding
   d. 4:52 – Hardy asks the homeowner for a pair of pliers
   e. 5:22 – Hardy calls for detectives
   f. 6:14–6:30 – Hardy uses the pliers to extract a metal fragment

In his report, however, Donovan placed the 5:22 call to detectives ahead of the 4:17 and 4:52 events — listing it as item (b). If that's not just a clerical mistake, which seems unlikely, it shifts the entire context. In fact, Donovan went so far as to write:

> *"Officers will not disengage the BWC until the entire incident has been recorded or when further recording of the incident will not serve a proper police purpose."*

> *"Officer Hardy is depicted and recorded on his body camera video as requesting that [redacted] get a tool (needle nose pliers) to extract the bullet/casing fragments from the side of the residence after he had called detectives to the scene."*

But by Donovan's own timeline, that statement is demonstrably false. Hardy asked for the pliers at 4:52 — before calling detectives at 5:22. Whether intentional or not, reordering the timeline presents a misleading narrative.

In investigative reports like this, perception is everything. And within the Methuen Police Department's internal politics, perception often trumps fact.

Ultimately, the case against Hardy came down to optics. And under Solomon's leadership, Hardy never had the optics on his side.

Donovan's Report

Donovan chose to use a stopwatch to track time instead of relying on the body-worn camera's (BWC) embedded timestamp — an immediate red flag.

BWC systems are equipped with embedded date and time precisely because they are reliable, court-admissible, and synchronized with CAD data, radio logs, and other time-sensitive evidence. Ignoring that and instead choosing an arbitrary "3:46 into the video" as a starting point — rather than the confirmed 1:38 PM arrival of Officer Hardy — raises serious questions.

Why would an experienced investigator bypass the objective timestamp? Why reshape the timeline around a subjective video marker? This wasn't a rookie oversight; it appears to be a deliberate decision to steer the narrative — particularly troubling given that this same investigator already made a material "error" earlier in the report, one I believe was intentional.

This isn't just poor methodology. It undermines the integrity of the entire report.

What follows are supporting materials that reveal inconsistencies, challenge the official timeline, and support the concern that the facts were manipulated to protect those in power — at the expense of truth and accountability.

The final decision came at a mayoral-level hearing held on March 7, 2019. The hearing officer was Mayor Jajuga's Chief of Staff, Paul Fahey. It's worth noting that impartiality might be at question, as Mayor Jajuga was a longtime family friend of Fountain's parents and had known Fountain since he was child.

Nearly two months passed before Hardy received the outcome. Fahey found Hardy guilty of four violations:

- Failing to wait for detectives to process the scene
- Attempting to retrieve evidence both before and after contacting detectives

2019

- Taking possession of evidence after calling for detectives, then losing it
- Failing to document those events in his official report

Hearing Determination

Fahey also considered Hardy's prior disciplinary history and concluded that the pattern amounted to incompetence. As a result, he issued a suspension of 270 working days without pay. All other restrictions placed on Hardy during his administrative leave — including the surrender of his badge, firearm, and equipment — remained in effect.

Additionally, official prohibited Hardy from exercising any police powers or acting in any capacity as a police officer. He was barred from entering the police station without a scheduled appointment, prohibited from accessing police reports, documents, or files, and was required to remain at home during his regular shift hours.

Exercising his rights under Civil Service, Hardy promptly filed an appeal with the commission, who scheduled an arbitration hearing for October 15th.

The Three Grievances

In 2018, three significant grievances were filed by the patrolmen's union, each illustrating the lengths Solomon and his loyal command staff were willing to go to assert control and reinforce their dominance within the MPD. These grievances, referenced in both Officer Souther's and Union President Hardy's accounts, reveal a concerning pattern of command behavior rooted in favoritism, manipulation, and disregard for established protocols. The following are their stories:

Grievance Number One

Officer Larry May had five days of vacation approved well in advance to plan a family trip. However, on the very first day of his vacation, he was contacted by his supervisor and ordered back to work. With no option to refuse, May and his family were forced to cut their trip short, pack up everything, and drive two hours home — losing both the financial investment in the trip and the much-need quality family time.

Unfortunately, this incident was not an isolated occurrence. In a Step I grievance letter submitted by union president Hardy to Solomon, Hardy wrote: "The Union therefore submits this grievance and demands that the City immediately cease this continual violation of officers' days off once approved weeks in advance."

In response, Solomon denied the grievance, citing language from the patrolmen's contract: "Notwithstanding the foregoing, the Chief, or his designee (with appeal rights to the Chief), retains the right to approve or disapprove the use of single vacation days requested during the course of the year."

Solomon then claimed that had the union appealed before May returned to duty, he would have instructed the commanding officer to find an alternative since May was on vacation with his family. He added that he remains mindful of officers' family needs — but placed the blame on the union for failing to act before MPD officials pulled May from his vacation.

The closing line of Solomon's letter, however, underscores a more troubling tone:

"Based on the clear language in the article you cited, I hereby deny the grievance. I hope this helps clear up your understanding of your contract."

This passive-aggressive remark reveals more than just a contract interpretation; it illustrates how Solomon wields his authority to undermine and control his officers. Those within the department widely understood that the approval or denial of vacation time occurs at the time of the request — not arbitrarily revoked after the fact. Using contractual language as a retroactive justification to disrupt officers' lives speaks volumes about the culture of command and the imbalance of power under Solomon's leadership.

Grievance Number Two

Officer Kevin Abraham was working a paid detail on a city street paving project for the Methuen Department of Public Works (DPW). During the shift, Sergeant Eric Ferreira contacted Abraham. He ordered him to return to the station to submit a

2019

TO/FROM report, demanding he explain who had authorized him to share police information with a civilian.

After completing the report, rather than allowing Abraham to return to the paid detail, Ferreira ordered him to go home — effectively stripping him of eight hours of detail pay. The sudden removal raised serious questions about motive and fairness.

Union President Hardy filed a grievance with Solomon, challenging the basis of the accusation. Hardy clarified that the so-called "civilian" in question was Jay Bonanno — the DPW Highway Superintendent and an intermittent officer with the Methuen Police Department — not an ordinary civilian. Bonanno was, at the time, operating an unmarked police-issued Chevy Tahoe equipped with emergency lights, underlining his formal ties to both city operations and law enforcement.

This added detail, likely included to emphasize the absurdity of the accusation, exposed the grievance for what it truly was: an example of Solomon and his command staff using technicalities to flex authority, assert rank, and punish officers arbitrarily. Instead of addressing the matter with proportionate professionalism, the command chose to escalate and financially penalize Abraham — further contributing to the climate of intimidation and favoritism within the department.

The whole incident, which likely had nothing to do with sharing police information with a "civilian," raises a more pressing question: What did Abraham actually do? Or, more to the point, what did Solomon *perceive* he did to land himself in Solomon's crosshairs?

Grievance Number Three

On August 9, 2018, Officer Brandon LaFlamme signed up for an extra paid detail. Several other full-time officers also expressed interest in working the assignment in the neighboring city of Lawrence. However, when officials filled the detail, the midnight shift supervisor, Lieutenant Valliere, failed to contact LaFlamme, as it was his turn on the list and instead assigned the work to a retired specialist officer.

The union filed a grievance on LaFlamme's behalf, arguing that MPD officials unfairly passed him over and requesting that the

2019

City reimburse him for the lost opportunity to work the detail due to what they described as a supervisor's error.

In his written response, Solomon denied the grievance. After reviewing the detail roster, Solomon asserted that LaFlamme was not next in line to receive the assignment and therefore lacked the standing to file the grievance. According to Solomon, the right to challenge the detail assignment belonged to whichever officer was next on the list.

Further, Solomon stated that even if an error had occurred, it was an unintentional oversight — not a deliberate violation of the union contract. On those grounds, he formally denied the grievance.

Though framed as a procedural technicality, the denial once again highlighted how the department's leadership often used process and interpretation of policy to avoid addressing fairness — or to sidestep accountability for decisions made by members of Solomon's command staff.

By October 2018, a troubling atmosphere had taken hold within the MPD. As the patrolmen's union pursued multiple grievances, rumors began circulating that Solomon was preparing to retaliate.

One rumor suggested that if the union persisted in pressing the grievances, Solomon would bar patrol officers from working details in neighboring Lawrence. This was no idle threat: at the time, the City of Lawrence was grappling with the aftermath of devastating gas explosions and was relying heavily on mutual aid from surrounding departments for paid detail coverage.

Solomon fueled further tension with his reported refusal to raise the hourly cap on detail rates — allegedly in direct response to the union's grievances involving detail-related disputes. The message was clear: if the union continued challenging decisions, it could cost officers real earnings.

As weeks passed and the grievances remained unresolved, the rumors grew more severe. One especially alarming claim was that if the union dropped the grievances, that concession would assist with the Union President's [Hardy] "situation." Whether this was a calculated rumor or a genuine threat from command, the pressure had its intended effect.

Ultimately, union contacted the officers involved in the grievances. Under mounting pressure, the officers agreed to withdraw their complaints.

2019

This episode didn't just underscore the fear of retaliation within the department — it exemplified how MPD officials used power not only to suppress dissent but to manipulate outcomes through implied threats. The use of internal rumors and administrative control over financial opportunities, like detail work created an environment where officers felt they had to choose between standing up for fairness and protecting their livelihoods.

June

In an interview with the *Eagle-Tribune*, Mayor Jajuga revealed that he would not seek a second term. He explained that he had delayed the announcement until the City Council approved the city's budget. "I wanted to be sure that my successor had a really solid foundation here," he said. "And I'm confident about that now."

Jajuga's term began amid significant challenges, including a school department overspending crisis and controversial police contract issues. With a state-appointed overseer guiding the city's finances and the appointment of Methuen's first-ever Chief Administration and Finance Officer (CAFO), Jajuga felt the timing was right to step aside. "Whoever succeeds me will be working with a community that has been put back together," he said.

Despite Mayor's assertion that the community had been "put back together," the reality told a different story. The police contracts remained unresolved and were heading to arbitration, and the city had taken on a $4 million loan due to the school department's overspending. Tensions between Jajuga and the City Council persisted, often manifesting in open hostility. Their relationship had grown so strained that it became uncommon for the mayor to attend council meetings at all.

Over the past year, Jajuga had developed a reputation for losing his temper during meetings, at times shouting in frustration. On the rare occasions he did attend, he would deliver his mayor's report and promptly leave, delegating any follow-up questions to his Chief of Staff, who would take his place at the council table.

Although Jajuga ultimately chose not to seek re-election, his campaign finances told another story. During his first term, his war chest steadily grew. Raising $63,563 before his initial election, contributions during his time in office surged an additional $121,187 by the time he announced his decision in June — nearly double the amount raised during his campaign.

It is worth noting that at least $23,875, nearly thirteen percent of Jajuga's total campaign contributions, came from MPD affiliated donors.

December

To address challenges inherited from their predecessors, the 2018–2019 City Council proactively sought assistance from multiple state and federal agencies to investigate the ethical and legal implications of costly decisions made by prior councils. One particularly troubling issue that emerged was the controversial invocation of the "Rule of Necessity" during a City Council vote on September 18, 2017.

On December 19, 2019, the Massachusetts State Ethics Commission found reasonable cause to believe that three former city councilors — James Atkinson, James Jajuga, and Lynn Vidler — violated conflict-of-interest laws by voting on the superior officers' contract despite direct family ties. The council had invoked the Rule of Necessity to justify their votes, but the Ethics Commission made clear: the rule had been misused and did not apply.

Under Massachusetts law, municipal employees, including elected officials, are prohibited from participating in official matters that involve their own financial interests, those of immediate family members, or entities with which they have an arrangement for future employment.

At the time of the vote, all three councilors had clear conflicts of interest: Atkinson had a pending job offer from the Methuen Police Department; Jajuga's son and Vidler's husband were both superior officers within the department. These relationships legally barred the councilors from taking part in the vote on the Superior Officers' contract.

Ethics Complaint

As detailed in the chapter addressing the Rule of Necessity, the Ethics Commission later clarified in formal correspondence that council improperly invoked the rule. The council was not legally obligated to vote on the Superior Officers' contract, thereby eliminating any valid basis for invoking the Rule of Necessity. Without a genuine necessity, the councilors' participation constituted a violation of conflict-of-interest statutes.

Rather than pursue formal charges, the Commission chose to issue "Public Education Letters" to the three councilors. This decision reflected a degree of leniency, influenced by several mitigating factors: the councilors had acted in good faith based on legal advice from the Methuen City Solicitor, had abstained from police-related matters in practice, were not involved in negotiating or drafting the superior officers' contract, and fully cooperated with the Commission's investigation.

Although the commission formally reprimanded the councilors, they appeared to take no public action against City Solicitor Richard D'Agostino, who had provided the flawed legal advice that underpinned their actions. Despite multiple controversies during his tenure — including erroneous guidance on the Rule of Necessity — which allowed the contract approval that nearly caused the city to be put into receivership. Despite the comedy of errors, D'Agostino remains listed as an attorney in good standing with the Massachusetts Board of Bar Overseers, with no record of disciplinary action as of this publication.

2020

January 6	Neil Perry is sworn in as Mayor of Methuen.
January 15	*Methuen Confidential*, a political blog, debuts online.
February 7	Chief Solomon has Mayor Perry sign Civil Service Form 67.
	Mayor Perry asks HR Director Anne Randazzo to provide background information regarding the City's use of intermittent police officers.
February 10	Randazzo submits Civil Service Form 67 to the state, listing Sean Fountain's name.
April 16	The arbitrator releases a decision on Officer Arthur Hardy's disciplinary appeal.
April 19	Councilor Mike Simard sends an email to Chief Solomon, criticizing him for failing to provide requested information.
	Solomon signs and submits a request to the MPTC for a 270-day training waiver for Officers Fountain and Abraham.
April 22	Solomon emails MPTC Director Robert Ferullo, attaching the waiver form.
April 24	Mayor Perry personally answers Councilor Mike Simard's questions in place of Solomon.
April 26	Simard requests that Mayor Perry ensure all intermittent officers have proper training certifications on file.
April 27	Officer Arthur Hardy returns to duty after his extended suspension.
May	The City selects a firm to conduct an audit of the Methuen Police Department.
May 1	HR Director Lisa Crowley requests that Solomon provide certifications for all intermittent officers.
	MPTC Director Ferullo emails Solomon expressing concerns about Sean Fountain's waiver.
	Ferullo and Solomon speak on the phone for 11 minutes.
May 4	Solomon sends Crowley three out of five requested certifications, promising that certifications for Fountain and Despins will follow.
May 5	Certifications for Officers Matthew Despins and Sean Fountain are emailed to Crowley.
May 7	Mayor Perry forwards the officer certification documents to Councilor Simard.

2020

May 11	Attorney Caruso, representing Solomon, Aiello, and Captain Greg Gallant, sends a letter to School Committee member DJ Deeb demanding the preservation of all relevant documents.
May 12	Mayor Perry sends a letter to Sean Fountain, demoting him from full intermittent to part-time intermittent status.
	Fountain files for whistleblower protection.
July 8	Due to COVID-19 budget cuts, the City lays off 10 patrol officers, 1 lieutenant, 3 sergeants, 2 dispatchers, and numerous intermittent officers.
August 31	The Methuen City Council votes "no confidence" in Chief Solomon.
October	Arbitration begins for the Superior Officers' Union's contract dispute.
October 8	Sean Fountain's attorney sends a formal "demand for settlement" letter to the City.
December 23	A new Massachusetts Inspector General report is released to the City.
	Chief Joseph Solomon and Captain Greg Gallant are placed on paid administrative leave.

January

Drawing inspiration from one of Solomon's tactics in 2009, an anonymous blog targeting the Methuen Police Department's leadership — primarily Solomon — emerged in January 2020. Written in a sharp, snarky tone, Methuen Confidential (MC) appeared just days after Neil Perry, a political newcomer, was sworn in as mayor. Initially seen as a puppet of former Mayor Sharon Pollard, Perry reinforced that perception by appointing Pollard's husband, Tom Lussier, to a position within the mayor's office.

But as the saying goes, blood proved thicker than water. Perry, a first cousin of retired MPD Chief Bruce MacDougall — who Pollard pushed aside to pave the way for Solomon's rise — soon broke ranks with the former mayor. The shift marked a clear turning point, signaling Perry's intent to settle an old family feud and assert his independence.

For six weeks, MC captivated and informed the public through more than 32 blistering posts, with eye-catching titles such as "Getting Rich on Taxpayers' Dollars," "Chief Solomon's Million

2020

Dollar Golden Parachute Scheme," "Chief Joe Solomon's Travel-with-a-Buddy Program," and "Solomon, Donovan & Shenanigan, Inc."

Several posts openly mocked Solomon's investigative acumen. According to the blog itself, Solomon was reportedly "steaming and pulling out all the stops to find the leakers and shut down the site." It was easy to imagine his desperation as he scrambled to contain the flood of information that captured the public's attention and was spreading rapidly.

The identity of the blog's author — known only as "Carlos P. Danger, Publisher" — remained one of Methuen's best-kept secrets. No one "in the know" ever floated credible theories as to whom was behind the blog, suggesting the creator had taken extraordinary care to remain anonymous. Many believed it was the work of someone inside the department — an insider who had finally reached a breaking point. The timing and accuracy of the posts led some to believe that justice might finally tilt away from Solomon and toward long-buried truths.

MC delved into both current events and long-rumored controversies, shedding light on topics that had previously circulated only in hushed conversations. Among them are Solomon's private business ventures, his lucrative employment contract, taxpayer-funded conferences in sunny destinations, questionable officer appointments, nepotism, conflicts of interest, and the highly controversial contract with his superior officers.

While the blog zeroed in on the police department, it didn't hesitate to expose dysfunction in other city departments or to spotlight broader municipal issues. That breadth of coverage only amplified its impact, transforming it into a lightning rod for public discourse and a symbol of growing discontent with city leadership.

February

Mayor Perry had only been in office a few weeks when Solomon arrived at his office with a document in hand — the annual Section 67 list required by the Massachusetts Civil Service Commission. The list, mandated by statute, must include all Civil Service employees and be posted in locations where five or more such employees begin their tour of duty.

Trusting the routine nature of the document, Perry signed it. What he didn't know was that this seemingly mundane list had already been the subject of extensive backchannel discussion between Solomon, then-HR Director Anne Randazzo (who also served as Assistant City Solicitor), and then-Chief of Staff Paul Fahey the previous year.

The roots of the controversy date back to 2018, when the city was grappling with the possibility of layoffs of patrol officers due to the unsustainable cost of the contract for superior officers. During that time, Fahey sent an email to Randazzo and Solomon, seeking clarity on the employment status of one officer in particular: Sean Fountain.

"I want to be clear about Sean's status," Fahey wrote. "Did Civil Service notify us that he can't be laid off due to the statute [Home Rule Petition] allowing for his hiring in the first place? Absent that, he needs to be part of the next layoffs. Please advise, thanks."

Randazzo quickly responded:

> *"I have not mentioned specifically Sean Fountain to Civil Service. I discussed the different titles of employees working for the City. Civil Service does not recognize our permanent intermittent officers who are not appointed through Civil Service. I have not been part of any conversation that discussed Fountain's status. However, I see no reason to treat him any differently than the other intermittent officers who were working full-time and who were notified of being laid off. I would think that the union will certainly object to an individual who a permanent intermittent officer is working full time when Civil Service employees are being laid off."*

Solomon, however, interjected with urgency:

> *"Anne, I thought you had an email from Civil Service that said Civil Service time transferred over for an employee. That is how Fountain was placed on the list. Can we meet today when everyone is available and review all the information? I am available all day."*

Randazzo's reply was curt and dismissive:

2020

> *"I'm not sure what that means, but I have no such email.
> — Anne."*

Whatever took place in the meeting that followed, it resolved in Solomon's favor. Sean Fountain was added to the final Section 67 list as entry No. 61 — with a Civil Service date of August 9, 1999, corresponding not to his police appointment but to his earlier tenure as a firefighter.

The next day, internal doubts continued to surface. In an email exchange with Randazzo, HR employee Jill Stackelin wrote:

"I made the changes; however, I don't agree with #61 being Civil Service, but I was also not privy to any discussions on it."

Randazzo replied: "Is that Fountain? We'll see what Civil Service says."

Stackelin responded: "Yes, but they might not say anything as he is listed as officer and not intermittent officer."

Randazzo, with characteristic brevity, replied: "Noted."

When she forwarded the final list to Fahey, Randazzo added a noteworthy disclaimer:

> *"This is the final Civil Service seniority list. Just for clarification purposes, I would not be surprised if Civil Service will be contacting us about Fountain's presence on this list, as he is a permanent full-time intermittent police officer and did not get appointed as a police officer through the Civil Service process. I will be sending this list to Civil Service."*

Yet, no objection came. The state's Human Resources Division (HRD) either overlooked the discrepancy or failed to act. It is worth noting that Solomon was the last to sign the Section 67 Report. Instead of signing it himself, he directed, via email, his confidential secretary to sign in his name – which she did. And now, months later, Solomon was standing in Perry's office, presenting that same list — with Fountain still on it — for the mayor's signature.

Unaware of the prior controversy or the questionable addition, Perry signed off, inadvertently legitimizing a decision that many believed lacked proper legal grounding.

Mayor Perry later recalled reaching out to Randazzo that same day, seeking background on the City's use of non-civil service intermittent police officers.

Later that morning, Randazzo followed up with an email, providing some of the information Perry had requested. In it, she wrote in part:

> "The intermittent officer who are appointed per the 1945 Methuen statute are not civil service appointments and therefore, those individuals do not belong on this list. Those would be the individuals on the list that you are referring to. I have confirmed with Civil Service that our statutory intermittent officer should not be there as they are not civil service employees."

Randazzo went on to state:

> "For your information, in civil service, the reserve and intermittent officer designation is often used interchangeably. Our reserves, on both fire and police, are appointed as permanent reserves through the civil service process. That is the interviewing process that we just concluded in the police department where 32 individuals were interviewed as we requested to add 16 certified civil service reserves to our police reserve list. The formula, as you have probably heard, is 2 plus 1. If we request to fill 16 spots, then Civil Service provides us with a certified list from which we can select 33 names (2 x 16 plus 1). I would be happy to meet with you to discuss this situation further."

Despite clearly acknowledging in her explanation that statutory intermittent officers were not civil service employees and should not appear on the Section 67 list, Randazzo — an attorney and the City's Assistant Solicitor — submitted a fraudulent report to the HRD anyway. This wasn't an isolated incident; she had done the same the previous year. The report, bearing the signatures of both Mayor Perry and Solomon, falsely listed Sean Fountain as a permanent, full-time civil service police officer with a seniority date of August 29, 1999.

2020

Meanwhile, City Councilor Mike Simard — chair of the Council's Public Safety Committee — was actively seeking information on the full-time intermittent officers then working for the City. In response, Solomon provided Simard with a list of names: Despins, Fountain, LaRosa, Gagne, and Abraham. Solomon informed the councilor that the department would need to retrieve the hiring packets for each officer from the archives to review their academy documentation.

Two months passed without any further information from Solomon to Councilor Simard or the Public Safety Committee. On April 19, Simard sent an email expressing his frustration with the delay. "As it pertains to training files," he wrote, "your response that these files were in the 'archives' of your department could be interpreted — and may appear — as deceptive and a direct attempt to delay and fail to respond to the Council's official request."

It was Perry — not Solomon — who ultimately responded to Simard, providing the names of the academies each of the intermittent officers had attended, along with the dates of their training. This included Sean Fountain, who had completed his training at the Northeast Regional Police Institute in Tewksbury, Massachusetts.

Armed with that information, Simard took the next step, formally requesting that the mayor and the Human Resources Department verify the documentation for each intermittent officer to ensure the city had the proper proof of training on file.

April

As COVID-19 strained Methuen's resources, six of nine city councilors urged Mayor Neil Perry to reinstate Officer Arthur Hardy early from a 270-working-day suspension, citing both the severity of the punishment and the department's urgent need for manpower. Hardy was scheduled to return May 18, but the letter — authored by Councilor D.J. Beauregard and shared with the *Eagle-Tribune* — urged the mayor to bring Hardy back.

The *Eagle-Tribune* reached out to Perry for comment, but he declined to speak, citing the arbitrator's pending decision. Chief Solomon also declined to comment.

Arbitrator Mary Ellen Shea of the American Arbitration Association heard testimony over three hearing days in late 2019.

Testifying on behalf of the City were Solomon and investigator Al Donovan. Officer Arthur Hardy was the sole witness for his side.

The facts of the August 1, 2018 incident weren't in dispute. Hardy had responded to a report of possible gunfire and discovered bullet holes in the home and a neighboring residence. Using his finger and a pair of pliers provided by the homeowner, he extracted a metal fragment and notified detectives.

While waiting for detectives, the homeowner handed him a small metal object from a neighbor — possibly related, but Hardy doubted its relevance. He accepted it but accidentally dropped it in the grass. A search turned up nothing.

The city accused Hardy of mishandling evidence, submitting an incomplete report, and violating department policy. They portrayed him as a reckless "cowboy" who ignored protocol, downplayed his mistakes, and refused accountability.

Hardy, in turn, claimed the punishment was personal — rooted in a long-running feud with Solomon. Years earlier, Hardy had been removed from a DEA task force and replaced with one of Solomon's favored supervisors, sparking tension between the DEA and Methuen. That tension, Hardy claimed, never faded. It only intensified when he became a union official.

Notably, during the arbitration hearing, the City did not challenge Hardy's account of his strained relationship with Solomon or the events that contributed to their ongoing conflict.

Hardy also challenged the integrity of Donovan's investigation. Donovan admitted he took no notes, couldn't recall key details, and didn't remember who hired him. He failed to produce documentation from other interviews and gave contradictory testimony about his visit to the scene. His conclusion — that Hardy left out key facts — was based solely on an early draft of the report. He'd never reviewed Hardy's final version, submitted at the start of his next shift due to a department policy prohibiting overtime.

Hardy argued the missing fragment had no evidentiary value. The cited policies, he contended, only applied to items known to be relevant.

On April 16, Arbitrator Shea issued her ruling.

She called Donovan's investigation "less than satisfactory," citing his poor memory, lack of documentation, and inconsistent process. Still, she found that these flaws didn't impact Hardy's rights, as the facts themselves weren't in dispute.

Arbitration Decision

Hardy claimed the discipline was retaliatory. Shea disagreed, citing a lack of direct evidence.

But the crux of her decision came down to proportionality. Could the city prove its policies were clearly communicated and consistently enforced?

Solomon claimed Hardy had acknowledged those policies back in 1996 and had access through the department's online system. Shea accepted that Hardy was aware of the rules — but that wasn't enough.

Hardy submitted evidence of a similar 2012 incident in which he removed a metal fragment from a shooting scene and filed a report. No discipline. No counseling. Testimony confirmed the same policies were in place.

That inconsistency was damning.

"Officer Hardy's conduct in 2012 did not warrant any response undermines [the City's] current argument that nearly identical conduct in 2018 warrants severe discipline," Shea wrote.

She acknowledged that while Hardy omitted mention of the dropped fragment in his report, he gave a full verbal account to detectives. Officers are allowed to leave out details they judge to be irrelevant, but given the time spent searching, the omission — while not malicious — was a mistake.

She found no evidence of deceit or intent to conceal.

Shea reduced the suspension from 270 working days to 60 **calendar** days — noting the City's use of "working days" was inconsistent with every other disciplinary case. She ordered the City to reimburse Hardy for lost wages, overtime, detail pay, and court time exceeding the 60-day suspension.

Hardy's Signoff Sheet

Hardy returned to duty on April 27, 2020 — 452 days after being placed on leave.

There was no welcome back. No briefing. No handshake.

Instead, Captain Greg Gallant and Lieutenant Jim Gunter met him at the station entrance and handed him a stack of documents: every MPD policy, procedure, and regulation. He was told to read and initial all 94 policies and 13 chapters of rules — something no other returning officer had ever been forced to do.

It took him four days.

At the bottom of the first page, Hardy left his final remark, scribbled under his initials:

"I was forced to sign these doc's – Art Hardy."

Message sent. Message received. Solomon didn't like to lose.

The 270-Day Waiver

On the very same day Councilor Simard emailed Solomon, demanding answers about several intermittent officers, Solomon abruptly sprang into action.

He submitted a formal memorandum to the Massachusetts Police Training Committee (MPTC), requesting a special waiver for Sean Fountain. Although Solomon was *not* the appointing authority, he signed the application in his limited capacity as "Police Chief – Non-Appointing," a designation clearly marked on the form. Notably, both Fountain's and Abraham's 270-day waiver applications were signed only in this capacity by Solomon; the next step should have involved forwarding the forms to Mayor Perry for proper authorization.

Instead, Solomon bypassed protocol. He skipped the required submission to the MPTC's Director of Training and sent the memo directly — through back channels — to Executive Director Robert Ferullo. Had the Director of Training received the application, it might have been flagged for lacking the necessary appointing authority's signature or mayoral approval. But Ferullo's decision to accept the memo outside of standard procedure effectively short-circuited those safeguards, inserting himself into a process designed to prevent precisely this kind of unchecked maneuvering.

The memo read in part:

> "*The Methuen Police Department is requesting that a temporary waiver be granted for a period of 270 days beginning on April 19, 2020, for Sean Fountain. The reason for this request is that the City of Methuen Police*

2020

> *"Officers will not disengage the BWC until the entire incident has been recorded or when further recording of the incident will not serve a proper police purpose."*

> *"Department is currently short on full-time officers, and during this COVID-19 pandemic, we need every position filled. Granting this waiver will allow one of the positions to be filled by Sean Fountain."*

What Solomon failed to mention in the letter is that Fountain had been working as a Methuen Police Officer for 1,388 days already. Solomon continues his letter:

> *"We have attempted to send officers to the Academy, but due to budgetary constraints, it is not feasible at this time. Sean Fountain attended and graduated from the Reserve/Intermittent Academy on May 13, 1995, but has since misplaced his graduation certificate. He has requested a copy of the certificate but has not received it yet. A copy of his request is included."*

"Your consideration during these challenging times is greatly appreciated."

At first glance, it reads like a practical — even noble — solution in the middle of a public health crisis. But dig even slightly beneath the surface, and the stench of misrepresentation becomes unmistakable.

To understand just how deceptive Solomon's actions were, we need to rewind. Back in early 2019, investigative reporter Tim Wood of *Loop Weekly* submitted a public records request for Fountain's police academy graduation record. The MPTC responded that no such record existed. The very next day, Sean Fountain himself requested the same document — and received the exact same response. The only difference? The name on the envelope.

Solomon knew all of this. For over a year, he was fully aware that no training record existed for Fountain. Yet now, in April 2020, Solomon falsely claimed in an official memo that Fountain had graduated from the academy — and even attached a copy of Fountain's prior transcript request as if it proved legitimacy, rather

333

2020

than confirming the opposite. Ironic, considering the agency had already denied the existence of any records on multiple occasions.

Three days later, Solomon doubled down. He emailed Ferullo directly, attaching the waiver request for Fountain, another for Officer Brady Abraham, both résumés, and Fountain's transcript request. He closed the message with casual familiarity:

"Please see attached requests for a 270-day waiver. Pls let me know if you have any questions? Thank you, Joe."

By this point, Solomon was clearly seeking cover. Fountain had been working full-time since at least 2016 — despite never having graduated from a full-time academy. Now, with mounting scrutiny from Simard and the press, Solomon was trying to retroactively legalize the appointment by exploiting the pandemic.

His memo painted a picture of an urgent need — a department strained by COVID-19 and unable to afford academy tuition. But city records show that since Fountain's questionable appointment, at least nine Methuen recruits had attended and successfully graduated from full-time academies.

Ferullo, to his credit, appeared uneasy. On May 1st, he emailed Solomon: "I am concerned about Fountain ... we can talk? I will call."

Phone records confirm they spoke for roughly eleven minutes. What exactly Ferullo said during that call remains unknown. But five days later, an old thread of 2019 emails landed on his desk — emails that may have changed everything.

MPTC Email Thread

The thread, between former MPTC Director Dan Zivkovich and officials at the Massachusetts Executive Office of Public Safety, responded to the same 2019 records request from Tim Wood. The subject line? *"Records request regarding Officer Sean Fountain of Methuen."* The messages made one thing painfully clear: Fountain was already serving as a full-time officer in 2019, despite lacking training credentials. They also included a newspaper article confirming his employment as an officer.

All of this — the emails, the denials, the public exposure — was now right in front of Ferullo. And if he hadn't already realized it on the phone with Solomon, the documentation now made it undeniable: Solomon had misrepresented Fountain's status in an

334

official waiver request. There was no COVID emergency. No recent appointment. No misplaced certificate. There was only a forgery of process, and a lie delivered at the highest level of law enforcement oversight.

Meanwhile, the new Human Resources Director, Lisa Crowley, who had been in her role for just under two months when, at the request of Mayor Perry, she began searching for academy certificates for the department's full-time intermittent officers. Unable to locate them in her records, she reached out to Solomon via email to ask if he had copies. Solomon responded by sending certificates for three of the five officers, noting that he would forward the remaining two — for Despins and Fountain — the following day, which he did.

Solomon's Email to Crowley with Certificates

With Fountain's certificate in hand, Perry was left with little choice. On May 12th, he issued a letter to Fountain informing him that, because he had completed only an introductory training course 25 years earlier — not a full-time academy, as required — he could no longer serve as a full-time intermittent officer.

Perry further stated that, to continue serving even as a part-time intermittent officer, Fountain would need to re-establish residency in Methuen, as he was currently living in New Hampshire. "It is incumbent upon each of us to follow the law, the guidelines, and the training requirements to minimize the risks and liabilities associated with the assignment of policing powers in the City of Methuen and the Commonwealth of Massachusetts," Perry wrote.

Perry's Letter

The following week, the MPTC held its regular business meeting. Abraham's request for a 270-day waiver was on the agenda — yet notably, the meeting plan did not included Fountain's application. Only Brady Abraham's request remained, and it was unanimously approved.

The reason for Fountain's omission remains unclear. However, it appears Ferullo may have discovered that Fountain had been working for years as a full-time police officer without ever having completed a required police academy. What's more troubling is the likelihood that his predecessor, Dan Zivkovich, along with senior officials at the Executive Office of Public Safety and Security (EOPSS) — including the then-Undersecretary of Public Safety, now Secretary of EOPSS, and Terrence Reidy— had been made aware of this more than a year earlier and had seemingly taken no action.

It is worth noting; both the MPTC and EOPS are the very agencies charged with ensuring that law enforcement personnel are properly trained and in compliance with the laws of the Commonwealth.

Demand Letter

Gallant, Aiello, and Solomon retained attorney Peter J. Caruso, who, in turn, issued a "Demand for Preservation of Electronically Stored Information" letter dated May 11. While the letter began by stating that the firm represented "members of the Methuen Police Superior Officers Association," it failed to clarify whether it was acting on behalf of the entire union or only select individuals within it.

Caruso sent the letter to all nine sitting city councilors as well as to Dennis "D.J." Deeb, a former school committee member and then-candidate for city council. It notified recipients of an ongoing investigation by Caruso's firm into the conduct of several councilors — both in their official roles and as private citizens — as well as the conduct of other individuals. The alleged wrongdoing under review included libel, defamation, invasion of privacy, intentional infliction of emotional distress, and doxing.

Attorney Caruso's Letter

The lawyer instructed the recipients to preserve all documents, physical materials, and electronically stored information that might be relevant to the potential claims. The remainder of the two-page letter outlined specific formats, devices, and measures to prevent the loss or destruction of data. It concluded with a request for the recipients' homeowner's insurance information.

The letter must have provoked a mix of concern, annoyance, and alarm among its recipients. However, Deeb responded with open defiance. In a sharply worded reply dated shortly after receiving the notice, he wrote:

> *"I have received your outrageous letter dated May 11, 2020. I am under no legal obligation to provide any of the information that you asked for. If civil litigation commences, I will obviously comply with all applicable statutes and procedures at that time. In the meantime, it is my intent to completely disregard your letter."*

Deeb further warned Caruso that the letter itself could violate Massachusetts' Anti-SLAPP statute (Strategic Lawsuit Against Public Participation), stating:

> *"As a respected law firm in the area, I would remind you that this letter constitutes a violation of the Anti-SLAPP statute... which I will raise under a potential counterclaim should civil litigation proceed in this matter. Given the exorbitant salaries that your clients are currently receiving or scheduled to receive under the contracts, I am sure that your clients will be able to pay a potential counterclaim that I file, along with my attorney and court filing fees that I incur with the salaries that they are making."*

D.J. Deeb's Response

Following Deeb's pointed response, there seem to be no further public references or legal actions taken in connection with this threat.

July

As the COVID-19 pandemic brought the economy to a grinding halt, Methuen was staring down the barrel of a projected $7 million budget shortfall for the upcoming fiscal year. The reduced state and federal aid, and declining municipal revenues — Methuen braced for a financial crisis.

Mayor Neil Perry acted swiftly. He imposed a hiring freeze across city departments and halted all scheduled pay increases

2020

until state or federal aid could be secured. Setting the tone from the top, Perry voluntarily reduced his own salary from $80,000 to $68,000.

But belt-tightening alone wouldn't solve the crisis. So Perry made a difficult request to every municipal union: accept either ten furlough days per employee or face layoffs within your ranks. Some unions chose the furloughs; others opted for layoffs. He presented the same choice to his department heads.

All but one agreed to the furloughs – Solomon, who chose neither.

The City Council responded with a pointed letter. The *Eagle-Tribune* obtained a copy and published it in full. It began with measured diplomacy:

"In a noble effort to help mitigate this impending loss of services, nearly every department head in our city has agreed to accept a reduction in pay by way of taking 10 furlough/unpaid vacation days during the upcoming fiscal year."

Then the message sharpened:

"We are aware that you are the only department head who has not."

Finally, they laid down the challenge:

"It is not too late to do the right thing by acting in the best interests of Methuen's residents and the patrol officers that keep them safe. By taking 10 furlough/unpaid vacation days during the upcoming fiscal year, you would join your fellow department heads in voluntarily accepting a reduction in pay."

And as a closing appeal:

"We hope you will earnestly consider putting service above self and helping us attempt to save the jobs of the employees you lead."

But Solomon wasn't moved. When contacted by the *Eagle-Tribune*, he fired back that the Council "needed to check their facts."

Mayor Perry, however, confirmed the facts were quite clear: Solomon had refused both the furlough and the pay freeze. His reasoning? He claimed his nearly $300,000 salary was already *below* what he was entitled to under his contract.

The controversy didn't fade with the news cycle. Solomon took to the airwaves, appearing on the *Paying Attention Podcast* hosted by Tom Duggan, where he attempted to rewrite the narrative. He

2020

argued that the so-called "furloughs" were merely vacation days in disguise and accused former Mayor Jim Jajuga of stripping him of both his 13 vacation days and his longevity pay. Solomon claimed that Mayor Perry had continued that practice, forcing him to absorb unjust compensation cuts.

It was a compelling story — if only it were true.

A review of payroll records from 2006 through 2021 told a different tale. In 2018, during Jajuga's tenure, Solomon received $21,893 in longevity pay. In 2019, the number rose to $22,578. Far from being stripped of his vacation time, Solomon was *paid out* for three weeks of unused vacation — totaling $14,420 — just days before Jajuga left office.

Even more telling, when Solomon ultimately retired, he cashed out nearly $100,000 in unused vacation time.

His public claim that he had been mistreated — financially victimized by the city — wasn't just misleading. It was false. And it landed hard in the face of a city workforce being asked to sacrifice in the name of survival.

While most department heads led by example, Solomon once again stood apart — not as a leader, but as someone unwilling to put the city's needs above his own.

Intermittent Layoff

At the direction of Mayor Perry, Human Resources Director Lisa Crowley sent letters to all full-time intermittent officers, stating:

> *"Due to the COVID-19 pandemic, the anticipated lack of state and federal funding, and the municipal shortfall in revenue, the City will be eliminating the position of full-time, permanent intermittent police officer effective July 31, 2020. Included in this letter is information on unemployment and COBRA benefits. Please accept our appreciation for your service while with the City of Methuen."*

Still advocating for his full-time intermittent officers, Solomon emailed Crowley to express his understanding that city officials were laying off this officer class — and, if they were ever to return, it would be at reduced hours.

Crowley, clearly frustrated and under the impression that everyone was on the same page after the last group meeting on the matter, emailed the mayor to confirm whether the city was eliminating the positions permanently or temporarily. Perry's response was brief and unequivocal: "It is not my intent to restore the intermittent officers."

Two days later, Fountain responded to his layoff letter with a three-paragraph rebuttal explaining why he believed the city could not legally terminate him. He first cited Massachusetts House Bill #3674, signed into law by Governor Charlie Baker on August 1, 2017, under Chapter 60 of the Acts of 2017, and referenced Massachusetts General Law (MGL), Chapter 31, Section 48, which pertains to appointments by the Governor and, according to Fountain, are not subject to layoff or elimination.

He then pointed to the Civil Service seniority summary sheet, posted by Methuen's HR Department per MGL Chapter 31, Section 67, and signed by Mayor Perry as the appointing authority on February 7, 2020. The document listed Fountain's employment status as "full-time officer" with a start date of August 29, 1999.

In the final paragraph, Fountain invoked protections under the Older Workers Benefit Protection Act (OWBPA), challenging the city to address his employment status and legal standing under the federal statute. The irony, of course, is that Fountain was, by law, over the age limit to be hired by the Methuen Police Department in the first place.

Fountain was pulling out all the stops to keep his position. He cc'd the letter to his own legal counsel, the patrolmen's union attorney, Solomon, and the Massachusetts Commission Against Discrimination.

October

A 10-page letter, accompanied by exhibits, dated October 8, 2020, was addressed to Mayor Neil Perry and Lisa Crowley, the City's Human Resources Director.

The letter, authored by attorney George Malonis, P.C., was submitted on behalf of his client, former MPD permanent intermittent officer Sean Fountain, as a formal demand for settlement. The document alleged a series of torts and civil rights violations that, according to the letter, led to and followed Fountain's wrongful termination from the department.

According to Malonis, shortly after the police contracts went into effect in 2018, Fountain became the target of a prolonged and deliberate campaign of harassment, retaliation, and other misconduct. The attorney asserted that this conduct sabotaged and ultimately destroyed Fountain's personal and business reputation in the City, as well as his career with the MPD.

Attorney Malonis' Letter

Fountain and his attorney further claimed that, as public criticism mounted over the police contracts — particularly the controversial Superior Officers' contract — City officials began seeking a "scapegoat" to absorb the political fallout. As scrutiny over the 2017 contract vote intensified during the 2019 election season, the alleged attacks took on a more personal tone, focusing on Fountain's employment with the MPD. Councilors James McCarty and Mike Simard, both running for re-election, allegedly began targeting Fountain through both direct and indirect innuendo. Examples cited included McCarty publicly stating he would not seek a job as a police officer after his council term, and Simard referring to the prior Council — of which Fountain was a member — as corrupt, stating it had included someone who had "skirted the system" and now worked for a "mismanaged police department."

Fountain also took issue with posts from Methuen Confidential (MC), which publicly criticized him using headlines such as "The Curious Case of Sean Fountain" and "Continuing Fiasco – Intermittent Police Officers." These posts accused Solomon of exploiting a "willfully deaf, dumb, and blind" mayor to appoint Fountain as an Intermittent Officer. MC further suggested that the Council at the time — again implicating Fountain — either "dropped the ball, or at worst, sold the ball" when approving the contracts. Malonis emphasized in the letter that these claims were "patently false."

Fountain asserted that he had cooperated extensively with state and federal authorities investigating the 2017 contract vote, despite knowing the results could harm the city. After the State Ethics Commission reprimanded three members of the 2017

2020

Council (Fountain was not among them), he claimed the Council's focus "drastically" shifted toward his role within the MPD.

In March 2020, a social media post criticized internal MPD politics and questioned why Fountain, a former City Councilor, was handling evidence rather than a veteran officer like Arthur Hardy. The following day, during a City Council meeting, Simard stated that "a detective who isn't certified and bypassed the hiring process is working major cases, even homicides."

The letter also referenced an April 2020 *Eagle-Tribune* article in which a reporter quoted Simard regarding the upcoming police audit: "I'm hoping the audit can explain why our police department would find the need to circumvent the civil service hiring process... Why was Fountain's training accelerated and modified, enabling him to become a detective in eight months?" Attorney Malonis characterized these statements as part of a "smear campaign" aimed at destroying Fountain's professional standing. He defended Fountain's assignment to the detectives' division by citing his "exemplary service" as an Intermittent Officer. The attorney stressed that it did not constitute a promotion that would require a Civil Service exam.

Fountain subsequently filed a whistleblower complaint with the city's HR department, alleging harassment in retaliation for his cooperation with investigators. The following day, May 12, 2020, Mayor Perry removed him from the detectives' division and reverted him to part-time intermittent officer status, citing Fountain's lack of completion of a full-time police academy program.

Despite this demotion, Fountain continued working "to the best of his abilities," including on a burglary case in progress. The MPD issued a public call for information on the case via social media, naming Fountain as the point of contact. McCarty responded by posting, "Contact former Methuen City Council Chairman Sean Fountain." Councilor D.J. Beauregard escalated the rhetoric, writing, "We must clearly point out how the Fountain situation is an insult to all academy-trained officers and has made a total mockery of the civil service appointment process. Progress is being made, but we will not stop fighting the corruption in that department. It is outrageous and unacceptable and needs to stop."

The letter continued to catalogue incidents of alleged harassment. During City Council budget workshops, Councilor

2020

Steve Saba questioned why a former firefighter without academy training was investigating homicides. He also asked Solomon why some officers were sent to the Methuen Police Academy while others, like Fountain, were not.

Solomon responded directly, stating he knew which officer Saba was referring to and asserted that the officer had more qualifications than most. In what appeared to be a rebuke to the Council, Solomon claimed he had repeatedly requested funding for academy training, only to be denied.

It is worth noting that Solomon had routinely sent officers to the academy in prior years, casting doubt on his claim that a lack of funding prevented him from doing so in this instance. Moreover, financial constraints do not legally justify deploying untrained officers to active duty. If funding truly was a concern, it is reasonable to question why Solomon did not reallocate existing "training" funds — particularly those reportedly used for travel by himself and his command staff — to support mandatory academy training.

The letter continued to chronicle the history with the MPD. The city later laid off Fountain during the COVID-19 pandemic due to budget shortfalls but he was still permitted to work paid details. While the city recalled other officers over the summer, Fountain and other intermittent officers were not. The police union filed a grievance on his behalf, but the city denied the grievance because the action was a layoff, not a termination.

The letter also detailed what Malonis described as an intolerable violation of privacy. Two months into Fountain's layoff, Solomon reportedly informed him that Human Resources had ordered the release of his complete employment and background application packets. These documents contained sensitive personal information, including credit reports, physical ability test results, psychological and medical exam records, and both Criminal Offender Record Information (CORI) and FBI background checks. Since the city no longer employed Fountain, the letter argued, there was no legitimate basis for accessing these records.

As a result of these events, Fountain engaged Malonis to seek damages on the following legal grounds:

- Federal and state civil rights violations
- Retaliation

2020

- Libel and slander
- Intentional infliction of emotional distress
- Interference with advantageous business relations
- Wrongful termination
- Civil conspiracy

To avoid the time, expense, and emotional toll of litigation, Fountain demanded a settlement of $1.5 million.

December

Amid growing concerns over the ethical, legal, and financial implications of the Methuen police contracts, many newly seated City Council members, joined by dozens of concerned residents, urged state agencies to intervene. They specifically requested an investigation into whether the contracts constituted a misuse of public funds and whether any fraudulent activity had taken place.

In response, in 2018, Inspector General Glenn Cunha of the Massachusetts Office of the Inspector General (OIG) launched a formal review of the Superior Officers' contract. By February 2019, the OIG issued a letter concluding that former Mayor Stephen Zanni and the 2017 City Council had violated multiple laws, regulations, and fiduciary duties owed to the city and its taxpayers.

What the public did not know at the time was that the OIG's inquiry did not end there. The investigation expanded to include Solomon's most recent employment contract, also approved by the 2017 Council, which raised additional red flags.

OIG Report

Nearly two years later, on December 23, 2020, the OIG released its formal report, "Leadership Failures in Methuen Police Contract," detailing six significant investigative findings:

The City's Negotiating Team Failed to Exercise Due Diligence

The OIG concluded that every member of Methuen's negotiating team had a legal and ethical duty to act with diligence, transparency, and integrity on behalf of the City's residents. That responsibility, the report emphasized, is rooted in the Massachusetts Declaration of Rights, which requires public officials to serve with "an eye single to the interest" of the people.

Yet during contract negotiations, the police union aggressively pushed to redefine "base pay" to include a slew of stipends and allowances — many of them newly created or significantly inflated. Though members of the City's team voiced concerns, they failed to demand a financial impact analysis or take meaningful steps to assess the long-term fiscal consequences.

One of the most glaring omissions was the absence of a salary schedule in the final contract — an intentional move by Captain Greg Gallant. Without it, the true financial impact of the agreement was obscured, leaving both city officials and the public in the dark about just how costly the contract really was.

While then-Mayor Zanni did ask the City Auditor to evaluate the cost of the COLA (cost-of-living adjustment), he made no effort to disclose the deeper financial giveaways buried throughout the agreement. According to the OIG, the City had a clear obligation to conduct — and make public — a full financial impact assessment before finalizing the contract. That never happened. In the end, basic standards of fiscal responsibility and transparency were not just overlooked — they were ignored.

Mayor Zanni Breached His Duty of Care

The OIG's second finding faulted then-Mayor Zanni for failing to carry out the duties of his office with even the most basic level of diligence. In his final year — widely seen as a "lame duck" term — Zanni approved two expensive police contracts without fully understanding their financial impact. While he claimed the COLAs were consistent with other union agreements, he also signed off on a range of new, costly provisions that significantly boosted officer pay.

The report cited a series of alarming missteps: Zanni took no notes during negotiations, never read the final contract before signing it, and excluded both the City Solicitor and City Auditor from the review process. He also misled the City Council, stating the only change was a "0-2-2" COLA — without providing any documentation to support that claim.

Worse, the signing lacked any of the standard safeguards: no witnesses, no page-by-page review, no initials on individual pages. The outcome: a blatant disregard for the most fundamental principles of oversight and transparency.

The City Solicitor May Have Breached His Duty of Care

The OIG's third finding sharply criticized City Solicitor Richard D'Agostino for failing to meet his obligations under the Methuen City Charter, which clearly required him to prepare and review all city contracts. Despite this mandate, neither D'Agostino nor Assistant Solicitor Ann Randazzo — who also served as the City's Human Resources Director — reviewed the final Superior Officers' contract submitted to the City Council just days before the crucial September 18, 2017 vote.

D'Agostino, a regular presence at Council meetings and the City's chief legal advisor, failed to disclose that his office had not reviewed the contract. Had he fulfilled his duty, his team would likely have flagged the now-infamous "Gallant Formula" — a provision that embedded stipends and educational incentives into base pay, triggering inflated salaries across the department.

Even as the contract's financial impact drew scrutiny in 2018, D'Agostino did not revisit his notes or examine the signed agreement. His inaction had real consequences. Then-Mayor James Jajuga, unaware of the unvetted provisions, negotiated a Memorandum of Understanding (MOU) under the false assumption that the contract had been lawfully negotiated and legally reviewed. In truth, many of the most expensive elements had never been formally approved — by anyone.

Captain Gallant Acted in Bad Faith

The OIG's fourth finding exposed a stunning breach of trust by Captain Greg Gallant, then-president of the Superior Officers' Union. Gallant deliberately inserted language into the final contract that had never been negotiated or approved by the City. Chief among these unauthorized changes: converting a flat $500 vest stipend into a percentage of base pay — 1 percent in FY2019, jumping to 2 percent in FY2020 — dramatically increasing its value.

2020

But he didn't stop there.

Gallant unilaterally redefined "base pay" to include holiday pay, uniform allowances, and the now-inflated vest stipend. Then, he introduced what would come to be known as the "Gallant Formula," embedding education incentives directly into base pay calculations. Because higher-ranking officers' salaries were based on a percentage of the patrol officers' base pay, this created a domino effect — patrol base pay rose, and so did every rank above it. The result: captains' salaries soared, all built on a manipulated foundation.

Gallant altered the contract's formatting to preserve the original pagination and signature page — making the edits harder to detect. He never disclosed the changes to Mayor Zanni. Nor did he notify the City's MOU negotiators once the contract was realized to be a problem, investigations were launched, and the city found this email exchange on their servers.

Gallant's email, dated September 4th, to the union's attorney, Gary Nolan:

> *"Signed today, looks good, it goes up for the council meeting on the 18th, hopefully goes ok,*
> *There will be four or five other contracts going up.*
> *We made some language changes at the last minute, added a paragraph in compensation, in which we break down the order of calculations to be made, i.e. base, the cleaning allowance, then holiday pay, then hazardous duty percentage, then Quinn. It makes a little difference. We also added prorated language to the longevity and firmed up the definition of base pay in each section."*

To which Nolan replied:

> *"You covered all bases Greg, nice work. Hopefully they don't have calculators at the meeting. Good luck."*

The OIG found that Gallant acted in bad faith, concluding that his manipulation of the contract and accompanying MOU amounted to an attempt to defraud the City.

2020

Emails between Nolan and Gallant

As an investigator with a financial background and a Certified Fraud Examiner, I would go further: Gallant *did* defraud the City of Methuen. The original intent of the negotiated contracts was straightforward — a 0-2-2 pay structure, with no raise in year one and two percent increases in each of the following two years. What ultimately passed, however, was a bloated and deceptive scheme, built on unauthorized figures and unverifiable calculations inserted by Gallant without oversight or approval.

His actions were not just unethical — they were a direct contributor to the fiscal disaster that followed. Even after public outcry forced a rollback of the most outrageous salaries, the damage was already done. The department had secured raises that far exceeded the agreed-upon 0-2-2 framework, saddling the city with long-term financial obligations rooted not in negotiation, but in manipulation and fraud.

Solomon Breached His Duty to *Ensure Public Safety*

The OIG's fifth finding held Solomon accountable for failing to uphold his fiduciary and managerial responsibilities as head of the Methuen Police Department. As a senior official charged with protecting both public safety and taxpayer resources, Solomon was expected to act in the city's best interest. Instead, the OIG found he knowingly enabled contract provisions that endangered both.

Solomon attended every negotiating session for the Superior Officers' contract and was fully aware that the union had not lawfully bargained the "Gallant Formula" or other costly additions. Yet he remained silent. Worse, he played an active role — offering input on contract language and cost implications, then forwarding the revised draft to the patrol officers' union just hours after receiving it from Gallant. He urged them to adopt the same language, knowing it would trigger massive salary increases — including his own.

Even after Mayor Jajuga publicly warned of the contract's unsustainable costs, Solomon said nothing. He continued participating in MOU negotiations as a union representative, concealing what he knew from city officials. When the City Council ultimately refused to fund the deal, the resulting budget crisis forced Jajuga to lay off more than half of the patrol division.

The OIG concluded that Solomon prioritized personal benefit over the well-being of the department and the public. His silence shielded Gallant's deceit, destabilized the department, eroded trust in city leadership, and put public safety at risk.

Solomon did not act in the best interests of the City and may have had a conflict of interest

The OIG's sixth finding concluded that Solomon was supposed to serve as a subject-matter advisor during police contract negotiations — offering the City expertise on law enforcement operations. Instead, he went far beyond that role, taking actions that directly benefited the police unions — and ultimately, himself.

State law bars public employees from participating in matters where they have a financial interest, including offering advice or recommendations in contract negotiations that could affect their own pay. Solomon flagrantly violated that standard when he promoted the "Gallant Formula" to the patrolmen's union, fully aware that his own compensation was tied to theirs. His actions were not just inappropriate — they were self-serving and unethical.

As the OIG bluntly put it: "By his own conduct, he put those interests above those of the City and the people of Methuen."

Two days before Christmas, Solomon was summoned to City Hall. There, in the mayor's office, a neighboring police chief relieved him of his badge, gun, and keys. Mayor Perry then placed him on paid administrative leave.

In a press release, Perry emphasized that the action was not disciplinary, but rather pending further review of the OIG's findings, the upcoming police department audit, and all applicable laws.

2021

January 8	Chief Joseph Solomon submits his letter of resignation, effective January 15.
January 15	The City of Methuen releases the results of the Police Department Performance Audit.
June	Arbitration concludes in the Superior Officers' Union contract dispute.
June 24	The Methuen Retirement Board rules that Solomon's salary exceeded the 10 percent allowable increase under the state's anti-spiking statute.
	Sean Fountain files a federal lawsuit against the City of Methuen alleging wrongful termination.
July 7	Solomon files an appeal of the Retirement Board's anti-spiking ruling.
September 30	The Retirement Board issues its final calculation of Solomon's pension benefit.
October 4	Solomon files an appeal of the Retirement Board's final pension calculation.
October 5	The City signs a contract with the STIRM Group to investigate Sean Fountain's police certification status.

Like many others, you're probably shaking your head in disbelief, wondering how Solomon managed to cling to power for so many years despite a pattern of misconduct. A friend of mine once summed it up with what he called the "Rivet-Popping Hypothesis."

Imagine an airplane in flight: each time Solomon committed an ethical breach or overstepped his authority, it was as if a rivet popped loose from the fuselage. At first, the damage didn't seem critical. A few missing rivets didn't compromise the plane's ability to stay in the air, just as Solomon's early controversies didn't immediately threaten his position. But over time, as more rivets gave way, the structure weakened. The integrity of the aircraft — and of his leadership — became increasingly unstable. The risk of catastrophic failure grew with each new incident until collapse felt not just possible, but inevitable.

2021

So, what's the tipping point? How many rivets have to pop before the whole thing goes down? At what moment does political survival give way to public accountability?

After being fired in 2008 and reinstated in 2010, Solomon appeared to have learned a key lesson: municipal elections acted like emergency patch jobs, sealing just enough of the cracks to keep his administration afloat. He became a master of political optics. Whenever scrutiny intensified or inquiries came too close to the truth, he deflected with remarkable agility. Solomon exercised tight control over the city's narrative — managing social media, issuing press releases, and making carefully staged television appearances with the precision of a campaign strategist.

His every word was measured, every appearance curated to reinforce his image as a capable, even indispensable, leader. And when Solomon could not avoid bad press, a well-timed public gesture — a generous donation, a heroic act or a positive headline — would appear, reinforcing his reputation and, in the public's eye, reattaching some of those loose rivets.

But politics can only defy gravity for so long.

As the scandals multiplied, so did the weight they placed on his administration. Financial crises, state oversight, and the public outrage over exorbitant raises in the superior officers' contract began to take a toll. The air of invincibility surrounding Solomon started to erode. Residents began paying closer attention. Voters elected new voices to the City Council — some running on platforms explicitly aimed at reforming city government and curbing Solomon's influence.

And then came Neil Perry, a newly elected mayor with both the public's trust and, ironically, a familial tie to the police chief that Solomon had replaced nearly two decades earlier.

It was beginning to look like too many rivets had popped for Solomon's operation to remain airborne. The descent had finally started.

January

As the new year began, Solomon — just sixteen days into his paid administrative leave — surprised many by submitting his notice of intent to retire to Mayor Perry on January 11. It was the first time in his 32-year career, including 18 years as police chief, that he had backed down from a challenge.

In typical Solomon fashion, he did not step aside quietly. In a five-page letter to the mayor, which sources later shared with the *Eagle-Tribune*, he began by expressing his love for his career and his gratitude to the men and women who had served under his command. He explained that his decision to retire was "made with the best interest of our community, the men and women of the MPD, and perhaps most importantly, the members of my family." He went on to write,

"While I remain confident in my ability to defend my personal and professional performance in any forum, the ceaseless baseless attacks on my integrity, together with the constant political interference in the management of the department, have created a negative environment that is detrimental to the city, the dedicated members of the department, and to my family and friends."

Solomon emphasized that he had always fought for what he believed to be in the best interest of the department and in line with his duty to serve and protect. He praised what he described as a "talented, well-educated, and highly trained group of police leaders," and expressed hope that they would one day be allowed to lead the MPD free from the political interference that had, in his view, become all too common in recent years.

The remaining four pages of his letter were devoted to listing and elaborating on what he considered the highlights of his personal and departmental accomplishments throughout his career. "During my tenure, we have achieved many things not believed possible," he wrote. "I have tried to be a transformational leader — a change agent — striving to foster a leadership environment that enabled us to work as a team to make each day better than the day before."

Solomon's Resignation Letter

We have documented many of Solomon's cited achievements in earlier chapters of this book. These initiatives included the launch of Community Policing programs, the establishment of the School Resource Officer Team, and the implementation of an internal automated gunshot detection system and a Body-Worn Camera Pilot Program. He also introduced technological advancements, including Nuance speech-to-text software, GPS tracking in cruisers, and the BOLO-Mobile app.

Beyond technology, Solomon played a pivotal role in founding the Methuen/NECC Police Academy and advancing initiatives related to substance use disorder. He oversaw the deployment of an Unmanned Aircraft System, supported underwater search and rescue capabilities, and managed the department's response during significant events, such as the Black Lives Matter protest. His broader leadership résumé included speaking at the National School Leadership Academy, serving on the boards of the Massachusetts Chiefs of Police and the Massachusetts Major City Chiefs, participating in White House meetings, and being featured on the cover of Time magazine.

Despite his departure, Solomon's letter made it clear that he intended to leave on his own terms, reminding both allies and critics of what he believed to be his legacy of innovation, leadership and unwavering service.

In closing his letter, Solomon took the time to address the report issued by the OIG, stating:

"I would be remiss if I failed to note my strong disagreement with the provisions of the recently released report of the Massachusetts OIG that relate directly to my personal performance. Since I was never interviewed by anyone from the OIG – never given the most basic common courtesy to respond to accusations I believe are blatantly false – I am frustrated and deeply disappointed. Although I am certainly willing and able to fight as I have in the past, as I noted earlier in this letter, I have decided to act in the best interest of our community and the department I love and respect. The impact that another long, drawn-out fight would have on the city, the department, and on my family is something I believe should be avoided at all costs."

With that said, the city breathed a sigh of relief. However, his retirement was a double-edged sword. On one hand, Solomon would no longer continue his micromanaged, authoritarian role as Chief of Police. On the other hand, he was retiring with a substantial monthly pension without facing consequences for the allegations against him.

2021

Police Department Audit

The Public Safety Committee, a subcommittee of the Methuen City Council, was established in 2018 in response to the 2017 Superior Officers' contract and other issues within the MPD. Councilor Mike Simard, the committee chair and a police sergeant in the City of Lawrence, lobbied newly elected Mayor Neil Perry to conduct an audit of the police department. As he told an *Eagle-Tribune* reporter, "Police mismanagement within the department has held the city back. I am asking Mayor Perry to conduct a complete audit, from top to bottom, which would help the mayor and council make changes based on facts, not emotions."

Perry, who committed funding for the audit, preferred to label it "risk management" rather than an audit, emphasizing that it was not a "witch hunt."

In May 2020, Perry selected CNA Center for Justice and Innovation (CNA), based in Alexandria, Virginia, to conduct the police audit. Coincidentally, CNA's principal, Edward Flynn, had succeeded James Jajuga, Sr., as Secretary of the Massachusetts Executive Office of Public Safety and Security (EOPSS) during the 2003 scandal involving grant misappropriation by Jajuga.

At the June 3rd City Council meeting, on the eve of the audit's commencement, tensions flared between several councilors and the mayor. Councilor Steve Saba accused Perry of breaking his word by failing to invite all Public Safety Committee members to the audit's kickoff meeting, inviting only the chair, Mike Simard. To further aggravate the situation, Perry had invited Solomon, frustrating several councilors who viewed him as the root of the department's problems.

The situation worsened when details surfaced that one of the auditors had to recuse themselves due to a conflict of interest, renewing concerns about the audit's integrity. As Saba expressed his frustration, Perry — clearly agitated — snapped, "Don't ever question my integrity. Ever!" The confrontation escalated, with Saba threatening to revoke funding for the audit and Perry insisting he was tired of the council challenging his integrity. Simard attempted to defuse the tension, noting that Solomon had been respectful and supportive of the audit and expressed confidence in Perry's ability to ensure a fair and impartial process.

2021

The city initially tasked CNA with auditing budget, equipment, training, staffing levels, hiring processes, equipment acquisition, and the development of policies and procedures. However, the team soon uncovered deeper issues at the MPD, including leadership problems, toxic organizational culture, and low morale. In discussions with council members, CNA acknowledged their concerns about the narrow scope of the audit and the need for impartiality. Although those additional areas were not part of the original contract, the issues raised were so compelling and relevant that CNA expanded the scope to include them.

The nationwide COVID-19 lockdown caused significant logistical delays. Nevertheless, in January 2021, CNA delivered the completed audit report to the mayor's office. Edward Flynn later presented CNA's findings via Zoom to the City Council and the public.

The report divided recommendations into five key categories: organizational structure and governance, budget and planning, operational policies and procedures, department culture, and professional standards and accountability.

The section of the audit that addressed department culture proved especially revealing. While its findings may not have surprised those who had been paying attention or had heard the long-circulating whispers, it was nonetheless striking to see the internal sentiments of MPD personnel laid out so plainly in black and white. For the rank and file, the audit offered a rare platform — one that listened, documented, and publicly exposed what had long remained hidden behind closed doors. Words like "toxic," "hostile," and "retaliatory" were frequently used to describe the station's atmosphere, shaped by a chief who viewed subordinates as either "with him" or "against him."

Those who felt safe enough to speak candidly with the auditors described a workplace where they constantly walked on eggshells, afraid of being written up for the slightest infraction. Meanwhile, those who enjoyed the Chief's favor appeared immune to discipline of any kind.

The auditors included several unfiltered quotes from department members, revealing the depth of dysfunction within the MPD:

> *"It's scarier to work inside the police station than outside the police station."*

2021

> *"Discipline is aimed at people, not conduct."*
> *"Improvement requires change at the top — nothing will change without that."*
>
> *"MPD is all about who you know."*
>
> *"Specialists have new SUVs while patrol officers drive cruisers with 125,000 miles on them."*

These candid remarks painted a stark portrait of a department in crisis — one plagued by fear, favoritism, and a leadership culture widely viewed as fundamentally broken.

Officers described the hiring, assignment, promotion, and disciplinary practices within the MPD as anything but impartial or transparent — more secretive and selective than fair. One example frequently cited was the department's shift to using assessment centers for promotions, which many believed was simply a way for Solomon to ensure his allies rose through the ranks.

The auditors noted with concern that the assessment centers chosen were run by individuals [Donovan and Stanley] who were not only friends and former colleagues of Solomon's, but that one of them also offered a promotional preparation course, despite being the same person who administered the test. What surprised the auditors even more was the lack of formal pushback: no grievances were filed, no complaints were lodged with Civil Service. But, as they quickly came to understand, that was the way in Methuen — those who dared to complain were usually the ones who ended up paying the price.

The report spends considerable time examining MPD's use of intermittent, reserve, and special officers, particularly in their role as supplemental staff.

Reserve officers have already passed the civil service exam and are waiting for full-time openings within the department. Intermittent officers are non-civil service hires, and special officers are typically retired MPD personnel who work paid details. After completing in-house training, both reserve and intermittent officers, may be assigned to patrol shifts to help address staffing shortages.

MPD Performance Audit

2021

At the time of the audit, investigators discovered that the MPD lacked a formal policy governing departmental discipline. This absence of clear guidelines contributed to what many officers described as inconsistent — but frequent — punishments across the department.

One particularly unusual practice stood out: officers reported a form of penalty they referred to as "house arrest-like." Under this arrangement, an officer would be suspended from duty with pay and ordered to remain at home between 8:30 a.m. and 4:30 p.m. The auditors, unfamiliar with this type of disciplinary measure in any other law enforcement setting, questioned Solomon about its purpose. He described it as a "non-disciplinary intervention."

When asked to provide examples of written orders tied to this so-called intervention, the auditors noted that none of the documents contained an explanation for the action. Solomon claimed the omission was intentional — meant to spare the officer from embarrassment by not including the reason in writing. Officers reported that they believed this form of punishment was a way for Solomon to bypass the formal grievance process. By labeling it a "non-disciplinary intervention" and omitting any written justification, they felt he could sidestep accountability and avoid challenges through official personnel procedures.

As with most departmental performance audits, many of the findings in this report were routine and non-sensational. It noted common issues, including unclear or missing policies and procedures, a lack of diversity in hiring practices, and delays in the accreditation process.

Still, the overarching theme that emerged was one of deep mistrust and fear between the rank and file and the department's leadership, particularly Solomon.

Retirement

In Massachusetts, public employees don't pay into Social Security. Instead, they contribute to a retirement system that vests after 10 years and calculates benefits based on age, years of service, and the average of their three highest-earning years — capped at 80 percent of that average.

When Solomon retired in January 2021, the Methuen Police Department submitted his retirement paperwork to the Methuen

2021

Contributory Retirement Board. The five-member board included two individuals with personal or professional ties to Solomon: one, a towing company owner whose business operated at the discretion of the police chief; the other, the fire chief, who had received a similarly controversial contract. His fiancée had also served as Solomon's executive assistant.

At its February meeting, the board began the process of calculating Solomon's pension. Because of his recent and significant salary increases, the board was required to apply the state's "anti-spiking" law, which prevents public employees from dramatically inflating their final year's salary to boost their retirement. Under the law, if an employee's last-year compensation exceeds the average of the previous two years by more than 10 percent, the excess must be excluded from pension calculations.

Solomon's contract had pegged his salary to a 2.6 ratio compared to a patrol officer's base pay — well above the 2.0 statutory minimum. The board disregarded the higher figure and recalculated his pensionable salary using the lower 2.0 ratio. Even with that adjustment, they found his final-year pay exceeded the allowed increase. They cut $9,857 from his pensionable salary and notified him on June 24. Less than two weeks later, Solomon appealed. When the board stood by its decision, he escalated the matter to the state's Division of Administrative Law Appeals (DALA).

Solomon argued that three exemptions to the anti-spiking law applied to his case:

1. *Salary "Specified by Law"*
   Solomon claimed his salary qualified for exemption because it was legally authorized through his contract. The magistrate disagreed. While his salary was permitted under the law, it wasn't "specified by law" in the way that, say, the Governor's salary is set by statute. Since his pay was negotiated and subject to approval, it didn't meet the legal definition.

2. *Bona Fide Change in Position*
   He argued that his 2017 contract reflected a substantial change in role, citing new titles like "Harbormaster" and

358

2021

"Emergency Management Director." But the magistrate found these titles weren't backed by any changes in duties or responsibilities. In fact, we — the authors of this book — obtained a résumé Solomon submitted to Northern Essex Community College in 2015, where he listed himself as Methuen's Emergency Management Director starting in January 2012 — five years before the contract that supposedly made it official.

3. *Salary Tied to a Collective Bargaining Agreement*
Finally, Solomon said his salary was derived from union pay formulas. The magistrate dismissed this as well, ruling that the exemption applies only when the salary is directly negotiated through a union contract — not when it simply references union scales.

Solomon v. Methuen Retirement Board

The magistrate upheld the anti-spiking adjustment but ruled that the board erred in using the 2.0 ratio. That figure, the ruling clarified, was a statutory floor, not a ceiling. Since Solomon had legally negotiated a 2.6 ratio, that higher figure should have been used when calculating his pensionable earnings.

In the end, Solomon failed to avoid the anti-spiking penalty but succeeded in restoring part of his higher salary to the final pension formula — a mixed outcome in an otherwise uphill legal fight.

October

Unsurprisingly, the city did not pay Fountain's $1.5 million demand for wrongful termination and slander.

The Patrolmen's Union did file a grievance on behalf of Fountain and two other full-time intermittent officers challenging their layoffs. However, the arbitrator ruled that the positions in question were governed by the 1945 Special Act, not by civil service regulations. The ruling emphasized that the Act explicitly stated intermittent officers "may be removed by the selectmen [later, the mayor] at any time for any reason." As a result, the City of Methuen was within its legal authority to terminate the three officers at its discretion, without cause.

With that ruling and Solomon no longer chief and unable to advocate for him, Fountain filed a lawsuit on June 24, 2021 in federal court against the City of Methuen, city councilors Beauregard, McCarty and Simard, as well as Perry. The lawsuit outlined 16 counts, including allegations of wrongful termination in violation of public policy, retaliation, defamation, intentional infliction of emotional distress, civil conspiracy, interface with advantageous and constructional relations, and abuse of process. The court complaint largely reiterated what was outlined in the demand letter sent in October 2020.

Fountain v. Methuen Court Papers

By September 2022, the court had dismissed Counts 2 through 16, which involved claims against Perry and the city councilors. The dismissal of the mayor and councilors from the lawsuit was based on the doctrine of qualified immunity. The court held that government officials are protected from liability for actions taken within the scope of their official discretion. The judge further explained that even if an official is partially motivated by personal reasons, their conduct may still fall within the scope of their duties — so long as the actions are tied to the employer's interests and remain within the bounds of their official authority. In this case, the alleged statements and actions by the defendants related to public safety and matters of public policy. As such, they were deemed to fall squarely within the scope of the defendants' official roles and could not serve as a basis for liability.

Only Count 1, wrongful termination, remained. Which was blown out of the water once the STIRM investigation began, as it was shown that Fountain had lied repeatedly on his employment and firearms application, about domestic violence, being arrested, and going to a police academy when he had never completed an academy.

2022

January 7	The arbitrator issues a ruling on the Superior Officers' Union contract dispute.
April 11	Former Chief Joseph Solomon appeals the Methuen Retirement Board's pension ruling to the Massachusetts Department of Administrative Law Appeals (DALA).
June 9	Captain Greg Gallant is officially terminated from the Methuen Police Department.

January

Denied. That single word jumped off the page in Arbitrator Loretta Attardo's decision on the long-running grievance over Methuen's Superior Officers' contract. Released on January 7, the ruling brought a definitive end to a contentious chapter that had dragged on for years.

The hearings spanned ten separate dates between October 2020 and June 2021. Over 150 exhibits, totaling more than a thousand pages were submitted. Fifteen witnesses took the stand. But in the end, Attardo's conclusion was blunt and unequivocal: the grievance was denied, and the contract was not binding on the City of Methuen.

Attardo acknowledged being aware of surrounding investigations involving collective bargaining agreements (CBAs), but made it clear her focus remained strictly on the contractual dispute before her. She claimed no stake in the political fallout, legal interpretations, or broader ramifications. Still, her conclusions closely echoed findings laid out by the Office of the Inspector General (OIG) back in 2020, enough so that the OIG issued a press release headlined: "Independent Arbitrator Corroborated OIG's Findings About Methuen's Superior Officers' Union Agreement, Ruled the Contract Not Binding on City."

Some of the reasons for her decision:

- No meeting of the minds. For a contract to be binding, both sides must share a mutual understanding of the terms. Attardo found that the City Council and mayor believed

they were approving a modest 0-2-2 percent raise structure, while the union understood — or at least claimed — something far more lucrative.
- Timing and funding. The argument that City Council "funded" the contract by approving its first year at 0 percent didn't hold water. The contracts had been signed after the budget was passed and before the next budget cycle began. At no point did the Council appropriate money for the 2017–2020 agreement or its accompanying Memorandum of Understanding (MOU). No funding meant no binding.

Attardo also took aim at the union's method for calculating base pay, particularly the use of Quinn Bill educational incentives. When the union attempted to argue that the Quinn amounts were never meant to be part of the compounding salary calculations, an argument offered after the financially outrageous totals were made public, she dismissed it outright, calling it a claim that "defies the very language that Gallant drafted."

In a particularly striking moment, the union floated what they called a "strawman" theory: that the City, beginning in May 2018, had deliberately rolled the Quinn into base to make calculations to manufacture public outrage and avoid paying the contract. They accused City Auditor Tom Kelly of being ordered to use those exaggerated numbers to turn the public against the Superior Officers. Attardo found no evidence of this. She made clear there was no indication that the City manipulated Kelly or his figures for any malicious purpose.

By this point, four and a half years had passed since the 2017 City Council approved what many now consider an economically reckless set of police contracts. What followed was a sprawling, costly saga that drained city resources, consumed countless hours, and eroded public trust — all in pursuit of a deal driven more by ambition and greed than by sound governance. And now, after all of it, the only thing left to do was go back to the table, reopen negotiations, and start all over again.

April

While much of the public's attention was on external investigations, a quieter but critical internal probe was also

2022

unfolding — the MPD's professional standards investigation into Captain Greg Gallant, who had been on administrative leave since December 2020. The inquiry was completed by new Police Chief Scott McNamara. It focused on Gallant's role in the controversial 2017 police contracts, discrepancies in his statements to investigators, and findings from the 2020 Inspector General's (OIG) report and a recent arbitration decision.

McNamara found that Gallant gave "widely divergent" accounts when comparing his interview with the OIG to his testimony during arbitration. Before the OIG, Gallant downplayed Chief Solomon's involvement in contract negotiations, initially claiming he couldn't recall discussing union benefits with him. He repeatedly insisted Solomon merely represented "management rights" and was not consulted on budgetary matters. But under oath in arbitration, Gallant painted a very different picture — stating that Solomon actively advised on budget implications and was central to the negotiating process.

Gallant's conflicting statements continued. In one instance, he told the OIG he couldn't recall who he gave the first contract draft to — Solomon or Mayor Zanni. Yet in arbitration, he said he gave it directly to Solomon, the City's "representative," and added that Solomon was the only management official who received draft versions. Gallant admitted working closely with Solomon to reformat and finalize the contract before submitting it to Zanni's office.

Gallant also falsely claimed responsibility for delivering controversial "stacking" language to the patrolmen's union president, David Gardner — a lie exposed by a city-retained email showing Solomon had provided the language himself. McNamara emphasized that without that email, Solomon's role might have remained hidden — and that Gallant's attempt to shield him was a deliberate act of deception.

Notably, Solomon was never interviewed by the OIG. Whether by choice or omission is unclear. During arbitration, he invoked his Fifth Amendment rights and refused to testify.

McNamara concluded that Gallant intended to deceive. Regarding the contract's finalization date, Gallant first told the OIG he made changes and signed it on August 31, 2017. Later in the same interview, he became unsure. But in arbitration, he claimed he completed the revisions on September 4 and was instructed by Solomon to backdate it to August 31.

To avoid detection, Gallant didn't retype the contract but physically cut, taped, and scanned sections to ensure the signature page remained in its original place. He claimed to have left a tabbed copy for Zanni — which Zanni denied ever receiving.

Once the contract's financial impact became public in 2018, Mayor Jajuga pushed to renegotiate and an MOU was brokered in just a day and a half. Gallant called it a compromise. But under oath, he admitted some officers would earn less than what he claimed the original contract entitled them to. In truth, every superior officer would earn *more* — between $2,000 and $4,000 more — under the so-called "compromise."

Gallant made it clear he didn't view protecting the public interest as part of his role. Instead, he blamed the City's negotiation team for letting him take advantage of the situation.

McNamara's report concluded Gallant violated three MPD rules: Conduct Unbecoming an Employee, Truthfulness, and Testifying. Gallant knowingly misrepresented Solomon's role in the contract's creation — a role that enabled significant, unwarranted raises for both officers and Solomon himself. McNamara noted that Solomon was the only management official who saw Gallant's last-minute changes, inserted *after* the agreement had supposedly been executed. These manipulations helped avoid renegotiation and hid key details from oversight.

Gallant's formatting tricks, his misrepresentations about the MOU, and his false statements in both forums showed not only an intent to deceive but a violation of the good faith and fair dealing required by Massachusetts labor law. According to McNamara, Gallant demonstrated he could not be trusted — a disqualifying trait for any law enforcement officer.

McNamara concluded:

"Gallant's conduct, both individually and collectively, demonstrates a failure to meet the basic standards of trustworthiness required of a police officer. His violations of department rules and the public trust warrant termination. I recommend the Appointing Authority proceed accordingly."

On June 7th, Mayor Perry accepted Chief McNamara's recommendation and officially terminated Captain Greg Gallant's employment with the City. Exercising his right under civil service law, Gallant promptly filed an appeal.

Investigative Report on Gallant

To make a long story short, Gallant's appeal was heard by the Massachusetts Division of Administrative Law Appeals (DALA). While the magistrate acknowledged that Gallant's negotiating tactics may have been aggressive, he ultimately concluded that Gallant "did not engage in any dishonest, untrustworthy, or improper conduct during the negotiations or in his testimony." The magistrate also noted that Gallant maintained contact with at least one member of the City's negotiating team throughout the process. Based on these findings, he ruled that the City lacked sufficient grounds for termination and ordered Gallant's reinstatement — pending final approval from the Civil Service Commission.

It took another year, but ultimately the Civil Service Commission rejected the magistrate's findings. The magistrate had reasoned that since Gallant communicated with Solomon about the contract changes, he reasonably believed Solomon would inform the rest of the City's negotiating team, and that any failure to do so wasn't Gallant's responsibility.

The Commission disagreed. It concluded that Gallant was fully aware Solomon had a personal stake in the deception and could not have credibly relied on him to act in the City's interest. The Commission upheld Gallant's termination from the City.

Civil Service Decision

2023

March 28	The STIRM Group completes its investigation into Officer Fountain's certification.
September 8	The Department of Administrative Law Appeals (DALA) issues a decision on former Chief Joseph Solomon's retirement appeal.
September 28	A grand jury returns indictments against Joseph Solomon and Sean Fountain.
November 10	Solomon and Fountain are arraigned in court.

January

Just when the citizens of Methuen thought nothing more would come of the past controversies surrounding the Methuen Police Department, the results of a long-running investigation by the Massachusetts Civil Service Commission (MCSC) surfaced. The Commission had been quietly investigating the department since January 2021, with a focus on the prior use of non-civil service intermittent police officers. On January 28th, the MCSC released their 43-page report with little fanfare, but it didn't stay quiet for long.

The report, plainly titled "Findings, Conclusions, Orders and Recommendations," went straight to the core of the issue: "For years, Joseph Solomon, former Chief of the Methuen Police Department, circumvented the civil service laws and rules by improperly allowing non-civil service intermittent police officers to serve as de facto, full-time, civil service police officers."

In Massachusetts communities where civil service governs police departments, the terms "reserve" and "intermittent" police officer are typically used interchangeably, both referring to part-time or non-regular roles that fall under civil service laws and regulations. However, Methuen stands as an exception. In Methuen, the appointment and use of reserve officers are subject to civil service oversight, while the appointment and use of intermittent officers are not.

According to city records submitted to the MCSC, the MPD paid an estimated $1.5 million to seven non-civil service intermittent officers who had been allowed to work in full-time roles within the MPD. Their employment was deemed impermissible for multiple reasons: in some cases, their full-time status violated the requirements outlined in the 1945 Special Act governing the use of intermittent officers; in others, they had not completed the mandatory MPTC police training required before performing law enforcement duties. In several instances, both conditions applied.

Civil Service Report

The Commission cited the employment of Sean Fountain as the most "brazen" example of the department's disregard for civil service laws and procedures, emphasizing that it occurred "in plain sight" and continued over several years. Fountain's appointment, they noted, was problematic on multiple fronts and should never have been allowed.

First, his employment violated the restrictions of the 1945 Special Act, which governed the structure and hiring practices of the MPD. Second, he was never certified as a full-time police officer by the MPTC, nor was he eligible for a waiver from that requirement. Additionally, there was no documented evidence that he had completed a mandatory physical or medical examination, a standard prerequisite for police service.

Fountain also exceeded the city's maximum age limit of 35 at the time of his appointment, rendering him ineligible under municipal hiring guidelines. To compound matters, after Solomon hired him, Fountain resided outside of Methuen, a violation of the city's residency policy for intermittent police officers. Despite these numerous and disqualifying factors, he remained employed in a full-time law enforcement capacity, highlighting what the Commission viewed as a systemic breakdown in oversight and compliance.

The Commission made clear that Fountain's unlawful employment was not the result of an oversight, administrative error, or a misinterpretation of the law — it was a deliberate act. The report stated that the evidence pointed directly to Solomon and other city officials from prior administrations who knowingly participated in the deception. Specifically, they submitted false information to the Civil Service Unit of the state's Human Resources Division (HRD), falsely certifying that Fountain was a permanent, full-time civil service police officer. The Commission emphasized that Solomon "unquestionably" knew this was not true.

The list of individuals interviewed by the Commission during its investigation was extensive. It included three former mayors, several former intermittent officers, the city's former solicitor, a former human resources director, a former city councilor, and several current members of the MPD. In contrast, the list of those that the MCSC attempted to interview but either declined or failed to respond was much shorter: Solomon, Fountain, Richard Stanley, and one former intermittent officer.

Some examples — among many — of the questionable, if not unlawful, actions by Solomon and others involved in Fountain's hiring are detailed in the report:

In July 2016, according to the State Ethics Commission, Fountain, while still serving as a city councilor, was required under Massachusetts General Law to sign a financial disclosure form to be eligible for appointment as a part-time intermittent officer. In doing so, he certified that he would not receive any compensation drawn directly from the City's treasury and that he would work only paid detail assignments. Solomon, in turn, had to certify that Fountain, as a municipal employee, was providing personal services to the department and that "no employee of my agency is available to perform the services described above as part of his or her duties."

The conditional offer of appointment issued to Fountain by Mayor Zanni in 2016 stood out in stark contrast to those given to other intermittent officers during Zanni's tenure. While the other letters outlined clear pre-employment conditions — such as passing medical, physical, and psychological examinations, and completing a reserve police academy within one year — Fountain's letter included none of those requirements. Instead, his appointment was conditioned only upon "compliance with the rules and regulations and policies and procedures of the Methuen Police Department," and "compliance with all the conditions determined by the Chief of Police."

When the Commission reviewed Fountain's personnel file, they found no evidence that he had ever completed any of the three mandatory pre-employment exams — either before his appointment or at any point during his time with the department.

In Methuen, the police department typically selected intermittent officers following an extensive background investigation, which includes a review of academic records, credit history, criminal background, and prior employment history. The MPD then interviewed character references. However, the Commission found no evidence that the MPD conducted any background check or interviews for Fountain.

The Civil Service Commission — which still included two members from the panel that had previously overturned Solomon's termination, including Commissioner Stein — offered a blunt assessment of Solomon's conduct:

Solomon's Defiance of the Law

Solomon blatantly subverted civil service law and the 1945 Special Act by appointing non-civil service intermittent officers to serve full-time in Methuen. The 1945 Special Act is explicit: intermittent officers may only serve full-time "so long as there are no members of the regular or reserve police forces available." The Commission was unequivocal: "Solomon simply ignored this restriction."

Solomon appointed seven individuals to full-time positions — including three who worked for his private security company — without regard to whether qualified civil service officers were available. Eventually, Solomon dropped even the pretense of compliance. On June 28, 2019, he issued a General Order stating: "Effective immediately, Intermittent officers who are working in a full-time capacity shall be called for extra work by seniority and by hours in the same manner as regular full-time officers."

The Commission concluded that Solomon "operated a parallel, unlawful, non-civil service system of police officers" right out in the open over several years.

This unlawful scheme had real consequences. The report noted: "Solomon's actions deprived deserving candidates of employment opportunities." Had he followed the law, "seven qualified individuals on a civil service eligible list or reserve roster likely would have been appointed."

2023

Fountain's Illegal Full-Time Role

Solomon knowingly allowed Fountain to serve full-time without completing the required full-time MPTC-approved academy. Despite this clear legal requirement, Solomon issued multiple personnel orders elevating Fountain to full-time intermittent status and assigning him to the Criminal Division as a detective.

The Commission emphasized: "The seriousness of this illegal appointment cannot be overstated." Arrests and charges stemming from Fountain's work are "open to challenge" because he was never legally authorized as a full-time officer.

Three others were similarly allowed to serve full-time without the required training.

Deception and Obstruction

When the City Council requested information on Fountain's employment, Solomon falsely claimed the files had been "archived" and would take time to retrieve, despite multiple MPD employees confirming the files were readily accessible. Solomon deflected responsibility to the press, stating media should direct inquiries to the city's HR Director.

Behind the scenes, emails revealed a coordinated effort to craft "carefully ambiguous" responses, avoiding any direct admission that Fountain lacked academy training and was unlawfully employed.

Backdated Waiver and Misrepresentation

In April 2020 — three years after Fountain was already working full-time — Solomon, who was not the official appointing authority, submitted a belated waiver request to MPTC Executive Director Robert Ferullo. Solomon claimed Fountain had "misplaced" his reserve/intermittent training certificate.

The Commission highlighted the deeper deception: Fountain had never produced such a certificate. Solomon's waiver request was a "deliberate misrepresentation" to justify an illegal appointment retroactively.

Mayors' Oversight Failures

Solomon asserted that the mayor, not the police chief, is the official appointing authority. Yet the Commission found it "painfully clear" that Solomon controlled the department as his fiefdom, fostering a culture of fear and retaliation.

Zanni admitted he was unaware that Fountain or any intermittent officers were working full-time and confessed he never read the 1945 Special Act — a "shocking lack of oversight" for a legally responsible supervisor.

Mayor Jajuga knew Fountain was working full-time without completing the academy, but accepted Fountain's false assurances that it was allowed. The Commission was blunt: "Jajuga knew — or should have known — that this was simply not true."

False Certification to the State

Paul Fahey, former Chief of Staff to Jajuga, and Anne Randazzo, former Assistant City Solicitor and HR Director, initially showed concern over Fountain's status. Randazzo rejected Solomon's false claim of Civil Service approval: "I have no such email." Fahey insisted that Fountain should be laid off first if necessary, as a non-civil service employee.

However, after a private meeting with Solomon, they submitted a false report to the state certifying Fountain as a permanent civil service officer, with seniority backdated to 1999, based on unrelated firefighter service. They could not explain this reversal. Even after Methuen's Personnel Coordinator flagged that Fountain "did not belong on the list," Randazzo seemingly ignored the warning. The Commission called this a "regrettable error in judgment."

Mayors Jajuga and Perry, who signed off on the report, said they were unaware of the false information. Their accounts were deemed credible.

MPTC's Inaction and Ignorance

The MPTC, charged with enforcing police training standards, failed spectacularly.

2023

Despite multiple warning signs, the MPTC looked the other way as Fountain served full-time without proper training. When Solomon emailed Interim Executive Director Ferullo seeking a waiver, he attached Fountain's resume boasting of leadership in "major cases including homicide, armed robbery, and missing persons."

A records analyst at the MPTC flagged an email from the prior year, clearly noting Fountain's full-time status. Ferullo and Solomon exchanged emails and had an 11-minute phone call. Ferullo claims no recollection of the discussion, but the evidence suggests he was informed and took no action. The MPTC never objected as Fountain continued to serve unlawfully.

By early 2019, the MPTC had fielded multiple public records requests questioning Fountain's credentials, yet, according to the MPTC, it had never initiated corrective action.

A system designed to enforce standards instead helped enable a blatant violation of them.

The 'Fountain Special Act' Was a Mistake

The City Council's decision to grant Fountain, then Chair of the Council with no police experience, the ability to serve simultaneously as a City Councilor and an intermittent police officer through a home rule petition had no merit.

This special exception did not override the 1945 Special Act or civil service law. The Commission called it "legally toothless and ethically indefensible." It should never have been proposed by the Council or enacted by the Legislature.

Acts of 2022 Abolishing the Intermittent Police Force

April

With an interim police chief from outside the department in place, long-simmering concerns about the credentials of City Councilor-turned-police detective Fountain finally spurred action. In October 2021, the City of Methuen reached out to several outside investigative firms to examine the legitimacy of

2023

Fountain's police academy certification. Two firms declined outright. Only one agreed to take on the assignment — my firm, the STIRM Group.

Forged Certificate

Our mandate was straightforward: verify the authenticity and integrity of Sean Fountain's MPTC NERPI graduation certificate. There was credible reason to believe the document had been forged. If it proved to be fake, we were to identify who created it, how it ended up in Fountain's official training file, and whether anyone had helped facilitate its inclusion. What began as a narrow inquiry into a single questionable document soon unraveled into one of the most consequential public corruption investigations in the state's history, and that is saying something for Massachusetts.

Eighteen months later, the investigation came to a conclusion. Under the leadership of Methuen's newly appointed permanent police chief, Scott McNamara, Captain Eric Ferreira filed a detailed affidavit — over fifty pages in length — outlining probable cause for multiple felony charges against Fountain. Attached to the affidavit was our 204-page investigative report, later referred to as The STIRM Report.

On April 6, 2023, officials submitted the affidavit to the Clerk Magistrate at Lawrence District Court. Finding sufficient probable cause, the magistrate issued an arrest warrant for Fountain. Methuen police then contacted Fountain's attorney and extended the opportunity for him to surrender voluntarily, which he did.

That same day, Fountain was arraigned in Lawrence District Court on charges including conspiracy, forgery, and violations of employee standards of conduct.

At the arraignment, the Essex County District Attorney's Office

STIRM Report

made an unusual request: to impound the affidavit and its supporting documentation. The official justification cited the need to preserve the integrity of an active investigation involving unnamed co-conspirators. In truth, the move was designed to suppress the politically explosive findings detailed in the report.

2023

Behind the scenes, resistance to pursuing the case had been persistent. Former Essex County District Attorney Jonathan Blodgett had previously declined to prosecute the matter three separate times. To us, the investigators, it was clear the DA's office avoiding moving forward with the case. Why? It was well established that Blodgett had a long-standing relationship with Solomon, although we have no direct evidence that this impacted the DA's office's decision-making process, Perhaps their reluctance was due to a desire to steer clear of an unfolding political firestorm.

Whatever the reason, the implications were troubling. Had the STIRM Report been made public, it would have exposed a disturbing pattern: under then-Attorney General Maura Healey, the Attorney General's Office had declined Methuen's formal requests for assistance or prosecution six times. Combined with the DA's three refusals, Federal, state and county prosecutors had turned the case down a total of eleven times. Was this political strategy ahead of Healey's gubernatorial campaign? Or did they genuinely see no prosecutable evidence? The indictments filed by her successor suggested the former.

One particularly notable figure was Assistant Attorney General James O'Brien, head of the Public Integrity Unit and liaison to the Municipal Police Training Committee (MPTC). As perhaps the most qualified official to evaluate the case, O'Brien's decision to decline prosecution due to "insufficient evidence" raised eyebrows. Soon after, he left the Attorney General's Office to become Chief of Staff and General Counsel for the MPTC — a post that came with a sizable salary increase.

The decision to impound the STIRM report had little to do with protecting an investigation. It had everything to do with shielding public officials — elected and appointed — who had failed in their duties and violated the public trust. The report exposed the actions of a corrupt police chief, a compromised city council president, and falsified police training credentials implicating high-ranking officials at the MPTC. It revealed that Sean Fountain had worn a badge and carried a gun without ever completing a certified police academy or the mandatory 96-hour firearms training. Even his firearm license, we found, had been obtained through false information, including omissions about a prior domestic violence arrest.

The STIRM Report was not just a collection of findings — it was a spotlight aimed into the darkest corners of institutional failure and political protectionism. For the residents of Methuen, it offered something long overdue: the unvarnished truth.

At the Methuen City Council meeting held a week and a half after Fountain's arraignment, tensions ran high as eight outraged councilors and an incensed mayor demanded action and the public release of the STIRM Report. Six councilors delivered impassioned speeches, with Steve Saba leading the charge.

"I have lived through this since it became public in 2018," Saba declared. "Every paragraph is shocking — every single paragraph." He expressed frustration over being repeatedly instructed not to discuss the issue while various agencies conduct their investigations.

Saba's Speech

Saba criticized the perceived inaction of these agencies, stating, "We have had a history of these agencies, in my opinion, burying this issue to the detriment of the very people they swore to protect and defend — the taxpayers."

He voiced exasperation with the council being "stifled" and unable to address the matter openly.

Saba emphasized the gravity of the STIRM Report, calling it the most significant document to date. "We've had two IG reports, a Civil Service report, an arbitrator report — and the report that dwarfs everything is this STIRM report." He concluded by praising the Methuen Police Department and its chief for their persistence in uncovering the truth and urged immediate action, declaring, "We need action."

Vice Chair Joel Faretra delivered a scathing critique of the broader inaction surrounding the Methuen police department scandal, highlighting the lack of accountability from state and county authorities. "All in all, the only department that acted is the Methuen Police Department," Faretra asserted. He criticized the handling of the situation by two Essex County district attorneys and two state attorneys general, one of whom is now the Governor of

Faretra's Speech

Massachusetts. "All of them have just buried their head in the sand, protecting each other, while the 53,000 citizens of Methuen sit here holding the bag after we were all ripped off hundreds of thousands of dollars. Certain people employed in the police department made a mockery of the city, using it for their own benefit."

Faretra expressed disbelief that no charges were filed despite the damning content of the various reports. "When you read these reports — and we have all read them, even the ones that weren't impounded — you sit there and wonder, 'How could somebody not be charged?'"

He speculated that the lack of action stemmed from individuals protecting themselves. "It's everyone protecting themselves, afraid of what would come out if somebody were charged because they're afraid of what doors that will open."

In a call for accountability, Faretra urged state and federal officials to take action. "Somebody — the District Attorney, the Attorney General, the U.S. Attorney — needs to step up for the citizens of Methuen. We need someone who will finally charge somebody and not worry about the ramifications." He reminded officials of their duty, emphasizing, "You took an oath to serve the citizens of the Commonwealth of Massachusetts, not to protect and serve your colleagues and buddies. Your responsibility is to protect the Commonwealth and the constituents who voted you into office."

Councilor Nick DiZoglio built on Faretra's remarks, expressing his frustration with the lack of accountability from high-ranking officials.

"It's amazing reading the paper and seeing the 'no comment' from some high officials," DiZoglio stated. "To me, that right there speaks guilt." He highlighted connections between the MPTC and influential figures, including the Lieutenant Governor and the Governor.

DiZoglio praised the collaborative efforts between the Methuen City Council and new zPolice Chief McNamara in bringing the issue to light. "It just shows that this city has taken the right steps, as a collaborator with the Chief, to really try to put this into light," he said.

Dizoglio's Speech

He also expressed disbelief at the speed with which the STIRM Report was impounded. "If you see how fast this was impounded, it blows my mind. It shows just how aligned some people were after this whole action went into place," DiZoglio remarked, underscoring his concerns about systemic efforts to suppress the report's findings.

Councilor Beauregard reiterated a stance he has expressed publicly in the past, now reinforced by recent events. He pointedly criticized several agencies, including the U.S. Attorney's Office, the Attorney General's Office, and the Essex County District Attorney's Office under John Blodgett, calling them "gutless, spineless, and absolutely nothing of use to the taxpayers of Methuen."

Beauregard's Speech

Beauregard lamented what he saw as a systemic failure to address corruption and misconduct. "Corruption in the community, attempts to pillage the public treasury — tough luck, you're on your own. That has been the message up to this point," he said. "And it's a damn shame, but thankfully it is not too late."

Regarding the STIRM Report, Beauregard advocated for transparency, asserting, "Sunlight is the best disinfectant. That report needs to be released."

The final speaker of the evening was Chair Eunice Zeigler, who reflected on the toll the ongoing scandal has taken on the City Council over the past six years. "This has been a dark cloud over Council," she began, aligning herself with her colleagues' frustrations.

"At every turn, we've faced people shutting doors at every level of government — on investigations we tried to launch, on truths we tried to expose," Zeigler said. She lamented the current predicament, where the city's $60,000 investment in a 200-page investigative report, the STIRM Report, cannot be discussed openly. "A Magistrate decided we can't do that because there's too much truth included in it, which is unfortunate," she noted.

Zeigler's Speech

Despite these obstacles, Zeigler emphasized the need for collective action to achieve justice the citizens of Methuen. "We are at this point where there are actions that need to be taken, but our hands are tied," she said. "We need help to get the justice our citizens deserve, and the way we can do that is together."

Zeigler called on the community to mobilize, urging the city's 53,000 residents to take a stand. "Call every single day — every single department: the IG's office, the AG's office, the Auditor's office, the District Attorney's office. Write letters, send them to the editor. Make your voices heard continuously so they do not drown us out," she implored.

She warned against complacency and fatigue, stating, "They are trying to weaken us, to make us tired, so we do not seek the justice we deserve." Zeigler concluded with a rallying cry: "I am asking, calling on our community members, to stand up with us."

City Council "Call to Action" Letter

But what about the unnamed co-conspirator? Why wasn't there a second arrest? Could it be Solomon, or someone else entirely?

These unanswered questions would hang in the air, leaving the community to speculate for several more months.

One thing the city and its residents no longer had to worry about was Fountain's federal lawsuit for wrongful termination. His arrest had an immediate and decisive impact on the case. On April 26, 2023, U.S. District Judge Angel Kelley issued an order for administrative stay and closure. While the ruling didn't dismiss the case outright, it effectively put it on ice, leaving the door open for either party to request its revival at a later date.

Reflections: Accountability Deferred is Accountability Denied

By 2023, Methuen's corruption was no longer rumor. It was fact, documented in a 203-page report, sealed in DA files, whispered about in courtrooms, and printed in headlines. And yet, accountability never arrived.

2023

Reports were sealed. Journalists were fired. Indictments were narrowed to the convenient few. The larger system — the state agencies, the prosecutors, the oversight boards — doubled down on delay. Delay became strategy. And strategy became survival.

Accountability delayed is accountability denied. Justice does not exist in theory. It exists in action — in prosecutions brought, in reports released, in leaders removed. When those actions are deferred, corruption doesn't weaken. It strengthens.

The most effective shield of corrupt is not defiance. It is delay. And delay, deployed long enough, becomes permanence. Methuen's story is proof that when those tasked with enforcing the law refuse to act, corruption does not wither away. It becomes the system itself.

July

On July 6th, Methuen received a bombshell: the Massachusetts State Ethics Commission dropped a press release that sent shockwaves through the city, titled: "State Ethics Commission's Enforcement Division Alleges Former Methuen Police Chief Joseph Solomon Violated Conflict of Interest Law." The subheading only added fuel: "Solomon allegedly caused changes to the CBA that would increase his salary and provide unwarranted benefits to five intermittent police officers, including one who was a City Councilor."

Ethics Commission Report

A collective wow swept through Methuen, followed by silence, as residents dove into the Commission's explosive 18-page Order to Show Cause, which laid out the formal charges in stark detail.

2023

Self-Dealing in Plain Sight

Massachusetts law strictly forbids public employees from participating in any matter where they have a financial stake. Solomon, however, sat at the bargaining table anyway, fully aware that his salary was tied to the base pay of the city's highest-paid patrolman.

Even worse, he emailed the patrolmen's union president with suggested edits to the contract, including how to calculate base pay, changes that would directly boost his own paycheck.

Power Used for Personal Gain

State law also prohibits public officials from using their positions to gain unwarranted perks of substantial value, for themselves or others.

Solomon, an accountant by training and the only official involved in sensitive contract discussions, privately worked with the head of the Superior Officers' Union on language that, if mirrored across both union contracts, he knew would result in a 30 percent salary increase.

Without consulting any of the City's bargaining team, Solomon forwarded the revised language to the patrolmen's union president, a blatant attempt to use his power to fatten his paycheck.

But the alleged misconduct didn't stop there.

According to the Ethics Commission, Solomon repeatedly abused his authority in his handling of intermittent officers:

- Hired and continued to employ at least five full-time intermittent officers in direct violation of the 1945 Special Act.
- Brought Fountain on full-time despite knowing there was no record of him completing the required police academy training.
- Reassigned Fountain's intermittent badge number to a badge reserved for civil service patrol officers.
- Issued an order giving intermittent officers the same seniority status as civil service officers, flouting state law.

- Placed Fountain on the Section 67 civil service seniority list submitted to the state Human Resources department, even though Fountain didn't qualify as a civil service officer.
- Backdated Fountain's civil service start date to include time served as a firefighter, time that he couldn't legally apply toward police seniority.
- And perhaps most damning, he submitted a training certificate for Fountain that he either knew, or had every reason to know, was fake.

Each of these acts could result in a $10,000 fine. Additionally, the Commission can order Solomon to repay any financial gain he obtained from the misconduct and require restitution to any third parties harmed in the process.

Fraudulent Claims

The Commission's Petitioner concluded that Solomon's actions crossed that threshold: he actively covered up Fountain's lack of qualifications, submitted false documents to maintain the illusion, and in doing so, ensured Fountain remained on the force, collecting pay he hadn't earned under the law.

The Commission scheduled Solomon's hearing for April 23–26, 2024, to be held at its Boston office.

September

It was the day many Methuen residents had waited years to see: a statewide Grand Jury, convened at the request of the Massachusetts Attorney General's Office, handed down indictments against Solomon and Fountain, charging them with multiple criminal offenses following a sweeping investigation.

The case was the result of a joint effort between Attorney General Andrea Campbell and Essex County District Attorney Paul Tucker. Investigators drew heavily from the damning STIRM report and the January 2023 findings of the Civil Service Commission — both of which painted a troubling picture of misconduct and manipulation within the Methuen Police Department.

2023

The Charges Against Solomon

Solomon's Booking Photo

Evidence presented to the grand jury revealed that Solomon had repeatedly sidestepped Civil Service laws to promote part-time intermittent officers to full-time roles without proper process, and falsely claimed that Fountain had graduated from the police academy when he had not. He now faces 17 felony charges:

- Perjury by Written Affidavit (2 counts)
- Obtaining Unwarranted Privileges in Violation of Civil Service Laws (7 counts)
- Civil Service Law Violations (6 counts)
- Uttering a Forged Document (1 count)
- Procurement Fraud (1 count)

The Charges Against Fountain

Fountain's role was no less severe. Prosecutors alleged he falsified his training records, lied on his employment application, and forged a training certificate to hide the fact that he lacked the minimum required police credentials. His indictment includes:

Fountain's Booking Photo

- Forgery (1 count)
- Uttering a Forged Document (1 count)
- Perjury (1 count)
- Procurement Fraud (1 count)
- Conflict of Interest Violations (1 count)

The grand jury returned its indictments on September 28, 2023, after hearing and deliberating on extensive evidence. The charges marked a decisive moment — an unmistakable declaration that no public official, however entrenched, was above the law.

A press release from the Attorney General's Office was blunt in its assessment:

2023

"The investigation demonstrated that Solomon repeatedly abused his authority as police chief, undermining the law for personal gain — including the improper hiring of six part-time officers and elevating them to full-time status. Fountain was one such officer, and he provided false information about his qualifications."

The release also revealed that Fountain falsely claimed to have graduated from the Northeast Regional Police Institute (NERPI) in 1996. Years later, when pressed, he produced a forged certificate claiming he had completed the part-time academy in 1995 — a graduation that never happened.

"Solomon knew the certificate was fake, yet acted as if it were authentic," the statement continued.

Together, Solomon and Fountain perpetuated a lie, asserting that Fountain was a certified civil service officer. Solomon even doubled down, swearing to the falsehood in two separate annual civil service reports — an act of perjury under Massachusetts law.

Because the allegations in the criminal indictments mirrored, or were materially similar to, those outlined in the Ethics Commission's Order to Show Cause, all parties agreed to pause the ethics proceedings until the criminal charges are resolved.

On the morning of November 10, 2023, both men found themselves standing before the Honorable Elizabeth Dunigan in Salem Superior Court. The surroundings may have been familiar, but this time, they were the ones in the defendant's seats.

Solomon, thinner and now bearded, stood on the left side of the podium, accompanied by his long-time legal counsel, Andrew Gambaccini. To his right stood Fountain — downcast and visibly exhausted — flanked by attorney Neil Faigel.

Absent from the courtroom were any family or friends offering support. But in the gallery sat five Methuen city councilors — Nicholas DiZoglio, Michael Simard, Joel Faretra, Jessica Finocchiaro, and Steve Saba — along with City Solicitor Kenneth Rossetti. Councilor Simard summed up their presence simply:

"We're here to support the prosecutors, our solicitor, and above all, the real victims — the citizens of Methuen."

After the clerk read out the charges in open court, both men pleaded not guilty.

Judge Dunigan ordered their release on personal recognizance, declining to impose bail but issuing a list of strict conditions:

2023

- Surrender passports
- Remain within the Commonwealth unless granted court permission
- Have no contact with victims
- Refrain from possessing firearms or dangerous weapons

Solomon received an additional restriction: The judge prohibited him from residing or spending the night in any location where he stored firearms.

The defendants had already fulfilled the first condition — Fountain did not have a passport, and Solomon had surrendered his to the State Police when booked. But the second condition quickly became a flashpoint.

Both men requested travel exceptions due to work obligations. Fountain, a night-shift tow truck driver whose job required interstate travel, pleaded for flexibility. The judge allowed him to drive his daughter to and from school in Salem, New Hampshire, but withheld judgment on broader travel, requesting more detailed documentation of his routes and responsibilities.

Solomon's lawyer made a similar request, noting that his security consulting business required regional travel and that he regularly crossed into New Hampshire for errands. His plea didn't persuade the judge. She kept his travel restrictions intact, denying both personal and professional exceptions.

The court set the joint trial date for March 2025 — a date that sparked mixed emotions in Methuen. Some residents breathed a cautious sigh of relief; others braced for disappointment, recalling Solomon's past ability to dodge serious consequences and often land on his feet.

But Solomon wasn't finished testing the limits. Five months after arraignment, he petitioned the court to ease his travel restrictions. This time, he succeeded. The judge allowed him to travel throughout New England and New York.

Another five months later, he returned with a second request: to lift the prohibition against possessing weapons. The court granted him a partial victory, allowing him to use a bow and arrow, but only within strict legal parameters.

For Methuen, it was another twist in a long-running saga — one that had seen power abused, trust eroded, and justice delayed. As the trial date approached, many wondered whether this time would be different. Whether this time, accountability would stick.

Reflections: Beyond Methuen

This is a book about Methuen. But it is not just Methuen's story.

Everywhere oversight bodies are weak, where journalists are silenced, where loyalty outweighs law, the same patterns repeat. It could be a small town in Massachusetts or a major city with millions of residents. Corruption adapts to its environment — but its DNA is the same. Fear. Favors. Fraud.

Methuen teaches us that corruption rarely arrives with force. It arrives quietly, wearing a smile, cloaked in normalcy, until the outrageous becomes routine. Over time, it embeds itself so deeply that rooting it out feels impossible.

But Methuen also teaches another lesson: corruption survives only as long as the public allows it. Whistleblowers, journalists, investigators, and citizens have always been the antidote. The question is not whether corruption can be stopped. The question is whether there are enough people willing to see it, to name it, and to fight it.

The final warning is this: if it can happen here, it can happen anywhere. The final hope is this: if it can be exposed here, it can be exposed everywhere. The choice belongs to us.

What if...

As I wrote this book, I found myself returning again and again to one persistent and unsettling question: *What might have been different?*

So much of what unfolded — so many of the missteps, the lost careers, the damage to public trust — can be traced back to a series of decisions, each seemingly isolated, yet collectively devastating. One appointment, one report, one moment of accountability embraced — or avoided — could have fundamentally altered the trajectory of the City of Methuen.

What if the Massachusetts Legislature had never passed the 1945 Special Act that allowed Methuen to deviate from Civil Service norms? A quiet piece of legislation, rarely scrutinized, ultimately opened the door to decades of political maneuvering and unchecked authority.

What if, at the very beginning of his career, police officials hadn't paired Joseph Solomon with Joseph Alaimo — planting the seeds of a long and controversial alliance that would later shape the department's internal culture?

What if Internal Affairs investigator Al Donovan had found Solomon guilty of abuse of power? Might it have marked an early and necessary course correction — one that could have prevented escalation and restored confidence in the system?

What if District Attorney Jonathan Blodgett hadn't ignored the explosive evidence stockpiled in Solomon's locker — evidence that pointed to serious ethical violations and misconduct? The opportunity for accountability was there. It simply wasn't taken.

What if Civil Service Commissioner Paul Stein had ruled against reinstating Solomon, considering the pattern of concerns raised and the potential risk to institutional integrity?

What if either Sharon Pollard or Stephen Zanni had never been elected mayor? Would different leadership at key moments have

What if...

disrupted the pattern of inertia and silence that allowed serious issues to fester?

How many careers could have flourished in a healthier environment? How many capable and committed officers might have stayed the course instead of walking away or being pushed out?

What would Methuen's financial health look like today had these preventable missteps been addressed in real time, rather than swept aside or rationalized?

And here's the hardest question of all: What if decent, hardworking people had just been allowed to do their jobs — without fear of being fired, demoted, or publicly smeared for refusing to play along?

The "what ifs" aren't just hypothetical. They are reminders of how fragile public institutions can be when critical moments are mishandled — or ignored. At each turning point, there was an opportunity to lead with integrity, to prioritize accountability, to protect the public interest.
Too often, those opportunities were missed. And the cost — though difficult to quantify — has been felt across every level of the city: in morale, in public confidence, in budget shortfalls, and in the erosion of trust that takes years to rebuild.
Methuen is a city full of good people — hardworking residents and public servants who care deeply about their community. It deserves principled leadership, honest governance, and a system that rewards integrity. Yet too often, what it receives instead is dysfunction, self-interest, and silence when it matters most. The people of Methuen deserve better — now, not someday.

The Fleecing was Just the Beginning

What's truly remarkable isn't just that Methuen survived this scandal — it's how many of the people responsible for it still walk free, untouched, unscathed, and seemingly unbothered.

Chief Joseph Solomon and Sean Fountain have now been indicted and are awaiting trial. And while that may represent a step toward accountability, it barely begins to address the full scope of what occurred in Methuen. If we're being honest, their indictments raise more questions than they answer — and lay bare a troubling truth: the corruption wasn't just deep. It was protected, sustained, and allowed to flourish for far too long.

Let's talk about Sean Fountain.

Methuen permitted a man with no academy training, no POST certification, and no legal authority to patrol the streets — armed with a badge, a gun, and the power to arrest. He wasn't a combat veteran. He wasn't a lateral transfer from another police department. He was an untrained civilian, with no law enforcement background, yet he was given a badge, issued a firearm, and told to begin work on Monday — as if the responsibilities of a police officer required no more preparation

Police officers are required to complete over 80 hours of firearms training during the academy before they can serve. Fountain's only firearms experience came *after* he was already on the street — through the department's annual requalification process. Not before. Not as a prerequisite. And even then, it wasn't a training course.

It's backwards. It's reckless. And it's utterly indefensible.

The City of Methuen — knowingly or through gross negligence — put an illegal police officer on the street for years. Fountain conducted traffic stops, executed search warrants, made arrests, filed reports, and testified in open court as if he were a legitimate officer of the law. He wasn't. He never was.

So how is it that not one charge of false arrest has been brought forward, despite Fountain reportedly making over 60 arrests or criminal summons? Under Massachusetts law, wouldn't that

The Fleecing was Just the Beginning

qualify as kidnapping? What about the three search warrant affidavits he signed under penalty of perjury? Or the two homicide trials — one in New Hampshire, one in Massachusetts — where he took the stand and falsely represented himself as a police officer under oath?

And yet, to date, no charges for perjury.
No charges for false imprisonment.
No civil rights violations.
No restitution.
No accountability.

Not for him — and certainly not for the co-conspirators who made his fraud possible.

As previously mentioned, both the affidavit and the STIRM Report were impounded — allegedly due to an ongoing investigation. At the time, we expected additional charges to follow. But that never happened.

So where are the investigations into the actions — and the consequences — such as former MPD Police Captain Greg Gallant, MPTC Director Robert Ferullo, former District Attorney Jonathan Blodgett, and former Attorney General turned sitting Governor, Maura Healey.

These individuals weren't innocent bystanders. They were part of the scaffolding that held this fraud upright for years.

So the real question is this: Why haven't *they* been charged? Why do the small fish take the fall while the higher-ups walk away untouched, continuing their careers as if nothing happened?

That's not an oversight. That's backroom politics — Massachusetts-style. A system deliberately designed to shield the powerful and protect the corrupt.

And the people of Methuen — and across Massachusetts — should be outraged. If you pay a single cent in taxes here, whether it's income, sales, or property tax, *you* are funding the salaries of the very people who enabled this.

You're footing the bill for their silence, their self-protection, and their unchecked power.

This wasn't a clerical error. It was a coordinated failure — one that stretches from a small city council chamber all the way to the steps of Beacon Hill. And while *The Fleecing of a City* exposed the mechanics of the corruption, it only began to reveal just how deep the rot truly runs.

The Fleecing was Just the Beginning

The second book in the series, *Six Degrees of Justice: The Investigation*, will take you inside the probe that uncovered what other investigators knew to avoid. You'll follow the trail of evidence, cover-ups, and calculated silence — and see exactly why this was the case no one wanted to see the light of day.

While Solomon and Fountain have finally begun to face some of the consequences for their roles, they were never acting alone. We'll expose the obstruction, the delays, and the deliberate interference — all calculated to shield the powerful. Because while a few have finally been held accountable, many of the key players still pray they won't get that 0600 knock at the door from one of the federal government's three-letter agencies.

They weren't indicted.
They weren't held accountable.
They weren't even questioned.

>And make no mistake — this story isn't over.
>Not even close.

>Coming Spring/Summer 2026
>*Six Degrees of Corruption: The Investigation*

Justice moves slowly, but secrets don't stay buried forever. As the trial unfolds, new evidence may surface — evidence that rewrites everything. Follow each turn at lpsmithauthor.com/trial-updates

or scan the code to see what's revealed next.

Acknowledgements

"Speaking out takes courage, but fear can make a compelling argument. I'm not saying it will be easy, but telling the truth gives you power....It sets you free."
Katie McGarry

First, and above all, to my business partner, who evolved into a lifelong friend during this endeavor — the one who nearly refused to be acknowledged at all. They remain unnamed here, just as requested. No aliases. No titles. No pronouns that can be pinned down. Is it *he* who helped shape this book? Or *she* who pulled history out of the shadows? Or perhaps *they* prefer the ambiguity. You won't find out — and that's entirely by design.

Privately, I refer to them as "DT." Not short for President Donald Trump — let's not get carried away — but in homage to the infamous anonymous Watergate source: Deep Throat. Like their namesake, DT didn't seek the spotlight. They operated behind the curtain, pushing for the truth to come out even when it was inconvenient — even when it was risky.

This — *right here* — is the only time they will be mentioned. It took some convincing to even get this far. What began as a business arrangement transformed into something more meaningful — a partnership, a collaboration, a trust built on shared values and a mutual disdain for corruption. I explained how much their role meant — not just to me personally, but to the integrity and scope of this book — and they finally, cautiously, agreed to this limited moment in the light.

Their contribution was nothing short of transformative. The depth, the context, the historical reach — that's the product of our combined effort. Without them, this story wouldn't have come together with the scope or precision it did. They unearthed the timeline others ignored, showing how this wasn't a sudden collapse, but a slow, calculated erosion of integrity. And while you won't see their name, feel their presence. It's there — between the lines, beneath the facts, guiding the spine of this book from page one.

To the rest of the quiet tribe — the researchers, analysts, and advisors who chose anonymity out of necessity — thank you.

Acknowledgements

Your concerns for your personal and professional safety are valid, and out of an abundance of caution, I have excluded all identifying information. But know this: over 34 pages of bibliography, source material, and documentation came directly from your tireless efforts. You chose truth over comfort, and I am humbled by your trust.

To the editors and proofreaders who sharpened this work without softening its punch — I may not be naming you, but I absolutely know who you are. And you should know how grateful I am. You elevated this project page by page, line by line, without ever dulling its edge.

To the victims of Joseph Solomon and his enablers — we deliberately stripped your names and redacted your cases. This wasn't an oversight; it was an act of respect. We refuse to let this book re-traumatize those who've already endured so much. Your voices guided our hands, even when your names did not.

To the marketing and social media professionals behind the scenes — the architects of visibility — thank you. Your talent helped turn a book into a campaign, a story into a spotlight. Your contribution cannot be overstated. We would not be positioned for impact without your vision.

Six Degrees of Corruption ~ The Fleecing of a City is just the beginning. Its counterpart, *Six Degrees of Justice ~ The Investigation*, is scheduled for release in late spring or early summer 2026. That book will complete the arc — diving deeper into the investigation, the forged records, the accountability still avoided. The timing is no accident. It will arrive just in time for election season, when the truth matters most and the stakes are highest.

By then, the truth will have been told. The curtain pulled back. The facts laid bare. What readers do with that knowledge is up to them. But one thing is certain: people are watching now. And for the first time in a long time — they're paying attention.

Author's Call

"That this nation, under God, shall have a new birth of freedom — and that government of the people, by the people, for the people, shall not perish from the earth."
Abraham Lincoln, Gettysburg Address

We are at a crossroads as citizens and taxpayers. Time and again, we see our elected officials placing personal fulfillment, political gain, or insider loyalty ahead of the people they swore an oath to serve. These abuses of power are not abstract scandals. They are real, and they cost us — millions of dollars every year in wasted funds, corruption schemes, and decisions made to protect the powerful rather than the public.

But here is the truth: corruption thrives only when good people look the other way.

This book is not just a story — it is a manual. It shows you how to investigate, how to question, how to dig. Every public records request, every document cited here is proof that you have the same tools in your hands. That is why I teach my Public Records and Open-Source Investigations class — a two-day program designed to put those tools in the hands of everyday citizens.

And this journey doesn't end here. When Six Degrees of Justice is completed, we'll go even further — into the investigative weeds, the step-by-step methods, and the behind-the-scenes tactics that expose corruption in real time. Book Two will not just tell the story; it will equip you with the investigative blueprint to take on your own fights for accountability.

The call to action is simple: demand more. Demand more courage from your leaders. Demand they make the hard, moral, ethical decisions, not just the popular or politically expedient ones. And when they refuse, stand up, speak out, and remind them who they work for — the people.

There is strength in numbers. Imagine the impact if thousands of citizens across Massachusetts — and across this country — used the same investigative tools that uncovered the abuses detailed in these pages. We've seen it happen before. In 2014, Market Basket employees, managers, and even customers united

Author's Call

in protest when a corporate board ousted beloved CEO Arthur T. Demoulas. Their boycotts and walkouts nearly crushed a billion-dollar empire, forcing shareholders to reinstate him. Ordinary citizens and workers proved they could defeat corporate greed when they stood together.

The same holds true locally. In Canton, citizens leveraged rules already in place — public procurement and governance laws — to compel leadership to act. They forced hearings, demanded transparency, and reminded officials that rules exist to protect taxpayers, not politicians. It was a reminder that when citizens show up, leaders can't simply hide.

And look beyond Massachusetts. One grieving mother's fight against drunk driving grew into Mothers Against Drunk Driving (MADD), a national movement that reshaped DUI laws, stiffened enforcement, and has saved tens of thousands of lives. It started with one voice — but it grew into millions.

Imagine if, instead of shrugging, we all asked the tough questions, submitted the public records requests, showed up at meetings, and refused to be silenced.

We are losing millions every year because politicians are serving their own agendas. That money belongs to our schools, our roads, our veterans, our first responders. It belongs to us.

Patriotism is not passive — it is active. It is a duty. And the most patriotic act you can take today is to hold your government accountable.

So take these lessons, take this story, and carry it forward. Stand shoulder to shoulder with your neighbors, your fellow taxpayers, and your fellow Americans. Demand better. Demand accountability. Demand integrity.

Because when the people lead, leaders have no choice but to follow.

With respect, gratitude, and unwavering belief in the people of this country, I remain in awe of your strength and humbled by your trust.

L.P. Smith, CFE, CPP
Author • Veteran • Investigator • Citizen

Glossary

Acronyms

ADL: Anti-Defamation League
AFSCME: American Federation of State, County and Municipal Employees
CBA: Collective Bargaining Agreement
CSC: Civil Service Commission
DALA: Division of Administrative Law Appeals
DA: District Attorney
DEA: Drug Enforcement Administration
DOJ: Department of Justice
EIS: Eagle Investigation Services, Inc.
EOPSS: Executive Office of Public Safety and Security
FBI: Federal Bureau of Investigation
HR: Human Resources
IA: Internal Affairs
IACP: International Association of Chiefs of Police
MCAD: Massachusetts Commission Against Discrimination
MGL: Massachusetts General Laws
MIT: Massachusetts Institute of Technology
MPD: Methuen Police Department
MOU: Memorandum of Understanding
MSP: Massachusetts State Police
NECC: Northern Essex Community College
OIG: Office of the Inspector General
PRR: Public Records Request
RFP: Request for Proposal
SJC: Supreme Judicial Court
SPD: Salem Police Department
SSAC: School Safety Advocacy Council
SWAT: Special Weapons and Tactics

Terms

270-Day Waiver Requirement (MPTC)
Under 550 CMR 3.03, a temporary waiver may be granted by the MPTC for up to 270 days to allow a reserve or intermittent

Glossary

officer to serve in a full-time capacity prior to completing the full-time police academy training. This waiver applies when there is a documented public safety emergency or other exigent circumstance and when the officer meets certain prerequisites.

The appointing or sponsoring agency must also furnish: A formal petition to MPTC explaining the emergency staffing need or exigent circumstance. Documentation demonstrating the officer meets the above criteria.

If the waiver is granted, the officer must begin attending the academy within that 270-day window. If not, the waiver expires and the officer may no longer serve full-time until academy attendance is complete.

Brady List

Derived from the landmark *Brady v. Maryland* (1963) it refers to an internal mechanism used by prosecutorial offices in Massachusetts to track law enforcement officers whose credibility may be compromised, typically due to misconduct or integrity issues.

Legal Basis & Purpose

Under Brady v. Maryland, prosecutors are constitutionally required to disclose to the defense any evidence favorable to the accused that is material to guilt or punishment

This includes exculpatory evidence or information that might impeach the credibility of government witnesses — including police officers.

What Is the Brady List?

A Brady List is a prosecutor's internal watch list of officers whose credibility is flagged by credible findings — such as proven misconduct, dishonesty, or rulings that question the reliability of their testimony.

Examples of conduct leading to inclusion:
1. Proven dishonesty or lying under oath
2. Internal investigations for excessive force, theft, or harassment
3. Credibility issues flagged in judicial proceedings.

Bridge Academy

The Bridge Academy was an MPTC-designed training initiative, launched under the 2020 police reform legislation, intended to help reserve or non-traditional law enforcement

Glossary

officers meet newly standardized certification requirements. Per 550 CMR 3.02, it specifically referred to training for officers who were certified by the Massachusetts Peace Officer Standards and Training (POST) Commission as of December 1, 2021, but who had not previously completed an MPTC-authorized full-time police academy.

This Bridge Academy Training consisted of approximately 200 hours of additional instruction. To qualify for an exemption from the full academy requirement, participants also had to document 2,400 hours of police duties.

The program launched its registration in March 1983 and officially concluded operations on June 30, 2024. During its run, over 1,300 officers completed the coursework, verified their required experience, and achieved POST certification. An additional 300 officers were still in the process of logging their 2,400 duty hours at the time the program closed.

Civil Service
Basics
"Civil Service" broadly refers to merit-based employment systems for government workers, established to reduce patronage, nepotism, and political favoritism.

At the federal level, this dates back to the Pendleton Act of 1883, which required competitive exams for many federal jobs.

At the state level, every state has some form of civil service, but not all states cover police and fire positions under it.

State-level variation
Full Civil Service Systems: Some states (e.g., Massachusetts, New Jersey, and New York) operate robust civil service commissions that govern hiring, promotion, discipline, and appeals for police, fire, and municipal jobs.

Partial Systems: Many states restrict civil service to state employees only, leaving local hiring up to municipalities (e.g., Texas, Florida). In these places, police hiring is usually governed by local ordinances or collective bargaining, not a centralized exam.

Home Rule states: Some states allow municipalities to opt in or out of civil service systems. For example:

In Illinois, cities can choose whether their police/fire departments fall under civil service protections.

Glossary

In California, state employees are civil service, but local police hiring is governed locally.

Right-to-work states: States with weaker union protections (e.g., South Carolina, Georgia) often have less extensive civil service frameworks, though state workers are still typically covered.

Police-specific coverage

Only a minority of states run centralized police hiring through civil service exams. Massachusetts is unusual in its strict residency, preference, and exam-based system.

In many states, police hiring is handled by POST (Peace Officer Standards and Training) agencies, local civil service boards, or directly by municipalities.

Universal elements

All states have civil service laws for at least state employees.

Not all states extend those systems to municipal police or firefighters.

States that do extend it often face debates like in Massachusetts: critics argue it limits flexibility, delays hiring, and protects poor performers; supporters argue it ensures fairness and prevents nepotism.

> *Clarification*: up until the Massachusetts Police Reform Law of 2020, part-time, intermittent, and special police officers' titles were terms that were often used interchangeably, despite having different meanings.

Freedom of Information Act/ Public Records Law

Federal FOIA

The Freedom of Information Act (FOIA), passed in 1966, gives the public the right to request access to federal agency records, subject to nine exemptions (e.g., national security, personal privacy, law enforcement). It applies only to federal executive branch agencies — not Congress, the courts, or state governments (foia.gov). Anyone, regardless of citizenship or residency, may file a FOIA request.

Massachusetts public records law

Massachusetts has its own public records law, codified in M.G.L. Chapter 66 and defined by Chapter 4, Section 7, Clause 26. It provides that all records made or received by a government entity are presumed public unless specifically exempt.

Glossary

Importantly, any person — resident or non-resident — may request records, and requests may be made anonymously. This makes Massachusetts one of the most accessible systems in the nation. Agencies must respond within 10 business days, though delays are common.

State variations

Each state has its own version of FOIA — sometimes called "sunshine laws," "right-to-know laws," or "public records acts." They differ in scope and accessibility:

Tennessee: Requests may only be made by Tennessee residents, and proof of residency (e.g., driver's license) is required.

Florida: The Sunshine Law is among the broadest — any person can request records, no residency requirement, and access is heavily favored.

Virginia: Restricted to state residents and media outlets published in the state.

Shared purpose

While the laws differ in access, exemptions, and enforcement, they all aim to promote transparency and accountability in government. The federal FOIA does this for federal agencies; state public records laws do the same for state and local government bodies. Together, they form a patchwork system of open government laws across the U.S.

Full-Time Police Academy
A state-approved training program required for anyone who wants to become a full-time police officer in Massachusetts. It covers the skills and laws officers need to know.

Full-Time Police Officer
A fully certified officer who works regular hours year-round and has completed the full-time police academy.

Home Rule Petition
In Massachusetts, a Home Rule Petition is a formal request by a city or town to the state legislature (the General Court) to enact a new law or grant new powers that aren't covered by general state law.

Glossary

Intermittent Police Officer
An officer who works only when needed, like filling in for others or helping during events. They complete a shorter version of the police academy called the Reserve/Intermittent training.

Municipal Police Training Committee (MPTC)
The state agency that sets the rules and training requirements for police officers in Massachusetts.

NERPI Academy (New England Reserve Police Institute)
A training center that offers the basic education needed to become a reserve or intermittent officer in Massachusetts and other parts of New England.

Part-Time Police Officer
An officer who has completed all required training to be a full-time police officer, but who works fewer hours than a full-time officer. They typically go through part-time, or reserve training approved by the state.

Peace Officers Standards & Training (POST)
A statewide agency that certifies police officers, sets professional standards, and handles discipline for misconduct.

Reserve Police Officer
A part-time officer who usually helps out when extra coverage is needed. They must complete a minimum level of training, usually through the Reserve/Intermittent academy.

Character Index

"The world is not run by laws written on paper, but by men. The laws are nothing if the men who enforce them refuse to obey."
Theodore Roosevelt

This index is provided for reference only. The inclusion of a name reflects documented involvement in events described and does not imply misconduct unless supported by cited sources.

Main Characters

Joseph Solomon
(pp. 1-2, 5, 7-8, 10, 13-15, 19-25, 28-29, 32-33, 35-39, 42-51, 55, 57-77, 81-82, 83-103, 107-115, 119, 121, 123-146, 151-156, 159-180, 184-185, 188-190, 192, 194-203, 207-210, 212, 215-220, 223-224, 226-230, 235-241, 243, 245-266, 269-272, 274-278, 280-283, 285, 289, 292, 294-297, 299-301, 305-312, 314-318, 323-336, 338-341, 343-344, 348-354, 356-361, 363-365, 367-373, 375, 379-385, 387, 389, 391)
Joined the Methuen Police Department (MPD) in 1987 and steadily rose through the ranks, becoming a Sergeant in 1993, a Lieutenant in 1995, a Captain in 2000, and ultimately Chief in 2003. He retired in 2021.

Loyal Methuen police supporters of Solomon

Joseph Aiello
(pp. 22, 55-56, 65-67, 81, 85-87, 96, 108, 110-111, 118-119, 138-140, 154-157, 159, 161, 167, 189-190, 197, 208, 211, 224, 248, 250-257, 261, 271-272, 301-302, 336)
Joined the MPD in 1994 and steadily advanced through the ranks, earning a promotion to Sergeant in 2014 and Lieutenant in 2017. He holds a master's degree in criminal justice from the University of Massachusetts Lowell. Before entering law enforcement, Aiello served in the U.S. Navy as a Seabee, attaining the rank of Petty Officer Third Class. His brother, Mark Aiello, also serves as a patrolman with the MPD.

Character Index

Angelo Michael "Mike" D. Alaimo
(pp. 74-77, 89, 100-101, 109, 135-137, 165, 185)
Joined the MPD in 1967 and dedicated 30 years to the force before retiring as a Lieutenant in 1997. Prior to his law enforcement career, he enlisted in the United States Navy before 1952, serving as an Aviation Machinist at Naval Air Station Whiting Field in Milton, Florida. He was honorably discharged in 1955 with the rank of Aviation Machinist Third Class Petty Officer. Following his retirement from the police department, Alaimo founded Eagle Investigation (EIS), a private investigative firm. He is the father of Deputy Chief Joseph D. Alaimo.

Joseph D. Alaimo
(pp. 14, 20, 23, 28-29, 32, 36-38, 42-45, 61-62, 64, 68-69, 71-72, 81-82, 86, 91, 99, 103, 105, 110-112, 121, 132-133, 137-139, 143, 148, 154, 157-158, 167-171, 187, 191-192, 197-198, 209, 213, 253, 273, 289)
Began his career with the MPD in 1981, serving with distinction until his retirement as Deputy Chief in 2008. A U.S. Navy veteran, he served aboard the USS *San Bernardino* before transitioning into law enforcement. In 2012, he assumed leadership of EIS, a private investigative firm founded by his father, Angelo Michael "Mike" D. Alaimo, partnering in the business with Chief Joseph Solomon. Alaimo is a magna cum laude graduate of Springfield College, where he earned a Bachelor of Science degree in Human Services. His son, Joseph Alaimo, is a patrolman with the MPD. His former wife, Lisa, also served the City of Methuen, beginning in Mayor Sharon Pollard's office before becoming the Administrative Assistant to the Police Chief.

Gregory Gallant
(pp. 20, 224, 241-244, 261, 264, 275, 282, 286, 290-291, 307, 331, 336, 345-349, 362-365, 390)
A Methuen native and graduate of Franklin Pierce University, he joined the MPD in 1993. Over the years, he served in a variety of roles, including patrol officer, community policing officer, school resource supervisor, patrol platoon commander, and platoon commander for the Massachusetts Regional Response Team. He was promoted to Sergeant in 2002, Lieutenant in 2007, and Captain in 2017. His specialized training includes SWAT tactics,

Character Index

hostage negotiation, emergency incident command, and active shooter instruction. He was dismissed from the department in 2022. His daughter currently works as a police dispatcher in Methuen, and his son is employed by the Department of Public Works.

Randy Haggar
(pp. 67, 70-71, 117, 126, 142, 159, 161-162, 176, 212, 214, 300)
Born and raised in Methuen, Haggar joined the MPD in 1994 and steadily rose through the ranks, promoted to Sergeant in 2000, Captain in 2005, and Deputy Chief in 2023. For the past year, he has served as the department's commander, overseeing both the Field Operations and Administrative Bureaus. He holds a bachelor's degree in criminal justice administration from Franklin Pierce College and a master's in criminal justice administration from Western New England University. He later returned to school to earn a second master's degree in public administration with a concentration in Emergency Management from Anna Maria College. Prior to his promotion to Deputy Chief, held various leadership roles, including court liaison supervisor, community policing officer, and traffic division supervisor.

Kevin Mahoney
(pp. 18, 62, 63, 103, 212, 248, 250)
He joined the MPD in 1993, advancing through the ranks to Sergeant in 2000, Lieutenant in 2004, and Captain in 2017. He holds a degree from Northern Essex Community College and retired from the department in 2021.

Kristopher McCarthy
(pp. 20, 62-63, 67, 103, 130, 160, 211-212, 301)
Joined the MPD in 1993, rising through the ranks to Sergeant in 1998, Lieutenant in 2002, and Captain in 2004.

Thomas F. McMenamon, Jr.
(pp. 66-67, 139-140, 170, 177, 212, 223, 250, 300-301)
Joined the MPD in 1998 and was promoted to Sergeant in 2016. His wife, Officer Kara (Lapides) McMenamon, began her career with the department as a dispatcher before becoming a patrol officer in 2012.

Character Index

Michael Pappalardo
(pp. 20, 155, 161, 212, 214-215)
Joined the MPD in 1994, rising to the rank of Sergeant in 2002 and Lieutenant in 2005.

Ronald Valliere
(pp. 70, 95-97, 121-122, 161-162, 248, 251, 277, 310)
Joined the MPD in 1993, earning promotions to Sergeant in 2016 and Lieutenant in 2017. Over the course of his career, he served in multiple divisions, including the Patrol Division, Community Policing Unit, Criminal Investigations Bureau, Drug and Gang Unit, and the FBI's Joint Terrorism Task Force. He retired from the department in 2021 and subsequently worked for EIS under Solomon and Alaimo. Notably, Solomon served as his best man at his wedding.

Other Methuen Police

Katherine Lavigne
(pp. 20, 61, 67, 71, 74, 85, 91-93, 96, 107-108, 111, 117-120, 139, 146, 154-156, 159, 161, 169, 241, 301)
Joined the MPD in 1990 and steadily advanced through the ranks, promoted to Sergeant in 1998, Lieutenant in 2002, and Captain in 2004. She served as Chief of Police from 2007 to 2010 and later retired as a Captain in 2017. She holds degrees from University of Massachusetts Lowell (undergraduate), and a master's in criminal justice from Western New England College. Her brother, Donald Lavigne, also served with the department and retired as a Sergeant in 2020.

Bruce MacDougall
(pp. 14-15, 19, 21, 110, 135-136, 201, 203, 324)
Began his career as a special police officer in Barnstable, Massachusetts, later serving as a provisional full-time officer in Wakefield. He joined the MPD in 1978, advancing from dispatcher to Sergeant in 1982, Captain in 1985, and ultimately Chief of Police in 1995. He served ten years as the Commander of Field Operations before his appointment as Chief and retired in 2002. He holds a Bachelor of Arts in American Government from Boston University and a Master of Science in Criminal Justice

Character Index

Administration from Northeastern University. Notably, Methuen Mayor Neil Perry is his first cousin.

Larry Phillips
(pp. 65-68, 88, 90, 95-97, 101, 121-122, 128-129, 138-140, 143, 159-163, 199)
Joined the MPD in 1982 and was promoted to Sergeant in 1991. He retired in 2013 after more than 30 years of service.

Michael Wnek
(pp. 65, 67, 89, 97, 101, 110, 121, 135-136, 138, 143, 160, 218-220)
Joined the MPD in 1988, rising to the rank of Sergeant in 1995 and Lieutenant in 2000. He retired in 2016. Once considered part of Chief Solomon's inner circle, Wnek later distanced himself from that group.

Methuen Mayors

Sharon Pollard
(pp. 19, 21, 23, 28-33, 35, 38, 42, 45, 59, 72-73, 77, 81, 103, 110, 114, 130, 132-133, 135-136, 270, 324, 387)
Served as a Massachusetts state representative from 1977 to 1983 and was appointed the first, and ultimately last Massachusetts Secretary of Energy, serving from 1983 to 1989. She later served as Mayor of Methuen from 2000 to 2006 and founded the nonprofit Festival of Trees in 1994. She is married to Thomas Lussier, a former state representative who served from 1979 to 1983. Both she and her husband later worked as lobbyists.

William "Bill" M. Manzi III
(pp. 22, 42, 58, 61, 63, 65, 69-77, 81, 81-85, 90-91, 94, 98, 100-103, 107-109, 111-115, 120, 124-125, 132-133, 143-147, 157, 164, 167, 177, 195, 270, 279)
Operated a liquor store in Methuen Square from 1978 to 2005 before entering public service. He served as a Methuen City Councilor from 2000 to 2006 and was elected Mayor of Methuen, serving from 2006 to 2011. Since 2013, he holds the position of Town Manager in Seabrook, New Hampshire.

Character Index

Stephen Zanni
(pp. 50, 64, 72, 164, 167, 169-174, 176,-177, 180-181, 194-195, 208-210, 219, 223, 225-227, 241-243, 248, 253-255, 261-264, 269-270, 274, 284, 344-345, 347, 363-364, 369, 372, 387)
Began his public service on the Lawrence School Committee, serving from 1974 to 1977. He ran unsuccessfully for Essex County Clerk of Courts in 1976 and for Massachusetts State Representative in 1978. He later served on the Methuen City Council from 1994 to 2000, and again from 2006 until his election as Mayor of Methuen in 2012, a role he held through 2018. In addition to his political career, Zanni was a high school science teacher in Hudson, New Hampshire, for 36 years, retiring in 2007. His daughter, Jana Zanni-Peche, followed in his public service footsteps, serving on the Methuen School Committee from 2018 to 2024 and currently serving on the Methuen City Council, beginning in 2024.

James P. Jajuga
(pp. 59-60, 117, 224-225, 240-241, 247-248, 264, 269-270, 272-275, 281-284, 287, 290, 297-298, 303-305, 314, 319-320, 339 346, 348-349, 354, 364, 372)
Joined the Massachusetts State Police in 1969 and retired as a Lieutenant in 1990. The following year, he was elected to the Massachusetts State Senate, where he served from 1991 until 2001. He then resigned to become the Massachusetts Executive Secretary of Public Safety, a role he held until 2003 when a new administration took office. After leaving state government, he worked for many years as a lobbyist and law enforcement consultant. He returned to public service as a Methuen City Councilor from 2014 to 2018, and was elected Mayor of Methuen in 2018, serving one term before retiring from politics in January 2020. His son, James Jajuga Jr., served as a Methuen Police Captain from 2000 until his retirement in 2020.

Neil Perry
(pp. 93, 280, 324-329, 332, 335, 337-340, 342, 349 351, 354, 360, 364, 372)
Began his professional career as a teacher in Methuen before joining Raytheon, where he worked for over 30 years and retired as Director of Supply Chain. Deeply involved in his community,

Character Index

he volunteered with the Festival of Trees and served on its Board of Directors. He was elected Mayor of Methuen in 2020 and served until his passing in office in 2024.

Methuen Solicitors

Maurice Lariviere
(pp. 28-29, 32-38, 40, 44-46, 68-73, 81-81, 167-168, 180)
He served as Methuen City Solicitor from 1980 until his resignation in 2005, after which he spent several years in private legal practice. He earned a bachelor's degree in political science from Northwestern University in 1972 and received his Juris Doctor from Suffolk University Law School in 1977. He passed away in 2015 from frontotemporal dementia.

Peter McQuillan
(pp. 38, 49, 58, 69, 72-73, 84, 99, 103, 146, 151, 156-157, 165, 170-172, 175-176, 179-181, 183-184)
Served as Methuen City Solicitor from the 1970s until 1980 before transitioning into private legal practice. He returned to the role in 2005 and served until 2013, when the City Council chose not to renew his contract. He then resumed his private practice. During the COVID-19 pandemic, he returned to City Hall once again, this time as Assistant City Solicitor. He holds a bachelor's degree from Suffolk University in 1971 and earned his Juris Doctor from Suffolk Law School in 1974.

Richard D'Agostino
(pp. 181-185, 230-242, 246, 260-262, 264,-265, 280, 282, 321, 346)
Began his career as a schoolteacher in Lawrence, Massachusetts from 1976 to 1977. Ran for the Lawrence School Committee in 1977, defeated by Stephen Zanni. Later elected Alderman of Engineering, serving from 1981 to 1985, and went on to become the city's Director of Public Works from 1985 to 1986. In 1984, he made an unsuccessful bid for Massachusetts State Representative. From 2005 to 2012, he served as Assistant City Solicitor for Lawrence until stepping away from the role due to health issues. In 2016, he was hired as Methuen City Solicitor and

Character Index

served until 2020, when the City Council opted not to renew his contract.

Essex County District Attorneys

Jonathan Blodgett
(pp. 9, 24, 31, 39, 47, 71, 92-93, 155, 375, 378, 387, 390)
Graduated from Suffolk University Law School in 1985 and immediately began serving as an Assistant Essex County District Attorney, a position he held from 1985 to 1986. In 2002, he ran for Essex County District Attorney, won the nomination, and was elected unopposed. He remained in office for 20 years, never facing an opponent in any election, before choosing not to seek reelection in 2022.

Paul Tucker
(pp. 9-10, 382)
Joined the Salem, Massachusetts Police Department in 1983, rising through the ranks to detective and chief of detectives before being appointed Chief of Police in 2009. He served as chief until his resignation in 2014. That same year, he was elected as a Massachusetts State Representative, a position he held until 2023, when he was elected Essex County District Attorney. He earned a master's degree from Anna Maria College.

Others

Alfred Donovan
(pp. 51, 188-189, 192-194, 197, 219-220, 247, 308, 312-314, 325, 329-330, 356, 387)
Joined the Tewksbury Police Department as a reserve officer in 1979 and was hired full-time in 1984. He was appointed Chief of Police in 2003 and served until his retirement in 2009. He earned a master's degree in law enforcement from Antioch University in 1980. In 1998, he founded APD Management Consultants.

Sean Fountain
(pp. 5, 8-10, 170, 179-181, 191, 222-224, 226-228, 230-231, 235, 240-242, 244-246, 248-249, 259-261, 264, 299-302, 306-309,

Character Index

314, 326-329, 332-335, 340-344, 359-360, 368-376, 379, 381-385, 389-391)
He served as a firefighter in North Andover, Massachusetts from 1999 until his retirement in 2017. He was elected to the Methuen City Council, serving three terms from 2012 to 2017. In 2016, he was appointed as a part-time intermittent police officer with the MPD and became a full-time permanent intermittent officer in 2017. He was laid off from the department in 2020.

Richard Stanley
(pp. 59, 188-192, 197-198, 247, 269, 276-277, 356, 369)
Joined the North Andover, Massachusetts Police Department in 1977, rising to the rank of Sergeant in 1982, Lieutenant in 1983, and Chief of Police in 1986, a position he held until 2011. He later served as Chief of Police in the Town of Wareham, Massachusetts from 2009 until his retirement in 2013. That same year, he founded RMS Associates, a public safety consulting firm, and co-founded Integrity Testing, a police promotional assessment center, alongside Al Donovan.

Supporting Characters

A
Abraham, Kevin MPD Officer [2004-present] (pp 70, 318)
Aiello, Mark MPD Officer [2006-present]; brother to Lt. Joseph Aiello (p.22)
Alaimo, Lisa Administrative Assistant for Mayor Sharon Pollard 2000 2006; MPD Administrative Assistant to Chief (p. 88)
Andrew, Robert Methuen City Councilor (1990s-2007) (pp. 64, 73-74)
Atkinson, James "Jamie" Methuen City Council (2012-2018); Council Chair (2014, 2017-2018) (pp.180-182, 224-225, 240242, 244-247, 249, 264-265, 279-280 320)

B
Bahan, Ellen *Rumbo* Columnist; Methuen resident (pp. 3-4, 11, 50)
Baker, Charlie Governor of Massachusetts [2015-2023] (pp. 247, 340)
Beauregard, D.J. Methuen City Councilor [2020-2024]; Methuen Mayor [2024-present] (pp.329, 342, 360, 378)
Bonanno, Clement "Jay" Methuen DPW Highway Superintendent (?-2019); MPD Intermittent Officer [1995-2020] (pp. 310, 317)
Broadhurst, Arthur Massachusetts State Representative [1993-2007]; Methuen Private Attorney [2007-present] (pp. 99, 180)

Character Index

Burke, Sean President, School Safety Advocacy Council; retired Lawrence PD Lieutenant (pp. 189, 254)

C

Campagnone, Joyce Methuen City Councilor; (?-2026) (pp. 152, 180)
Campbell, Andrea Massachusetts Attorney General [2023-present] (p. 382)
Capanelli, Anthony Husband of Fulya Metin (pp. 34, 68)
Capanelli, Fulya (Metin) Secretary to the Methuen Solicitor [2003-2004] (pp. 34-36, 44-46, 68-69, 167-168)
Ciulla, Thomas Methuen City Councilor; [2012-2018] (pp. 180, 181, 224. 230, 240-241, 246)
Condon, Michael Methuen City Councilor [?-2013] (pp. 170, 179-181)
Cote, Brandon MPD reserve candidate (pp. 211-213)
Cronin, Shaun MPD Officer [1987-?] (2008-2019) (pp. 42-44, 49-50, 69, 94, 95-98, 152)
Crowley, Lisa Methuen Human Resource Director [2020-?] (pp. 335, 339-340)
Cunha, Glenn Massachusetts Inspector General (2012-2022) (p. 344)

D

Deeb, Dennis "D.J." Methuen School Committee (pp. 336-337)
Deleon, Eric MPD Sergeant [2000-present] (pp. 48, 66, 138)
Despins, Matthew MPD full-time intermittent officer [2012-2020] (pp. 300, 329, 335)
DiZoglio, Nick Methuen School Committee [2020-2024]; Methuen City Councilor [2024-present] (pp. 377-378, 384)
Dorgan, Ryan MPD reserve candidate (bypassed) [2015] (p. 210-211, 216-218)
Drouin, Anne Assistant City Clerk [2002-2021]; City Clerk [2021-present]; (p. 225)
Duggan, Tom Host of Paying Attention Podcast; founder of *The Valley Patriot* (pp. 57, 71, 279, 338)
Dugan, Ryan Methuen resident (pp. 296-297)
Dwinells, Stephen MPD reserve candidate [2015] (pp. 211-213)

E

Eddings, Keith *Eagle-Tribune* journalist (pp. 7, 8, 208)
Estes, Andrea *The Boston Globe* Journalist (pp. 8-11)

Character Index

F

Fahey, Paul Chief of Staff to Mayor Jajuga (pp.274, 304, 306, 307, 314-315, 326-327, 372)

Faretra, Joel Methuen City Councilor [2020-2026] Chair [2024] (pp. 93, 376-377, 384)

Ferreira, Eric MPD Captain [2012-2022] (pp. 9, 223, 316-317, 374)

Ferullo, Robert Woburn, MA Police Chief [1980-2011]; Director of the MPTC [2019-2024] (pp. 332, 334-335, 373, 375, 390)

Ferry, Lisa Yarid Methuen City Councilor [2011–2017] (pp. 180, 224, 231, 240-241)

Fleming, Patrick MPD officer [2017-present] (p. 211)

Fleming, Thomas Former Lowell PD Sergeant; NECC/Methuen Academy Director [2015-2018] (pp. 206-208, 287-289)

Fleming, Walter MPD Sergeant [1993-present]; father of Patrick Fleming (pp. 110, 211)

Flynn, Edward Auditor, CNA; oversaw 2021 police audit; former EOPSS Secretary [2003-2006] (pp. 59, 354-355)

Fram, Thomas MPD Captain [1985-2013] (pp. 43, 49, 85, 108, 111, 120, 154-156)

G

Gambaccini, Andrew Attorney for Solomon (pp. 44, 58, 69, 72, 84, 100, 114-115, 162, 172, 384)

Gardner, David MPD Patrolmen [2000-present] Union President (pp. 299-300, 311, 363)

Giordano, Larry Methuen City Councilor [1990s-early 2000s] (pp. 64, 117)

Gradzewicz, Andrew Lawrence District Court Clerk (pp. 182-183)

H

Haggar, Kristopher MPD Intermmittent Officer, nephew of Randy Haggar [2006-2011] (p. 117)

Harb, Joseph MPD Captain [retired] (p. 43)

Healey, Maura Massachusetts Attorney General [2015-2023], Governor of Massachusetts [2023-present] (pp. 297, 375, 390)

Henrick, Brian MPD Recruit Canidate (p. 117)

Henrick, Kenneth Methuen City Councilor [early 2000s] (p. 23)

Himmer, Tod MPD Sargeant [1986-2016] (pp. 65, 218-220)

J

Jajuga, James Jr. MPD Captain [2000-2020] (pp. 117, 282, 320, 407)

Jenness, Kerry (Regan) Methuen City Solicitor [2013-2016] (pp. 184, 222-223, 241)

Character Index

K

Kalil, George Owner of Merrimac Marine; wife Emily Solomon, Joe Solomon's sister (p. 88,108-110, 131, 133-134)

Kannan, Jennifer Methuen City Councilor [2008-2020, 2016-2020] Chair [2012, 2019, 2018-20] (pp. 177, 180 224-226, 230, 240-242, 247-248, 264, 290, 296)

Kannan, William MPD Officer [2012-present] son of Jennifer Kannan (pp. 117, 177, 180 224-226, 230, 240-242, 247-248, 264, 290, 296)

Kara (Lipides) Mc Menamon MPD Officer [2012-present] previously MPD dispatcher; wife of Sergeant Thomas McMenamon (pp. 66, 139, 161, 177)

Kazanjian, George Methuen City Council [2014-2020] (pp. 224, 240-242, 290)

Kelly, Thomas Methuen Purchasing Agent [1980s-1990] City Auditor [1990-2018] (pp. 72, 109, 126, 131-132, 274, 284, 289, 290, 362)

Klein, Darren KP Law attorney (pp. 219-220)

Korn, Frank MPD Lieutenant [1987-2018] (pp. 20, 95, 97, 122, 170, 241, 243)

L

LaFlamme, Brandon MPD Officer [2012-present] (pp. 317-318)
Lahey, Phil Methuen City Councilor [early 2000s (p. 64)
Lantigua, William "Willie" Former Lawrence Mayor (pp. 182-183)
LeBlanc, Robert Methuen Town Manager [1990s] (p. 73)
Lever, Scott MPD Patrolman [1996-2023] (p. 23)
Lussier, Tom Husband of Sharon Pollard (p. 31, 324)

M

Marks, Michael Hearing Officer (pp. 58, 60-61, 84, 87, 119, 134)
Martin, Kevin MPD Lieutenant [1988-2019] (p. 43)
McCarty, James Methuen City Councilor [2018-2024] (pp. 295-296, 341-342, 360)
McLaughlin, Michael Methuen Town Manager [1990s] (p. 18)
McLaughlin, Neil Tewksbury, MA dispatcher, brother-in-law Al Donovan (pp. 192-194)
McNamara, Scott MPD Chief [2021-present] (pp. 9, 93, 363-364, 374, 377)

N

Neve, Michael Methuen resident (pp. 71, 101-4, 107)
Nolan, Gary Attorney for Methuen Superior Officers' Union (pp. 283, 305, 347)

Character Index

O

O'Brien, James Massachsuetts Assistant Attorney General; MPTC Chief of Staff (p. 375)

O'Connell, Dan MPD Sergeant [2006-present]; spouse of Councilor Vidler (pp. 247-248, 289)

P

Pappalardo, Jeanne Methuen City Couselor (pp. 151, 180, 184)
Parolisi, Mark MPD Officer [2015-present] (p. 211)
Peterson, Dennis Tewksbury Police Detective (p. 194)
Phillips, Michael MPD Canidate (pp. 211, 213-216)
Pilz, Kenneth MPD Officer [2012-present] (p. 177)
Pilz, Richard MPD Officer [1986-2018] (p. 177)

R

Randazzo, Anne Methuen HR Director/Asst. Solicitor (pp. 5, 261-262, 306-307, 326-328, 346, 372)
Reidy, Terrence Massachusetts Secretary of Public Safety [2021-2025] (p. 336)
Rynne, Joseph MPD Sergeant [2003-present] (pp. 66, 218)

S

Saba, John Methuen Resident (p. 297)
Saba, Steve Methuen City Councilor [2018-2024] (pp. 274, 2887, 297, 343, 354, 3786, 384)
Silva, Daryl Independent filmmaker, Methuen native (p. 70)
Sirois, Chad MPD Officer [2006-present] (p. 199)
Smith, Stephen MPD Lieutenant [1996-2020] (pp. 215, 223)
Souther, David MPD Officer [2012-present] (pp. 299-302, 311, 315)
Stackelin, Jill Methuen Human Resource Department (p. 327)
Stein, Paul Commissioner, Massachusetts Civil Service Commission [2008-present] (pp. 98-99, 113, 115. 123-126, 128-146, 155, 181, 192, 370, 387)

T

Torrisi, Jeffrey MPD Officer [1999-present] (p. 176)

U

Uliano, Pat Methuen resident or city hall employee (p. 151)

Character Index

V
Vidler, Lynn Methuen City Councilor [2014-2020] (pp. 224, 240-241, 245, 247-248, 264, 289-290, 320)

W
Waldron, Patrick MPD Officer [2013-present] (p. 117)
Willette, Kenneth Jr. Methuen City Councilor (p. 64)
Wnek, Michael MPD Lieutenant [1988-2016] (pp. 65, 67, 89, 97, 101, 110, 121, 135-136, 138, 143, 160, 218-220)
Woekel, Todd Methuen City Councilor (p. 23)
Wood, Tim Owner/reporter, Loop Weekly; (pp. 5, 6, 279-280, 306-309, 333-334)

Z
Zeigler, Eunice Methuen City Councilor [2018-2024] (pp. 283, 378 379)
Zivkovich, Dan MPTC Executive Director [?-2019] (p. 334, 336)

Investigator's Dossier

(Bibliography)

Arbitration
American Arbitrator Association
- **Notice of Hearing**, Methuen Police Patrolman's Union v City of Methuen, August 12, 2019
- **Methuen Police Superior Officers' Association and the City of Methuen**, Loretta T. Attardo, January 7, 2020
- **City of Methuen and Methuen Police Patrolman's Association**, Mary Ellen Shea, April 16, 2020

Blogs
- **Methuen Police Blotter**, September 17-November 6, 2009
- **BillManzi.com**
    - 'Mayor's Statement Re Civil Service Case, July 31, 2010
    - 'State of the City Address' April 28, 2018
- **Methuen Confidential**
- **Mondoweiss**, Detroit Michigan, December 5, 2018
- **Numismatic News** 'Charges Against roofers Dismissed' July 21, 2008

City of Methuen, Massachusetts
City Council
- **Council Rules & Procedures**
- **Meeting Agenda**
    - March 7, 2016
    - August 1, 2016
    - February 21, 2017
    - January 10, 2019
- **Meeting Votes**
    - October 17, 2016
    - July 10, 2017
- **Minutes**
    - March 6, 2017
    - April 18, 2023
- **Meeting Video**

(Bibliography)

- March 7, 2016 [mark 1:28]
- July 11, 2016
- October 17, 2016 [Mark 3:18]
- February 21, 2017 [22:43]
- March 6, 2017 [41.20 mark]
- April 18, 2017
- May 30, 2017 [24:33 mark]
- June 1, 2017 [19:01 mark]
- September 18, 2017
- January 10, 2019 [mark 1:15:25]
- February 7, 2019
- April 18, 2023 [Mark 51:42]

Finance
- **Budget**
  - Fiscal Year 2009-2021
- **Payroll**
  - Joseph Solomon city payroll records, 2006-2021

Purchasing
- Hard Rock Hotel, Las Vegas, NV, July 22-29-2017
- JetBlue Itinerary Confirmation, July 22, 2017 & July 29, 2017
- MPD Out of State Meal allowance slips, July22-29, 2017
- **Vendor Reports**
  - February 2011
  - April 2011
  - May 2011
  - June 2011
  - August 2011
  - September 2012
  - August 2012
  - December 2012
  - May 2014
  - July 2014
  - August 2014
  - June 2017
  - August 2017
  - October 2014
  - May 2015
  - August 2015
  - October 2015
  - December 2015
  - January 2016
  - June 2016
  - August 2016
  - September 2016

(Bibliography)

- November 2016
- April 2017,
- May 2017
- September 2017
- November 2017
- January 2018
- December 2018
- March 2019
- October 2019
- December 2019
- January 2020

Human Resources
- **Collective Bargaining Agreements and Employment Contracts**
  - Collective Bargaining Agreement Between the City of Methuen and the Methuen Police Patrolman's Association
  - Collective Bargaining Agreement Between the City of Methuen and the Methuen Police Superior Officer's Association, N.E.P.B.A., Local 17, C-18-21, September 18, 2017
  - Police Chief Employment Contract between the City of Methuen and Joseph Solomon, C-17-15, February 21, 2017
  - Memorandum of Agreement between Methuen Police Superior Officers Association and City of Methuen,

Letters and Correspondences
- **William Manzi to Joseph Solomon**, Notice of Decision, April 11, 2007
- **Nolan Perroni to City of Methuen**, February 7, 2019
- **KP Law to Massachusetts State Ethics Commission**, September 26, 2019
- **Solomon's Retirement Letter to Mayor Perry**, January 8, 2020
- **Attorney Caruso to Methuen City Council & DJ Deeb**, May 11, 2020
- **Attorney George Malonis to City of Methuen**, Sean Fountain, October 8, 2020
- **Lawrence Mayor Lantiqua to Methuen City Council,** March 29, 2013
- **Methuen City Council to Various State Agencies**, Methuen's Call for Action, April 26, 2023

Police Department
Final Report: Methuen Police Department Performance Audit, Flynn, E., Friedl, D., Richardson, K., Jenkins, M., & Bond, B., CAN, January 2021
- **MPD Disciplinary Records**, Al Tracker, Public Records Request, September 30, 2021, Eric Ferreira
- **Methuen Discipline Hearing Decision**, Paul Fahey, April 9, 2019
- **Methuen Police Department, Investigative Report 22-01**, Chief Scott McNamara, April 14, 2022
- MPDnews.com

(Bibliography)

- 'Chief Solomon and Mayor Zanni Host Promotional Swearing in Ceremony for Four Officers' February 1, 2016
- 'Methuen Police Department Announces Promotions of Three Officers' March 9, 2017
- **Valliere Accident Report**, May 26, 2016
- **MPD Investigative Report, Matter of Arthur Hardy**, APD Management, October 10, 2018
- **Methuen Police Department, Notice of Administrative Leave**, Arthur Hardy, January 30, 2019
- **Methuen Police Department, Notice of Internal Investigation**, Hardy, September 10, 2018
- **MPD Policy & Procedure No. 840 Body Worn Cameras**, April 29, 2016, page 4
- **Police Report**, January 10, 2019
- **Possessed Property Report**, Locker of Joseph Solomon, May 8, 2008
- **STIRM Report**, STIRM Group, Lawrence Smith, March 27, 2023

Solicitor
- **Methuen Charter and General Ordinances of the City**, 2000

Commonwealth of Massachusetts

Civil Service Commission, Boston, Massachusetts
- **Modified Interim Order**, Commissioner Christopher C. Bowman, Case Nos: G1-09-20, G1-09-33, G1-09-253, G1-09-261, July 9, 2009
- **Conclusion of Civil Service Commission Investigation Case No: 1-09-290**, Commissioner Christopher C. Bowman, August 20, 2009
- **Civil Service Commission Findings/Conclusions/Orders**, Case No. I-09-290, August 29, 2009
- **Joseph Solomon v. City of Methuen**, Commissioner Paul Stein, Cases no: D-07-159 & D1-08-114, July 29, 2010
- **Conclusion of Civil Service Commission Investigation**, Commissioner Christopher C. Bowman, Case No. I-09-290, January 27, 2011
- **Whitehouse vs Town of Wareham**, Commissioner Paul Stein, Case No: I-12-184, September 20, 2012
- **Ryan Dorgan v. Methuen**, Response to Joint request for relief, Commissioner Christopher C. Bowman, Case No. G1-15-24, April 30, 2015
- **Michael Phillips v. Methuen**, Decision, Commissioner Christopher C. Bowman, Case No. G1-15-45, July 9, 2015
- **Stephen Dwinells v. Methuen**, Decision, Commissioner Cynthia A. Ittleman, Case No. G1-15-46, August 6, 2015

(Bibliography)

- **Brandon Cote v. Methuen**, Commissioner Cynthia A. Ittleman, Decision, Case No. G1-15-25, August 6, 2015
- **Ryan v. Methuen, Decision**, Commissioner Cynthia A. Ittleman, Case No. G1-15-24, September 3, 2015
- **Discipline Appeal Form**, Arthur L. Hardy, May 8, 2019
- 2023 Statewide Police Sergeant, Lieutenant and Captain Exams
- **Findings, Conclusions, Orders and Recommendations**, Commissioner Christopher C. Bowman, Case No. I-20-182, January 26, 2023
- **Final Orders and Conclusions of Investigation**, Commissioner Christopher C. Bowman, Case No. I-20-182, July 13, 2023
- **Gregory Gallant v. City of Methuen**, Decision, Yakov Malkiel, Administrative Magistrate, Case No. D1-22-084, October 21, 2024

Division of Administrative Law Appeals, Boston, Massachusetts
- **Solomon v. Methuen Retirement Board**, Docket numbers: CR-21-0371 & CR-21-0274, September 8, 2023

Massachusetts General Laws
- **Part I, Title VII, Chapter 43, Section 20** Passage of Ordinances
- **Part I, Title III, Chapter 30B, Section 4**, Submission of quotations
- **Part I, Title III, Chapter 44, Section 33A**, Salary provisions in budget; requirements and limitations
- **Part I, Title IV, Chapter 32, Section 5(2)(f),** Superannuation retirement
- **Part I, Title VII, Chapter 41,**
    - Section 96B Police Training schools; supervisory training; attendance by persons exercising police powers; wages and expenses; exceptions; removal for failure to attend
    - Section 97B, Rape reporting and prosecution units within police departments; training and funding; personnel; retention and preservation of forensic evidence
- **Part I, Title VII, Chapter 48, Section 57G** Compensation of certain heads of fire and police departments
- **Part IV, Title I, Chapter 268A**
    - Section 19 Municipal employees, relatives or associates; financial interest in particular matter
    - Section 20 Municipal employees; financial interest in contracts; holding one or more elected positions
    - Section 23 (B)(1), Supplemental provisions; standard of conduct
- **Part IV, Title I, Chapter 270, Section 22(3)** Smoking in public places

Human Resource Department, Boston, Massachusetts
- **Methuen Captain Eligibility List**, November 3, 2014

Office of Attorney General, Boston, Massachusetts
- **Indictments Announced in Case Against Former Methuen Police Chief, Police Officer,** September 28, 2023

Office of Campaign and Political Finance

(Bibliography)

- William Manzi III
- James P. Jajuga
- Stephen Zanni
- Neil Perry

Office of Jury Commissioner, Boston, Massachusetts
- **Grand Jurors Handbook**, February 16, 2024

Office of the Comptroller
- **Statewide Payroll**
- **Statewide Spending**

Office of Secretary of State, Boston, Massachusetts
- **Corporation Lookup**
    - APD Management, Inc.
    - Assessment Center Training, LLC
    - Bolo Mobile, LLC
    - Eagle Investigations, Inc.
    - Integrity Testing, LLC
    - International Association of School Resource Officers, Inc.
    - Municipal Police Institute
    - Police Assessment Center for Training
    - School Safety Advocacy Council
    - Methuen Festival of Trees, Inc.

Office of the Inspector General, Boston, Massachusetts
- **Leadership Failures in Methuen Police Contracts**, December 23, 2020

State Ethics Commission, Boston, Massachusetts
- **Advisory, 86-02: Nepotism**, December 15, 1986
- **Opinion EC-COI-97-1**, March 12, 1997
- **Matter of Thomas Lussier**, Docket No. 661, July 2, 2002
- **Matter of Sharon Pollard**, Docket No. 07-0010, April 26, 2007
- **Thomas Fleming**, August 6, 2018
- **Matter of Thomas Fleming**. August 8, 2018
- **Advisory 05-05: The Rule of Necessity**, pages 841-842, May 16, 2019
- **Public Education Letter in the Matter of Lynn Vidler**, April 30, 2020
- **Public Education Letter in the Matter of James Atkinson**, April 30, 2020
- **Public Education Letter in the Matter of James Jajuga**, April 30, 2020
- **Matter of Joseph Solomon**, Docket No. 23-0010, June 30, 2023

State Legislature
- **Acts of 1945, Chapter 201**, An Act Providing a Permanent Intermittent Police Force for the Town of Methuen, Regulating Appointments Thereto and the Service Thereof, April 9, 1945
- **Acts of 2002, Chapter 42**, An Act Exempting Herbert Stacey And Timothy Getchell From The Maximum Age Requirements As A Police Officer In The City of Methuen, February 21, 2002

(Bibliography)

- **Acts of 2008, Chapter 141**, An act to exempt the position of chief of police in the city known as the Town of Methuen from Civil Service Law, June 20, 2008
- **Acts of 2017, Chapter 60**, An Act Authorizing the Appointment of Sean Fountain to the Position of Permanent Intermittent Police Officer of the Police Department of the City Known as the Town of Methuen, August 1, 2017
- **Acts of 2017, Chapter 149**, Authorizing appointment of James Atkinson to the position of junior accountant of the police department of the City of Methuen, December 13, 2017
- **Acts of 2022, Chapter 251**, an act abolishing the permanent intermittent police force in the City of Methuen, November 1, 2022

Courts
Essex County Superior Court, Lawrence, Massachusetts
- **Capanelli et al v. Methuen**, Civil Action, 0777CV01595 August 27, 2007
- **Eagle Tribune Publishing Company v. Solomon**, Civil Action, 0577CV00523, April 1, 2005
- **Lariviere v. Solomon et al**, Civil Action, 0577CV01155, July 1, 2005
- **Cronin v. City of Methuen**, Civil Action, 0677CV00549, March 30, 2006
- **Solomon v. Kelly et al**, Civil Action, 00777CV01749, September 19, 2007
- **Alaimo v. Kelly et al.**, Civil Action, 0777CV01750, September 19, 2007
- **Vasques v. Solomon**, Civil Action, 0977CV0167, August 28, 2009
- **City of Methuen v. Massachusetts Civil Service Commission and Joseph Solomon**, Civil Action, No. 2010-1813D, August 25, 2010
- **Despin v. City of Methuen**, Civil Action, 1877CV01398, September 27, 2018
- **Commonwealth of Massachusetts v. Fountain, Sean** Criminal 2377CR00449 & 2377CR00450
- **Commonwealth of Massachusetts v. Joseph E. Solomon**, Criminal 2377CR00451 & 2377CR00452

United States District Court, D. Massachusetts, Boston, Massachusetts
- **Aiello v. Manzi et al.**, Civil Action, 1:08-cv-10635, April 15, 2008
- **Phillips v. City of Methuen**, Civil Action 1:11-10171, January 31, 2011
- **Solomon v. Manzi et al.**, Civil Action, 1:11-cv-10794, May 5, 2011
- **Fountain v. City of Methuen**, United States District Court, 1-21-cv-11046, June 24, 2021

United States Bankruptcy Court, Eastern District of New York
- **Fulya Capanelli**, Case No. 8-11-74009-AST, June 6, 2011

(Bibliography)

Middlesex County District Court, Lowell, Massachusetts
— **Commonwealth v McLaughlin, Neil F.**. Case # 0581CR01215,

Magazines
Time Magazine
November 5, 2018, 'Guns in America'

Miscellaneous
Death Certificate, Richard Henry St. Louis, February 17, 2004
Contract between Northern Essex Community College and EIS, Inc, January 2015
State of New York, Insurance Department
Stipulation Surrendering Licenses, Fulya Capanelli, No. 2009-0080
Gloucester, Massachusetts Police Department, press release, 'Gloucester Police Department Unveils Details for Drug Recovery Initiative' May 27, 2015
Florida Department of State, Department of State, Division of Corporations, Corporations Search, School Safety Advocacy Council
Response Letter from DJ Deeb to Attorney Caruso, May 13, 2020
Northern Essex Community College Academic Catalog, p244 & 254
John Guilfoil Public Relations
- 'Methuen Police Department Announces Promotions of Three Officers' March 9, 2017
- 'Methuen Police Department Announces Promotions' July 14, 2017

Casetext.com, Cronin v. City of Methuen, Memorandum of Decision and Order on Defendants Joseph E. Solomon and Joseph Alaimo's Motion for Summary Judgement,

Newspapers
The Boston Globe, Boston, Massachusetts
- '2 witnesses say they saw police chief's speeding car' September 3, 1992
- 'Judge finds N. Andover chief was drinking' September 4, 1992
- 'N. Andover police chief suspended in driving case' September 12, 1992
- 'Chief won't appeal drunken driving case' November 19, 1992
- 'Top Cop to remain a Civil Servant' August 29, 2002
- 'Crime-fighting Program makes Inroads' October 3, 2002
- 'Alaimo eyed for police deputy post', November 14, 2002
- 'Reserve Police May Increase' June 1, 2002
- 'City Acts Fast to Grab Police Grants', January 26, 2003

(Bibliography)

- 'Permanent Police Chief' August 7, 2003
- 'Federal Money for Police' October 19, 2003
- 'FBI probe of grants is said to narrow' December 6, 2003
- 'Jajuga awarding of grants probed' December 27, 2003
- 'Sexual Misconduct Alleged in Methuen' March 17, 2005
- 'Questions are Raised on Money Discovery' April 29, 2005
- 'Police call Methuen treasure story a tall tale' April 30, 2005
- 'Council Questions use of Gift.' May 15, 2005
- 'Brooks Funds go to the City' July 10, 2005
- 'Financial claim filed in harassment case' July 14, 2005
- 'Chief's Daughter Faces Hearing' October 29, 2006
- 'Police Chief's Daughter not Charged' November 9, 2006
- 'Union Assails Chief's Action in Methuen Police Probe' November 28, 2006
- 'Police probe has Methuen on edge' November 30, 2006
- 'In Methuen, police chief's pursuit continues' December 7, 2006
- 'Police Union Head Defeated' January 4, 2007
- 'Sanction Against Chief is Weighed' April 5, 2007
- 'Mayor of Methuen Suspends Police Chief' April 13, 2007
- 'Two got most of grants for policing' May 3, 2007
- 'Council Votes Against Chief' May 10, 2007
- 'US Seeks Details of Police Payroll Records' June 7, 2007
- 'US Wants City Police to Repay $170,472' July 31, 2007
- 'Methuen Delays Repaying US $170,000' August 5, 2007
- 'Alert Sent on Officer's Guilty Plea' September 2, 2007
- 'City Moves to cut pay of chiefs' September 9, 2007
- 'Methuen's police chief sues city over cut in pay' September 22, 2007
- 'Interim Chief Seeks to mend Morale' October 4, 2007
- 'Federal Funds Examined' December 6, 2007
- 'Lawsuit alleges police coercion' December 16, 2007
- 'Jury rejects claim' January 31, 2008
- 'Early retirement' February 21, 2008
- 'Police chief hearings set to resume' March 23, 2008
- 'Police union's leader sues Methuen over demotion' April 20, 2008
- 'Police Officer Rehired' September 21, 2008
- 'Chief Wins Unemployment Benefits' October 19, 2008
- 'Fired Chief's Appeal' January 4, 2009
- 'The cost for school shooter detection system? Maybe $100K, but Methuen got it for free' November 11, 2014
- 'Methuen may rescind police accords' February 5, 2019
- 'Methuen's police chief is one of the highest paid in the country' August 2, 2020
- 'Methuen police chief gets vote of no confidence' September 1, 2020

(Bibliography)

- 'In Methuen, a question of favors by chief' December 1, 2020
- 'Methuen police chief placed on leave after inspector general finds he violated his duty by orchestrating exorbitant police contracts' December 23, 2020
- 'Methuen police chief retiring' January 12, 2021
- 'Arbitrator nixes Methuen police pact' January 11, 2022

BU Today, Boston University, Boston, Massachusetts
- Training police to effectively investigate sexual assault cases, March 14, 2017

Boston Voyager, Bostonvoyager.com,
- 'Meet Joseph Alaimo and Joseph Solomon of Eagle Investigation Services' July 3, 2018

Daily Item, Lynn, Massachusetts
- 'Buried Treasure too good to be true' April 30, 2005

Daily News, New York, New York
- 'Mob-mole cop testifies to select few' April 23, 2003
- 'Pen to go with his ink' June 17, 2003

The Daily Universe
Brigham Young University School of Communications, Provo, Utah
- 'Salt Lake honored for community policing' October 28, 1997

Lawrence Eagle Tribune, North Andover, Massachusetts
- 'Former Methuen mayor fined $4,000 for funneling city money to her non-profit' April 26, 2007
- 'Councilors want Solomon to stay on; No-confidence vote called symbolic, not message to step down' May 9, 2007
- 'Correction', August 24, 2007
- 'Fights $25,610 pay cut, wants his full $158,295' September 27, 2007
- 'Police Chief sent home' September 29, 2007
- 'Methuen Police Chief Solomon to go Public' October 26, 2007
- 'Solomon: I Will Fight' November 3, 2007
- 'Manzi re-elected to second term in Methuen, November 6, 2007
- 'Testimony: Lariviere said 'I gotta resign' Police chief, deputy defend themselves in U.S. District Court' January 18, 2008
- 'Ex-Secretary testifies against Lariviere' January 19, 2008
- 'Methuen Chief could face reprimand to termination at hearing' January 31, 2008
- 'Methuen officers seek extra holiday pay' March 31, 2008
- 'Solomon misses job, ready for hearing to conclude' April 4, 2008
- 'Our view: No extra pay for Methuen Police' April 4, 2008
- 'Methuen Mayor has report on police chief will make decision on Solomon's fate within two days' May 6, 2008
- 'Illegal Drugs, Weapons, evidence found in Solomon's locker' May 13, 2008
- 'Mayor says it's 'very likely' former officer will be rehired' June 19, 2008

(Bibliography)

- 'No Criminal Charges against Solomon for storing evidence in locker' July 18, 2008
- 'Officer injured in training exercise' August 27, 2008
- 'Former Methuen chief's brother-in-law charged in theft case' September 11, 2008
- 'Police: Caron knew tractor, machine were stolen' September 12, 2008
- 'Cop says superior officer attacked him' September 22, 2008
- 'Methuen officer cleared of wrongdoing at training session' September 25, 2008
- 'Fighting for his job: Solomon's Civil Service hearing set for Tuesday' October 6, 2008
- 'Public allowed at Solomon Hearing' October 7, 2008
- 'Lawyer: 'A trial of the mayor, as well as a trial of Joe Solomon' October 8, 2008
- 'Solomon wins fight for unemployment benefits' October 8, 2008
- 'Mayor Manzi to testify against Solomon' October 14, 2008
- 'Fired Methuen police chief Solomon hopes to return Mayor Manzi to testify Tuesday when hearing reconvenes' October 17, 2008
- "Mayoral money bag allegation to come up at Solomon hearing' October 19, 2008
- 'Three Officers to testify against fired chief today' October 22, 2008
- 'Manzi accuses Solomon of Blackmail and says ex-chief threatened to reveal untrue sexual secrets about the mayor at a rally' October 22, 2008
- 'Sergeant Describes Solomon's Tirade' October 23, 2008
- 'Resident says Manzi refused $15K bribe – Testimony comes during ex-police chief's civil service hearing' October 31, 2008
- 'City Purchasing chief told to "stay out" of police business – boat bought from chief's sister' November 7, 2008
- 'Solomon hearing on hiatus until 2009' December 5, 2008
- 'Chief: Solomon wanted Neve to wear a wire to catch Manzi accepting bribe' January 7, 2009
- 'Cop says mayor called police chief midget' January 7, 2009
- 'Former Methuen Mayor Pollard sticks up for ex-Chief Solomon – Denies she told purchasing employee to stay out of police business' January 9, 2009
- 'Retired cop says former chief would have left quietly for $500k' January 21, 2009
- 'Baddour wants to speed up civil service hearings' January 28, 2009
- 'Property checks at issue in fired chief's hearing' January 28, 2009
- 'Lawyer wants information about FBI investigation into Methuen mayor' January 30, 2009
- 'Cop: FBI recorded conversations he had with Mayor' February 11, 2009
- 'Solomon too sick to testify today' February 12, 2009

(Bibliography)

- 'Cop: Mayor said he was going to get me between the eyes – cop claims Manzi threatened him' February 13, 2009
- 'Solomon's brother-in-law testifies for him' February 20, 2009
- 'Solomon: I'm still working with FBI – Ex-police chief says he kept diary of Manzi investigation' February 24, 2009
- 'Solomon: Never thought my job was on the line – Ex chief testifies in final day of civil service hearing to win back job' February 25, 2009
- 'Fired police chief says song parody shows political bias' March 13, 2009
- 'Warning: political satire – Politicians trade good-natured barbs at St. Patrick's Day lunch' March 15, 2009
- 'Chief ignored mayor's order on movie shoot – Dispute over mob film hastened deterioration of relationship with Manzi' March 22, 2009
- 'Chiefs offered to call in the troops for Solomon' April 10, 2009
- 'Solomon hearing ends; Methuen still owes $170k in grant money' April 10, 2009
- 'Lawyers receive extension in Solomon case' July 1, 2009
- 'Former in-law of ex-chief gets probation over stolen tractor' July 10, 2009
- 'Lawyers receive another extension in Solomon hearing' July 16, 2009
- 'Cop claims chief's call sent him to hospital – Officer denied injured in the line of duty benefits' July 29, 2009
- 'Residents, councilors unsure if city should appeal police chief's reinstatement' August 1, 2010   'North Andover police chief has part-time gig on Cape Cod – Stanley starts as interim chief in Wareham' August 5, 2009
- 'Cop loses fight to have sergeant punished' November 23, 2009
- 'Methuen compiles new list of reserve police candidates' February 10, 2010
- 'Commissioner Stein on Manzi' July 31, 2010
- 'A look at the charges and the rulings' July 31, 2010
- 'Solomon can come back as Methuen Police Chief' July 31, 2010
- 'Mayor calls Solomon ruling a political diatribe' August 1, 2010
- 'A timeline of the Solomon case', Oct 1, 2010
- 'North Andover police chief's future unclear' November 5, 2010
- 'Editorial: Chief's charade has gone on too long' November 8, 2010
- 'Aiello: Mayor threatened me" November 16, 2010
- 'Chief says Mayor threatened to beat up cop' November 17, 2010
- 'Wiretapped calls aired in lawsuit trial, November 18, 2010
- 'Jury out in police lawsuit' November 20, 2010
- 'Mistrial in Aiello trial' November 22, 2010
- 'Methuen cop's lawsuit ends in hung jury' November 23, 2010
- 'Judge explains why he let jury hear FBI tapes' November 28, 2010
- 'City, Aiello to talk about settling civil suit' December 8, 2010

(Bibliography)

- 'Chief's return has gone smoothly' January 9, 2011
- 'Sergeant sues city, police for slander – Demands $750,000 for stress, health problems from Methuen' February 21, 2011
- 'Methuen man creates mob movie' March 31, 2011
- 'Lawyer: City on the hook for $300K' April 13, 2011
- 'Wareham is welcome to Stanley's services' April 14, 2011
- 'Council approves $120K settlement for Methuen cop' April 20, 2011
- 'Judge approves $120K settlement for Methuen cop' April 27, 2011
- 'Solomon back-pay trial halted as judge recuses himself' October 26, 2011
- 'Solomon earned $77k teaching after firing' December 14, 2011
- 'Solomon sues to regain his old salary lawyer: action filed at legal deadline to protect his rights' May 7, 2011
- 'Judge grants Solomon lost wages, $31K raise' March 17, 2012
- 'Police Unions support Solomon after court decision' March 20, 2012
- 'Time to move forward – Potential Solomon appeal faces opposition' March 25, 2012
- 'Methuen Police department Solomon suit deal proposed – Mayor wants to end wrangling with chief' April 5, 2012
- 'Solomon deal talks continuing despite appeals' April 18, 2012
- 'Wants more" April 24, 2012
- 'Solomon submits settlement proposal to Methuen Mayor' April 26, 2012
- 'City argues Solomon job ruling was wrong' May 18, 2012
- 'Methuen police chief 'stunned' by sudden negotiations collapse' June 8, 2012
- 'Solomon case on way to federal court' June 21, 2012
- 'Methuen's Mayor Stephen Zanni: Six months on the job' July 2, 2012
- 'Chief seeks 'severe sanctions' for Zanni – Solomon angered mayor detailed settlement talks' July 10, 2012
- 'Do your job' July 13, 2012
- 'Methuen officials not cited after speeding' July 15, 2012
- 'Methuen lawyer: Solomon trying to intimidate the city into settling' July 17, 2012
- 'Judge upholds ruling reinstating Solomon as chief Civil Service acted correctly' July 28, 2012
- 'Mayor offers Solomon proposal' November 11, 2012
- 'Methuen Police add 7 new Patrolman' December 23, 2012 'Solomon says city owes him $200K' December 26, 2012
- 'Methuen police add 7 new patrolmen – some familiar names join force' December 23, 2012
- 'Zanni's final offer to go to Solomon by end of week" January 30, 2013
- 'Deal or no deal' February 26, 2013
- 'Zanni and Solomon meet but can't settle' February 28, 2013

(Bibliography)

- 'Methuen to pay Solomon $100K' March 26, 2013
- 'Council wants details of $100,000 Solomon deal' March 28, 2013
- Council approves spending $100,001 to pay settlement' March 29, 2013
- 'Methuen Council to reorganize' January 6, 2013
- 'Council ousts city solicitor – 5-4 vote seals his fate' January 8, 2013
- 'Smooth transition sought in replacing Methuen solicitor' January 15, 2013
- '12 apply for Methuen solicitor job' January 29, 2013
- 'Solicitor search conflicts with law' February 12, 2013
- 'Interviews with finalists now to be made public – Solicitor search' February 14, 2013
- 'City to release names of solicitor finalists' February 21, 2013
- 'Finalists revealed for solicitor job' March 4, 2013
- 'Two finalists drop out of solicitor search' March 12, 2013
- 'Secret meeting held last month – Councilors praise hiring process despite violation' March 19, 2013
- 'Finalist blames corrupt mayor for firing in Lawrence – Solicitor search' March 27, 2013
- 'Text Backlash Methuen solicitor finalist calls for an investigation' March 29, 2013
- 'Council votes to start solicitor search over' April 2, 2013
- 'The search for a city solicitor Methuen retrial' April 2, 2013
- 'New Contract near for Solomon' March 31, 2014
- 'Chief, Zanni agree to deal – Solomon on verge of $200K settlement and new contract' April 17, 2014
- 'Pollard gets her place of honor' November 3, 2014
- 'Methuen live test active shooter system' November 11, 2014
- 'Hi-tech help: Shooter detection demonstrated in Methuen school' November 12, 2014
- 'Police Recruit Training Academy Opens on NECC's Haverhill campus' January 21, 2015
- 'Zanni earns national anti-bullying honor' March 1, 2015
- 'Narcan saves 35 OD victims in Methuen' March 8, 2015
- 'Northern Essex police academy graduates first recruits' June 30, 2015
- 'Methuen solicitor's job an issue for Council candidates' October 22, 2015
- 'Outside law firm vs. City solicitor' October 25, 2015
- 'Methuen solicitor leaving post' February 4, 2016
- 'Methuen uses law firm to fill in for outgoing solicitor' February 19, 2016
- 'Methuen council holding off on city solicitor decision' March 11, 2016
- 'Gloucester police blasts defeat of opioid funding' July 6, 2016
- 'Council chairman named intermittent police officer' July 28, 2016
- 'City Council is rethinking legal services' August 3, 2016
- 'Methuen Council wants D'Agostino as interim solicitor' August 5, 2016

(Bibliography)

- 'Councilor's votes on solicitor raise conflict questions' August 23, 2016
- 'Methuen Police officers promoted' March 7, 2017
- 'Jaujga kicks off campaign for Methuen mayor' May 5, 2017
- 'Methuen's $160M budget passes with little debate' June 1, 2017
- 'Methuen Police officers promoted' July 24, 2017
- 'Atkinson seeks accountant job for Methuen police' August 7, 2017
- 'Methuen's councilor's police job could create conflict' August 8, 2017
- 'Councilor's votes on solicitor raise conflict questions' August 23, 2016
- 'Councilor gets police post not held by anyone in years' August 27, 2017
- 'Police hold shooter training at churches' April 10, 2018
- 'Mayor warns of police layoffs if unions won't deal' April 18, 2018
- 'Methuen mayor, police unions to meet about contract' April 17, 2018
- 'Jajuga touts progress, discusses budget issues in State of the City' April 24, 2018
- 'Methuen police chief, lieutenant honored for school safety work' May 15, 2018
- 'With job as mayor, Jajuga drives new SUV' May 19, 2018
- 'Jajuga proposes first budget as mayor' May 26, 2018
- 'Methuen Auditor: Police contracts are bankrupting the city' June 17, 2018
- 'Zanni defends his role in police contracts' June 18, 2018
- 'Methuen Council rejects mayor's budget' June 19, 2018
- 'Methuen police contract resolution not a guarantee to pass' July 11, 2018
- 'Methuen Police, city sign agreement lowering officers' salaries' July 18, 2018
- 'Methuen council passes budget' July 20, 2018
- 'Fault lines harden over Methuen police contract' July 24, 2018
- 'Councilors postpone decision on police salaries' July 26, 2018
- 'Methuen police superiors will file wage complaint' July 23, 2018
- 'Fault lines harden over Methuen police contract' July 24, 2018
- 'Methuen mayor intends to pay police compromise' July 31, 2018
- 'NECC Police Academy director admits to ethics violations' August 6, 2018
- 'Solomon's pay would soar under police contracts' June 6, 2018
- 'Police contracts sow confusion at budget meeting' June 6, 2018
- 'City could face damages if contracts aren't honored' June 7, 2018
- 'Fleming quit Lowell police amid cheating allegations' August 7, 2018
- 'Former Methuen councilor let go from city job' August 8, 2018 'NECC opens new investigation into former police academy director' August 19, 2018
- 'Mayor: Superiors salaries will revert to former contract' February 4, 2019
- 'Solomon will travel to Washington to discuss opioid crisis' February 6, 2019

(Bibliography)

- 'Council restores money to police department' February 7, 2019

'Police layoffs to begin in Methuen tonight' January 24, 2019
- 'Layoffs and furloughs hit Methuen as revenues plunges, July 10, 2020
- 'City Councilors ask Solomon to take pay cut, July 15, 2020

'Lussier addresses 2002 ethics probe' January 4, 2020

'Methuen: Perry, council to take close look at Police Department' January 26, 2020
- 'Methuen Mayor, councilors push ahead with audit' February 16, 2020
- 'Methuen Council rejects mayoral appointment' March 3, 2020 'Methuen council Oks $87K for police audit, April 28, 2020
- 'Tempers flare on eve of police audit' June 3, 2020
- 'Solomon, Gallant placed on leave in Methuen.' December 24, 2020
- 'A synopsis of Joseph Solomon's career with the PD' January 24, 2021
- 'Captain Gallant fired from Methuen police over contract controversy' June 9, 2022
- 'State board orders Methuen to rehire police captain' August 8, 2022
- 'Former Methuen police chief Solomon and officer Fountain indicted on criminal charges" September 28, 2023
- 'Former Methuen Chief, officer arraigned on fraud, forgery charges' November 10, 2023

Loop Weekly (later Methuen Today), Methuen, Massachusetts
- 'Atkinson Fired from City Job after Charter Review' August 8, 2018
- 'Taxpayer Thrown out of Council Meeting After Incident with Police Chief' January 16, 2019

Lowell Sun, Lowell, Massachusetts,
- 'Former Methuen solicitor loses case against city' January 25, 2008
- 'Veteran Lowell cop put on leave as part of cheating probe' July 3, 2014
- 'Veteran Lowell cop retires two weeks after being put on paid leave' July 15, 2014
- 'The Column: New Year, same old divisive Dracut' January 4, 2015 'Rape suspect on tape: "I did it" July 13, 2019
- 'DA criticizes Donovan in McLaughlin rape case' July 13, 2019

NECC News
Northern Essex Community College, Haverhill, Massachusetts
- 'NECC/Methuen Police Academy Graduates First Class' June 29, 2015

NECC Observer
Northern Essex Community College, Haverhill, Massachusetts
- 'NECC to bid public safety' September 3, 2014
- 'NECC holds security seminar' November 8, 2014

New York Post, New York, New York
- 'Stop the presses: Rob plot at Times' April 9, 2003
- 'Mafia cop's 'inside' story' April 10, 2003
- 'Jury nails pressman in Times rob plot' April 23, 2003

(Bibliography)

- 'Pressman jailed in mob plot to rob Times' June 17, 2003

Rumbo, Lawrence, Massachusetts,
- 'The package a.k.a. the kiss off' September 1, 2002, page 15
- 'Ellen Bahan's Short Stories' September 15, 2002, page 17
- 'Ellen Bahan's Short Stories' September 15, 2003
- 'Ellen Bahan's Short Stories' October 1, 2003, page 15
- 'Letter objecting to Ellen Bahan's recent articles' October 8, 2003
- 'For your eyes only...' November 1, 2003, pages 19 & 25
- 'A Mother's Story' December 1, 2003
- 'Am I the only one who sees these things' September 8, 2006
- 'Racism Plain and Simple' December 8, 2006
- 'Methuen Police Department Holds Active Shooter Training at Local Churches' April 8, 2018
- 'Methuen Police Awarded by School Safety Advocacy Council' June 23, 2018

Salem Evening News, Salem, Massachusetts
- 'Methuen Police Chief disciplined by the city again' January 31, 2008

Seacoastonline.com
- 'Police: Man Found with Hallucinogenic Mushrooms' September 18, 2008

Tewksbury Advocate, WickedLocal.com, Tewksbury, Massachusetts
- 'Lawsuit filed for assault' December 25, 2007

The Tufts Daily, Tufts University, Medford, Massachusetts
- 'Tufts Police Chief travels to Israel for counterterrorism seminar' January 26, 2018

Valley Patriot, North Andover, Massachusetts

'Harassed" Secretary in Methuen Gets Workers' Comp' April 4, 2006

'Methuen's Police Chief Joe Solomon Speaks Out' February 3, 2007
- 'Methuen Police Chief Solomon alleges federal corruption probe of Mayor Manzi' February 18, 2008
- 'Mayor Steve Zanni's Inauguration Speech' January 6, 2012
- 'Solomon Decision was Right for Methuen' September 11, 2012
- 'Methuen Police Chief Announces Retirement' January 11, 2021

Wareham Week, Wareham.theweektoday.com, Wareham, Massachusetts
- 'Unclear when Police Chief Richard Stanley will return to duty' August 21, 2013

Organizations

- **International Association of Chiefs of Police**
- **Methuen Festival of Trees, Inc.**
- **School Safety Advocacy Council**
  - National School Safety Conference, July 24-28, 2017, Schedule

(Bibliography)

- School Safety Leadership Academy'

Podcast
- **Paying Attention Podcast**, Tom Duggan, July 9, 2020
- **Looped in Live!**, Tim Wood, MPD Chief Joseph Solomon and Superior Officers Union President Greg Gallant, September 13, 2018

Radio
WHAV, Haverhill, Massachusetts
- 'Methuen Police Lt. Aiello Receives National School Safety Award, July 31, 2017

Social Media
Facebook
- **Curt Laverello**
  - November 11, 2016
  - May 18, 2017
  - August 4, 2017
  - May 5, 2018
  - July 25, 2019
  - September 4, 2018
  - September 5, 2018
  - October 8, 2018
  - October 25, 2018
  - October 30, 2018
  - December 7, 2018
- **EIS, Inc.**
  - March 13, 2017
  - April 26, 2017
  - December 9, 2017
  - March 2, 2018
  - March 7 2018
  - May 10, 2018
  - May 21, 2018
- **International Association of School Resource Officers** July 29, 2019
- **Joe Solomon** May 19, 2017
- **Lisa Kashinsky** February 7, 2019
- **Methuen Police Department**

(Bibliography)

- - February 7, 2016
  - May 21, 2018
- **NeasroInfo**
  - March 7, 2018
  - September 26, 2022
- **School Safety Advocacy Council**
  - September 16, 2016
  - June 20, 2017
  - August 2, 2017
- **Valley Patriot**, September 17, 2018
  - Facebook, March 1, 2015,
- Methuen Today, Facebook, [formally Loop Weekly], August 7, 2018

Linkedin.com
- Joseph Alaimo
- Mike Alaimo
- James Atkinson
- Al Donovan
- Curtis Lavarello
- Bruce A. MacDougall
- Joseph Solomon

X (Twitter).com
- **Blair Miller** February 7, 2019
- **Curt Lavarello** May 18, 2017
- **Fabulous Finn** May 23, 2018
- **Gina Scanlon** April 3, 2017
- **Methuen Police Department**
  - March 1, 2015
  - February 24, 2016
  - July 3, 2017
  - July 25, 2017
  - July 26, 2017
  - May 31, 2018
  - October 25, 2018
  - February 28, 2019
- **Natioal Information Officers Association** January 25, 2019
- **School nSafety Advocacy Council**
  - March 17, 2015
  - February 25, 2016
  - May 18, 2017
  - July 25, 2017
  - September 4, 2018
  - October 17, 2018
  - December 7, 2018

(Bibliography)

- December 13, 2018
- **Scott Wood**
  - 8, 2019
  - February 28, 2019
  - March 3, 2019
- March **StarChase**
  - November 29, 2016
  - February 22, 2017

YouTube.com
- **BOLO Mobile**
  - 'A critically needed tool for law enforcement', 2018
  - BOLO Mobile on Boston25 News, May 30, 2018
- **Freedom of Speech Ltd**
  - Nuance Dragon Speech Recognized for Law Enforcement August 21, 2018
- **Shooter Detection System**
  - WBZ4, 'Shooter Detection Systems and Methuen Police Demonstrates Active Shooter Detection Technology' February 16, 2018
  - SDS Gunshot detection featured on NBC's Today Show May 3, 2023
  - Welcome to Shooter Detection Systems, April 5, 2019
- **Tom Duggan**,
  - Methuen Police Lt. Mike Pappalardo, Deputy Director, Emergency Management at Methuen Command Center' February 9, 2013
- **ZDNET**
  - 'How police work is evolving, thanks to voice recognition and the cloud, July 20, 2018
- 'L'Italien St Patricks Day 2008'
- 'Rep. Barbra L'Italien St. Pat's 2009'

Television

10Boston.com, Boston, Massachusetts
- 'Mayor: Gloucester Police Chief Fired Over 'Unethical' Actions' October 3, 2016

Boston 25 News, Boston, Massachusetts
- 'Mass. Police department testing GPS darts to deter chases' October 31, 2016
- 'Crime reporting app lets Methuen police, community share real-time crime info' March 22, 2017
- 25 News Investigates: Police tap new smartphone app to find missing kids, May 30, 2018

(Bibliography)

- Embattled former Methuen police chief indicted on slew of charges, September 28, 2023

GBH, Boston, Massachusetts
- 'Walsh asked to stop BPD from attending Israeli training' November 29, 2018

United States Federal Government
Department of Justice, Office of the Inspector General, Washington, DC
- Glendinning Report, Special Agent David Glendinning

Websites
Anti-Defamation League, adl.org
APD Management, apdmanagement.com
Bolo-Mobile, BoloMobile.com
City of Methuen, CityofMethuen.net, Cityofmethuen.org, Cityofmethuen.com
EIS, Inc., Eagleinvestigations.com
The Foundation for School Safety and Security
foundationforschoolsafetyandsecurity.org
Integrity Testing, integritytestingllc.com
International Association of School Resource Officers, iasros.org
Municipal Police Institute, mpitraining.com
Police Assessment Center Training, policeassessmentcenter training.com
School Safety Advocacy Council, schoolsafety911.org
Wayback Machine, web.archive.org

Yearbooks
Methuen High School Yearbook
- Randy Haggar, 1987, page 46
- Daryl Silva, 1991, page 85

Sojourn, University of Lowell
- Joseph E. Solomon, Class of 1983, page 412

www.ingramcontent.com/pod-product-compliance
Lightning Source LLC
Chambersburg PA
CBHW060448030426
42337CB00015B/1519